冨 樫 義 博

A vow on the ocean—or not.

Yoshihiro Togashi

Yoshihiro Togashi's manga career began in 1986 at the age of 20, when he won the coveted Osamu Tezuka Award for new manga artists. He debuted in the Japanese **Weekly Shonen Jump** magazine in 1989 with the romantic comedy **Tende Shôwaru Cupid**. From 1990 to 1994 he wrote and drew the hit manga **YuYu Hakusho**, which was followed by the dark comedy science-fiction series **Level E**, and finally this adventure series **Hunter x Hunter**. In 1999 he married the manga artist Naoko Takeuchi.

HUNTER X HUNTER Volume 3
The SHONEN JUMP ADVANCED Graphic Novel Edition

STORY AND ART BY
YOSHIHIRO TOGASHI

English Adaptation/Gary Leach
Translation/Lillian Olsen
Touch-up Art & Lettering/Mark Griffin
Design/Amy Martin
Editor/Pancha Diaz

Managing Editor/Elizabeth Kawasaki
Director of Production/Noboru Watanabe
Vice President of Publishing/Alvin Lu
Vice President & Editor in Chief/Yumi Hoashi
Sr. Director of Acquisitions/Rika Inouye
Vice President of Sales & Marketing/Liza Coppola
Publisher/Hyoe Narita

HUNTER x HUNTER © POT(Yoshihiro Togashi)1998. All rights reserved. First published in Japan in 1998 by SHUEISHA Inc., Tokyo. English translation rights in the United States of America and Canada arranged by SHUEISHA Inc. The stories, characters and incidents mentioned in this publication are entirely fictional.

Printed in the U.S.A.

Published by VIZ, LLC
P.O. Box 77010
San Francisco, CA 94107

SHONEN JUMP ADVANCED Graphic Novel Edition
10 9 8 7 6 5 4 3 2 1
First printing, June 2005

www.viz.com

PARENTAL ADVISORY
HUNTER X HUNTER is rated T+ for Older Teen. It contains realistic violence. It is recommended for ages 16 and up.

THE WORLD'S MOST CUTTING-EDGE MANGA

SHONEN JUMP
ADVANCED
www.shonenjump.com

SHONEN JUMP ADVANCED GRAPHIC NOVEL

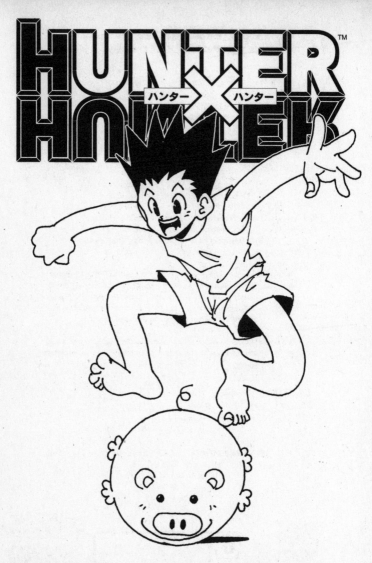

HUNTER × HUNTER™

ハンター × ハンター

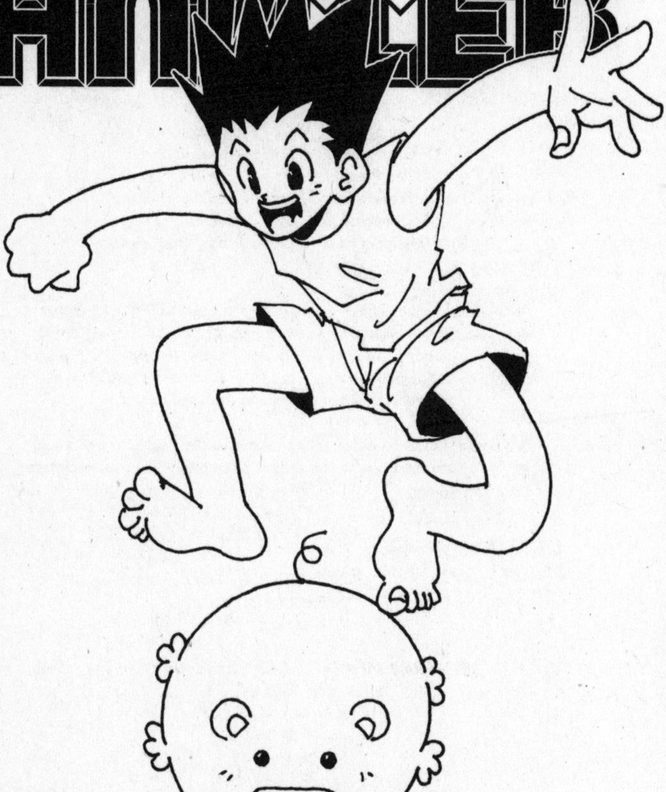

Story & Art by

Yoshihiro Togashi

Volume 3

CHARACTERS

The Story Thus Far

GON DREAMS OF BEING A HUNTER LIKE HIS FATHER, AND SETS OUT TO TAKE THE ULTRA-TOUGH LICENSING EXAM. ALONG THE WAY, HE MEETS FELLOW APPLICANTS KURAPIKA, LEORIO, AND KILLUA. THE FOUR PASS THE SECOND PHASE OF THE EXAM AND MOVE ON TO THE THIRD, WHICH REQUIRES THEM TO FIND THEIR WAY DOWN THE TRICK TOWER WITHIN THE ALLOTTED TIME. GON'S GROUP, JOINED BY THE TREACHEROUS TONPA, MAKES PROGRESS THROUGH "THE PATH OF MAJORITY RULES," BUT WAITING FOR THEM ARE PRISONERS HIRED AS TASKMASTERS IN EXCHANGE FOR SHORTER SENTENCES. IF GON'S TEAM CAN GET THE "BEST OF FIVE" IN THE ONE-ON-ONE MATCHES, THEY MAY CONTINUE ON THEIR WAY. TONPA THROWS HIS MATCH, BUT GON WINS HIS, PUTTING THE SCORE AT 1-1...!!

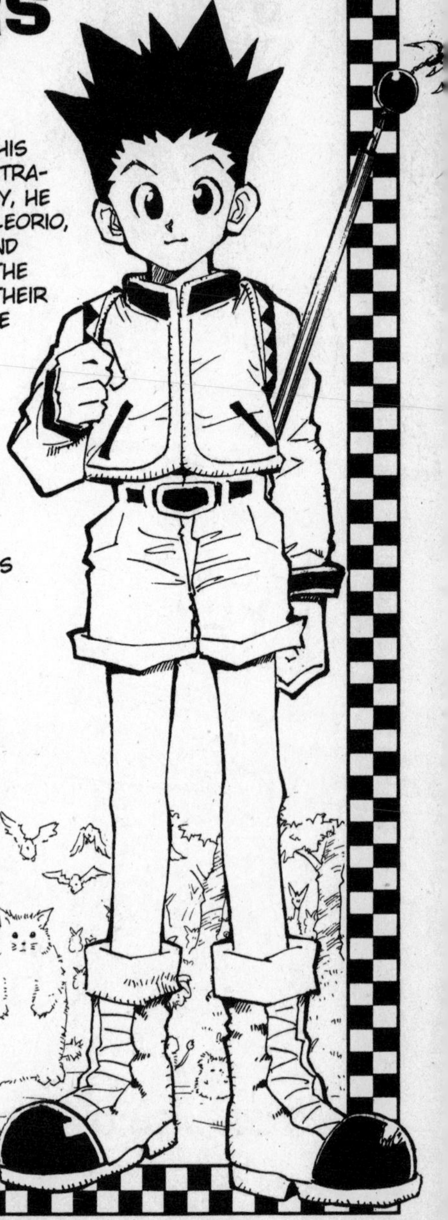

Gon

OUR HERO ASPIRES TO BECOME A HUNTER, AND REUNITE WITH HIS FATHER!

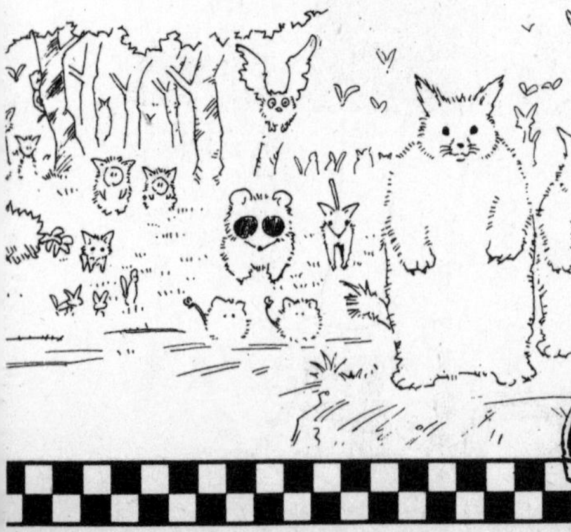

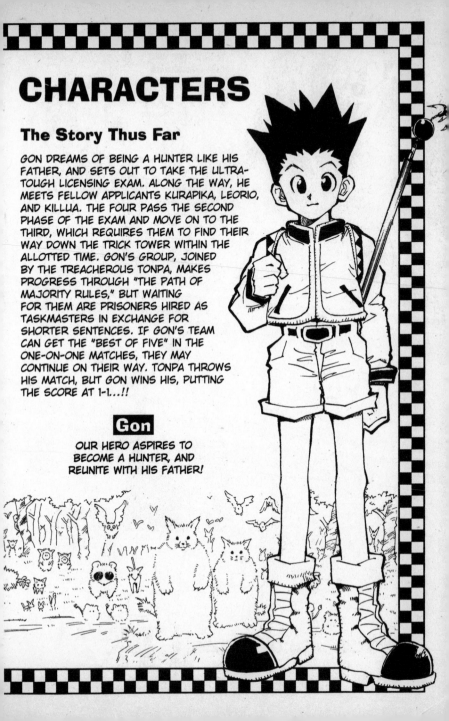

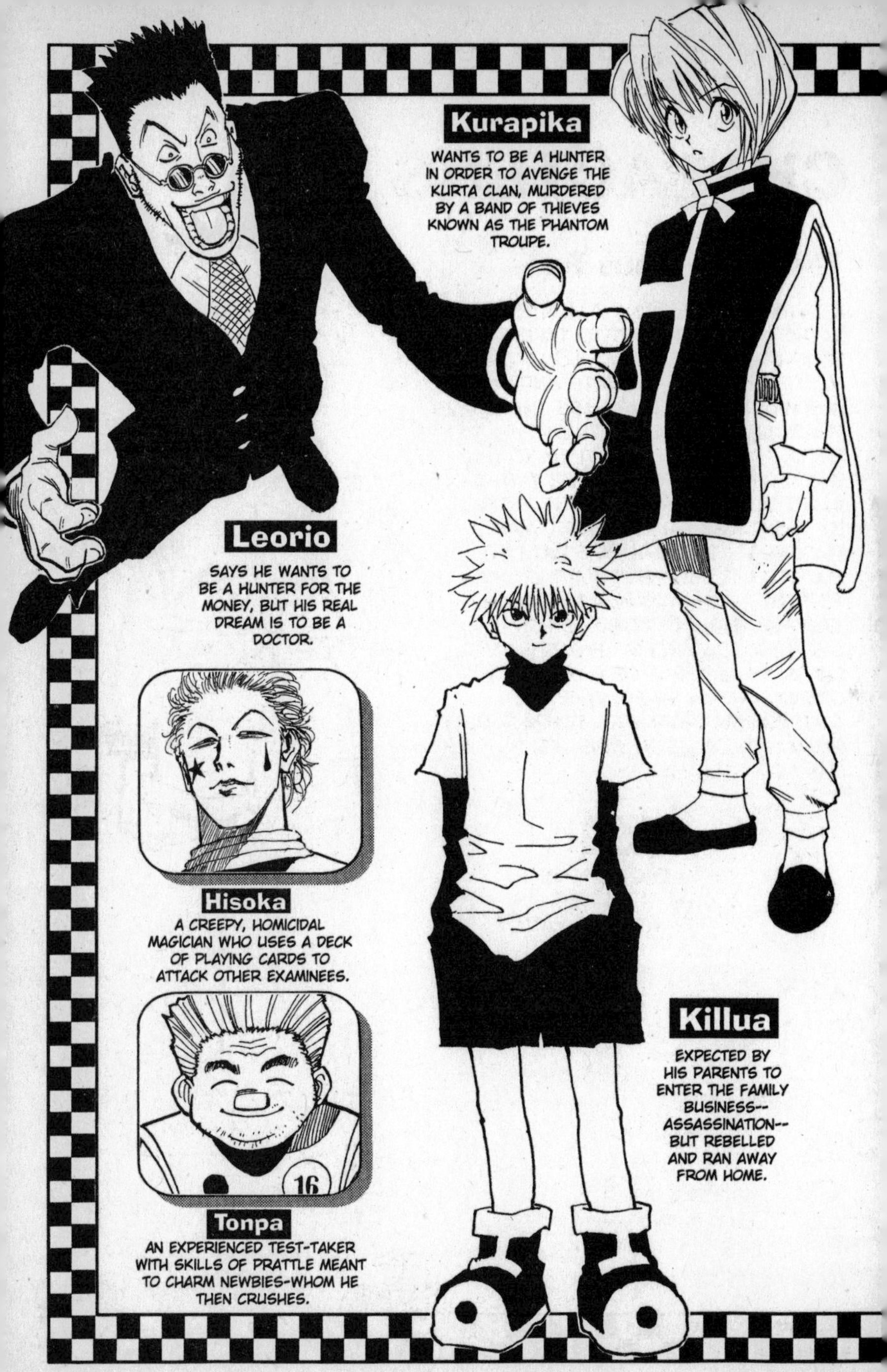
Kurapika
WANTS TO BE A HUNTER IN ORDER TO AVENGE THE KURTA CLAN, MURDERED BY A BAND OF THIEVES KNOWN AS THE PHANTOM TROUPE.
Leorio
SAYS HE WANTS TO BE A HUNTER FOR THE MONEY, BUT HIS REAL DREAM IS TO BE A DOCTOR.
Killua
EXPECTED BY HIS PARENTS TO ENTER THE FAMILY BUSINESS--ASSASSINATION--BUT REBELLED AND RAN AWAY FROM HOME.
Hisoka
A CREEPY, HOMICIDAL MAGICIAN WHO USES A DECK OF PLAYING CARDS TO ATTACK OTHER EXAMINEES.
16
Tonpa
AN EXPERIENCED TEST-TAKER WITH SKILLS OF PRATTLE MEANT TO CHARM NEWBIES-WHOM HE THEN CRUSHES.

HUNTER × HUNTER

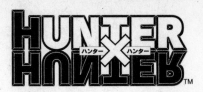

Volume 3

CONTENTS

Chapter 18
THE TWO ACES IN THE HOLE

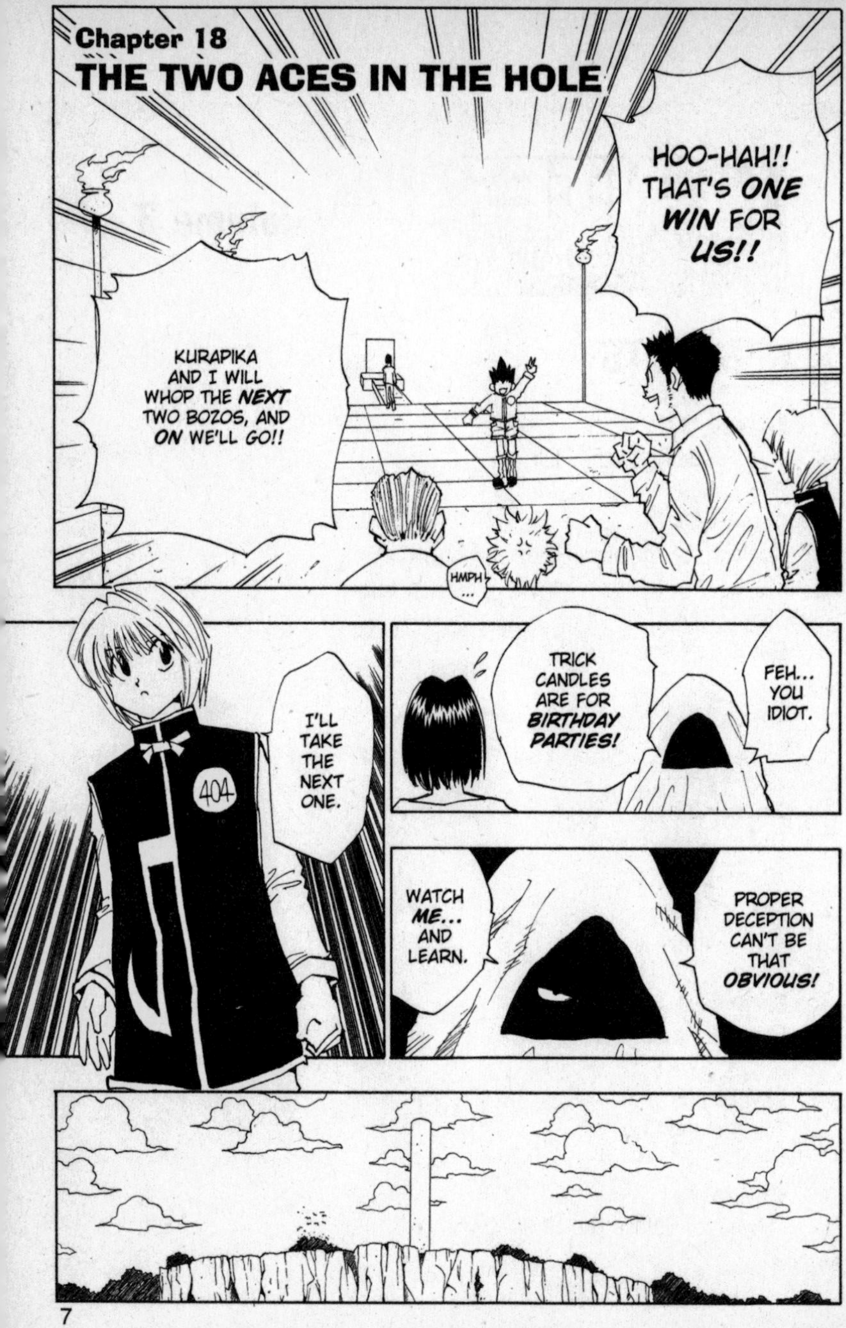
HOO-HAH!! THAT'S ONE WIN FOR US!!
KURAPIKA AND I WILL WHOP THE NEXT TWO BOZOS, AND ON WE'LL GO!!
HMPH...
FEH... YOU IDIOT.
TRICK CANDLES ARE FOR BIRTHDAY PARTIES!
PROPER DECEPTION CAN'T BE THAT OBVIOUS!
WATCH ME... AND LEARN.
I'LL TAKE THE NEXT ONE.
404

Chapter 18

THE TWO ACES IN THE HOLE

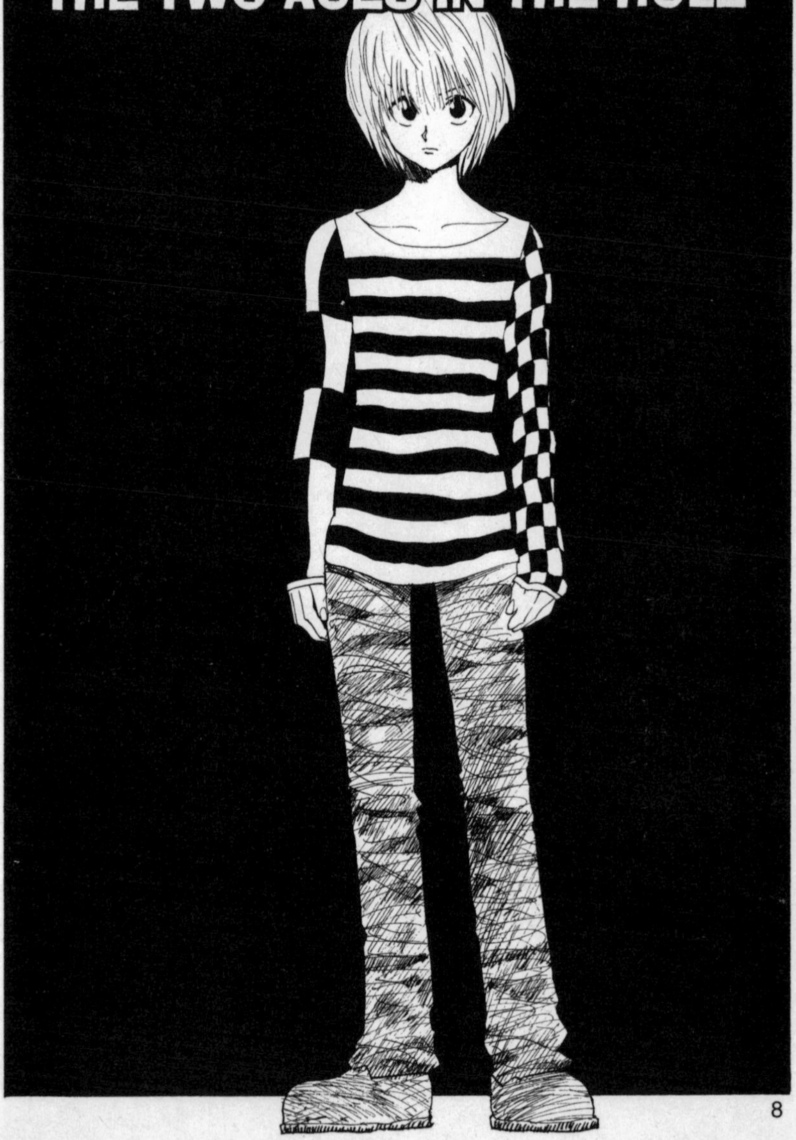

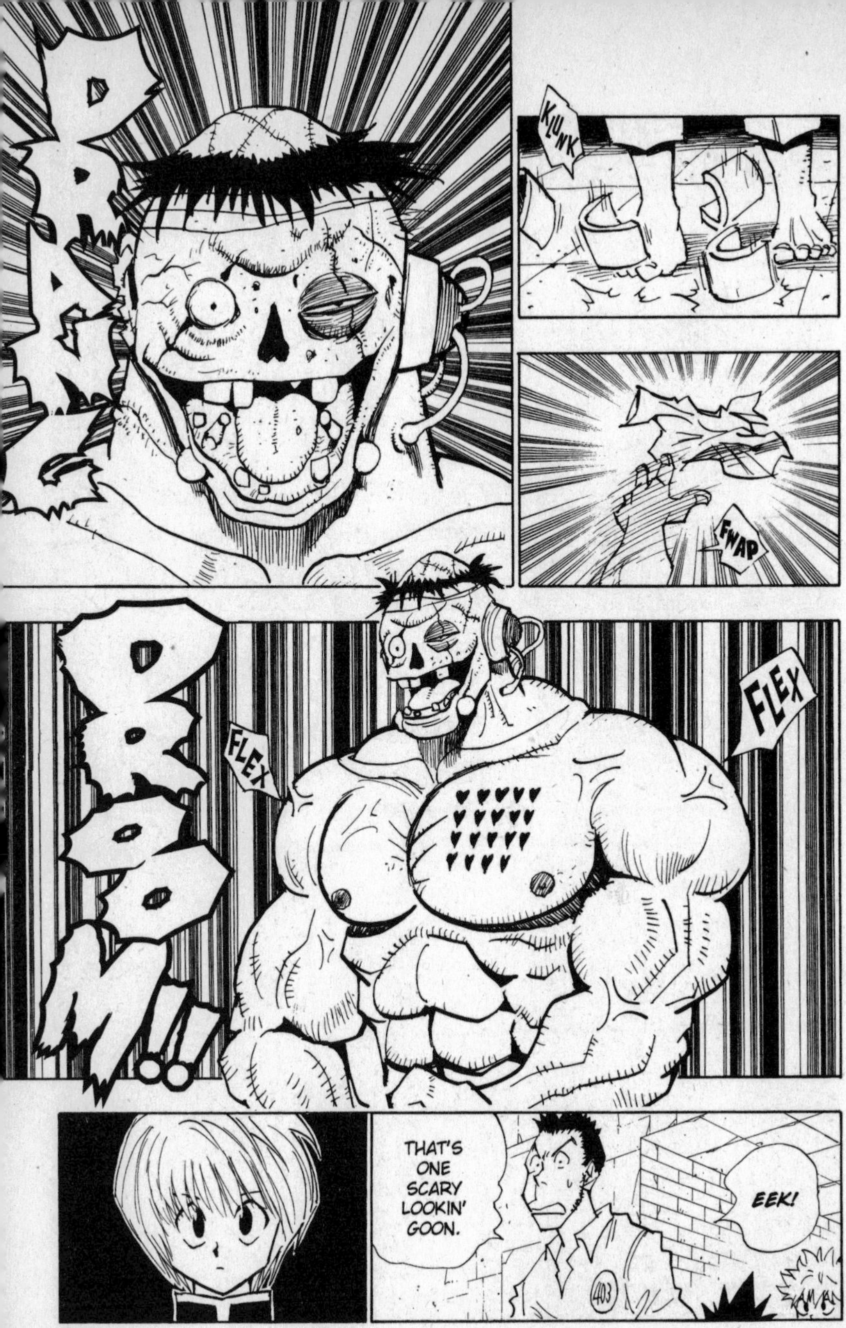
KLUNK
FWAP
FLEX
FLEX
EEK!
THAT'S ONE SCARY LOOKIN' GOON.

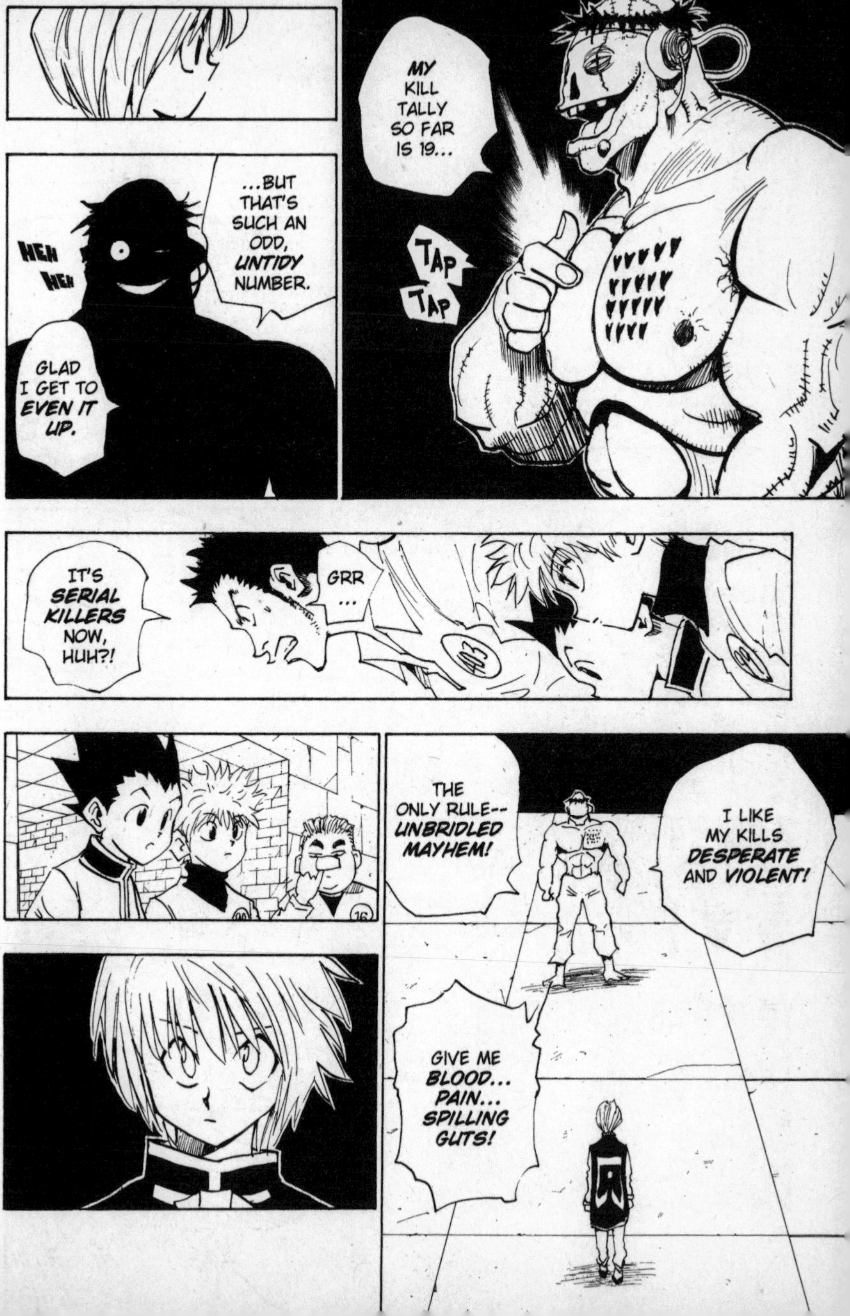
MY KILL TALLY SO FAR IS 19...
TAP TAP
...BUT THAT'S SUCH AN ODD, UNTIDY NUMBER.
HEH HEH
GLAD I GET TO EVEN IT UP.
GRR ...
IT'S SERIAL KILLERS NOW, HUH?!
I LIKE MY KILLS DESPERATE AND VIOLENT!
THE ONLY RULE-- UNBRIDLED MAYHEM!
GIVE ME BLOOD... PAIN... SPILLING GUTS!

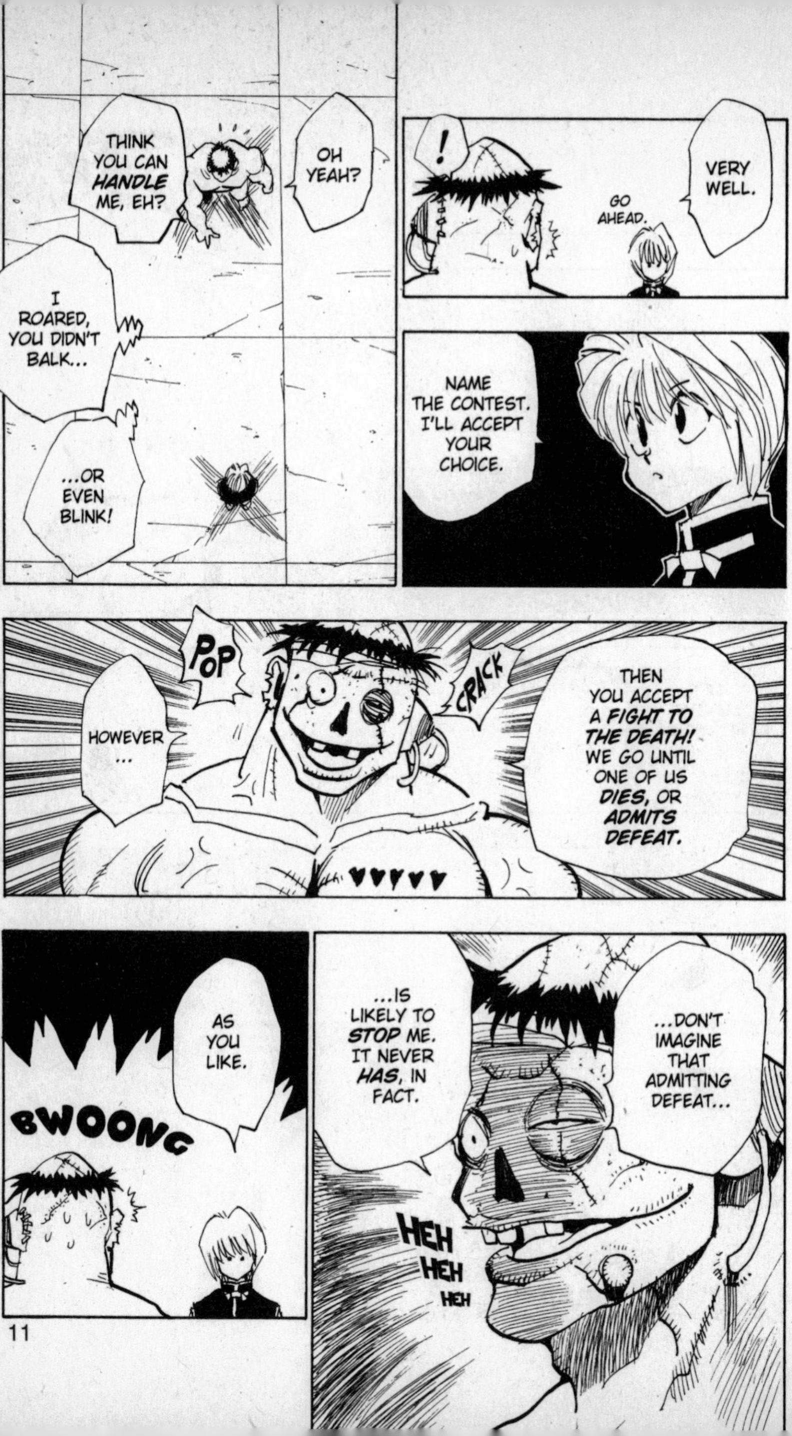
!
GO AHEAD.
VERY WELL.
NAME THE CONTEST. I'LL ACCEPT YOUR CHOICE.
OH YEAH?
THINK YOU CAN *HANDLE* ME, EH?
I ROARED, YOU DIDN'T BALK...
...OR EVEN BLINK!
THEN YOU ACCEPT A *FIGHT TO THE DEATH!* WE GO UNTIL ONE OF US *DIES,* OR *ADMITS DEFEAT.*
CRACK
POP
HOWEVER...
...DON'T IMAGINE THAT ADMITTING DEFEAT...
...IS LIKELY TO *STOP* ME. IT NEVER *HAS,* IN FACT.
HEH HEH HEH
AS YOU LIKE.
BWOONG

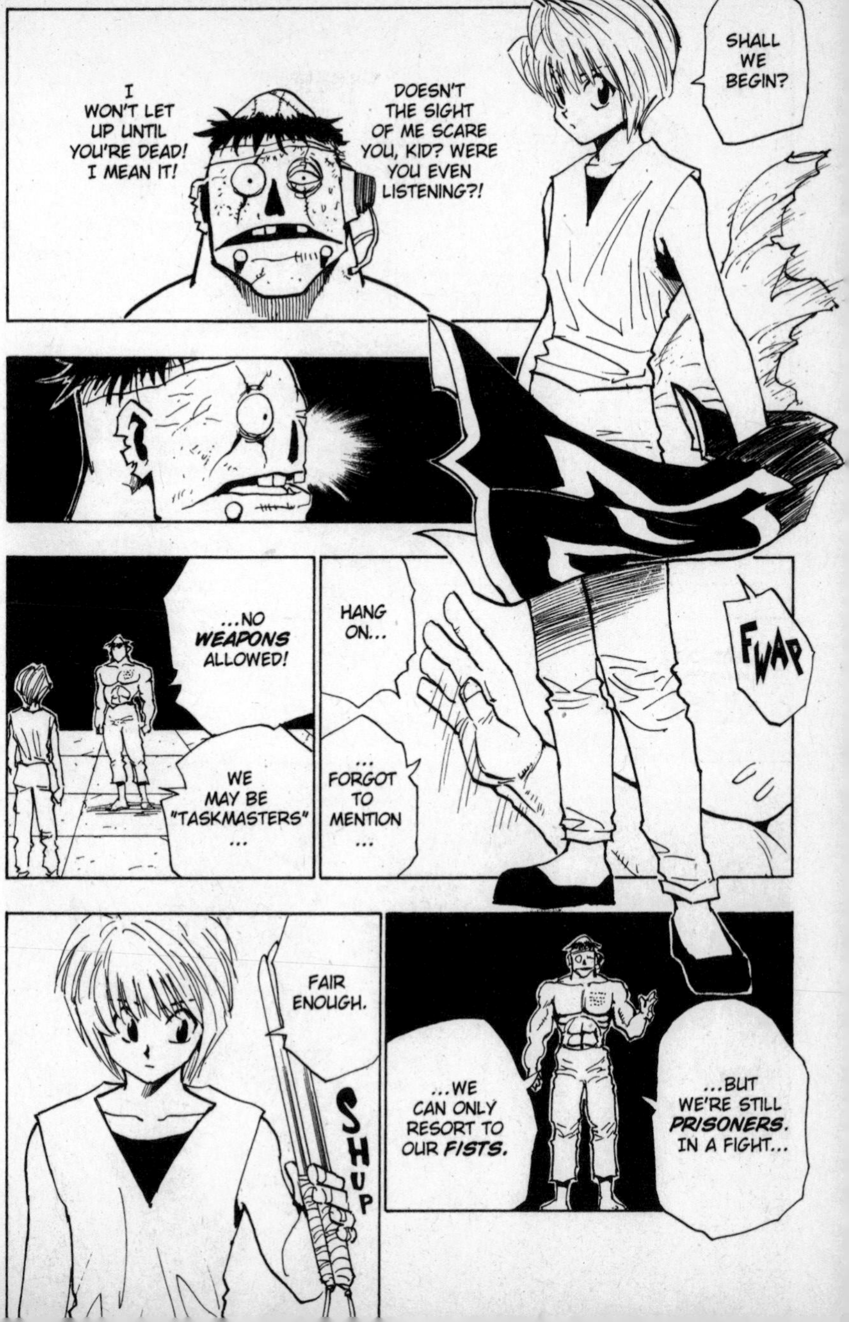
SHALL WE BEGIN?
DOESN'T THE SIGHT OF ME SCARE YOU, KID? WERE YOU EVEN LISTENING?!
I WON'T LET UP UNTIL YOU'RE DEAD! I MEAN IT!
FWAP
HANG ON...
...FORGOT TO MENTION...
...NO **WEAPONS** ALLOWED!
WE MAY BE "TASKMASTERS"...
...BUT WE'RE STILL **PRISONERS.** IN A FIGHT...
...WE CAN ONLY RESORT TO OUR **FISTS.**
FAIR ENOUGH.
SHUP

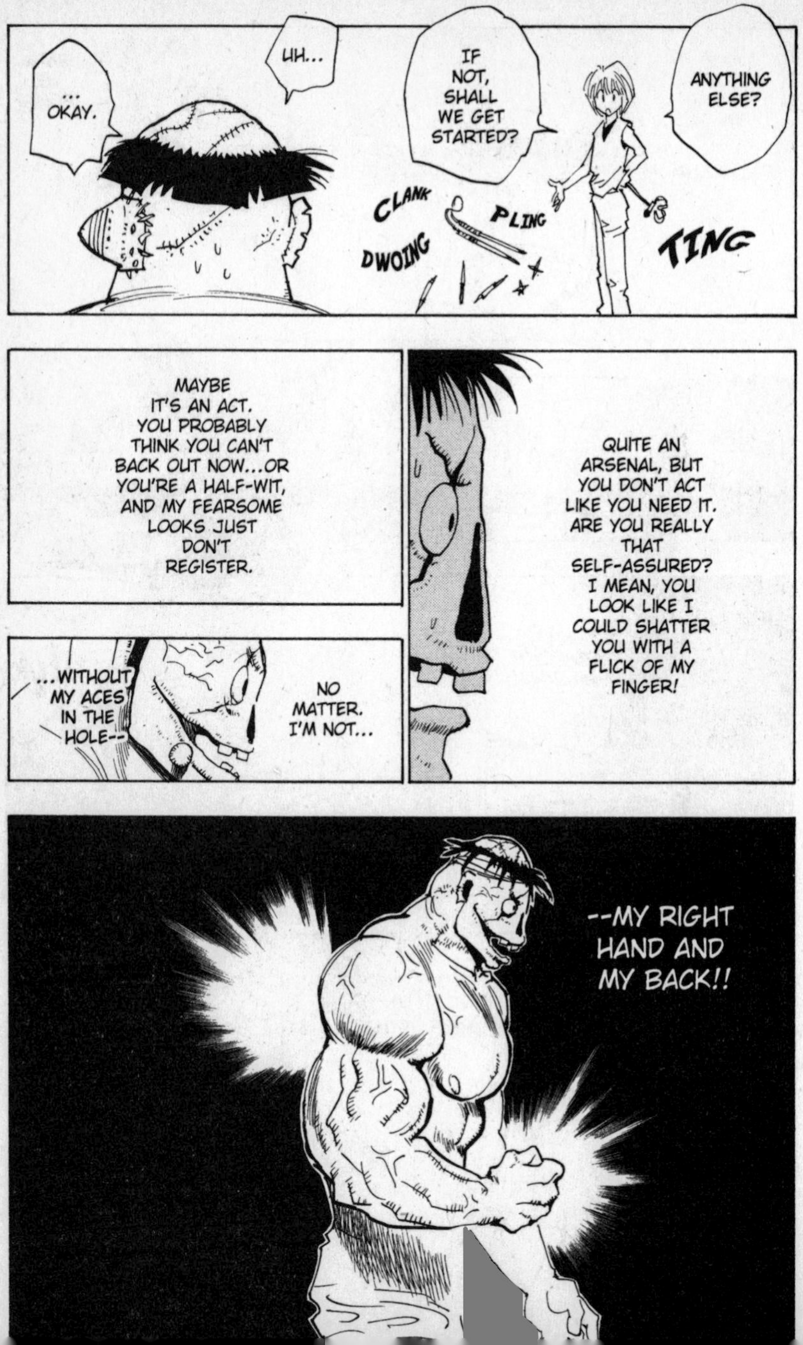
ANYTHING ELSE?
IF NOT, SHALL WE GET STARTED?
TING
PLING
CLANK
DWOING
UH...
... OKAY.
QUITE AN ARSENAL, BUT YOU DON'T ACT LIKE YOU NEED IT. ARE YOU REALLY THAT SELF-ASSURED? I MEAN, YOU LOOK LIKE I COULD SHATTER YOU WITH A FLICK OF MY FINGER!
MAYBE IT'S AN ACT. YOU PROBABLY THINK YOU CAN'T BACK OUT NOW...OR YOU'RE A HALF-WIT, AND MY FEARSOME LOOKS JUST DON'T REGISTER.
NO MATTER. I'M NOT...
...WITHOUT MY ACES IN THE HOLE--
--MY RIGHT HAND AND MY BACK!!

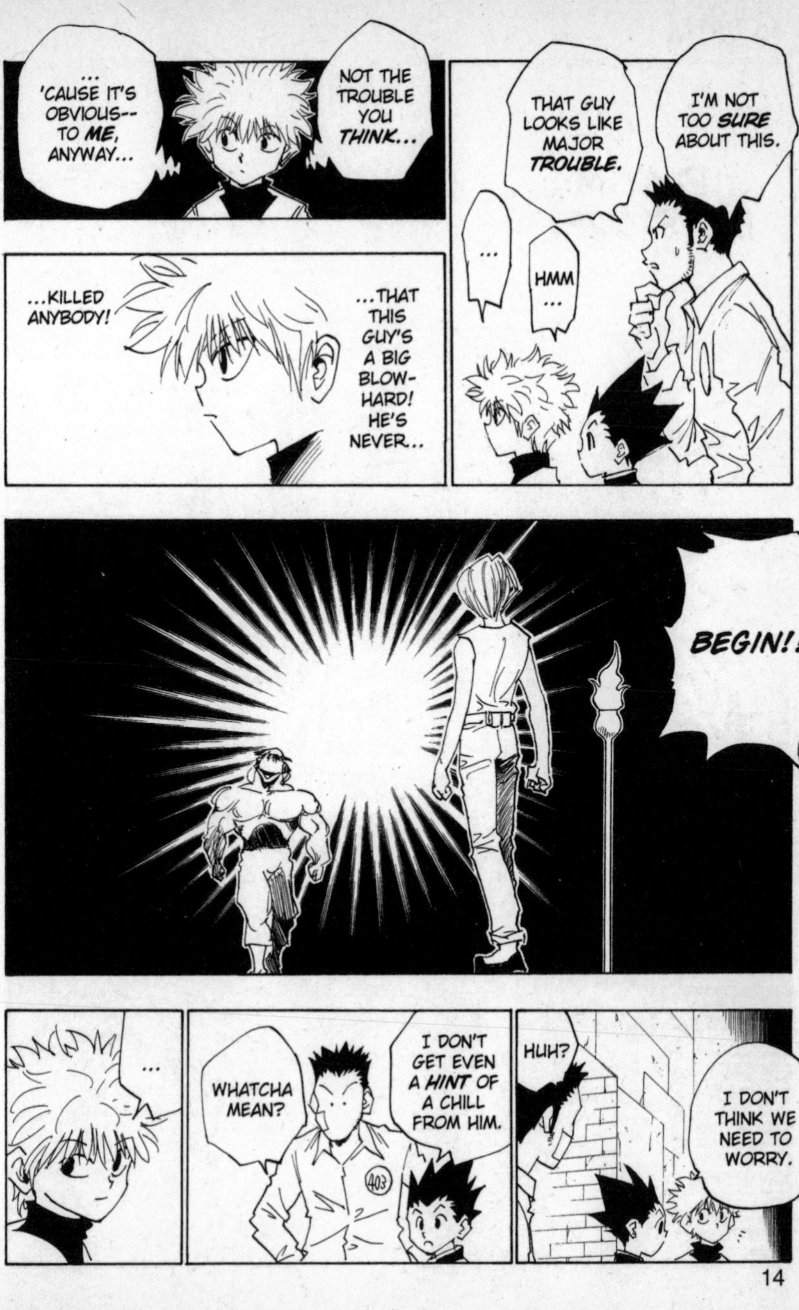
I'M NOT TOO SURE ABOUT THIS.
THAT GUY LOOKS LIKE MAJOR TROUBLE.
HMM ...
...
NOT THE TROUBLE YOU THINK...
... 'CAUSE IT'S OBVIOUS-- TO ME, ANYWAY...
...THAT THIS GUY'S A BIG BLOW-HARD! HE'S NEVER...
...KILLED ANYBODY!
BEGIN!!
I DON'T THINK WE NEED TO WORRY.
HUH?
I DON'T GET EVEN A HINT OF A CHILL FROM HIM.
WHATCHA MEAN?
...

READ THIS WAY

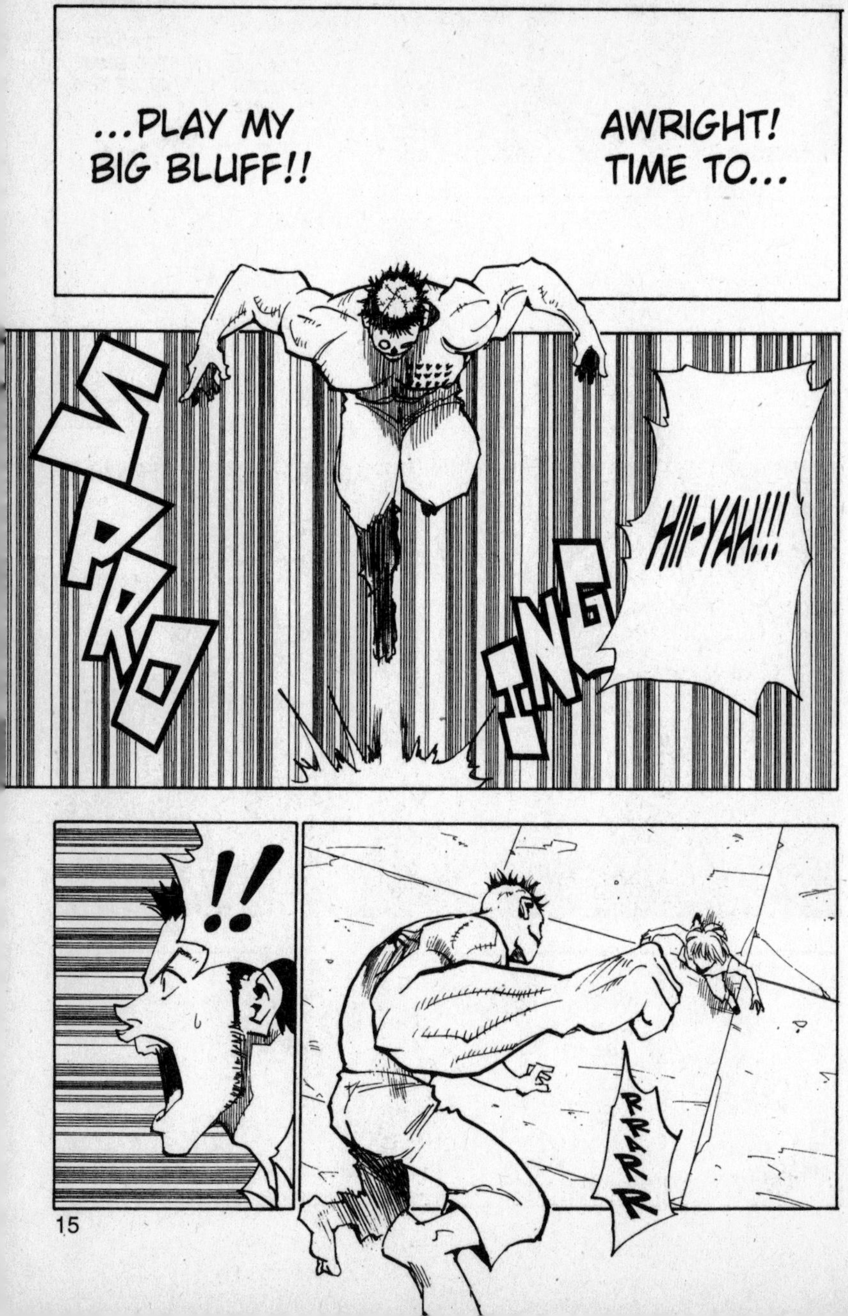

AWRIGHT! TIME TO...
...PLAY MY BIG BLUFF!!
HII-YAH!!!
SPROING
RRRRR
!!

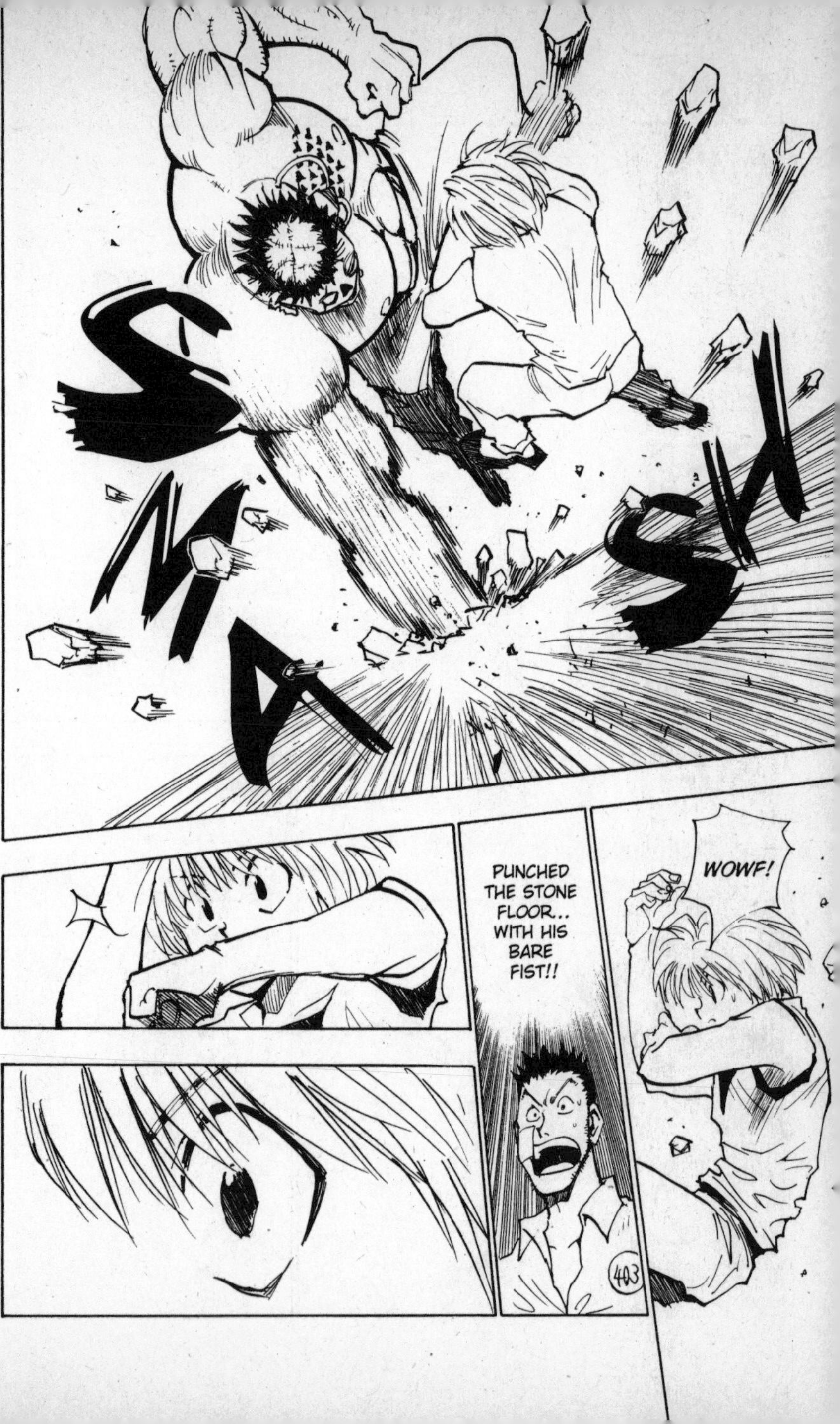
SMASH
WOWF!
PUNCHED THE STONE FLOOR... WITH HIS BARE FIST!!
403

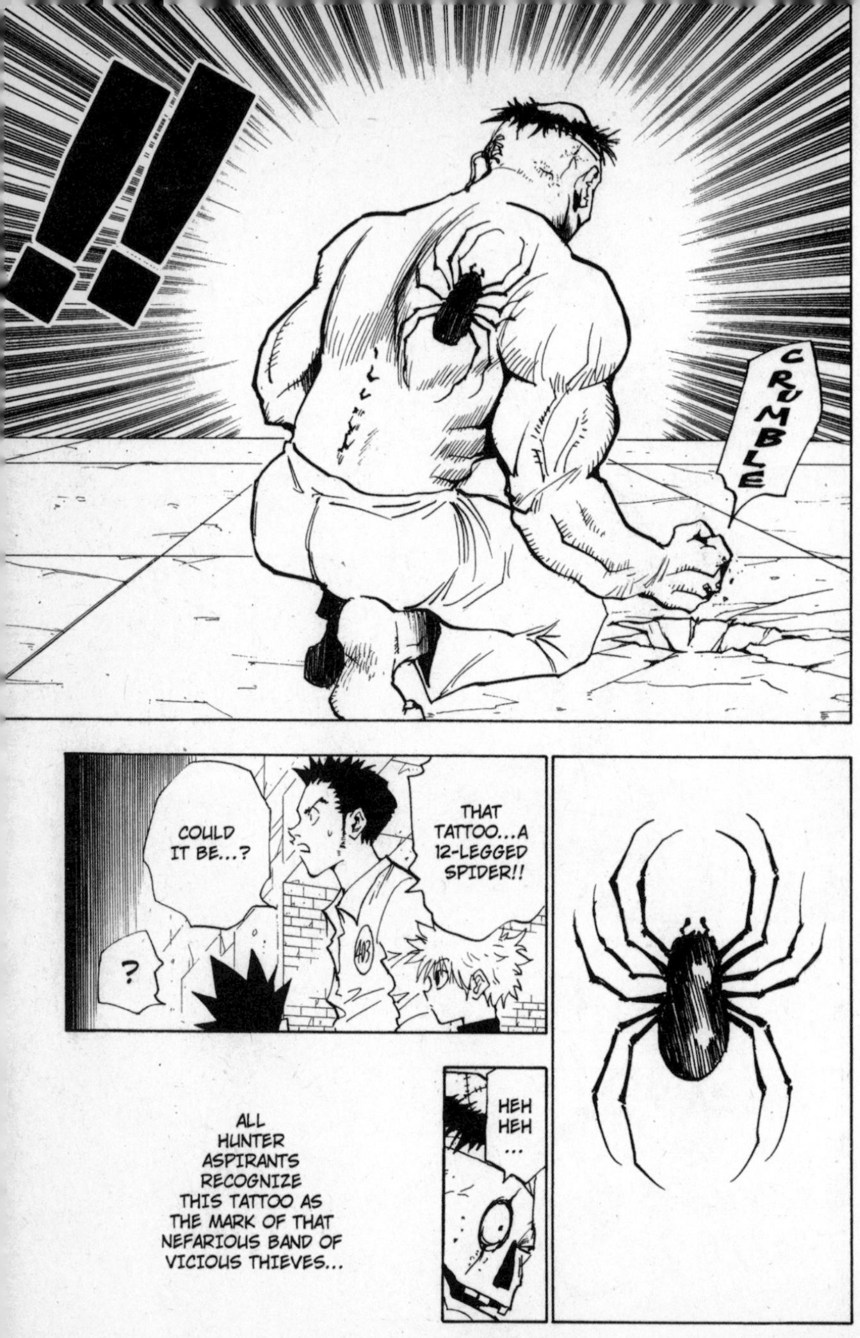
!!
CRUMBLE
THAT TATTOO...A 12-LEGGED SPIDER!!
COULD IT BE...?
?
HEH HEH ...
ALL HUNTER ASPIRANTS RECOGNIZE THIS TATTOO AS THE MARK OF THAT NEFARIOUS BAND OF VICIOUS THIEVES...

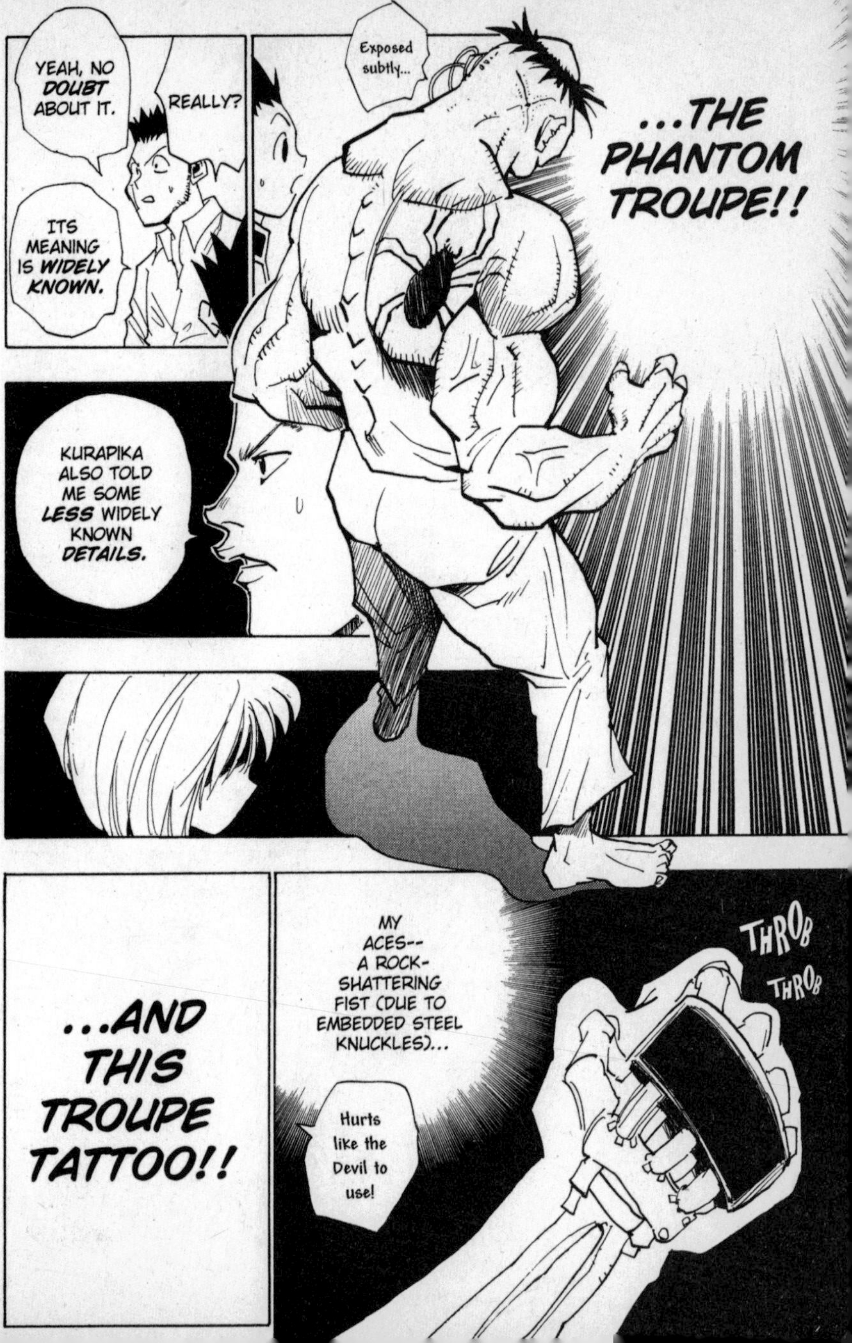

Exposed subtly...
...THE PHANTOM TROUPE!!
REALLY?
YEAH, NO DOUBT ABOUT IT.
ITS MEANING IS WIDELY KNOWN.
KURAPIKA ALSO TOLD ME SOME LESS WIDELY KNOWN DETAILS.
THROB THROB
MY ACES-- A ROCK-SHATTERING FIST (DUE TO EMBEDDED STEEL KNUCKLES)...
Hurts like the Devil to use!
...AND THIS TROUPE TATTOO!!

READ THIS WAY

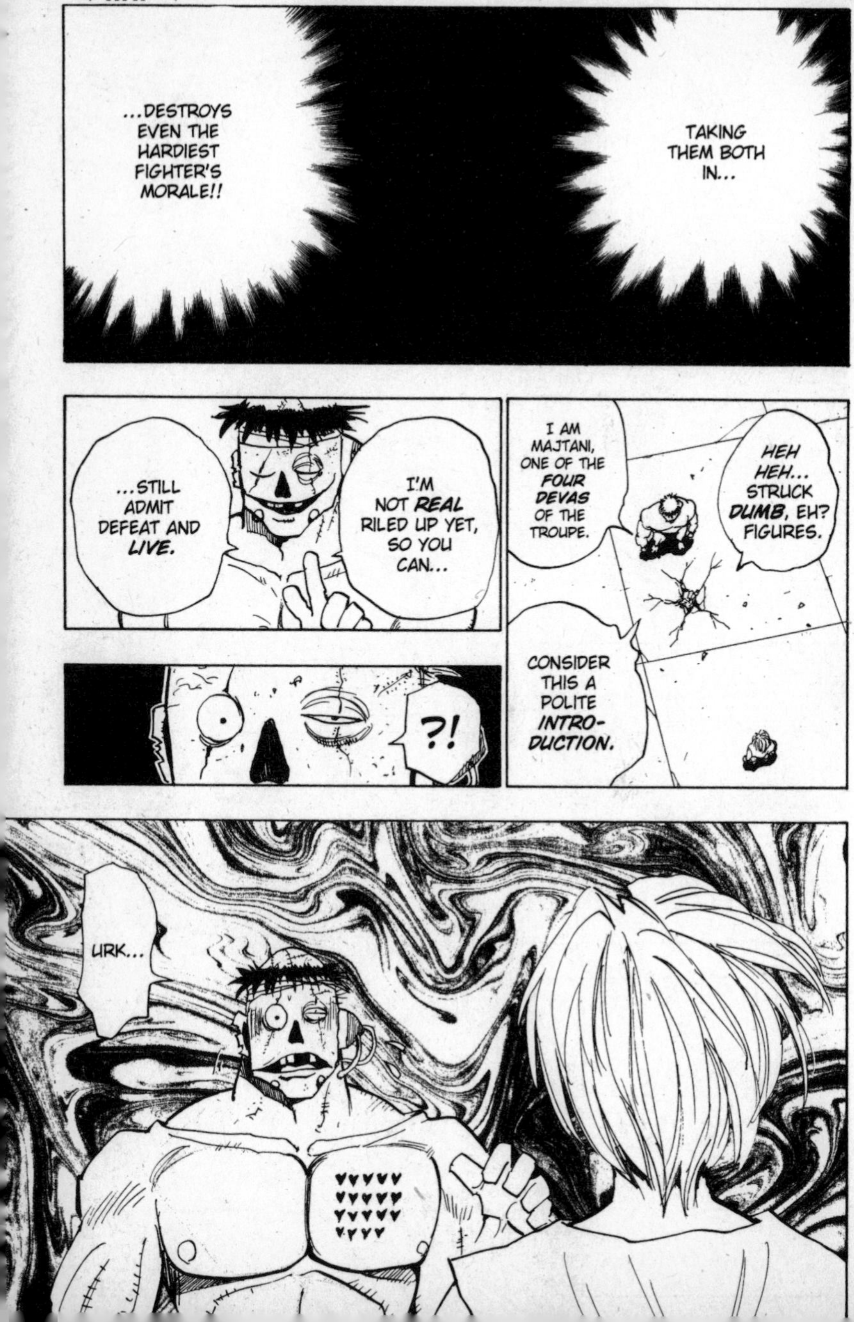
TAKING THEM BOTH IN...
...DESTROYS EVEN THE HARDIEST FIGHTER'S MORALE!!
HEH HEH... STRUCK DUMB, EH? FIGURES.
I AM MAJTANI, ONE OF THE FOUR DEVAS OF THE TROUPE.
CONSIDER THIS A POLITE INTRODUCTION.
I'M NOT REAL RILED UP YET, SO YOU CAN...
...STILL ADMIT DEFEAT AND LIVE.
?!
URK...

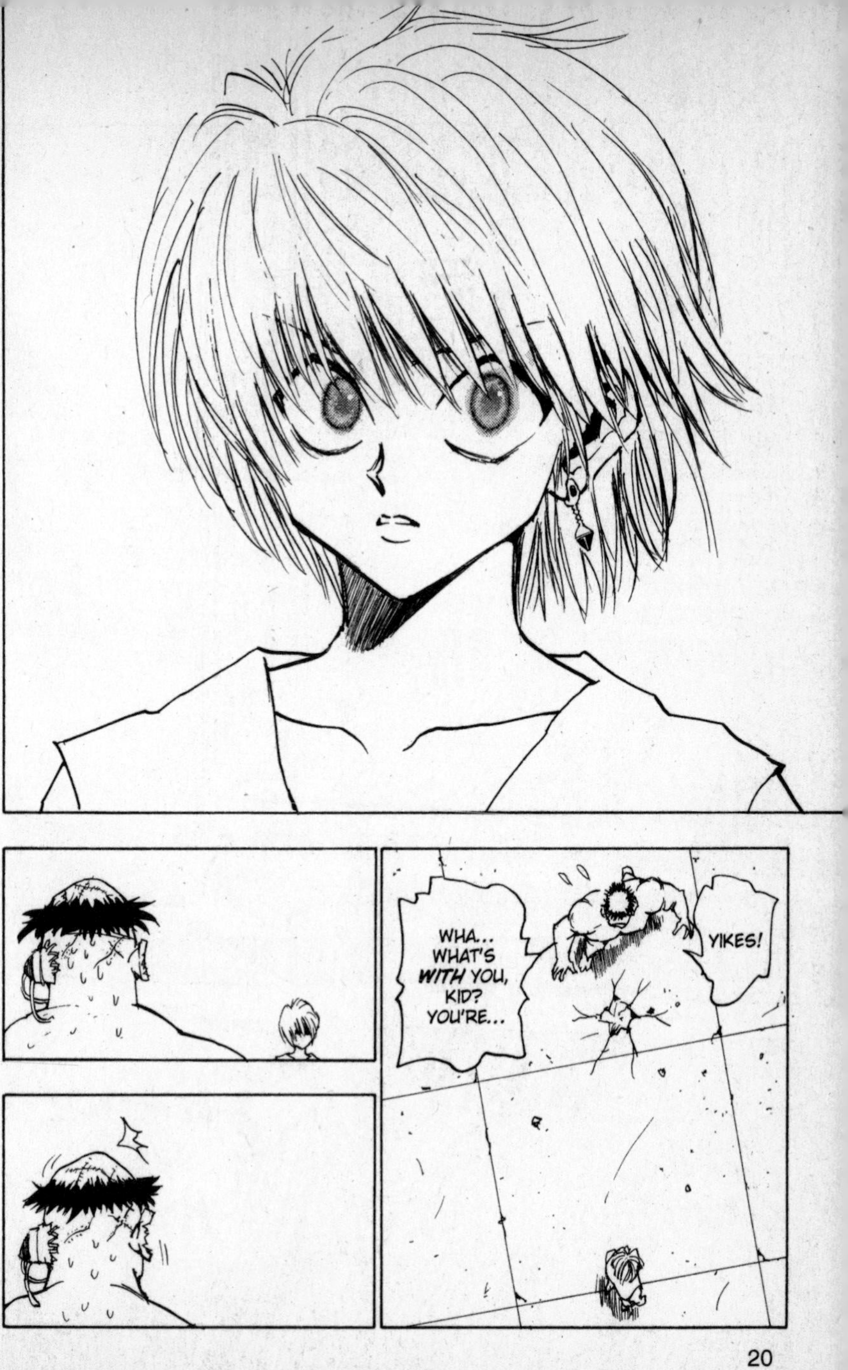
YIKES!
WHA... WHAT'S *WITH* YOU, KID? YOU'RE...

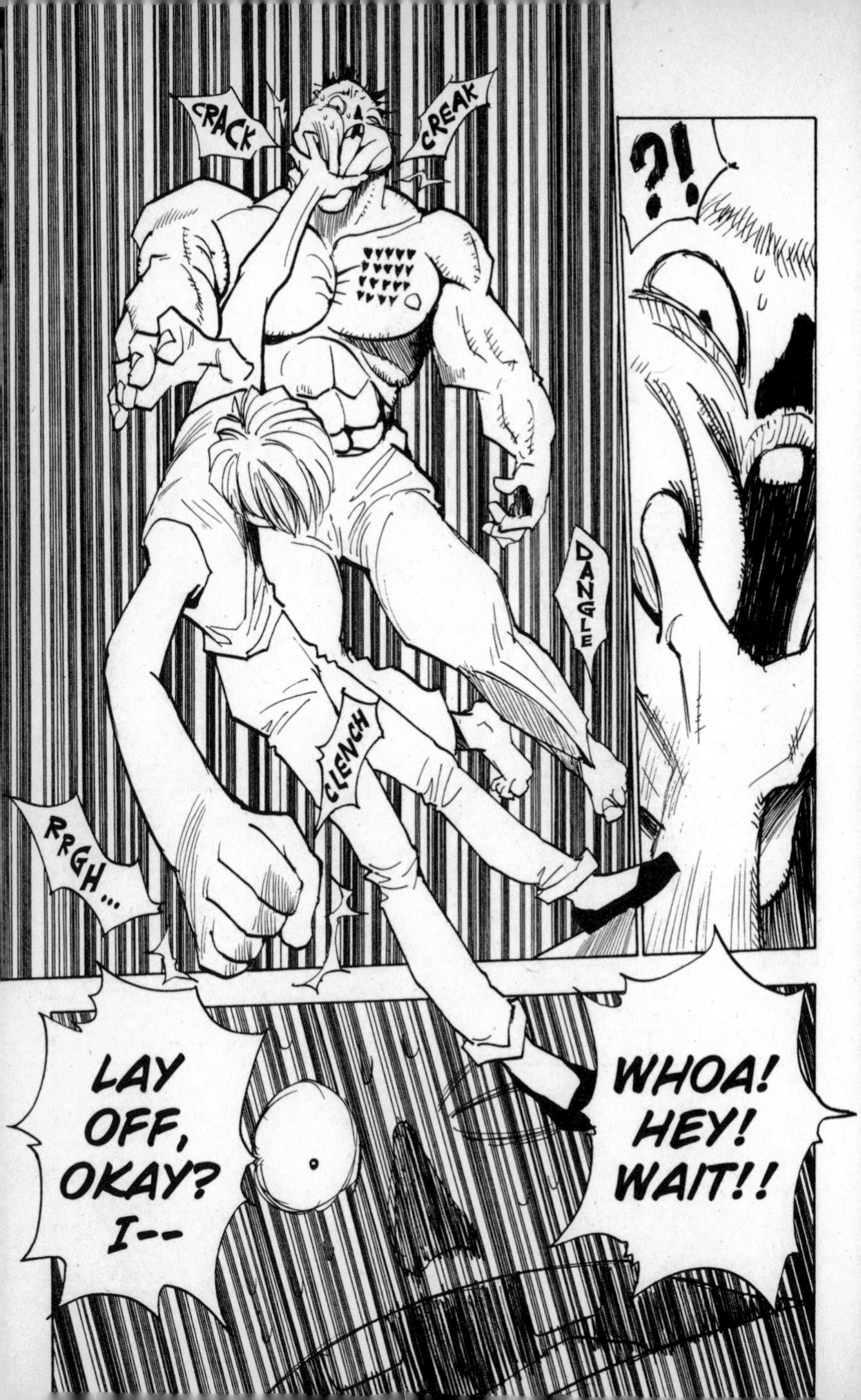
?!
CREAK
CRACK
DANGLE
CLENCH
RRGH...
WHOA! HEY! WAIT!!
LAY OFF, OKAY? I--

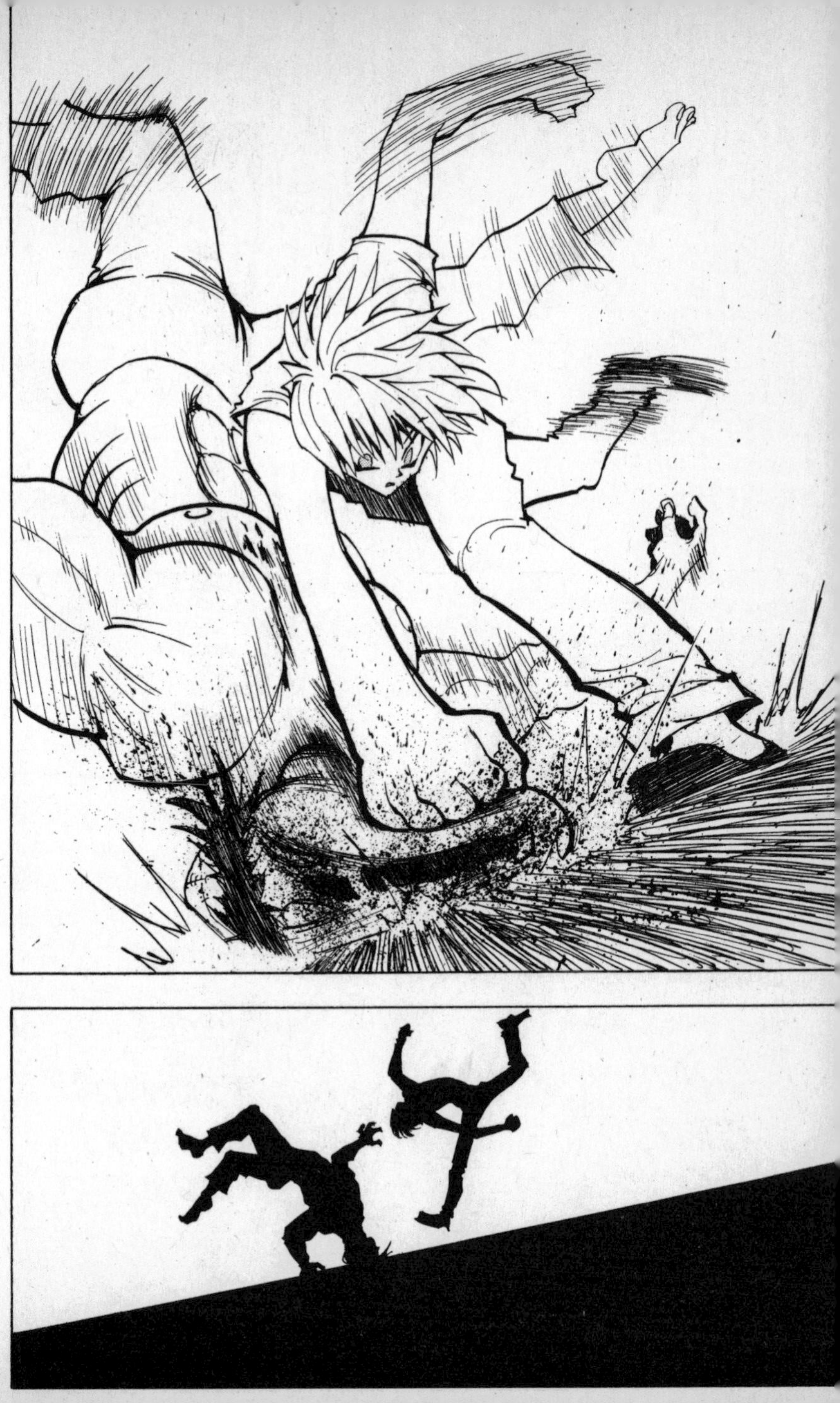

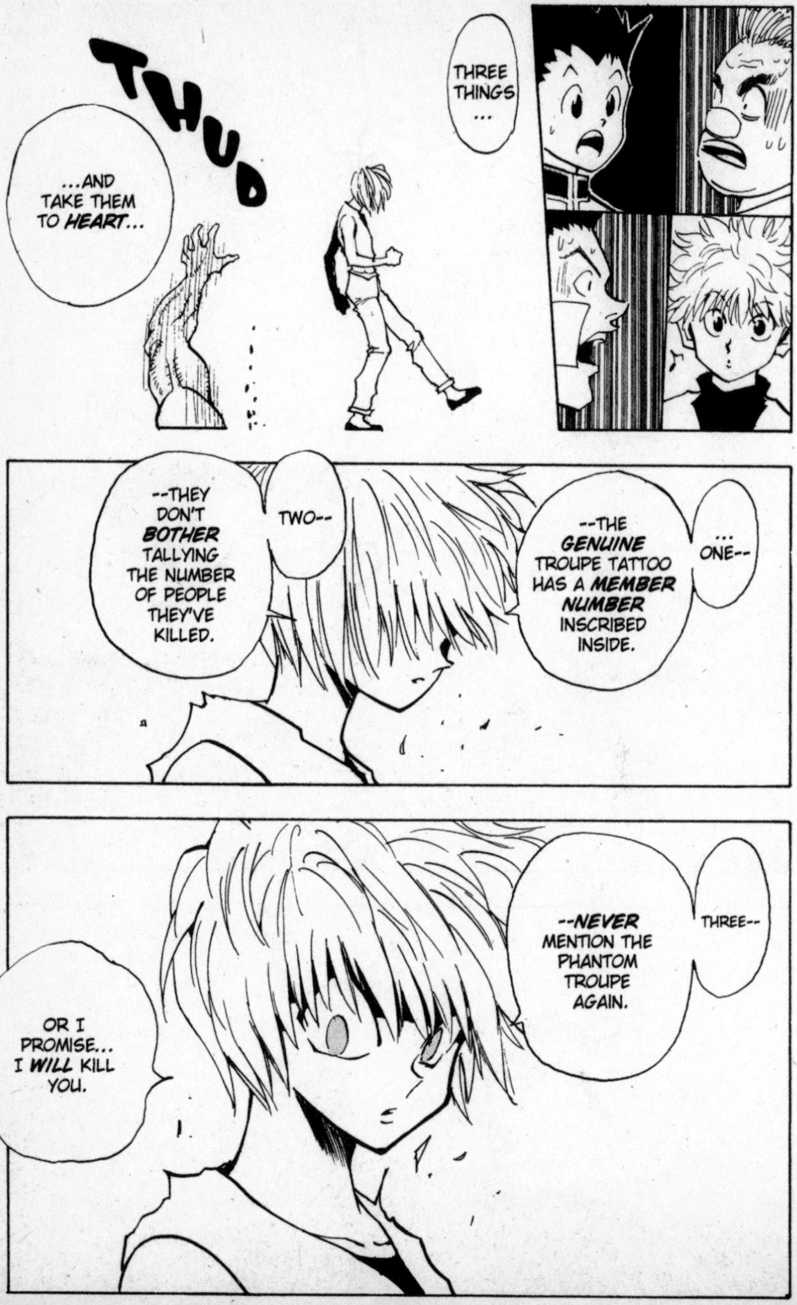
THREE THINGS ...
THUD
...AND TAKE THEM TO HEART...
... ONE--
--THE GENUINE TROUPE TATTOO HAS A MEMBER NUMBER INSCRIBED INSIDE.
TWO--
--THEY DON'T BOTHER TALLYING THE NUMBER OF PEOPLE THEY'VE KILLED.
THREE--
--NEVER MENTION THE PHANTOM TROUPE AGAIN.
OR I PROMISE... I WILL KILL YOU.

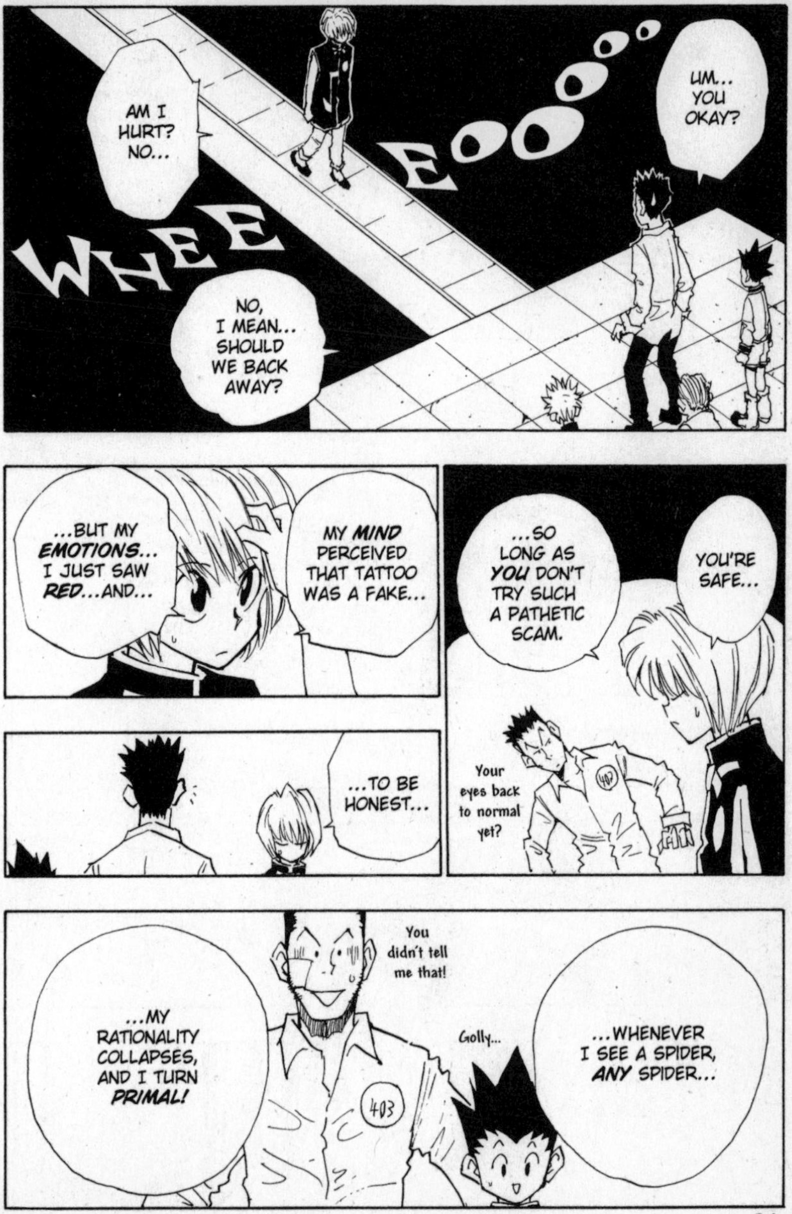
UM... YOU OKAY?
WHEEEOOOOO
AM I HURT? NO...
NO, I MEAN... SHOULD WE BACK AWAY?
YOU'RE SAFE...
...SO LONG AS ***YOU*** DON'T TRY SUCH A PATHETIC SCAM.
Your eyes back to normal yet?
MY ***MIND*** PERCEIVED THAT TATTOO WAS A FAKE...
...BUT MY ***EMOTIONS***... I JUST SAW ***RED***...AND...
...TO BE HONEST...
...WHENEVER I SEE A SPIDER, ***ANY*** SPIDER...
You didn't tell me that!
Golly...
...MY RATIONALITY COLLAPSES, AND I TURN ***PRIMAL!***

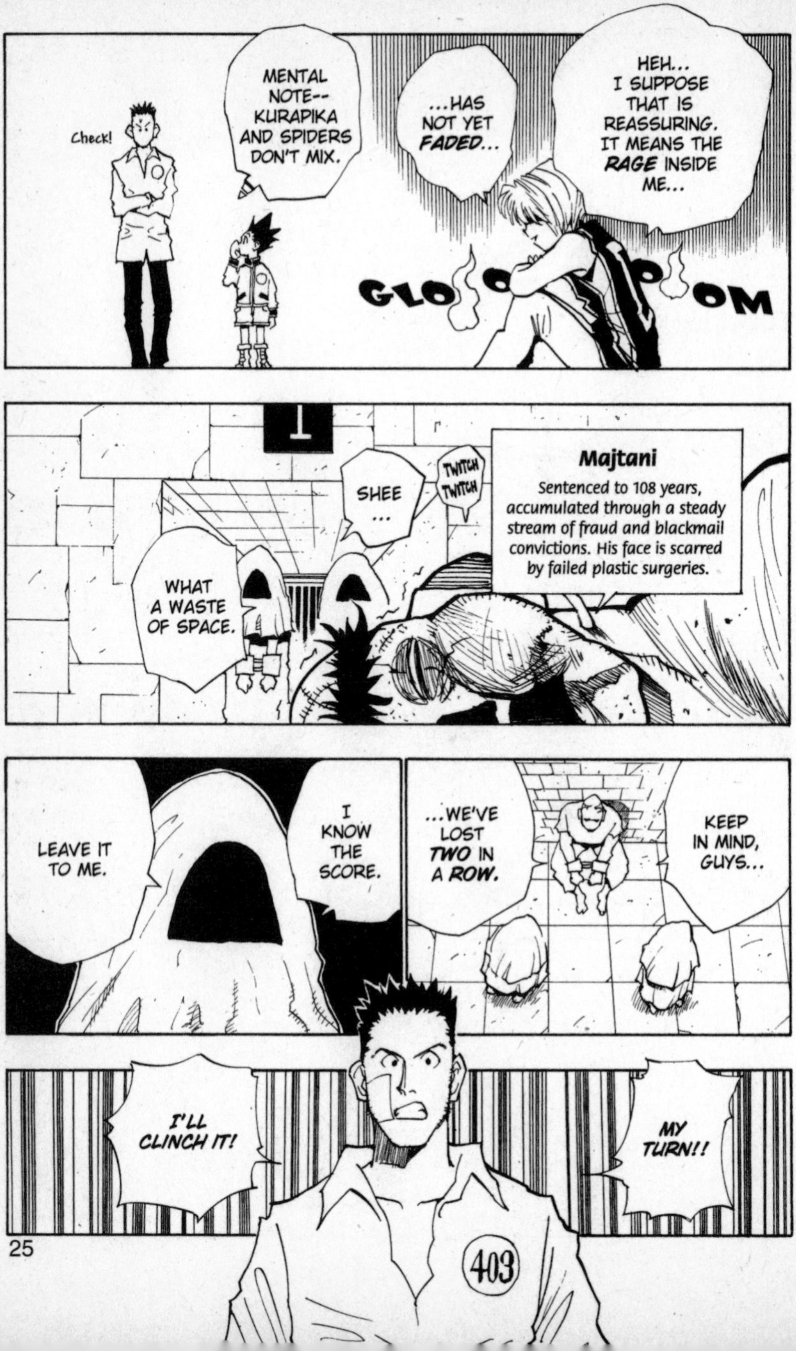
HEH... I SUPPOSE THAT IS REASSURING. IT MEANS THE RAGE INSIDE ME...
...HAS NOT YET FADED...
GLOOOOM
MENTAL NOTE-- KURAPIKA AND SPIDERS DON'T MIX.
Check!
Majtani
Sentenced to 108 years, accumulated through a steady stream of fraud and blackmail convictions. His face is scarred by failed plastic surgeries.
TWITCH TWITCH
SHEE...
WHAT A WASTE OF SPACE.
KEEP IN MIND, GUYS...
...WE'VE LOST TWO IN A ROW.
I KNOW THE SCORE.
LEAVE IT TO ME.
MY TURN!!
I'LL CLINCH IT!
403

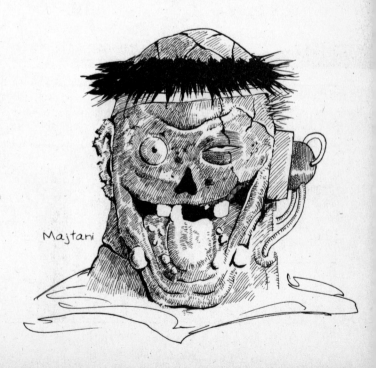
Majtani

Chapter 19

THE TRAP OF MAJORITY RULES

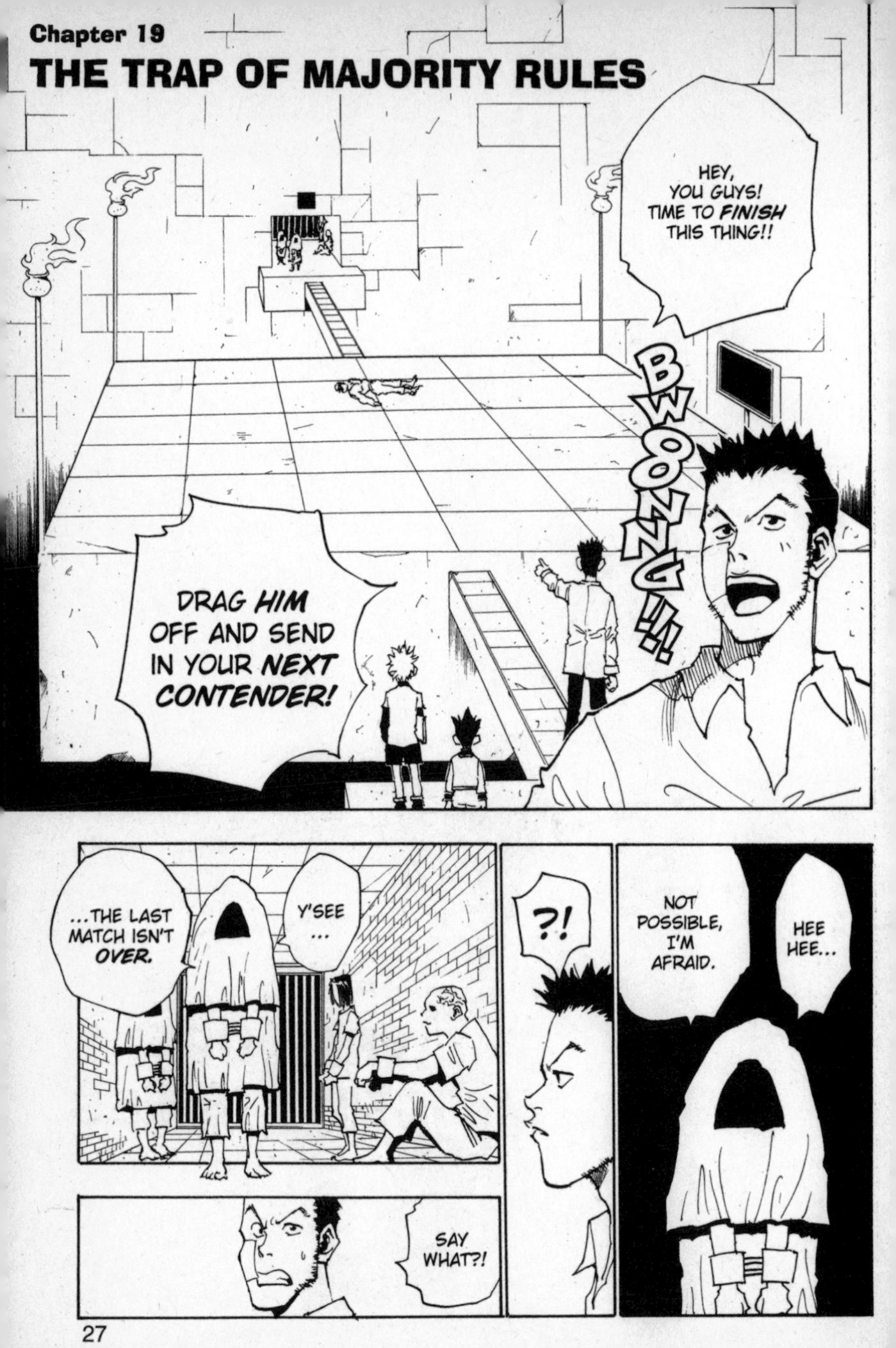
HEY, YOU GUYS! TIME TO *FINISH* THIS THING!!
BWOONG!!!
DRAG *HIM* OFF AND SEND IN YOUR *NEXT CONTENDER!*
HEE HEE...
NOT POSSIBLE, I'M AFRAID.
?!
Y'SEE ...
...THE LAST MATCH ISN'T *OVER.*
SAY WHAT?!

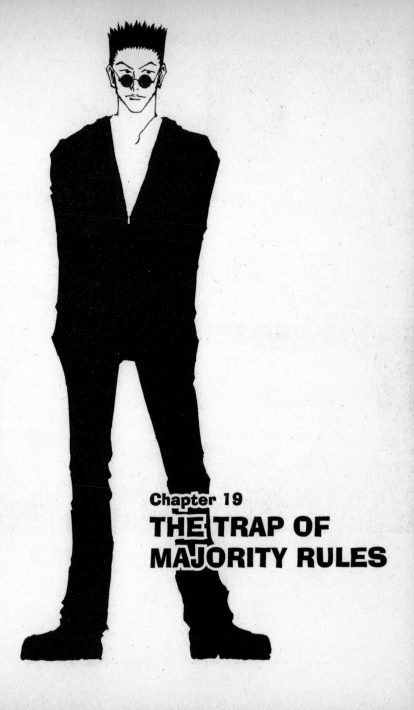

Chapter 19
THE TRAP OF MAJORITY RULES

READ THIS WAY

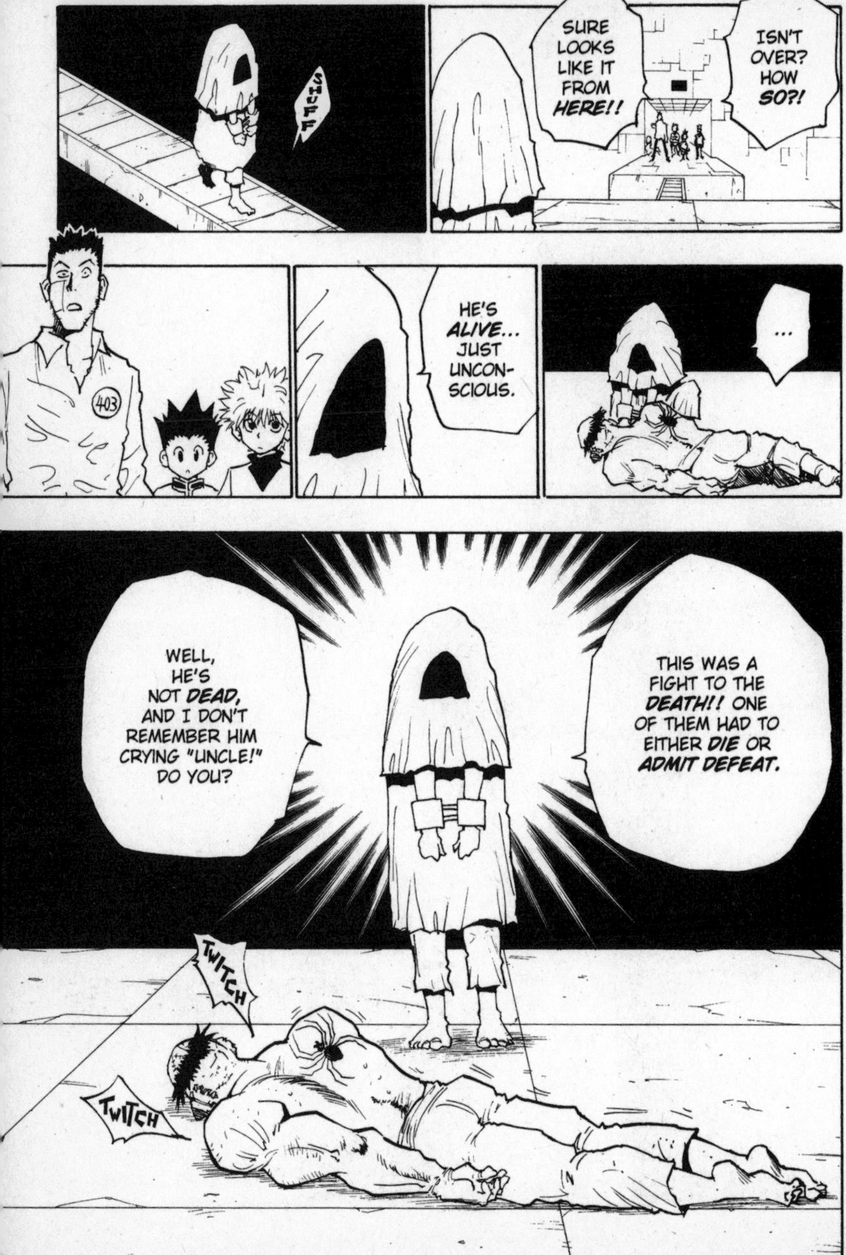
ISN'T OVER? HOW SO?!
SURE LOOKS LIKE IT FROM HERE!!
SHUFF
...
HE'S ALIVE... JUST UNCON-SCIOUS.
403
THIS WAS A FIGHT TO THE DEATH!! ONE OF THEM HAD TO EITHER DIE OR ADMIT DEFEAT.
WELL, HE'S NOT DEAD, AND I DON'T REMEMBER HIM CRYING "UNCLE!" DO YOU?
TWITCH
TWITCH

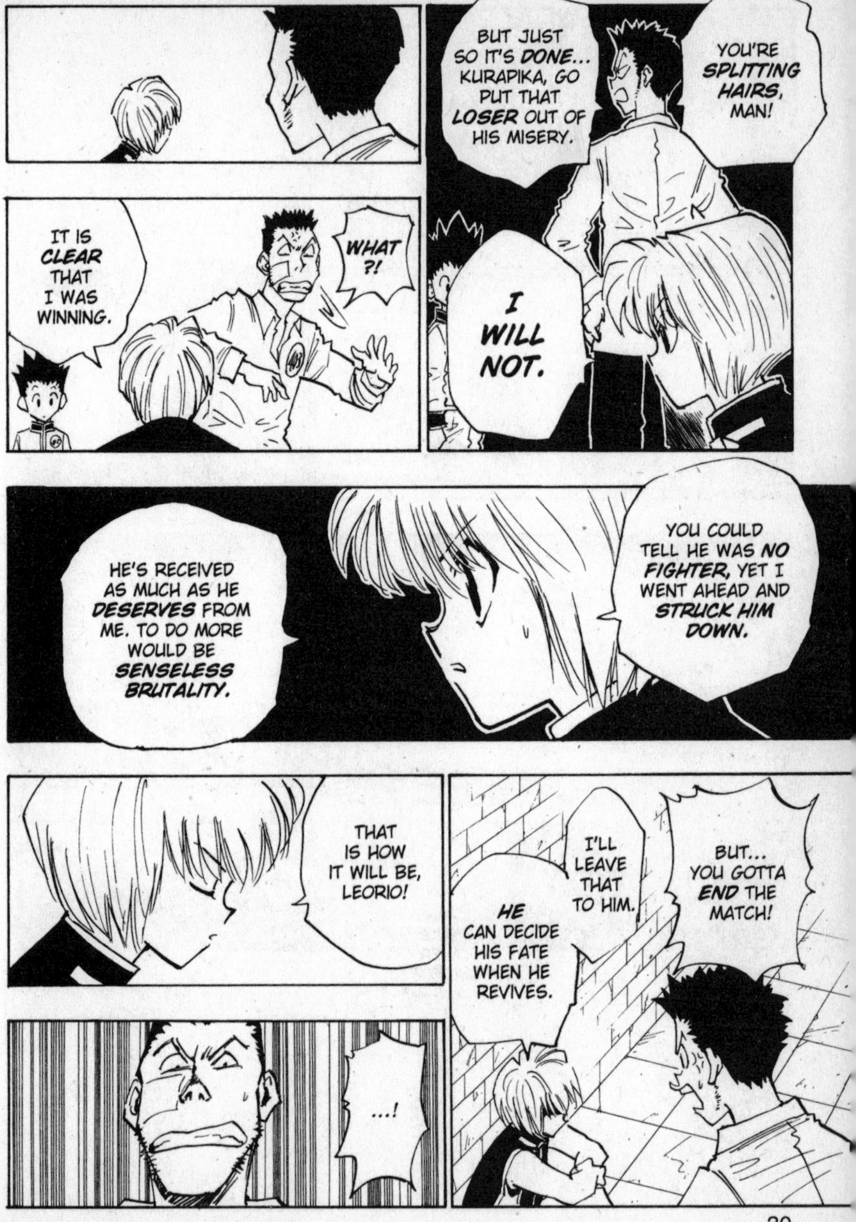
YOU'RE SPLITTING HAIRS, MAN!
BUT JUST SO IT'S DONE... KURAPIKA, GO PUT THAT LOSER OUT OF HIS MISERY.
I WILL NOT.
WHAT?!
IT IS CLEAR THAT I WAS WINNING.
YOU COULD TELL HE WAS NO FIGHTER, YET I WENT AHEAD AND STRUCK HIM DOWN.
HE'S RECEIVED AS MUCH AS HE DESERVES FROM ME. TO DO MORE WOULD BE SENSELESS BRUTALITY.
BUT... YOU GOTTA END THE MATCH!
I'LL LEAVE THAT TO HIM.
HE CAN DECIDE HIS FATE WHEN HE REVIVES.
THAT IS HOW IT WILL BE, LEORIO!
...!

READ THIS WAY

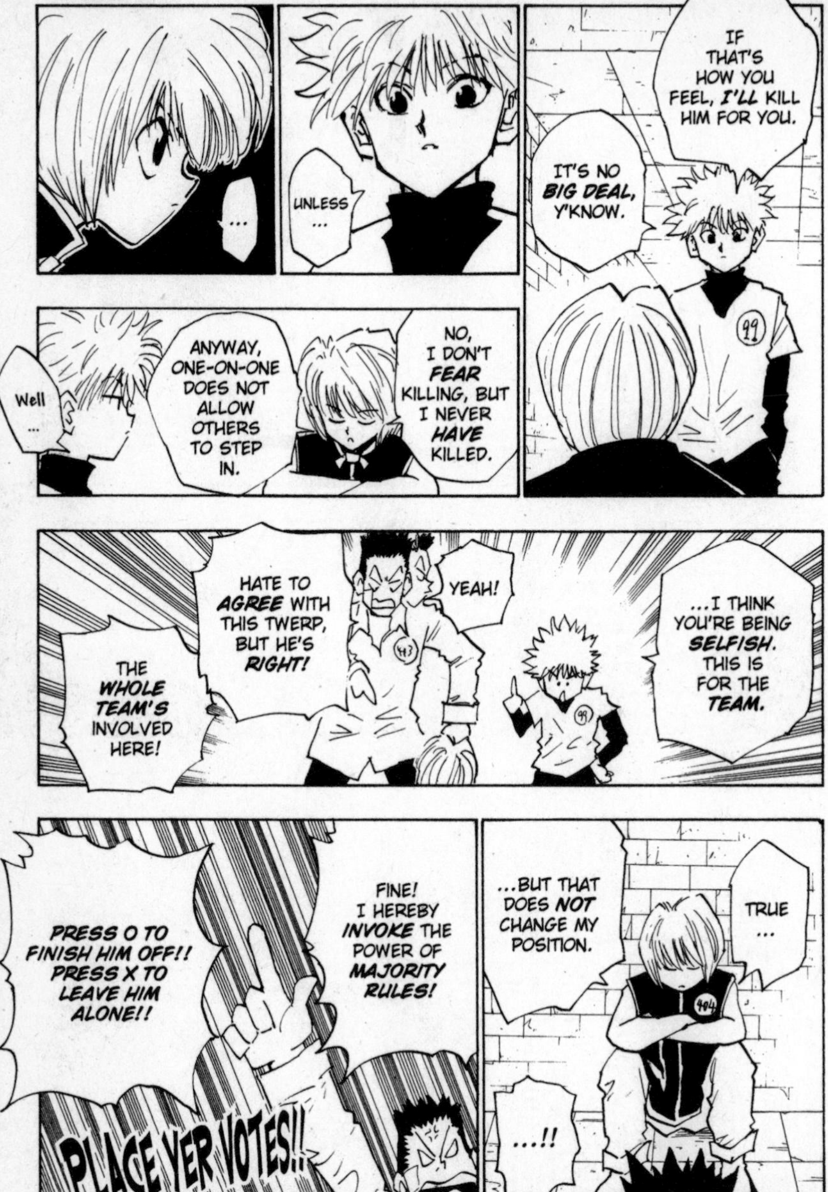

IF THAT'S HOW YOU FEEL, I'LL KILL HIM FOR YOU.
IT'S NO BIG DEAL, Y'KNOW.
UNLESS ...
...
NO, I DON'T FEAR KILLING, BUT I NEVER HAVE KILLED.
ANYWAY, ONE-ON-ONE DOES NOT ALLOW OTHERS TO STEP IN.
Well ...
...I THINK YOU'RE BEING SELFISH. THIS IS FOR THE TEAM.
YEAH!
HATE TO AGREE WITH THIS TWERP, BUT HE'S RIGHT!
THE WHOLE TEAM'S INVOLVED HERE!
TRUE ...
...BUT THAT DOES NOT CHANGE MY POSITION.
...!!
FINE! I HEREBY INVOKE THE POWER OF MAJORITY RULES!
PRESS O TO FINISH HIM OFF!! PRESS X TO LEAVE HIM ALONE!!
PLACE YER VOTES!!

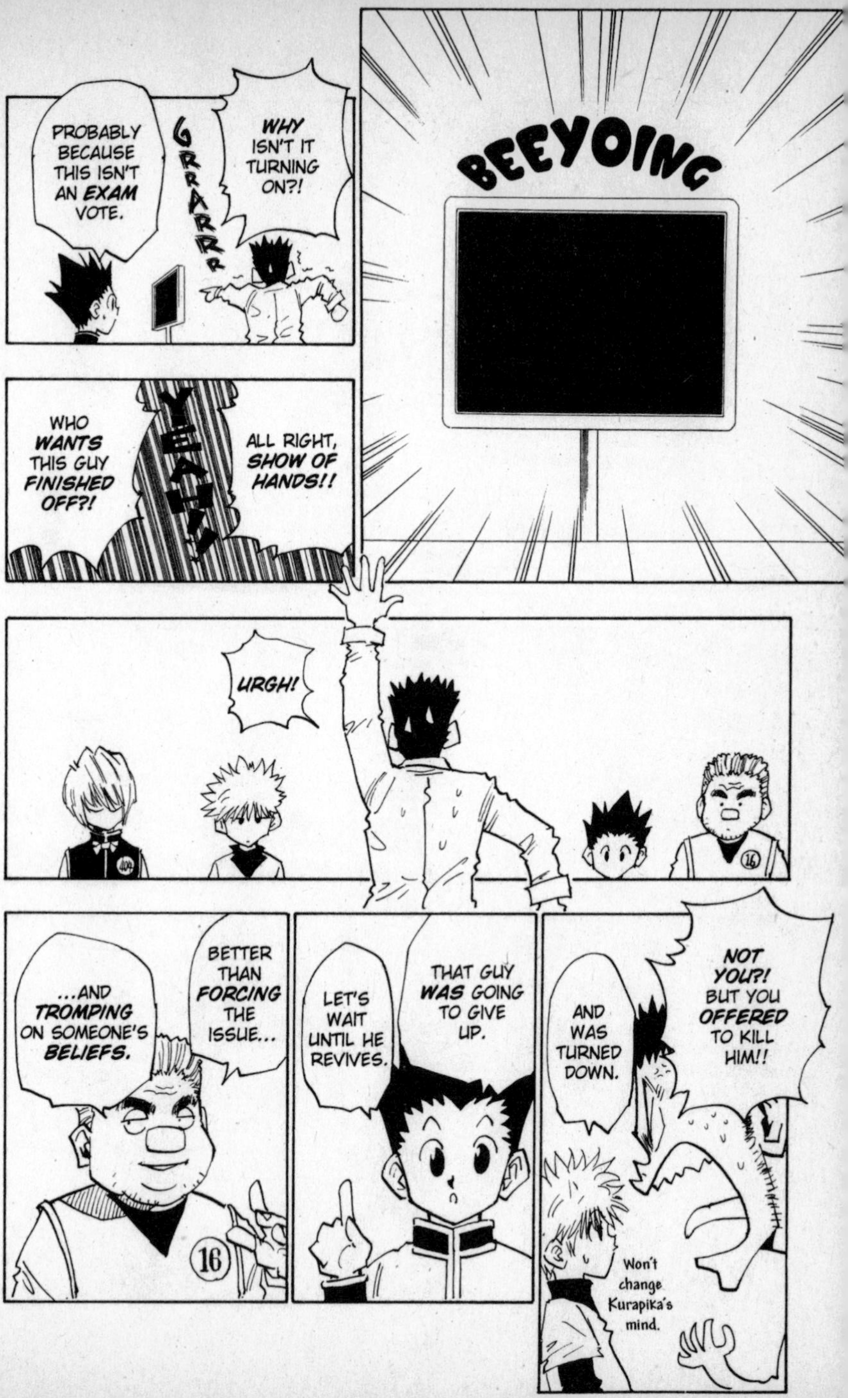
BEEYOING
WHY ISN'T IT TURNING ON?!
GRRARRRR
PROBABLY BECAUSE THIS ISN'T AN EXAM VOTE.
ALL RIGHT, SHOW OF HANDS!!
WHO WANTS THIS GUY FINISHED OFF?!
YEAH!!
URGH!
NOT YOU?! BUT YOU OFFERED TO KILL HIM!!
AND WAS TURNED DOWN.
Won't change Kurapika's mind.
THAT GUY WAS GOING TO GIVE UP.
LET'S WAIT UNTIL HE REVIVES.
BETTER THAN FORCING THE ISSUE...
...AND TROMPING ON SOMEONE'S BELIEFS.

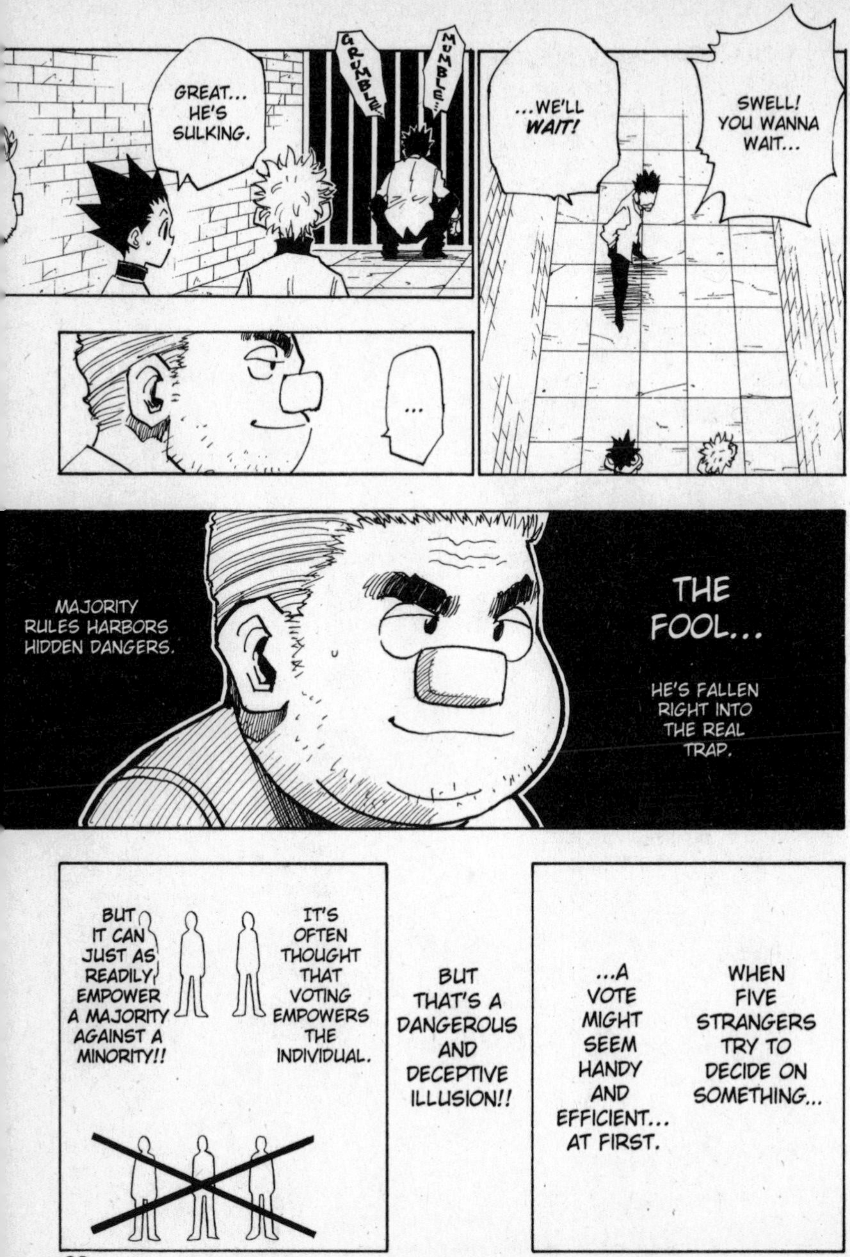
SWELL! YOU WANNA WAIT...
...WE'LL WAIT!
MUMBLE...
GRUMBLE
GREAT... HE'S SULKING.
...
THE FOOL...
HE'S FALLEN RIGHT INTO THE REAL TRAP.
MAJORITY RULES HARBORS HIDDEN DANGERS.
WHEN FIVE STRANGERS TRY TO DECIDE ON SOMETHING...
...A VOTE MIGHT SEEM HANDY AND EFFICIENT... AT FIRST.
BUT THAT'S A DANGEROUS AND DECEPTIVE ILLUSION!!
IT'S OFTEN THOUGHT THAT VOTING EMPOWERS THE INDIVIDUAL.
BUT IT CAN JUST AS READILY EMPOWER A MAJORITY AGAINST A MINORITY!!

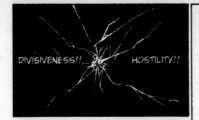

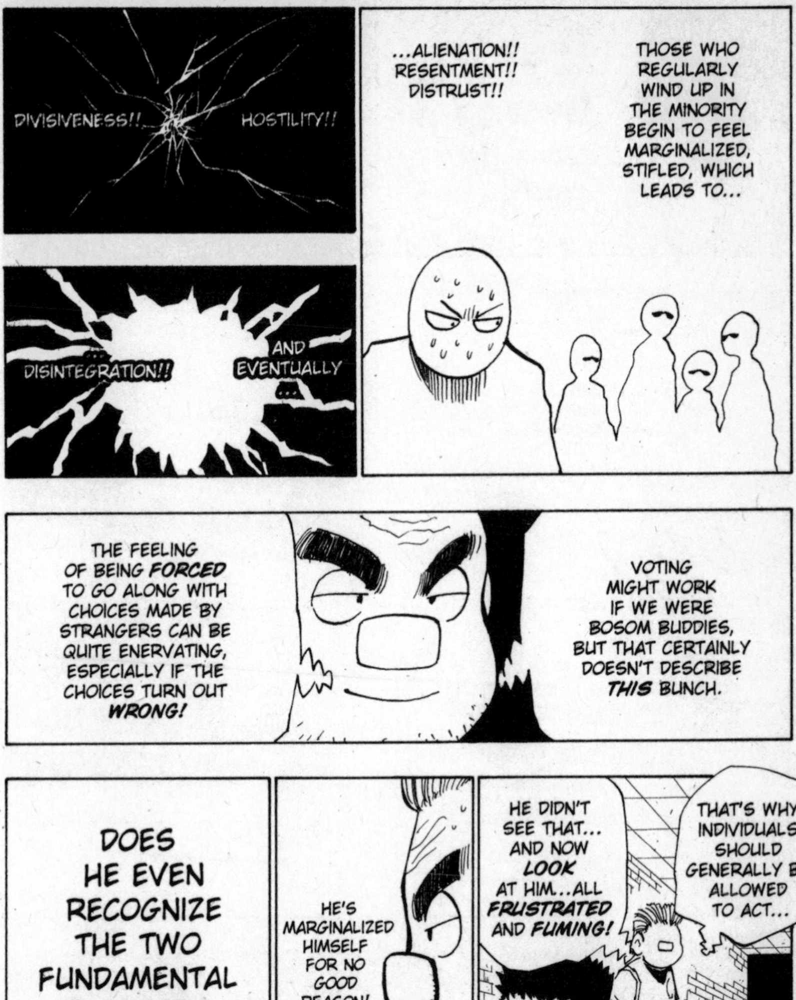
THOSE WHO REGULARLY WIND UP IN THE MINORITY BEGIN TO FEEL MARGINALIZED, STIFLED, WHICH LEADS TO...
...ALIENATION!! RESENTMENT!! DISTRUST!!
HOSTILITY!!
DIVISIVENESS!!
AND EVENTUALLY ...
...DISINTEGRATION!!
VOTING MIGHT WORK IF WE WERE BOSOM BUDDIES, BUT THAT CERTAINLY DOESN'T DESCRIBE THIS BUNCH.
THE FEELING OF BEING FORCED TO GO ALONG WITH CHOICES MADE BY STRANGERS CAN BE QUITE ENERVATING, ESPECIALLY IF THE CHOICES TURN OUT WRONG!
THAT'S WHY INDIVIDUALS SHOULD GENERALLY BE ALLOWED TO ACT...
HE DIDN'T SEE THAT... AND NOW LOOK AT HIM...ALL FRUSTRATED AND FUMING!
...AS THEY SEE FIT. VOTES JUST CREATE TENSION AND DESTROY INITIATIVE.
MUMBLE...
GRUMBLE...
HE'S MARGINALIZED HIMSELF FOR NO GOOD REASON!
DOES HE EVEN RECOGNIZE THE TWO FUNDAMENTAL BLUNDERS HE MADE, ALLOWING DISCUSSION AND...

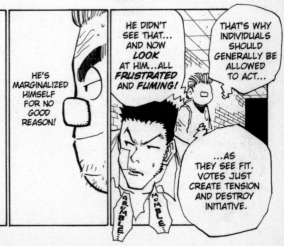

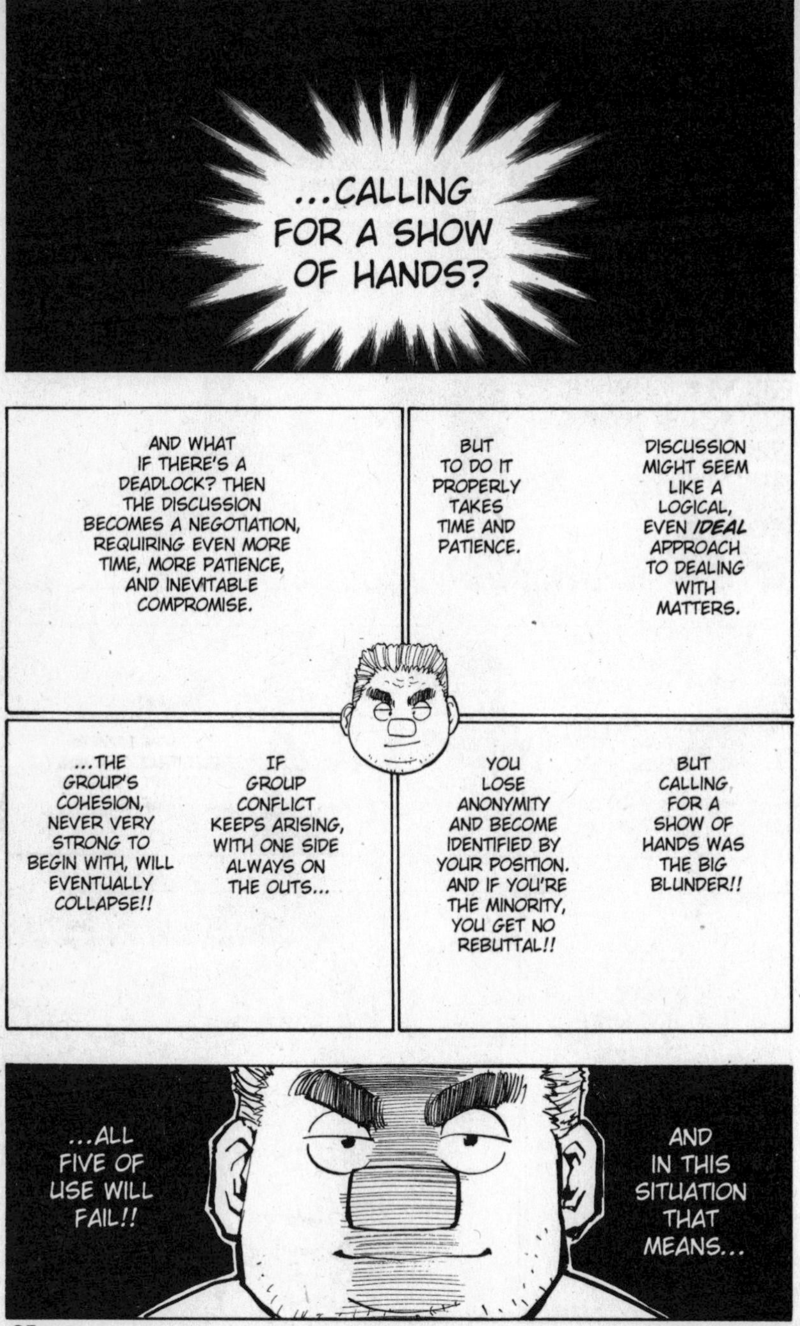
...CALLING FOR A SHOW OF HANDS?
DISCUSSION MIGHT SEEM LIKE A LOGICAL, EVEN *IDEAL* APPROACH TO DEALING WITH MATTERS.
BUT TO DO IT PROPERLY TAKES TIME AND PATIENCE.
AND WHAT IF THERE'S A DEADLOCK? THEN THE DISCUSSION BECOMES A NEGOTIATION, REQUIRING EVEN MORE TIME, MORE PATIENCE, AND INEVITABLE COMPROMISE.
BUT CALLING FOR A SHOW OF HANDS WAS THE BIG BLUNDER!!
YOU LOSE ANONYMITY AND BECOME IDENTIFIED BY YOUR POSITION. AND IF YOU'RE THE MINORITY, YOU GET NO REBUTTAL!!
IF GROUP CONFLICT KEEPS ARISING, WITH ONE SIDE ALWAYS ON THE OUTS...
...THE GROUP'S COHESION, NEVER VERY STRONG TO BEGIN WITH, WILL EVENTUALLY COLLAPSE!!
AND IN THIS SITUATION THAT MEANS...
...ALL FIVE OF USE WILL FAIL!!

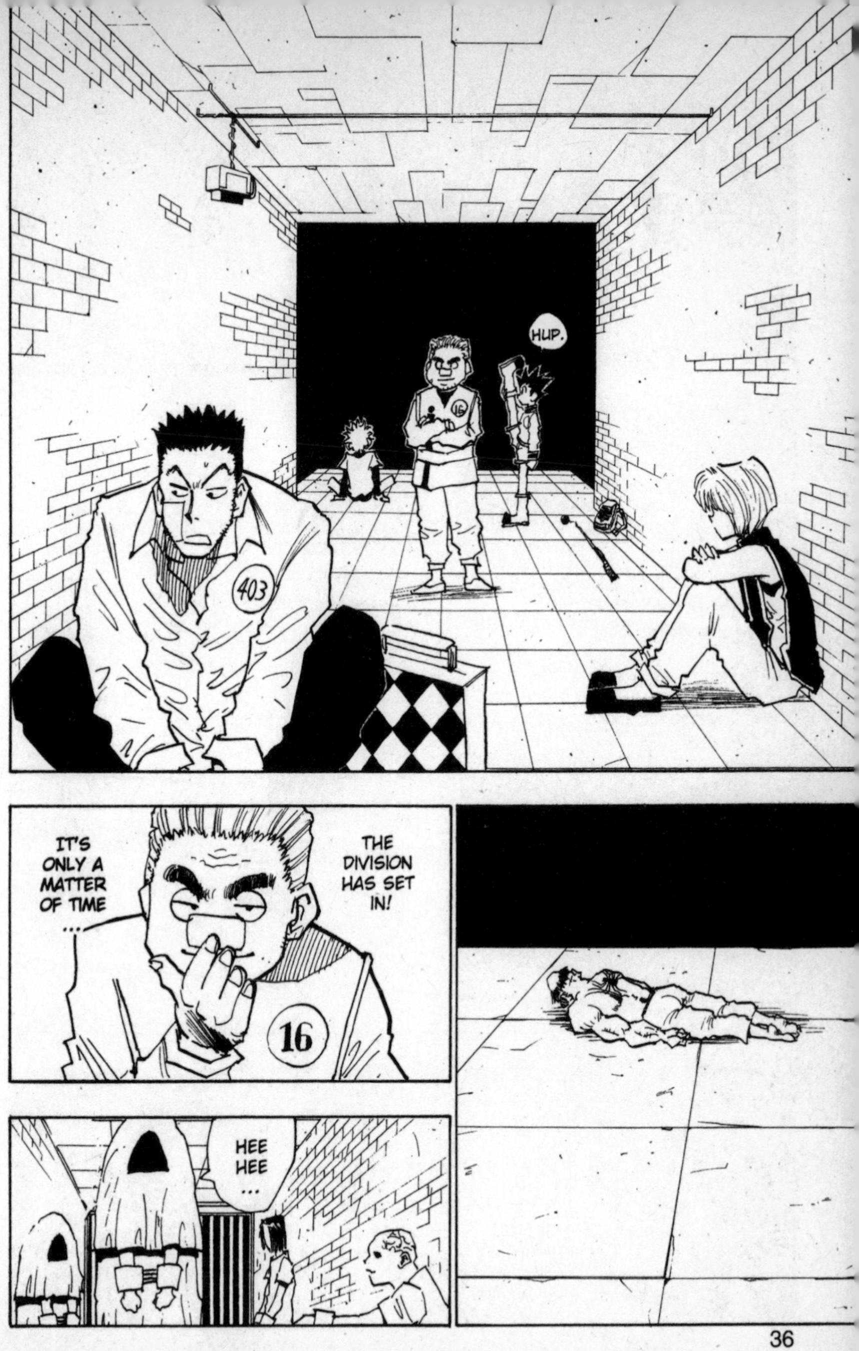
HUP.
THE DIVISION HAS SET IN!
IT'S ONLY A MATTER OF TIME ...
HEE HEE ...

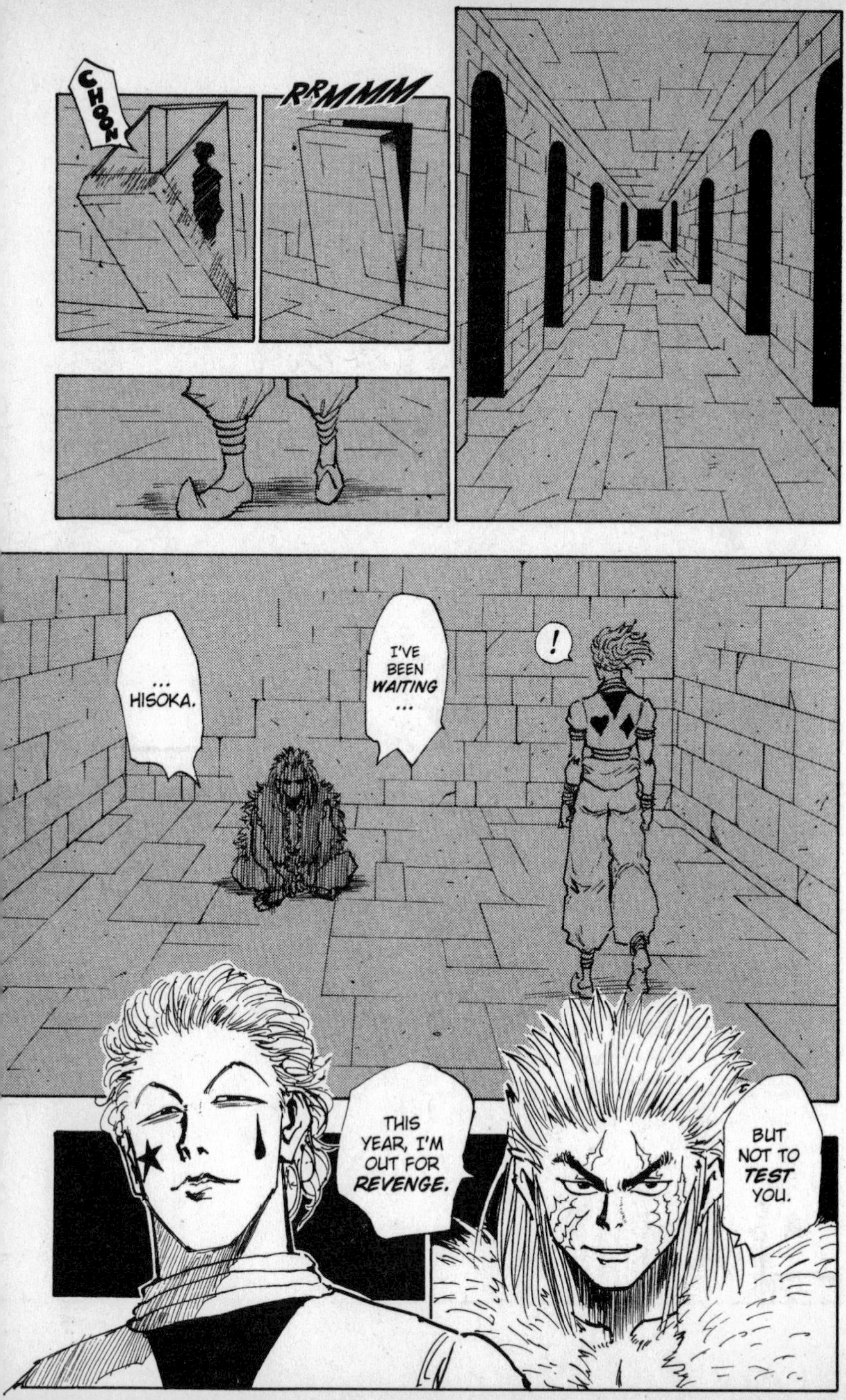
RRMMM
CHOON
!
I'VE BEEN WAITING ...
... HISOKA.
BUT NOT TO TEST YOU.
THIS YEAR, I'M OUT FOR REVENGE.

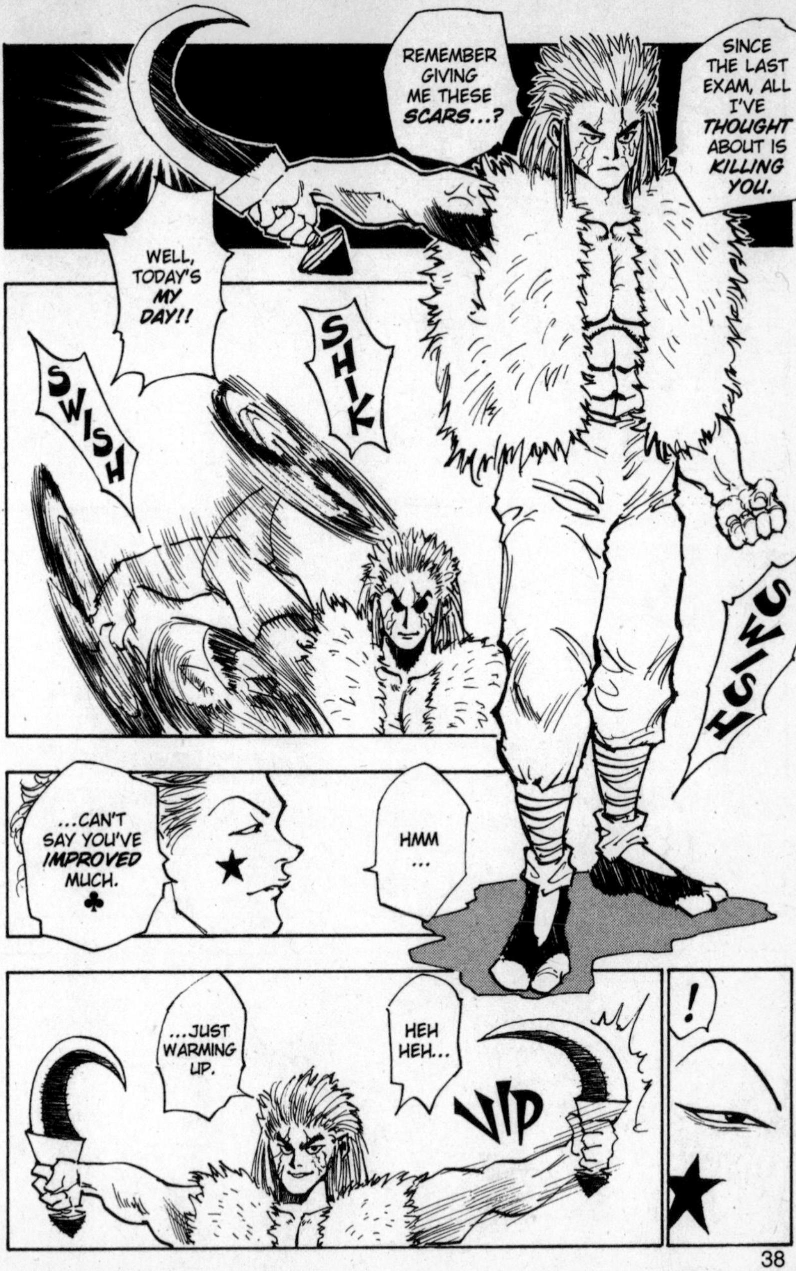
SINCE THE LAST EXAM, ALL I'VE *THOUGHT* ABOUT IS *KILLING YOU.*
REMEMBER GIVING ME THESE *SCARS...?*
WELL, TODAY'S *MY DAY!!*
SWISH
SHIK
SWISH
HMM ...
...CAN'T SAY YOU'VE *IMPROVED* MUCH. ♣
!
HEH HEH...
VIP
...JUST WARMING UP.

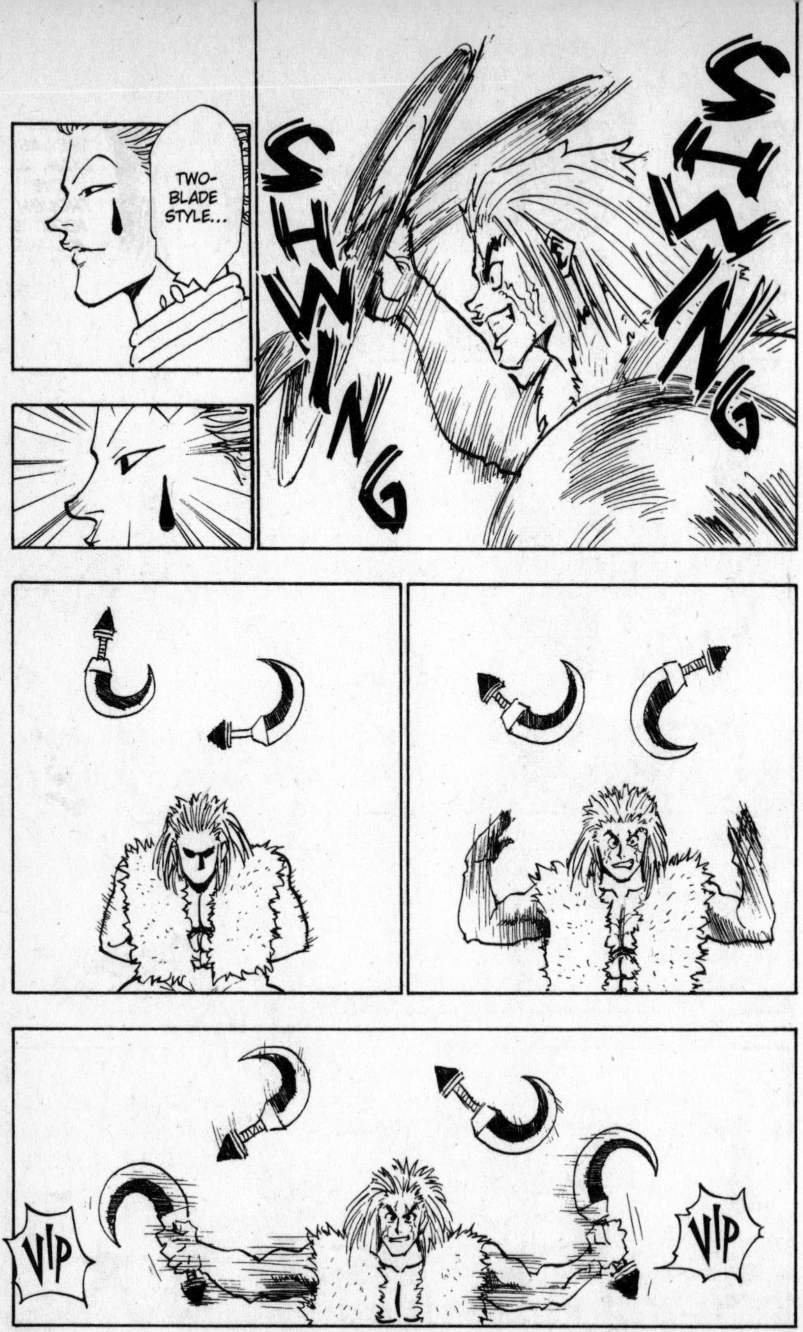
SHWING
SHWING
TWO-BLADE STYLE...
VIP
VIP

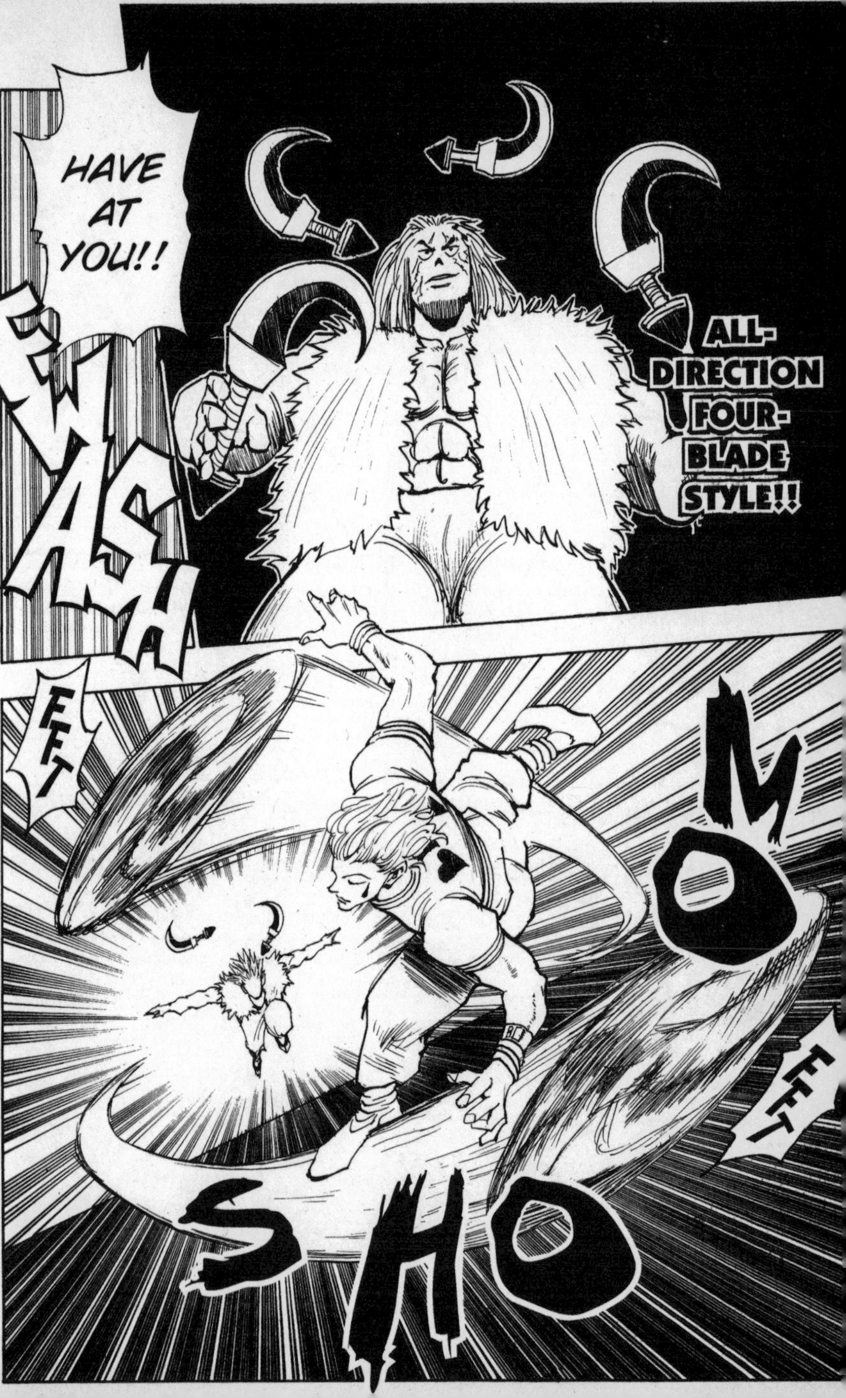
ALL-DIRECTION FOUR-BLADE STYLE!!
HAVE AT YOU!!
FFT
FFT

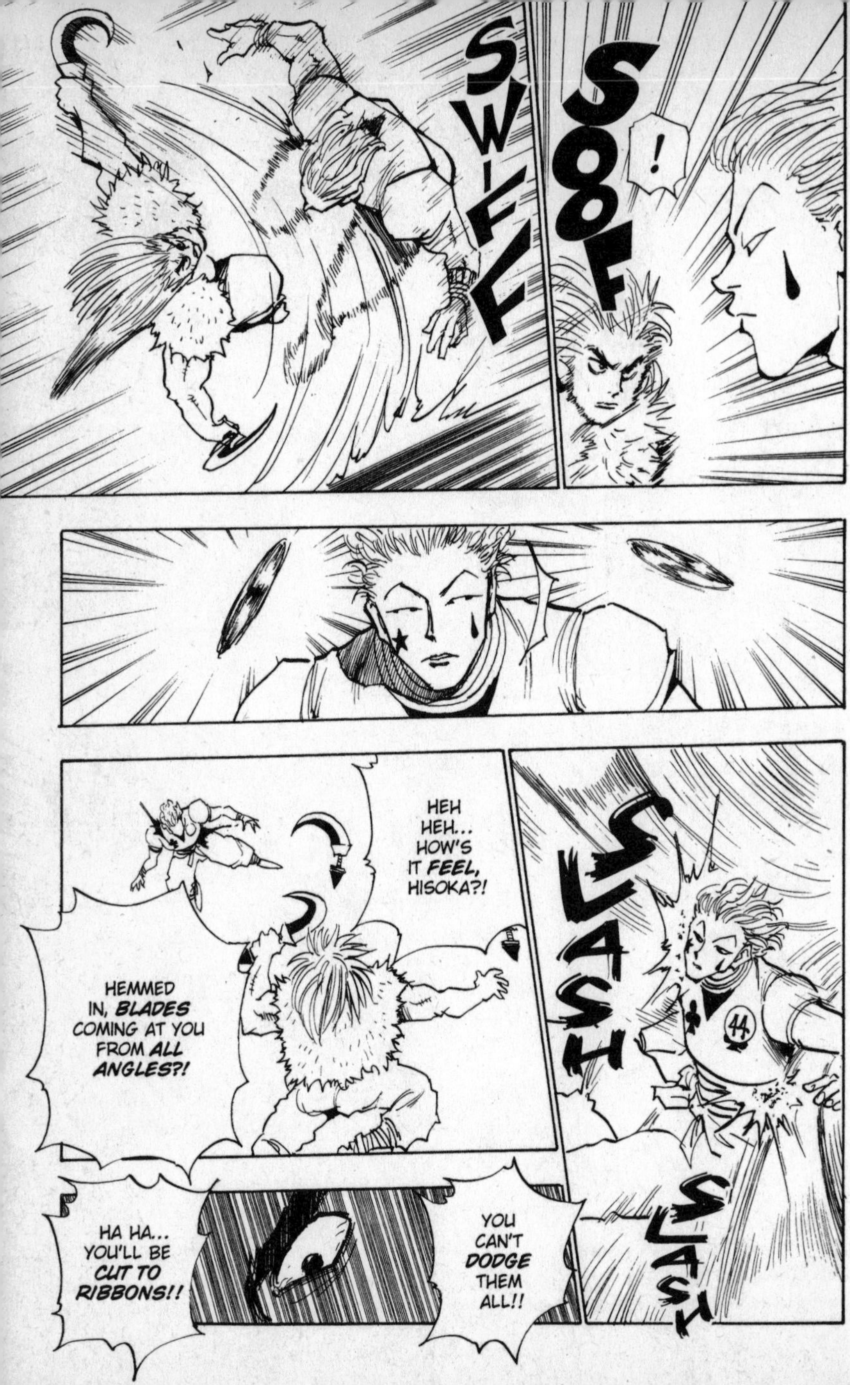
SOOF
!
SWIFF
SLASH
SLASH
HEH HEH... HOW'S IT FEEL, HISOKA?!
HEMMED IN, BLADES COMING AT YOU FROM ALL ANGLES?!
YOU CAN'T DODGE THEM ALL!!
HA HA... YOU'LL BE CUT TO RIBBONS!!

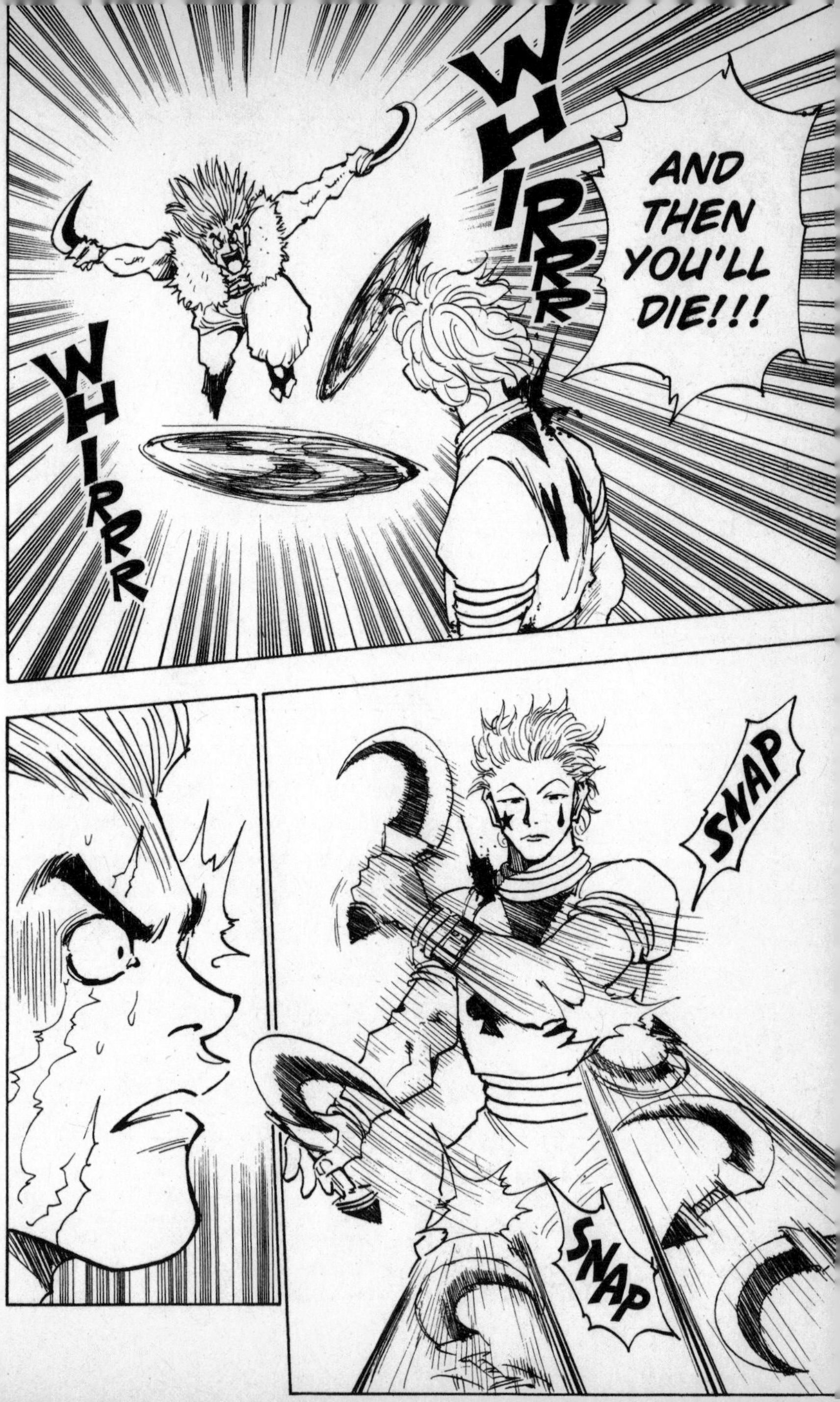
WHIRRR
AND THEN YOU'LL DIE!!!
WHIRRR
SNAP
SNAP

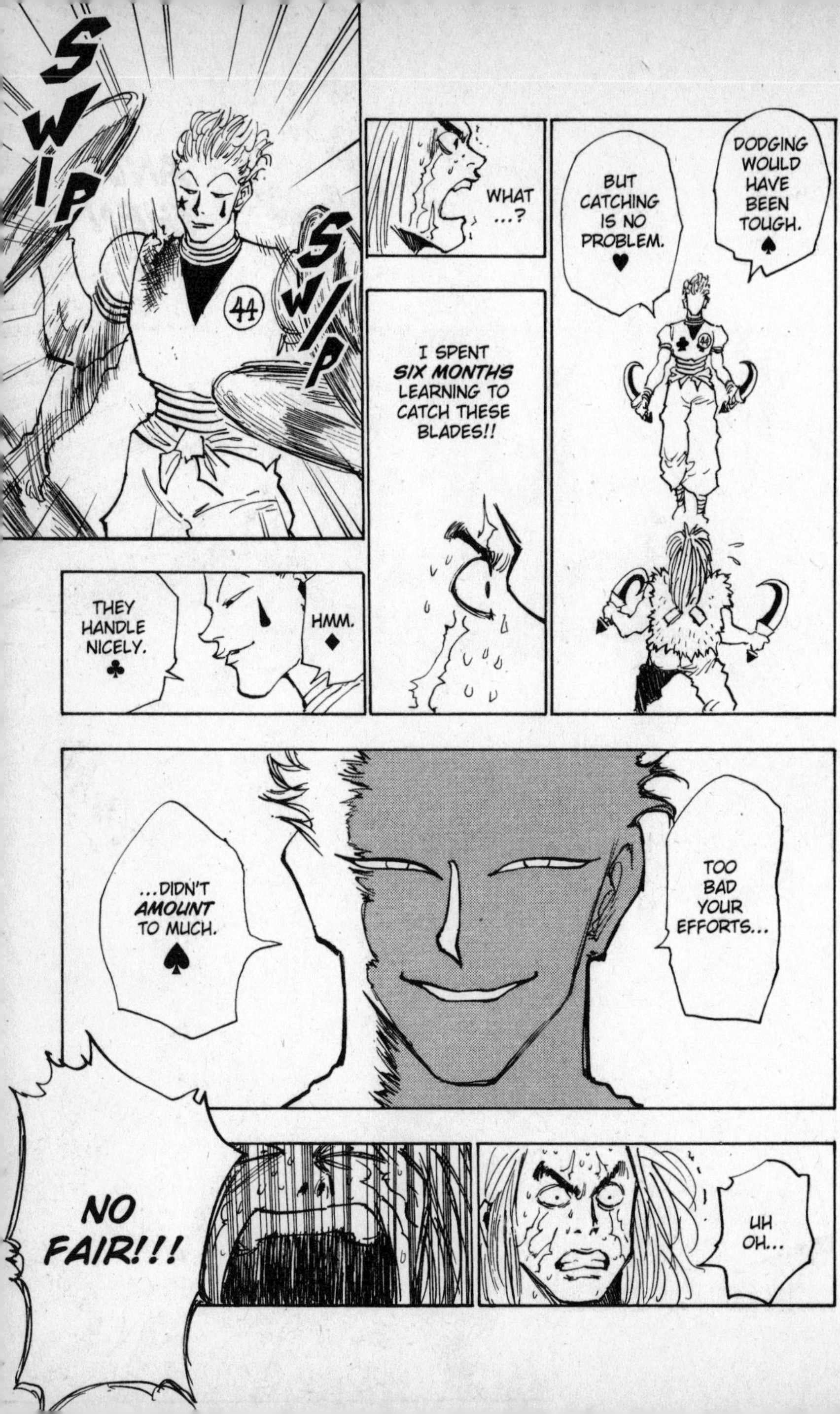
DODGING WOULD HAVE BEEN TOUGH. ♠
BUT CATCHING IS NO PROBLEM. ♥
WHAT ...?
I SPENT *SIX MONTHS* LEARNING TO CATCH THESE BLADES!!
SWIP
SWIP
HMM. ♦
THEY HANDLE NICELY. ♣
TOO BAD YOUR EFFORTS...
...DIDN'T *AMOUNT* TO MUCH. ♠
UH OH...
NO FAIR!!!

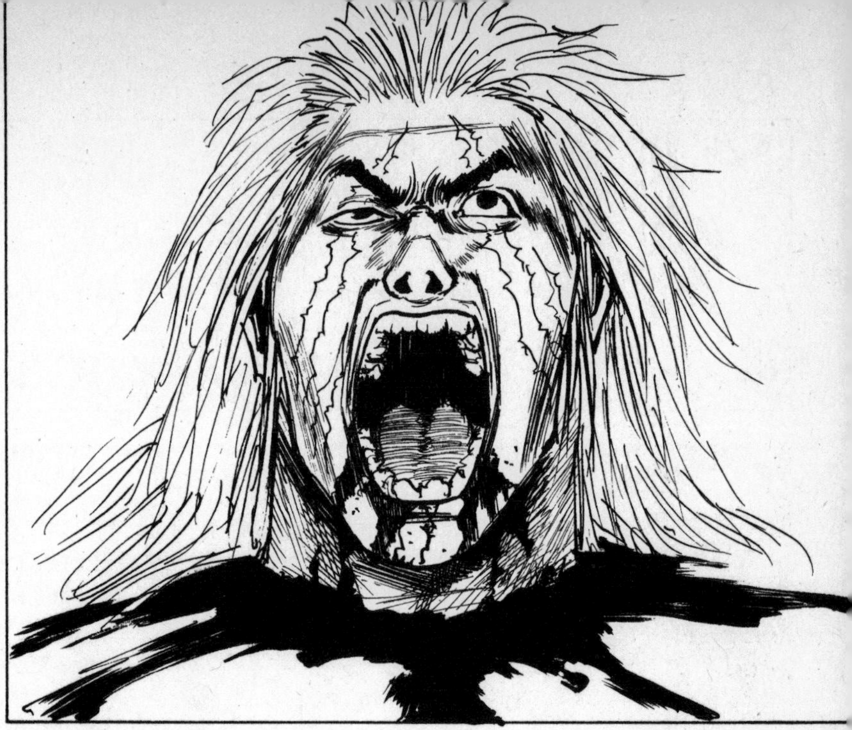

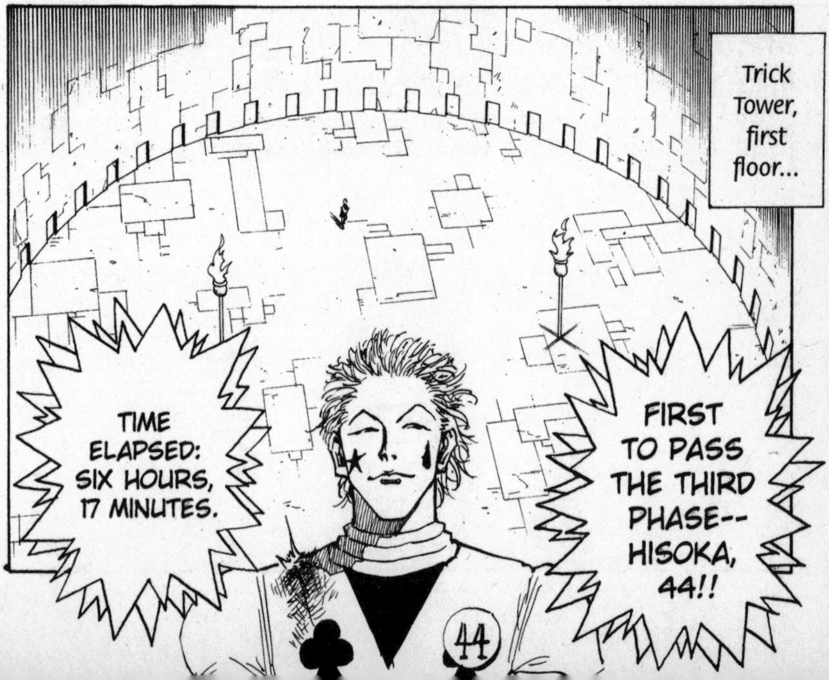
Trick Tower, first floor...
FIRST TO PASS THE THIRD PHASE-- HISOKA, 44!!
TIME ELAPSED: SIX HOURS, 17 MINUTES.
44

READ THIS WAY

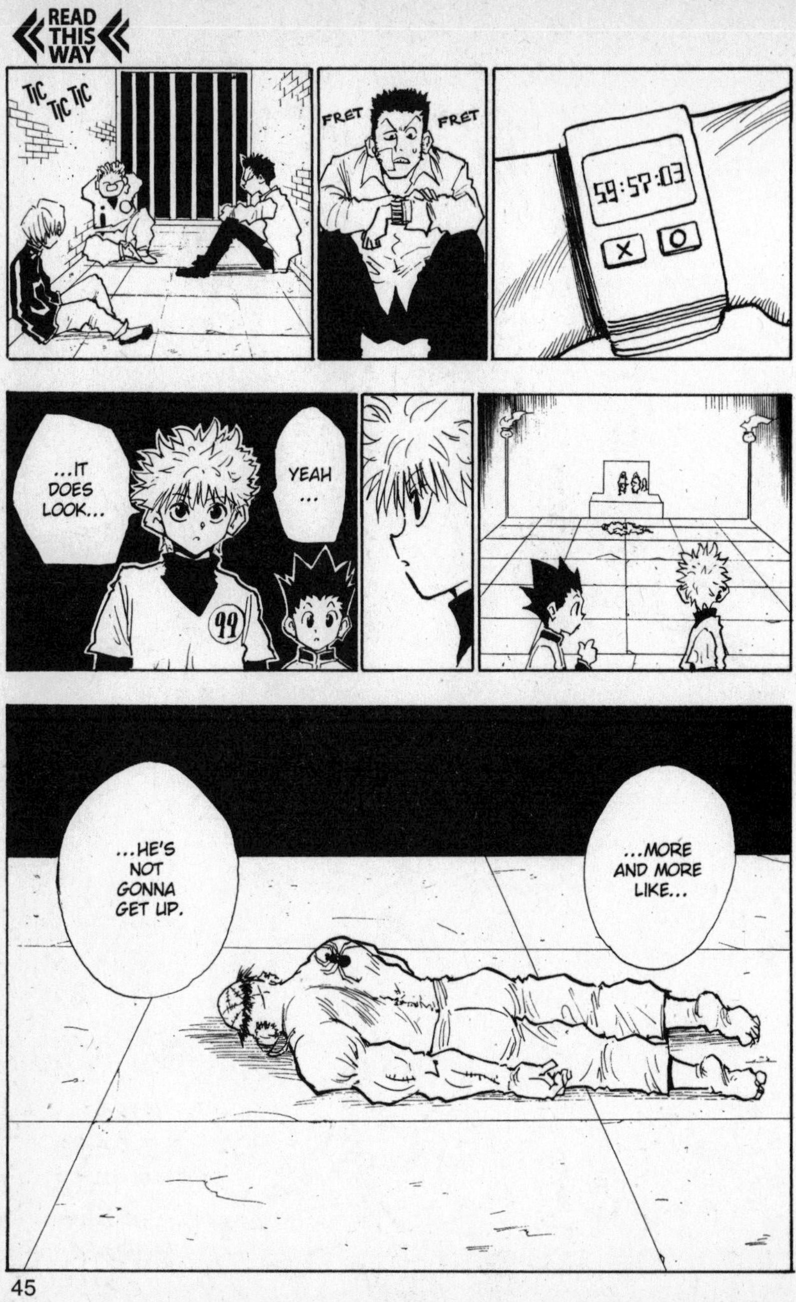
59:57:03
X
O
FRET
FRET
TIC
TIC TIC
YEAH ...
...IT DOES LOOK...
...MORE AND MORE LIKE...
...HE'S NOT GONNA GET UP.

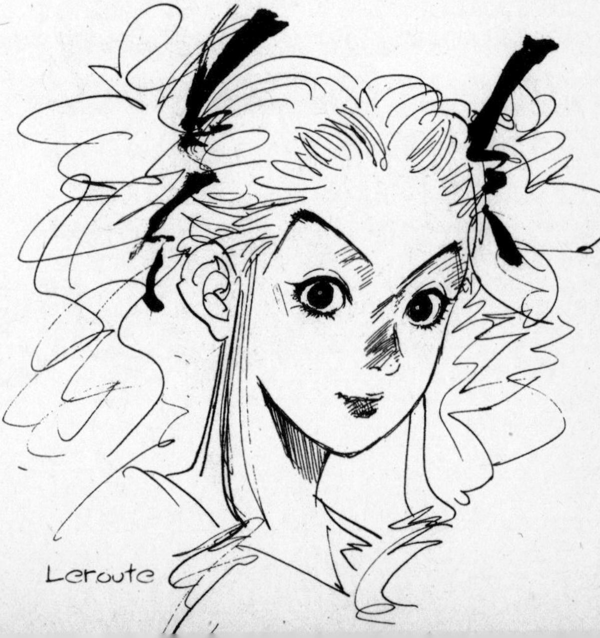
Leroute

Chapter 20
Gambling Time

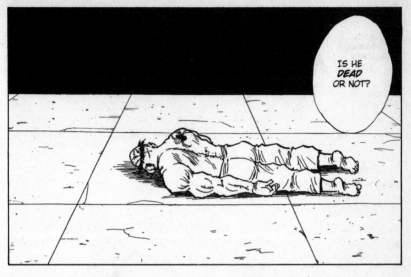

IS HE *DEAD* OR NOT?

CAN'T TELL FROM *HERE*...

...AT THIS DISTANCE, IN THIS DIM LIGHT.

SHUFF

403

48

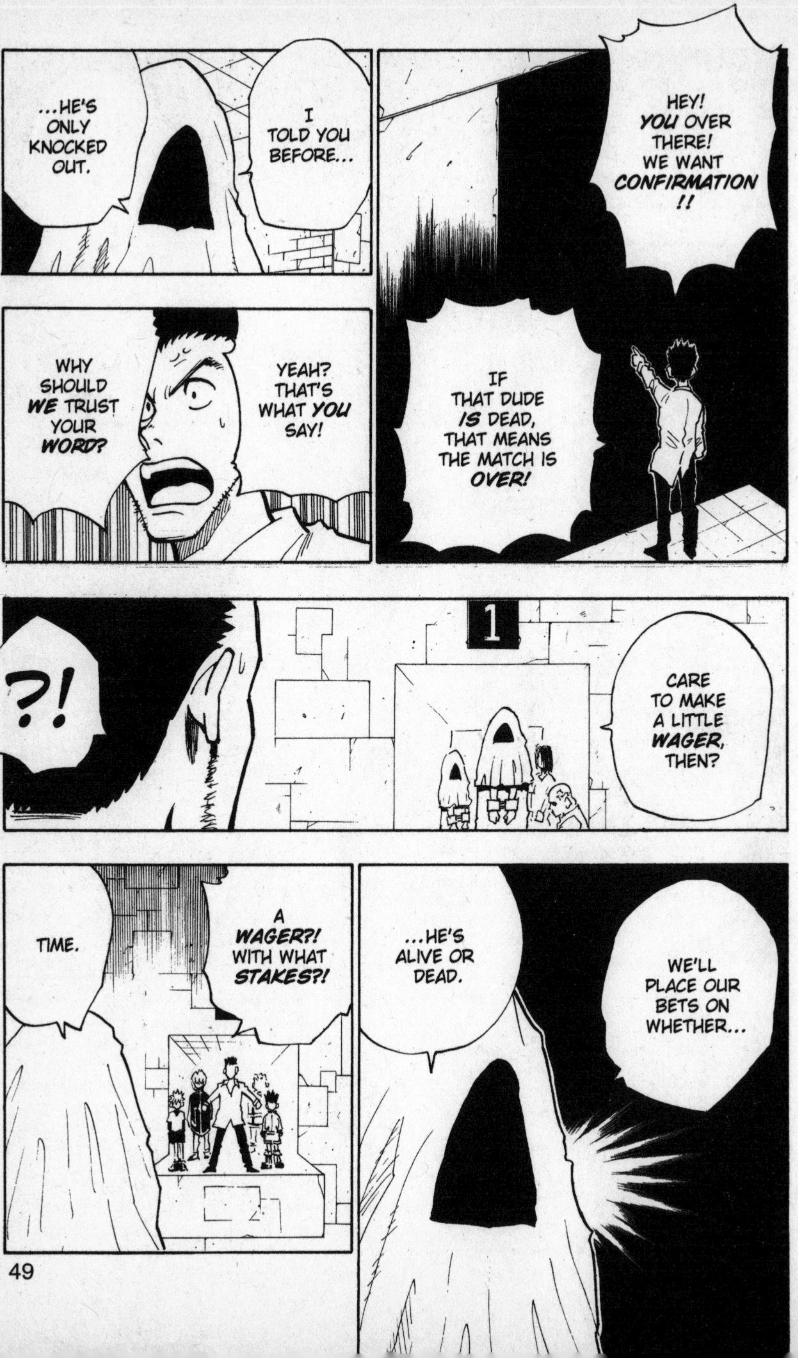
HEY! YOU OVER THERE! WE WANT CONFIRMATION !!
IF THAT DUDE IS DEAD, THAT MEANS THE MATCH IS OVER!
I TOLD YOU BEFORE...
...HE'S ONLY KNOCKED OUT.
YEAH? THAT'S WHAT YOU SAY!
WHY SHOULD WE TRUST YOUR WORD?
1
CARE TO MAKE A LITTLE WAGER, THEN?
?!
WE'LL PLACE OUR BETS ON WHETHER...
...HE'S ALIVE OR DEAD.
A WAGER?! WITH WHAT STAKES?!
TIME.

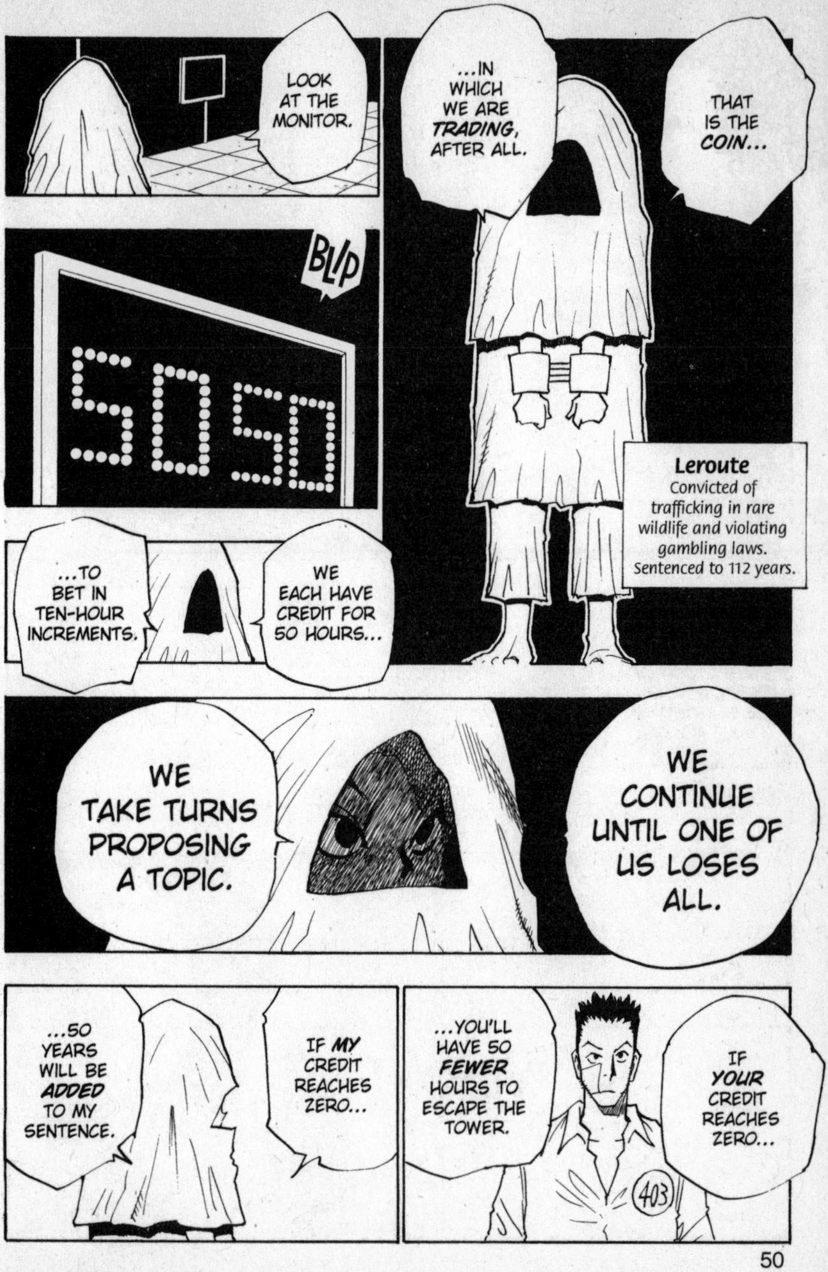
THAT IS THE *COIN*...
...IN WHICH WE ARE *TRADING*, AFTER ALL.
Leroute
Convicted of trafficking in rare wildlife and violating gambling laws. Sentenced to 112 years.
LOOK AT THE MONITOR.
BLIP
50 50
WE EACH HAVE CREDIT FOR 50 HOURS...
...TO BET IN TEN-HOUR INCREMENTS.
WE CONTINUE UNTIL ONE OF US LOSES ALL.
WE TAKE TURNS PROPOSING A TOPIC.
IF *YOUR* CREDIT REACHES ZERO...
...YOU'LL HAVE 50 *FEWER* HOURS TO ESCAPE THE TOWER.
403
IF *MY* CREDIT REACHES ZERO...
...50 YEARS WILL BE *ADDED* TO MY SENTENCE.

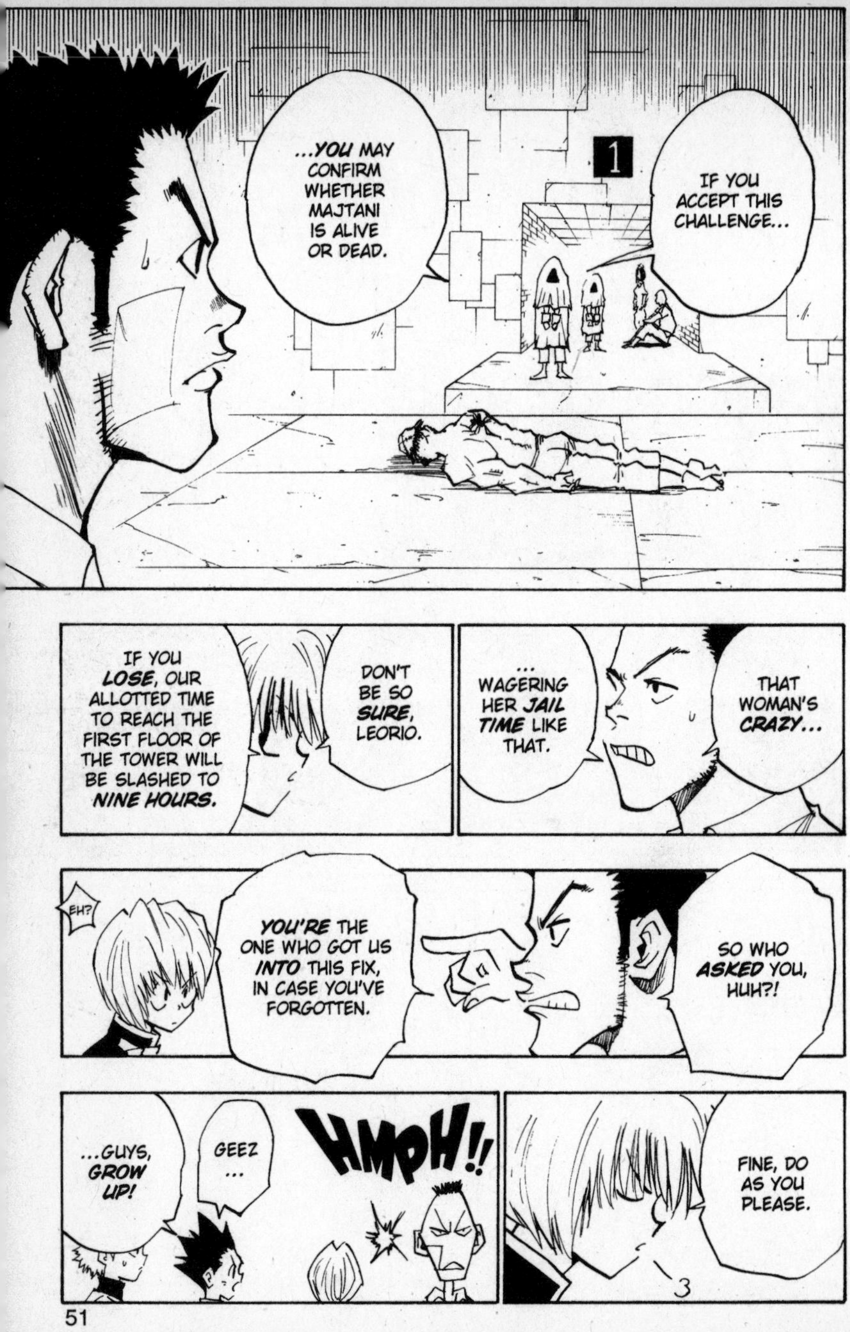
1
IF YOU ACCEPT THIS CHALLENGE...
...YOU MAY CONFIRM WHETHER MAJTANI IS ALIVE OR DEAD.
THAT WOMAN'S CRAZY...
...WAGERING HER JAIL TIME LIKE THAT.
DON'T BE SO SURE, LEORIO.
IF YOU LOSE, OUR ALLOTTED TIME TO REACH THE FIRST FLOOR OF THE TOWER WILL BE SLASHED TO NINE HOURS.
SO WHO ASKED YOU, HUH?!
YOU'RE THE ONE WHO GOT US INTO THIS FIX, IN CASE YOU'VE FORGOTTEN.
EH?
FINE, DO AS YOU PLEASE.
HMPH!!
GEEZ ...
...GUYS, GROW UP!

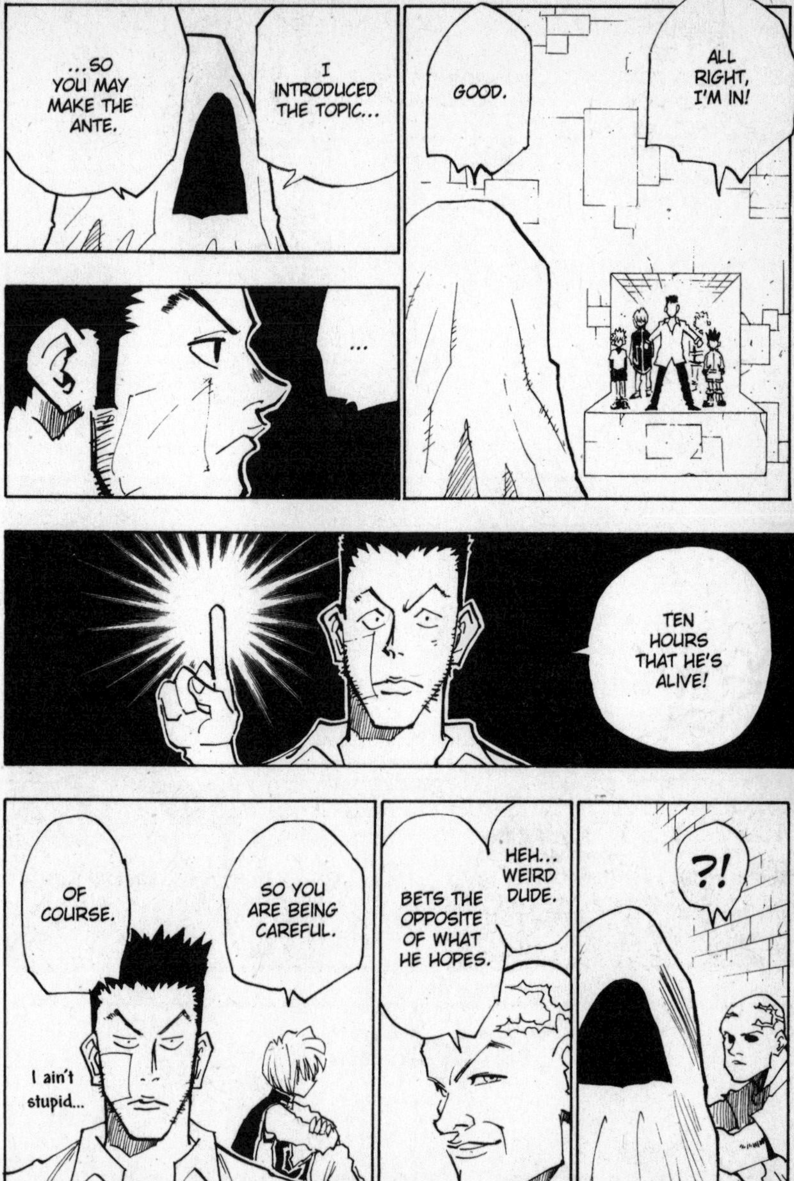

ALL RIGHT, I'M IN!
GOOD.
I INTRODUCED THE TOPIC...
...SO YOU MAY MAKE THE ANTE.
...
TEN HOURS THAT HE'S ALIVE!
?!
HEH... WEIRD DUDE.
BETS THE OPPOSITE OF WHAT HE HOPES.
SO YOU ARE BEING CAREFUL.
OF COURSE.
I ain't stupid...

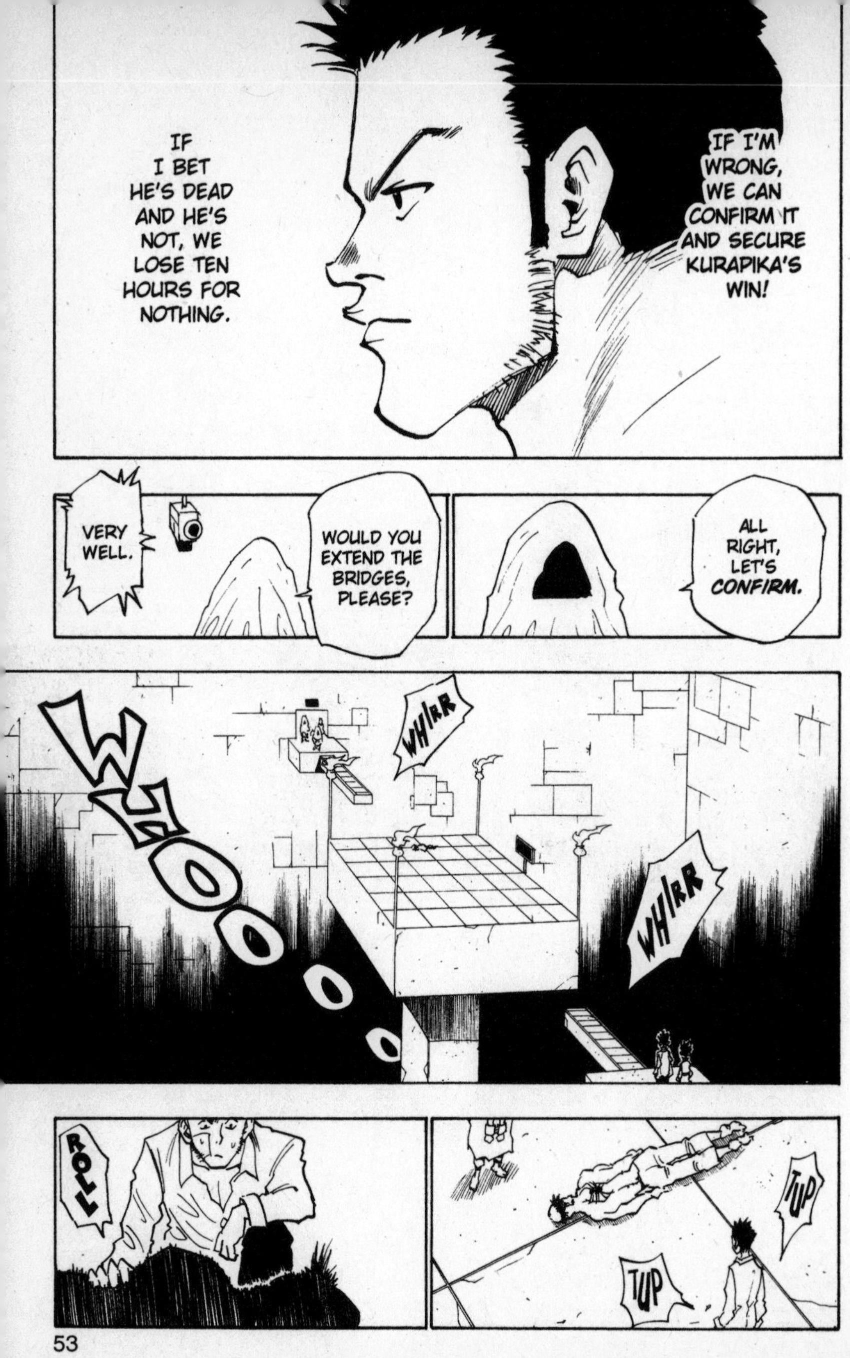
IF I'M WRONG, WE CAN CONFIRM IT AND SECURE KURAPIKA'S WIN!
IF I BET HE'S DEAD AND HE'S NOT, WE LOSE TEN HOURS FOR NOTHING.
ALL RIGHT, LET'S *CONFIRM.*
WOULD YOU EXTEND THE BRIDGES, PLEASE?
VERY WELL.
WHIRR
WHIRR
WHOOOOOO
TUP
TUP
ROLL

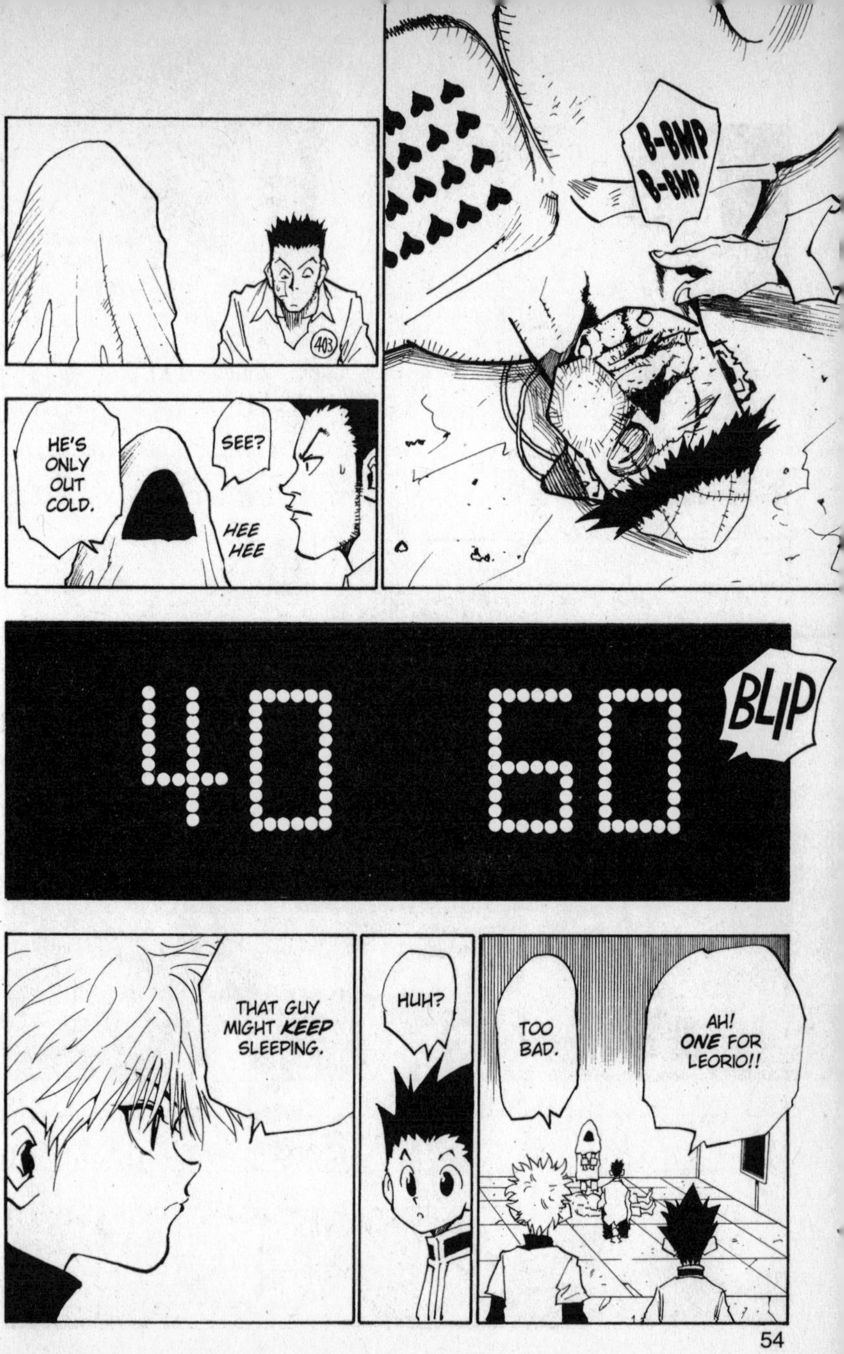
B-BMP B-BMP
SEE?
HEE HEE
HE'S ONLY OUT COLD.
40 60
BLIP
AH! ONE FOR LEORIO!!
TOO BAD.
HUH?
THAT GUY MIGHT KEEP SLEEPING.

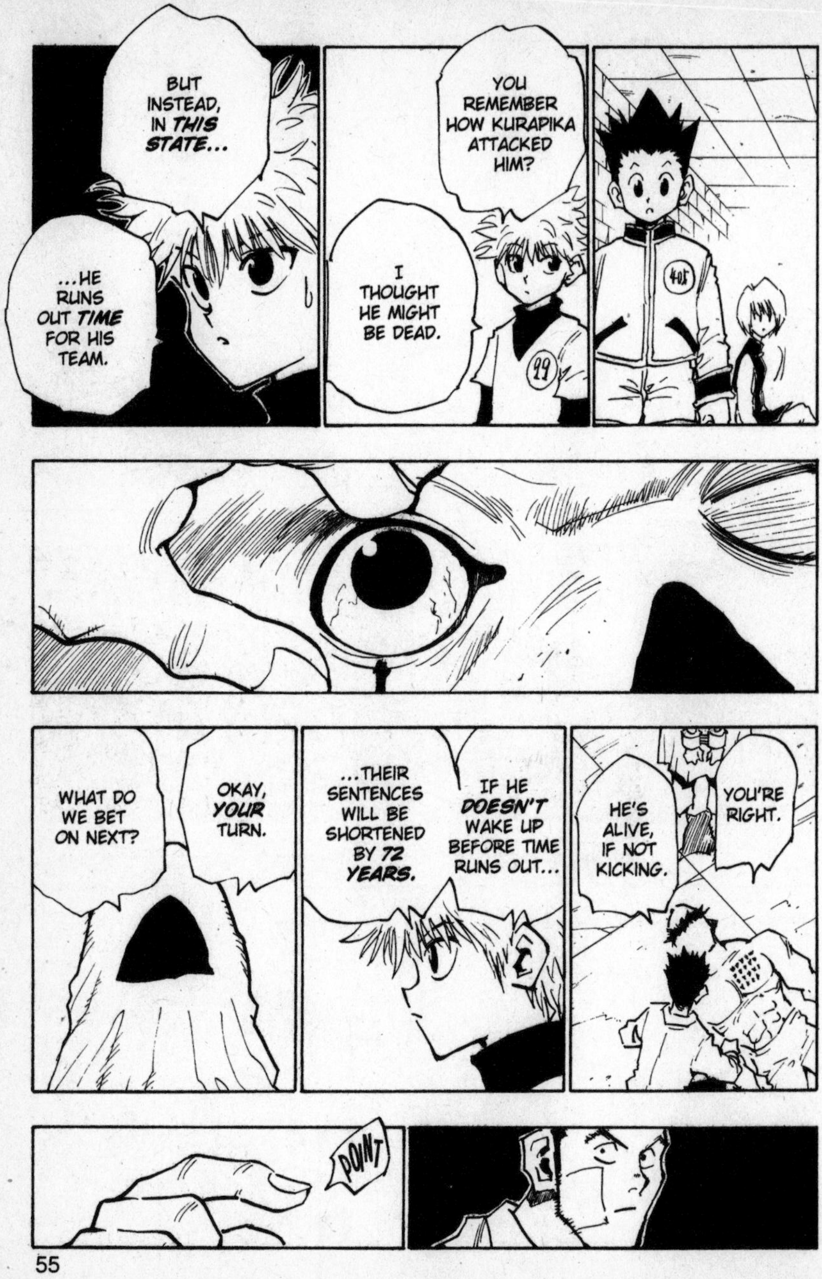
YOU REMEMBER HOW KURAPIKA ATTACKED HIM?
I THOUGHT HE MIGHT BE DEAD.
BUT INSTEAD, IN THIS STATE...
...HE RUNS OUT TIME FOR HIS TEAM.
YOU'RE RIGHT.
HE'S ALIVE, IF NOT KICKING.
IF HE DOESN'T WAKE UP BEFORE TIME RUNS OUT...
...THEIR SENTENCES WILL BE SHORTENED BY 72 YEARS.
OKAY, YOUR TURN.
WHAT DO WE BET ON NEXT?
POINT

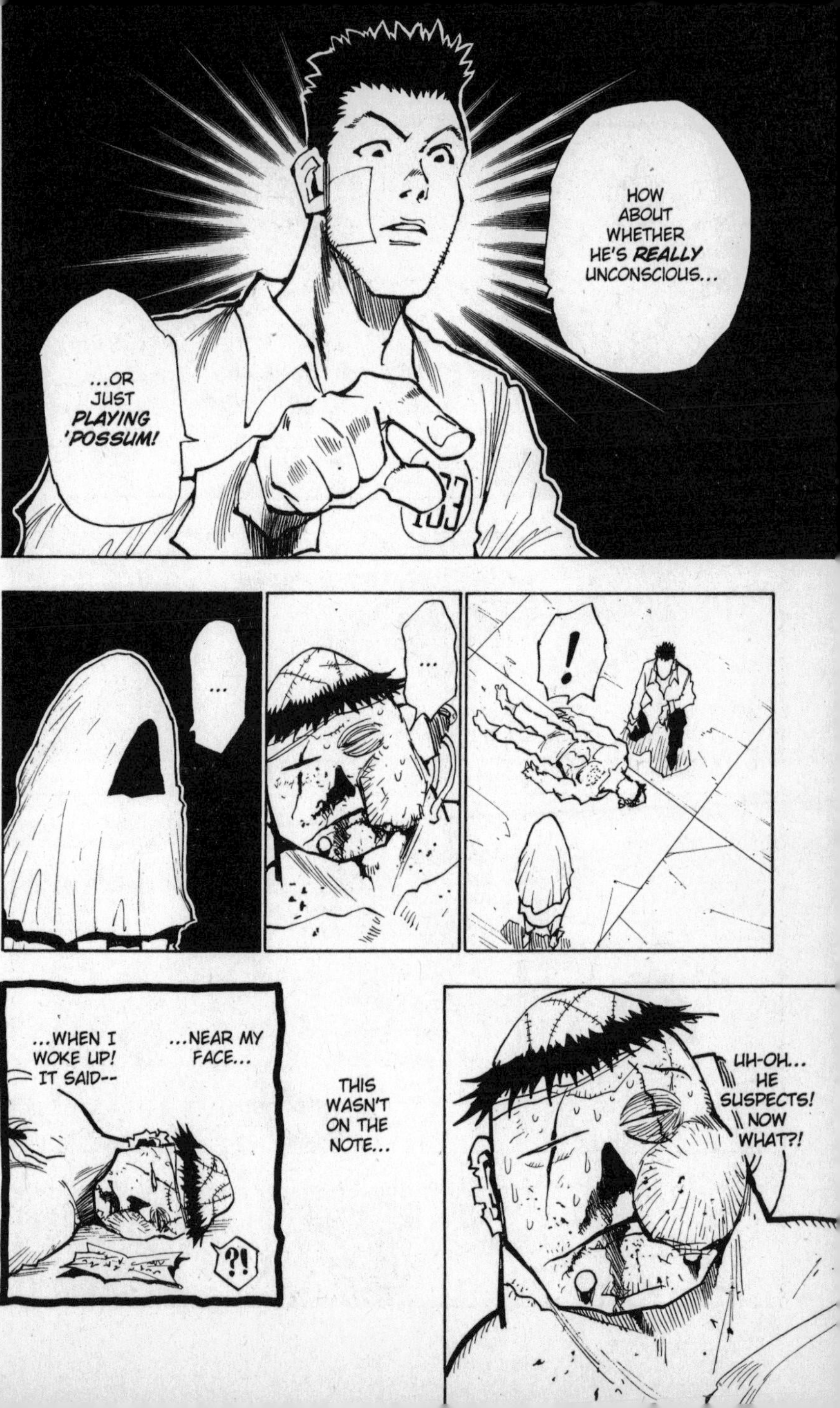
HOW ABOUT WHETHER HE'S *REALLY* UNCONSCIOUS...
...OR JUST *PLAYING 'POSSUM!*
!
...
...
UH-OH... HE SUSPECTS! NOW WHAT?!
THIS WASN'T ON THE NOTE...
...NEAR MY FACE...
...WHEN I WOKE UP! IT SAID--
?!

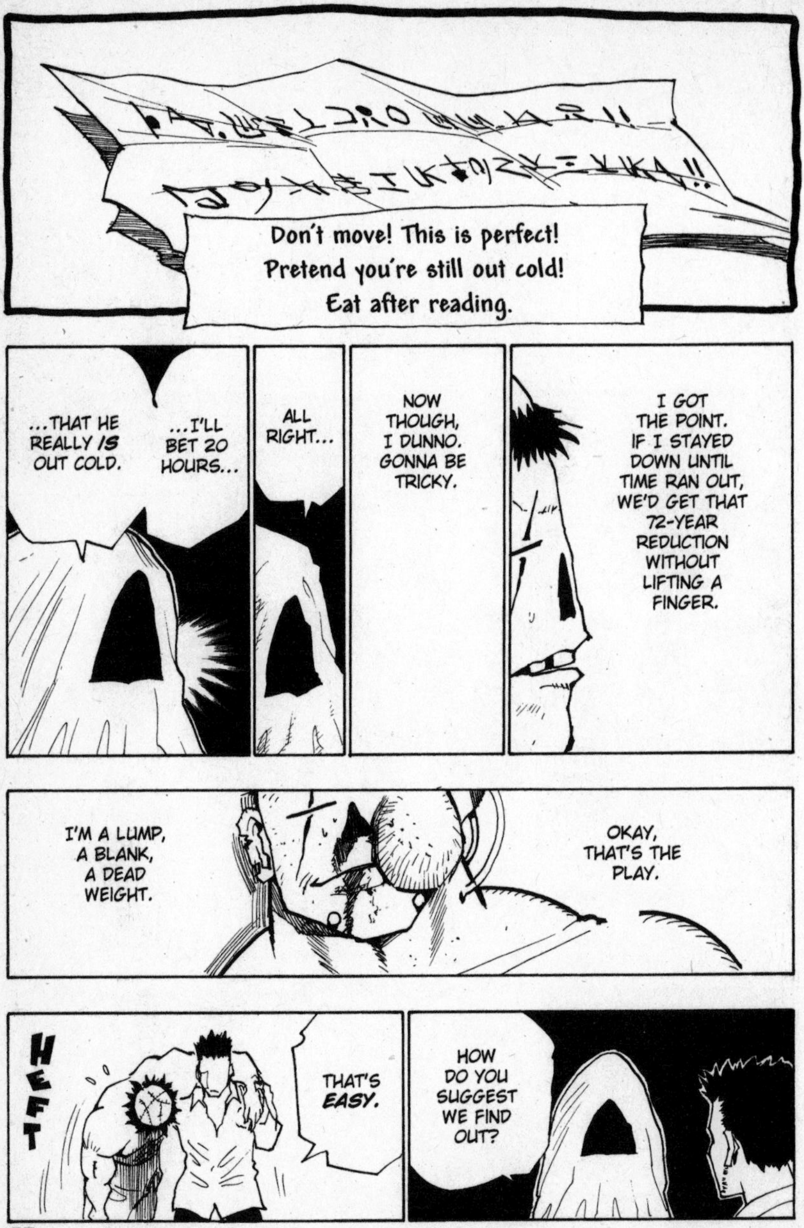
Don't move! This is perfect!
Pretend you're still out cold!
Eat after reading.
I GOT THE POINT. IF I STAYED DOWN UNTIL TIME RAN OUT, WE'D GET THAT 72-YEAR REDUCTION WITHOUT LIFTING A FINGER.
NOW THOUGH, I DUNNO. GONNA BE TRICKY.
ALL RIGHT...
...I'LL BET 20 HOURS...
...THAT HE REALLY *IS* OUT COLD.
OKAY, THAT'S THE PLAY.
I'M A LUMP, A BLANK, A DEAD WEIGHT.
HOW DO YOU SUGGEST WE FIND OUT?
THAT'S *EASY.*
HEFT

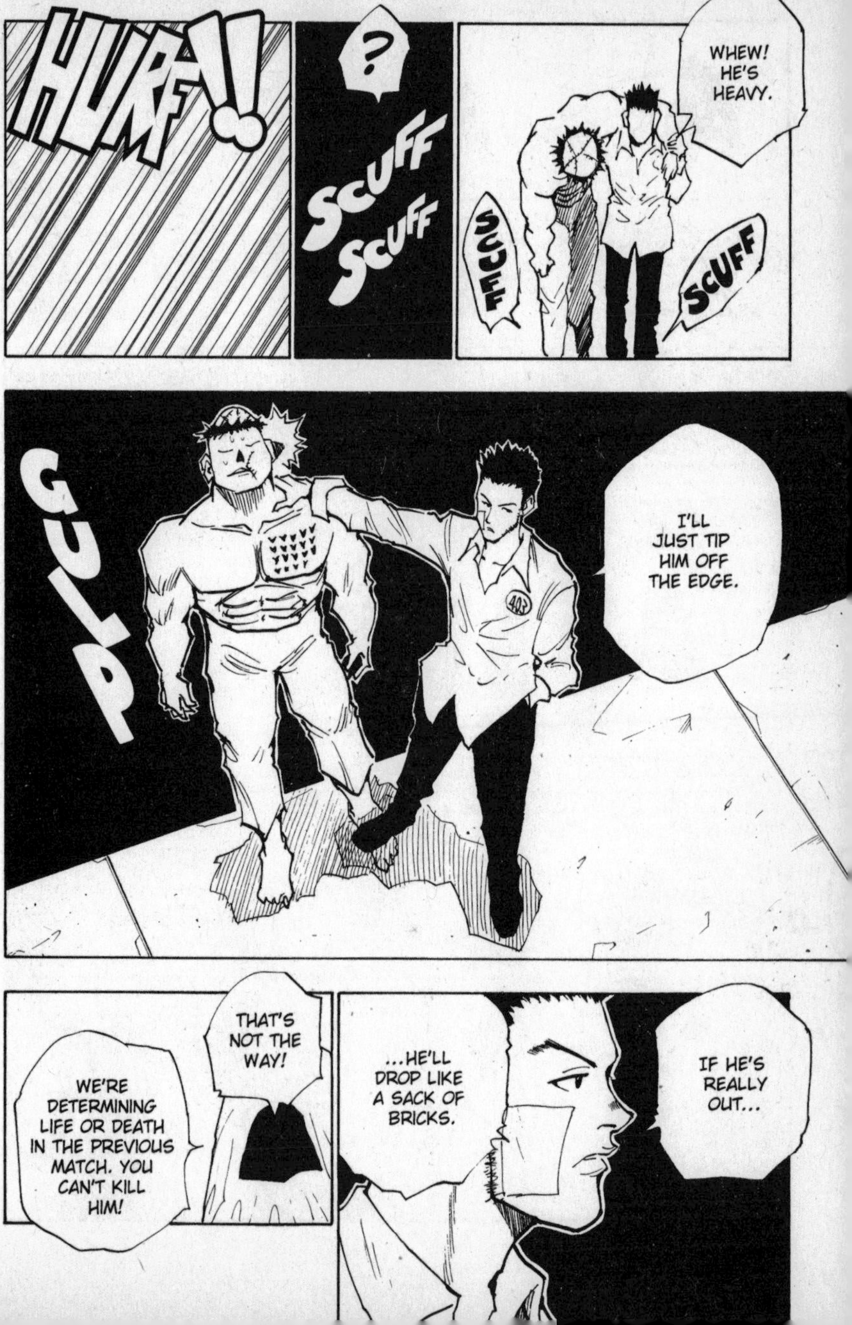
WHEW! HE'S HEAVY.
SCUFF
SCUFF
?
SCUFF SCUFF
HURF!!
I'LL JUST TIP HIM OFF THE EDGE.
GULP
IF HE'S REALLY OUT...
...HE'LL DROP LIKE A SACK OF BRICKS.
THAT'S NOT THE WAY!
WE'RE DETERMINING LIFE OR DEATH IN THE PREVIOUS MATCH. YOU CAN'T KILL HIM!

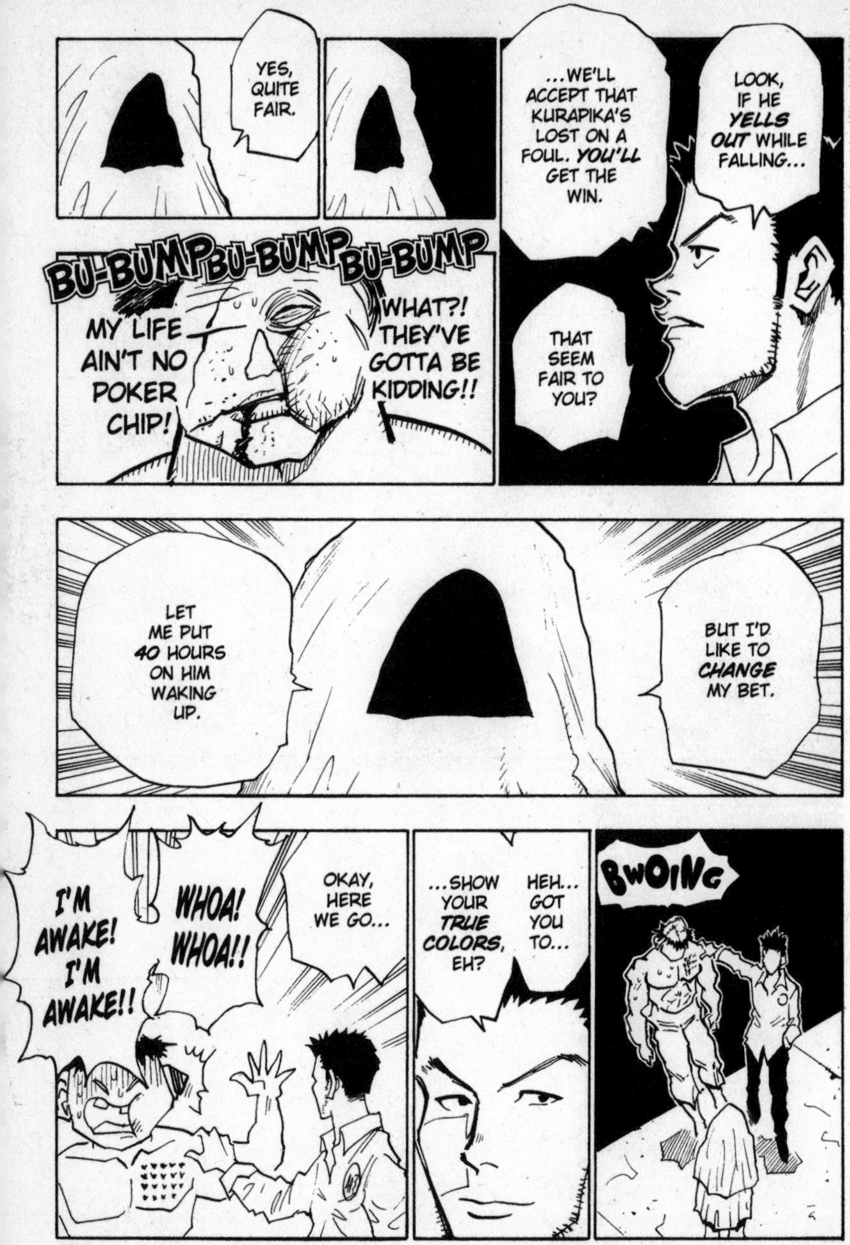
LOOK, IF HE YELLS OUT WHILE FALLING...
...WE'LL ACCEPT THAT KURAPIKA'S LOST ON A FOUL. YOU'LL GET THE WIN.
THAT SEEM FAIR TO YOU?
YES, QUITE FAIR.
BU-BUMP BU-BUMP BU-BUMP
WHAT?! THEY'VE GOTTA BE KIDDING!!
MY LIFE AIN'T NO POKER CHIP!
BUT I'D LIKE TO CHANGE MY BET.
LET ME PUT 40 HOURS ON HIM WAKING UP.
BWOING
HEH... GOT YOU TO...
...SHOW YOUR TRUE COLORS, EH?
OKAY, HERE WE GO...
WHOA! WHOA!!
I'M AWAKE! I'M AWAKE!!

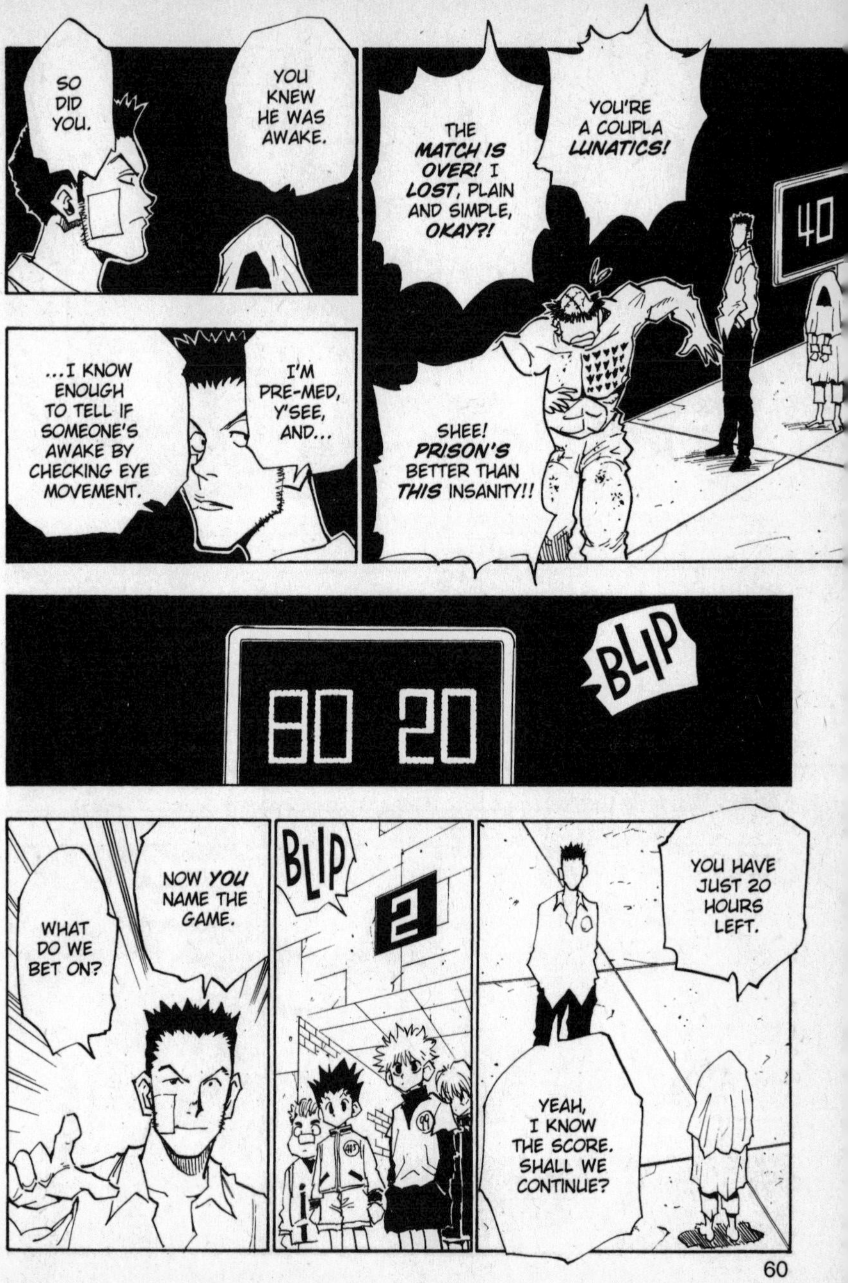
YOU'RE A COUPLA LUNATICS!
THE MATCH IS OVER! I LOST, PLAIN AND SIMPLE, OKAY?!
40
SHEE! PRISON'S BETTER THAN THIS INSANITY!!
YOU KNEW HE WAS AWAKE.
SO DID YOU.
I'M PRE-MED, Y'SEE, AND...
...I KNOW ENOUGH TO TELL IF SOMEONE'S AWAKE BY CHECKING EYE MOVEMENT.
BLIP
80 20
YOU HAVE JUST 20 HOURS LEFT.
YEAH, I KNOW THE SCORE. SHALL WE CONTINUE?
BLIP
2
NOW YOU NAME THE GAME.
WHAT DO WE BET ON?

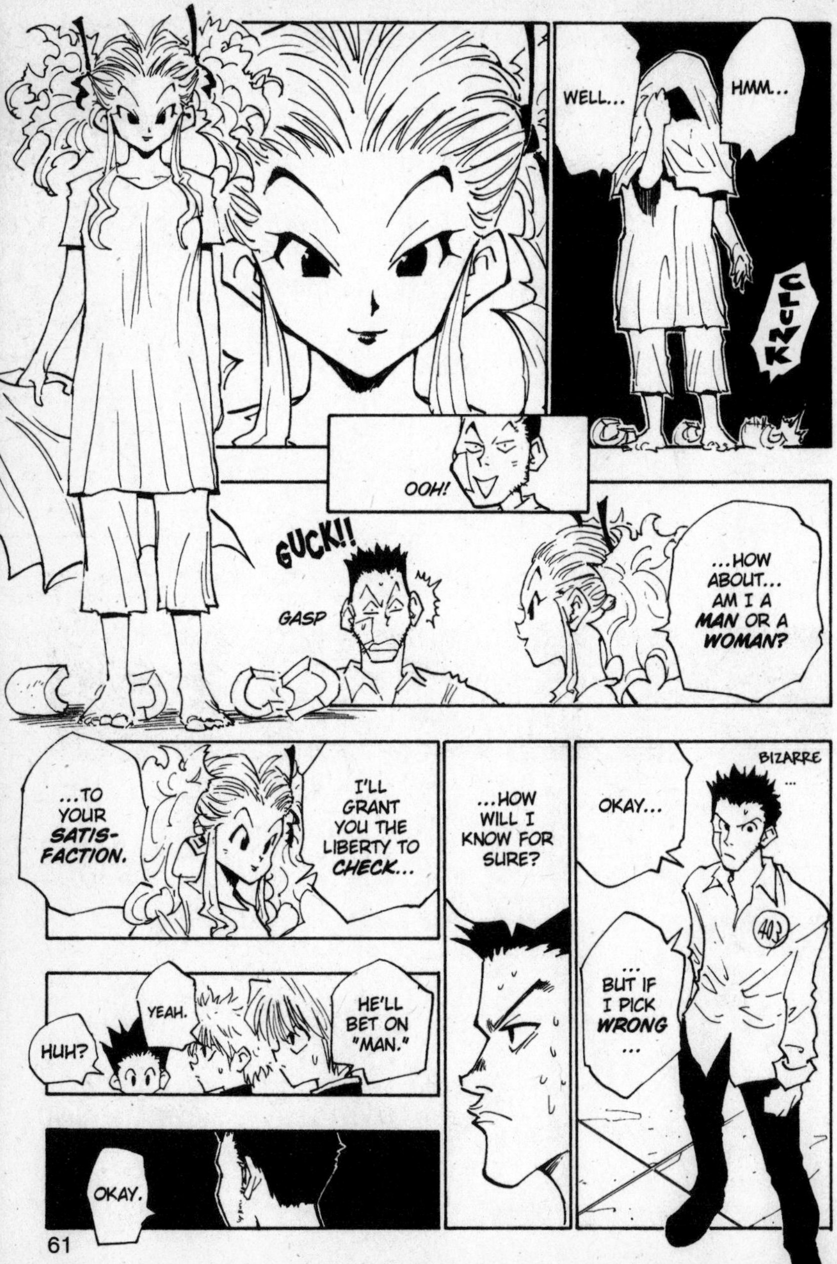
HMM...
WELL...
CLUNK
OOH!
...HOW ABOUT... AM I A *MAN* OR A *WOMAN?*
GUCK!!
GASP
BIZARRE...
OKAY...
...BUT IF I PICK *WRONG*...
...HOW WILL I KNOW FOR SURE?
I'LL GRANT YOU THE LIBERTY TO *CHECK*...
...TO YOUR *SATIS-FACTION.*
HE'LL BET ON "MAN."
YEAH.
HUH?
OKAY.

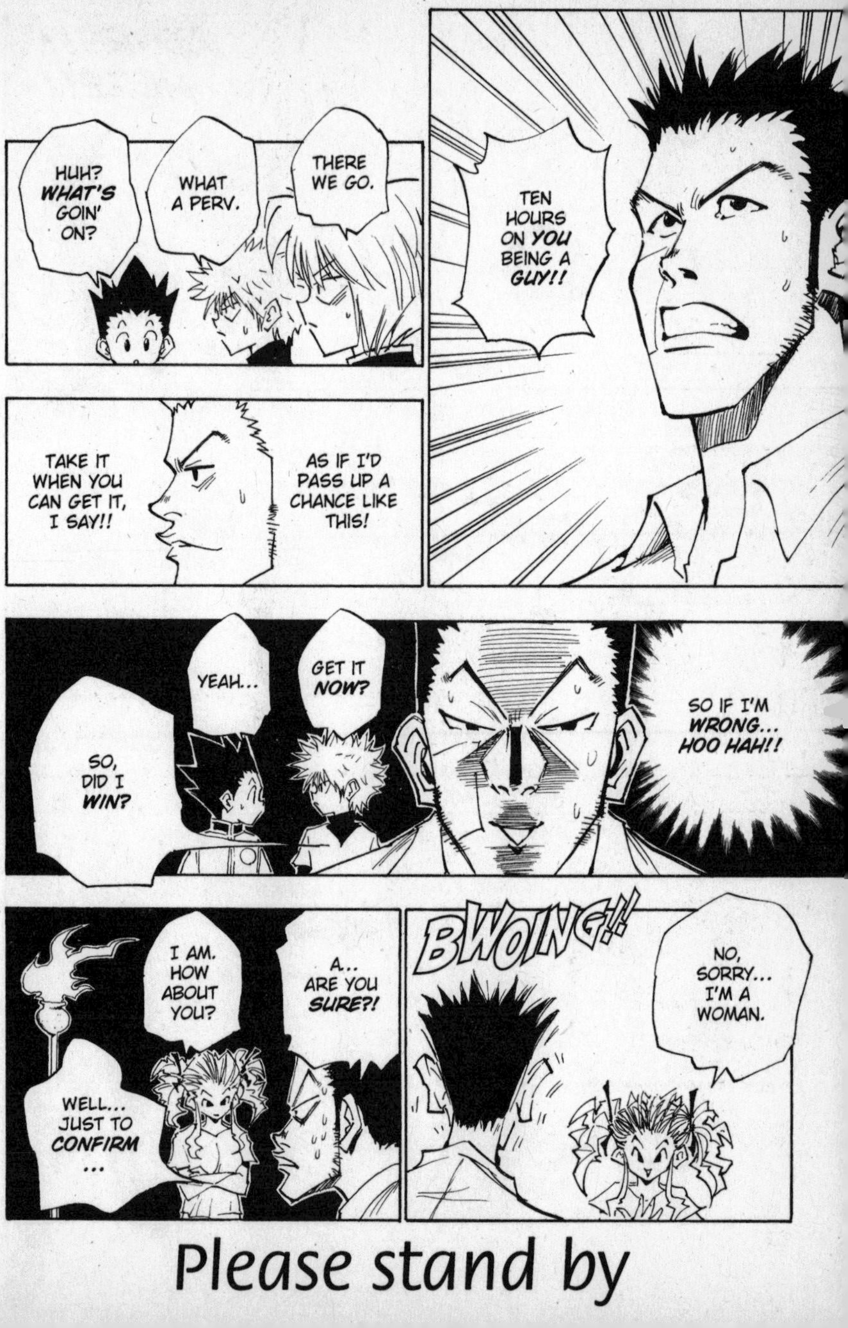
TEN HOURS ON YOU BEING A GUY!!
THERE WE GO.
WHAT A PERV.
HUH? WHAT'S GOIN' ON?
AS IF I'D PASS UP A CHANCE LIKE THIS!
TAKE IT WHEN YOU CAN GET IT, I SAY!!
SO IF I'M WRONG... HOO HAH!!
GET IT NOW?
YEAH...
SO, DID I WIN?
BWOING!!
NO, SORRY... I'M A WOMAN.
A... ARE YOU SURE?!
I AM. HOW ABOUT YOU?
WELL... JUST TO CONFIRM ...

Please stand by

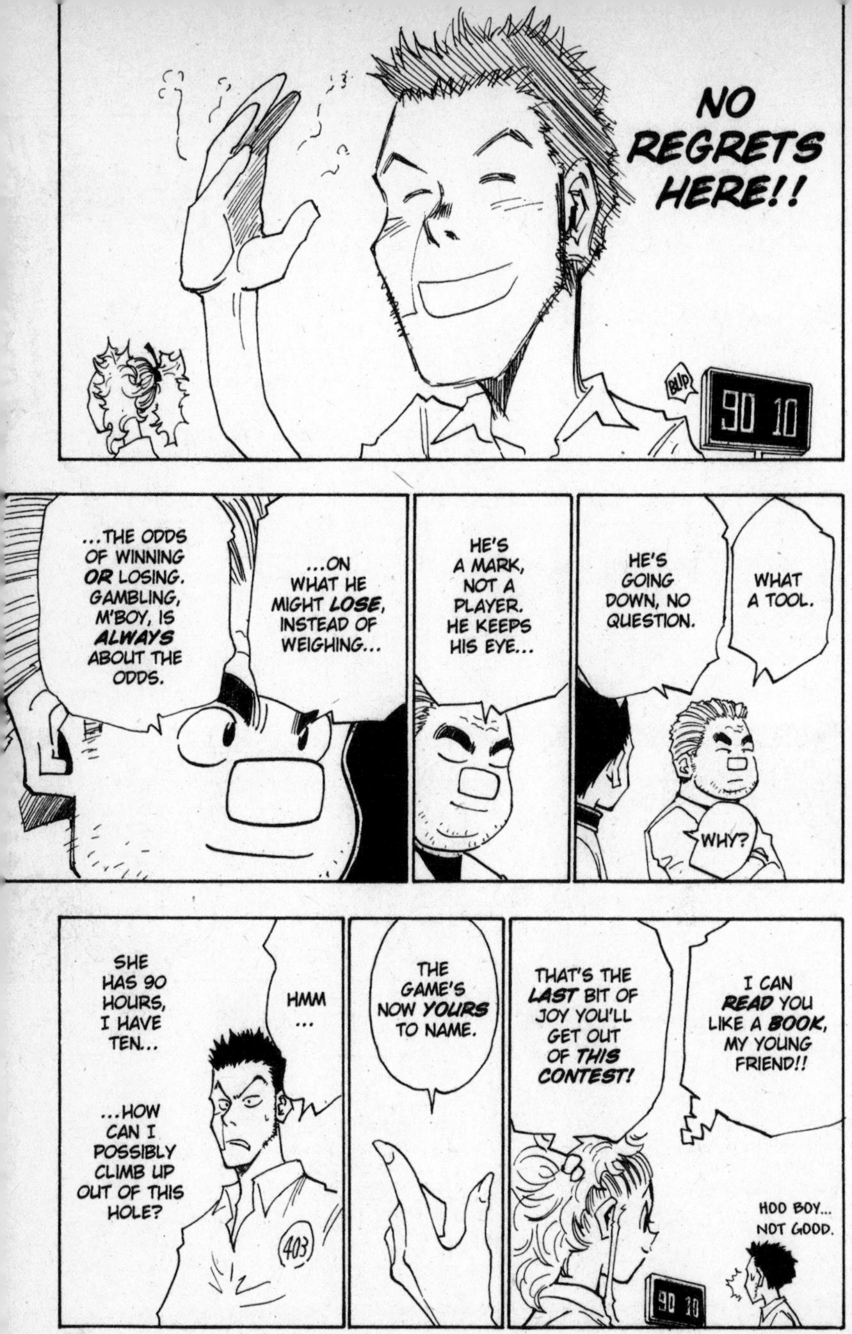
NO REGRETS HERE!!
BLIP
90 10
WHAT A TOOL.
HE'S GOING DOWN, NO QUESTION.
WHY?
HE'S A MARK, NOT A PLAYER. HE KEEPS HIS EYE...
...ON WHAT HE MIGHT LOSE, INSTEAD OF WEIGHING...
...THE ODDS OF WINNING OR LOSING. GAMBLING, M'BOY, IS ALWAYS ABOUT THE ODDS.
I CAN READ YOU LIKE A BOOK, MY YOUNG FRIEND!!
THAT'S THE LAST BIT OF JOY YOU'LL GET OUT OF THIS CONTEST!
HOO BOY... NOT GOOD.
90 10
THE GAME'S NOW YOURS TO NAME.
HMM ...
SHE HAS 90 HOURS, I HAVE TEN...
...HOW CAN I POSSIBLY CLIMB UP OUT OF THIS HOLE?
403

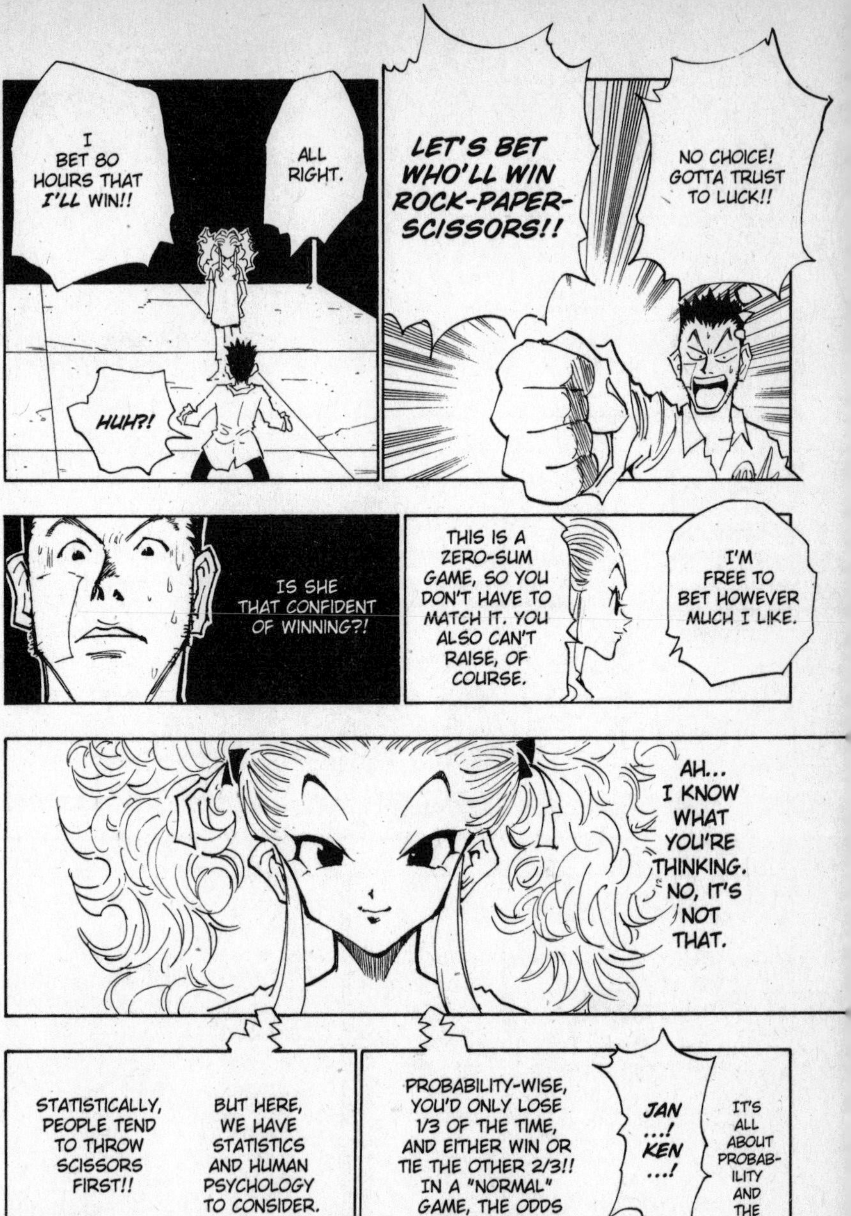
NO CHOICE! GOTTA TRUST TO LUCK!!
LET'S BET WHO'LL WIN ROCK-PAPER-SCISSORS!!
ALL RIGHT.
I BET 80 HOURS THAT I'LL WIN!!
HUH?!
I'M FREE TO BET HOWEVER MUCH I LIKE.
THIS IS A ZERO-SUM GAME, SO YOU DON'T HAVE TO MATCH IT. YOU ALSO CAN'T RAISE, OF COURSE.
IS SHE THAT CONFIDENT OF WINNING?!
AH... I KNOW WHAT YOU'RE THINKING. NO, IT'S NOT THAT.
IT'S ALL ABOUT PROBABILITY AND THE MIND.
JAN...! KEN...!
PROBABILITY-WISE, YOU'D ONLY LOSE 1/3 OF THE TIME, AND EITHER WIN OR TIE THE OTHER 2/3!! IN A "NORMAL" GAME, THE ODDS ARE YOU WON'T LOSE.
BUT HERE, WE HAVE STATISTICS AND HUMAN PSYCHOLOGY TO CONSIDER.
STATISTICALLY, PEOPLE TEND TO THROW SCISSORS FIRST!!

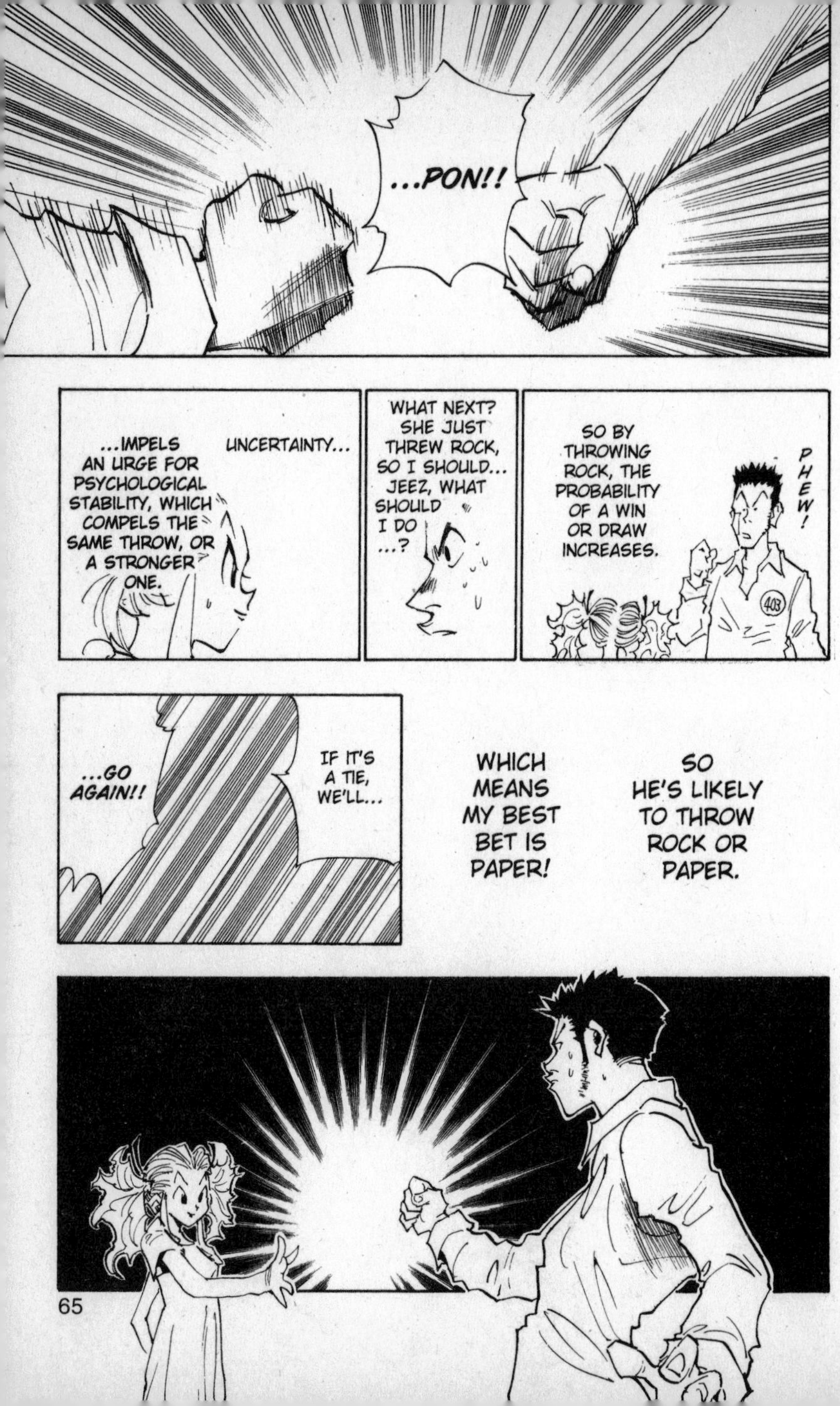
...PON!!
PHEW!
SO BY THROWING ROCK, THE PROBABILITY OF A WIN OR DRAW INCREASES.
WHAT NEXT? SHE JUST THREW ROCK, SO I SHOULD... JEEZ, WHAT SHOULD I DO ...?
UNCERTAINTY...
...IMPELS AN URGE FOR PSYCHOLOGICAL STABILITY, WHICH COMPELS THE SAME THROW, OR A STRONGER ONE.
SO HE'S LIKELY TO THROW ROCK OR PAPER.
WHICH MEANS MY BEST BET IS PAPER!
IF IT'S A TIE, WE'LL...
...GO AGAIN!!

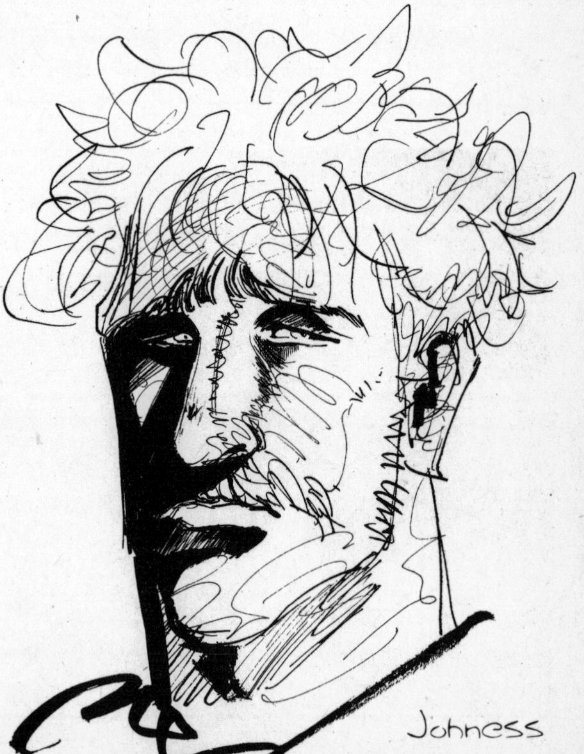
Johness

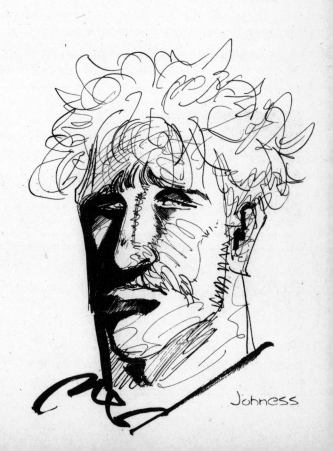

Chapter 21
Resolution

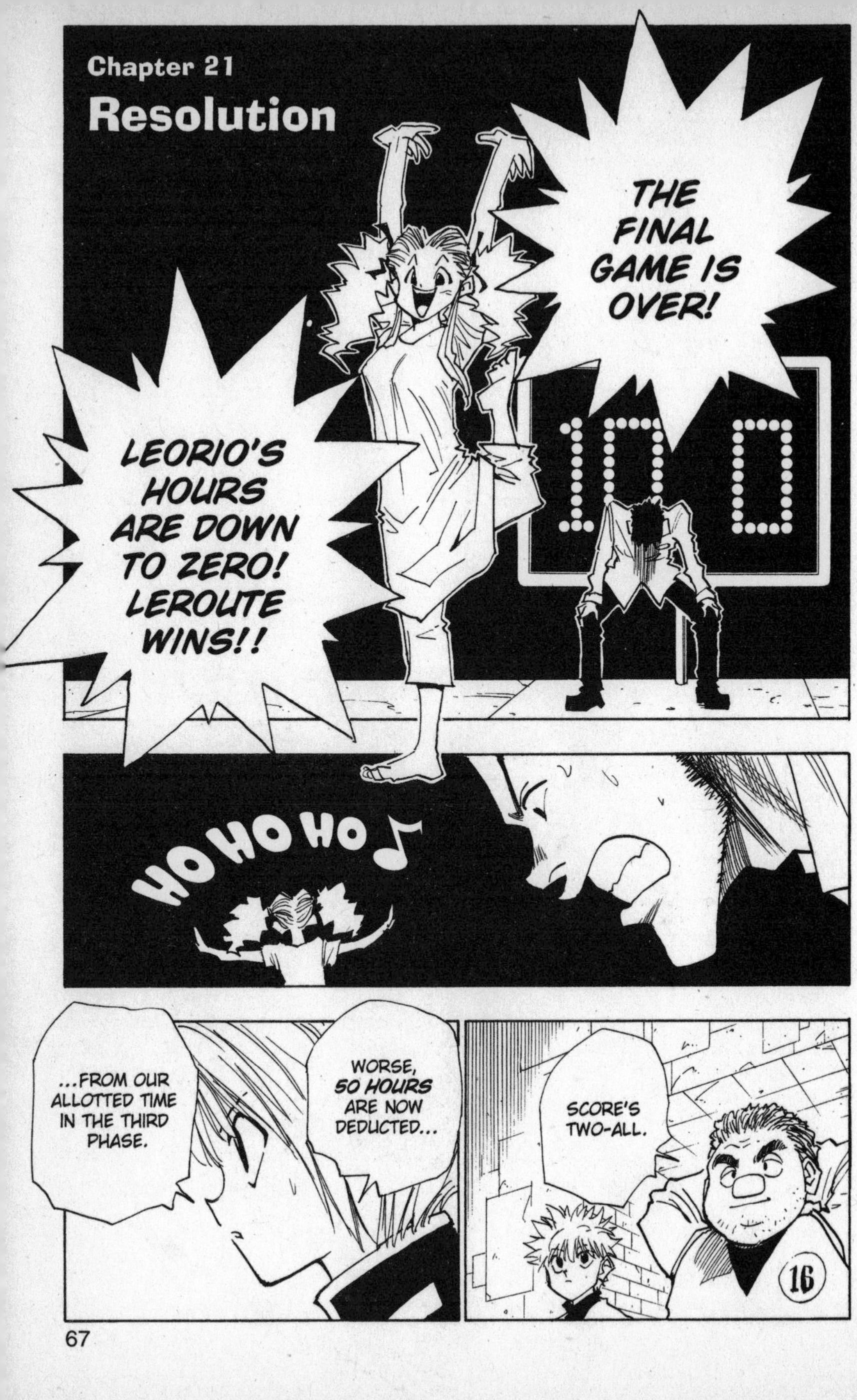
THE FINAL GAME IS OVER!
LEORIO'S HOURS ARE DOWN TO ZERO! LEROUTE WINS!!
HO HO HO HO ♪
SCORE'S TWO-ALL.
WORSE, 50 HOURS ARE NOW DEDUCTED...
...FROM OUR ALLOTTED TIME IN THE THIRD PHASE.

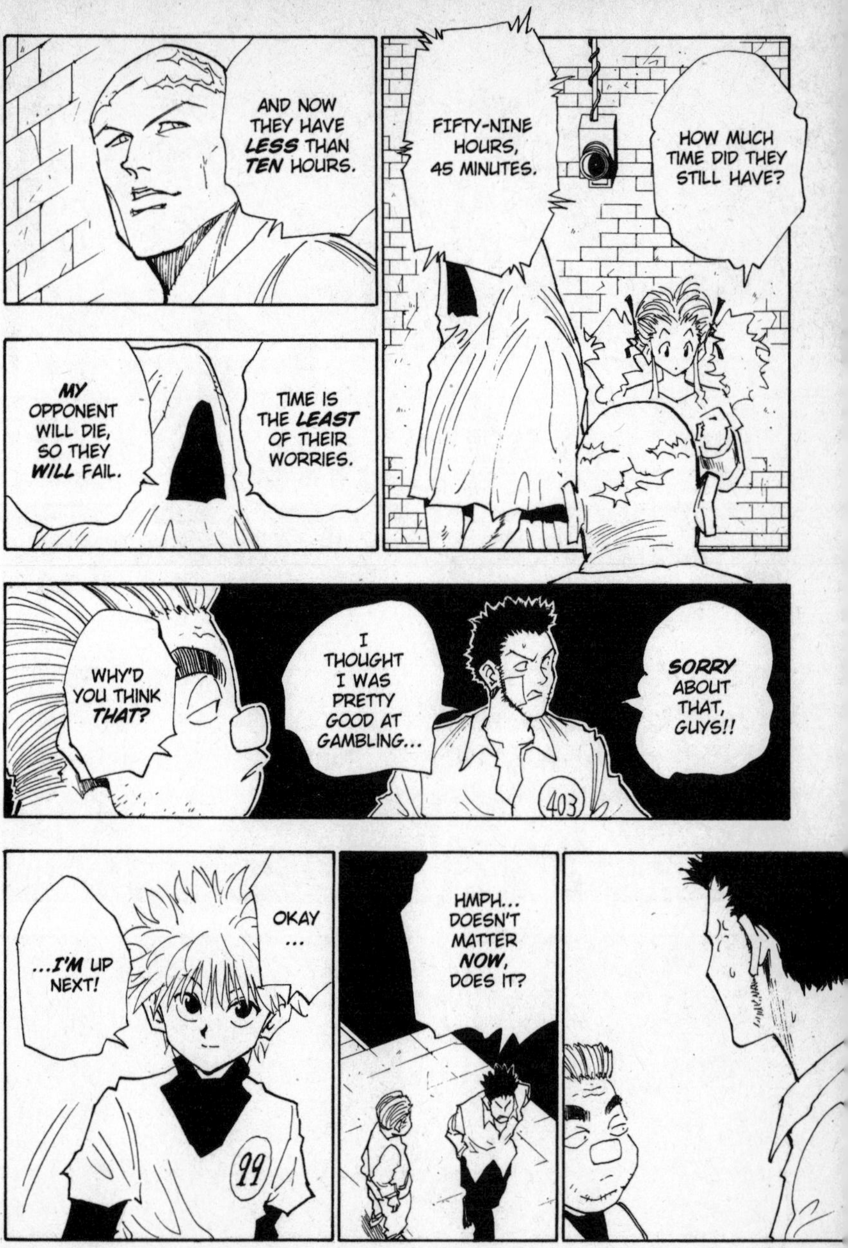
HOW MUCH TIME DID THEY STILL HAVE?
FIFTY-NINE HOURS, 45 MINUTES.
AND NOW THEY HAVE LESS THAN TEN HOURS.
TIME IS THE LEAST OF THEIR WORRIES.
MY OPPONENT WILL DIE, SO THEY WILL FAIL.
SORRY ABOUT THAT, GUYS!!
I THOUGHT I WAS PRETTY GOOD AT GAMBLING...
WHY'D YOU THINK THAT?
HMPH... DOESN'T MATTER NOW, DOES IT?
OKAY ...
...I'M UP NEXT!

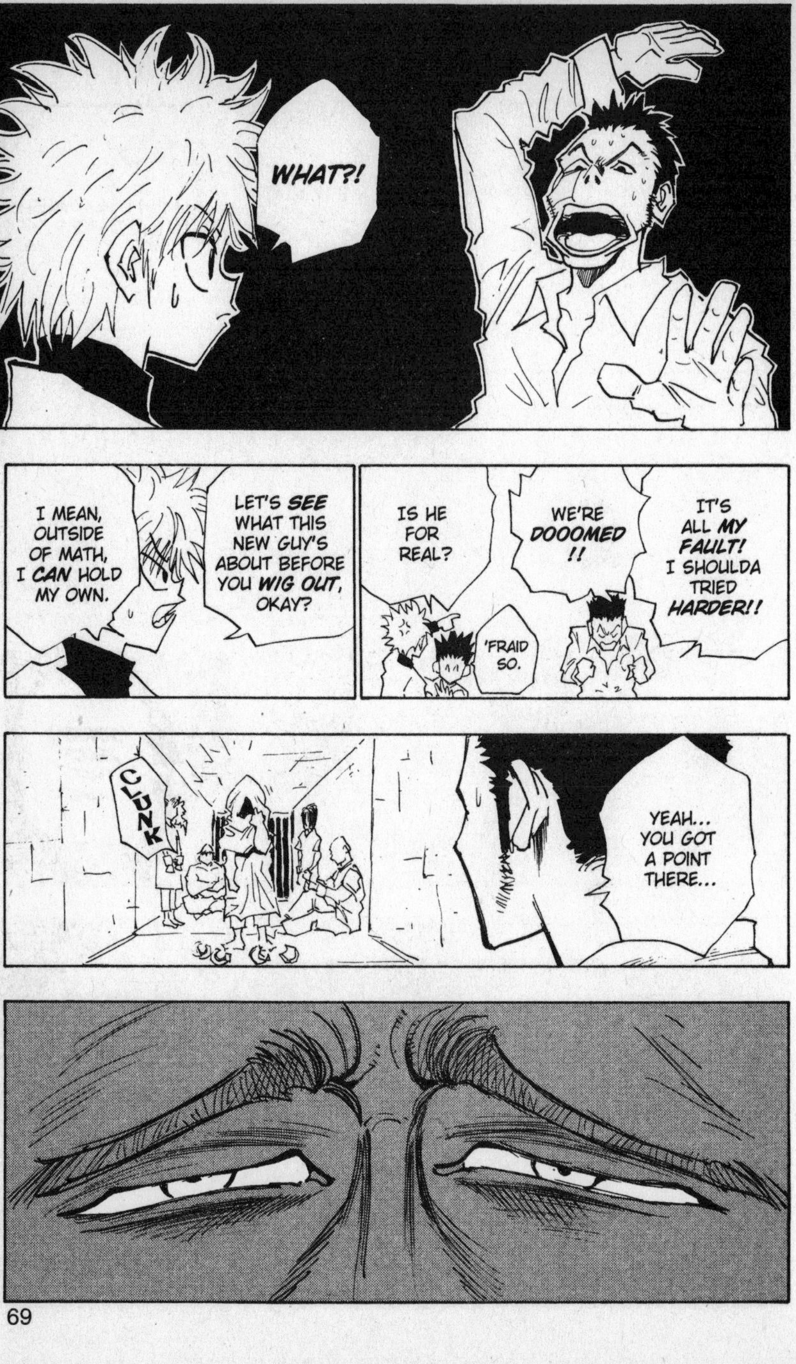
WHAT?!
IT'S ALL MY FAULT! I SHOULDA TRIED HARDER!!
WE'RE DOOOMED!!
IS HE FOR REAL?
'FRAID SO.
LET'S SEE WHAT THIS NEW GUY'S ABOUT BEFORE YOU WIG OUT, OKAY?
I MEAN, OUTSIDE OF MATH, I CAN HOLD MY OWN.
YEAH... YOU GOT A POINT THERE...
CLUNK

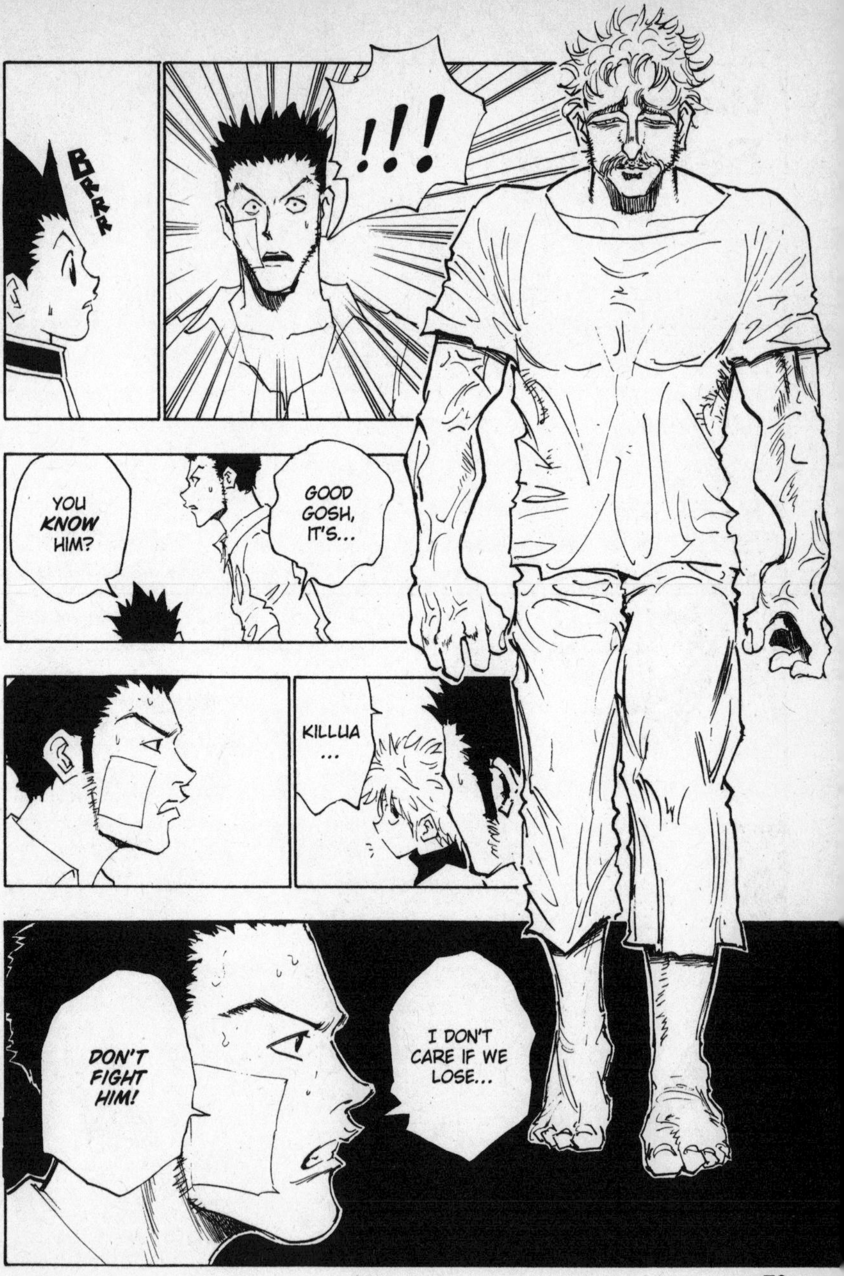
!!!
BRRR
GOOD GOSH, IT'S...
YOU KNOW HIM?
KILLUA...
I DON'T CARE IF WE LOSE...
DON'T FIGHT HIM!

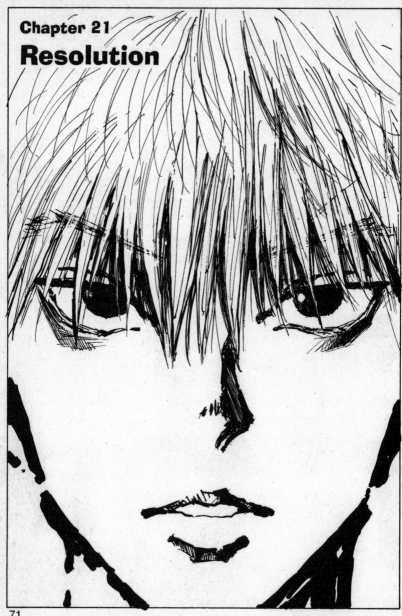

Chapter 21
Resolution

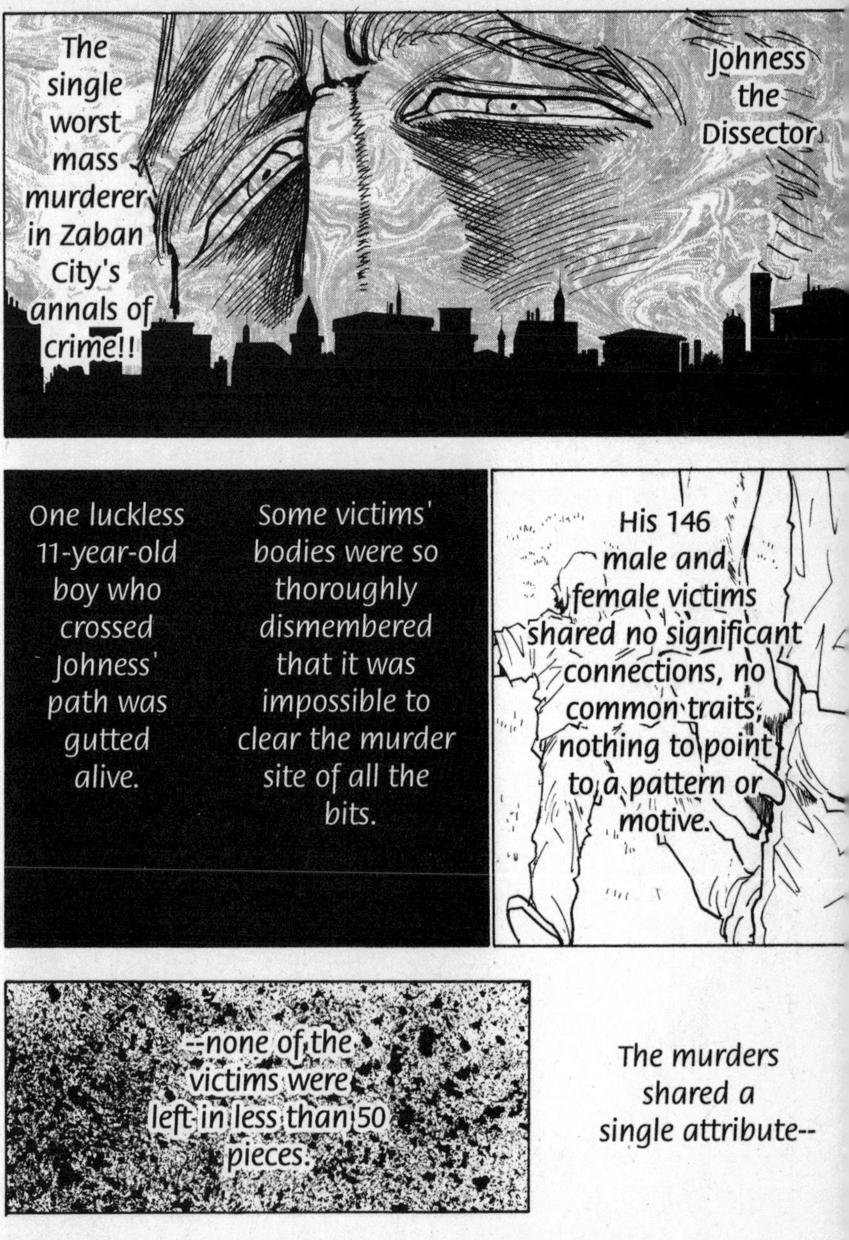
Johness the Dissector
The single worst mass murderer in Zaban City's annals of crime!!
His 146 male and female victims shared no significant connections, no common traits, nothing to point to a pattern or motive.
Some victims' bodies were so thoroughly dismembered that it was impossible to clear the murder site of all the bits.
One luckless 11-year-old boy who crossed Johness' path was gutted alive.
The murders shared a single attribute--
--none of the victims were left in less than 50 pieces.

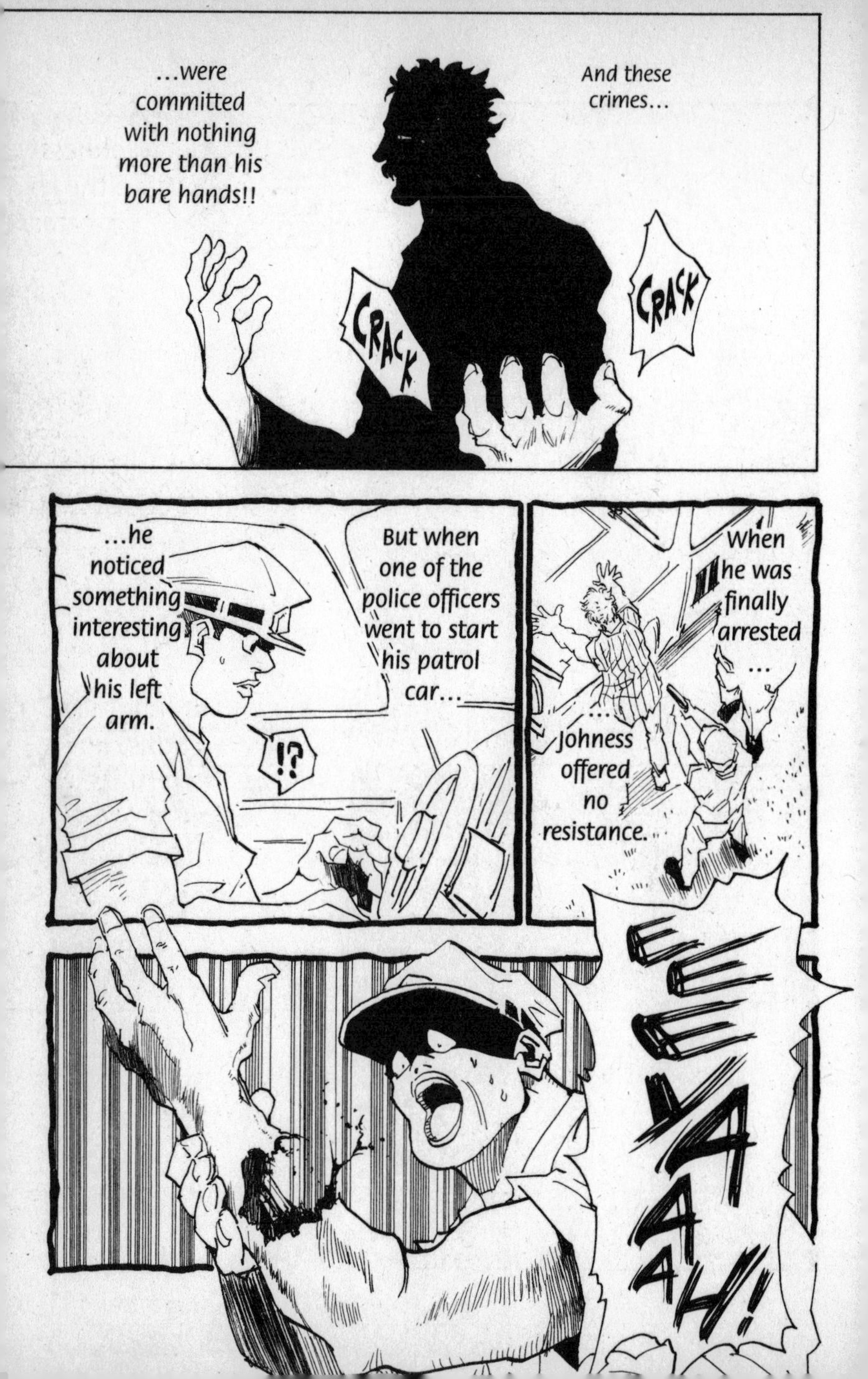
And these crimes...
CRACK
...were committed with nothing more than his bare hands!!
CRACK
When he was finally arrested...
...Johness offered no resistance.
But when one of the police officers went to start his patrol car...
...he noticed something interesting about his left arm.
!?
EEEYAAAH!

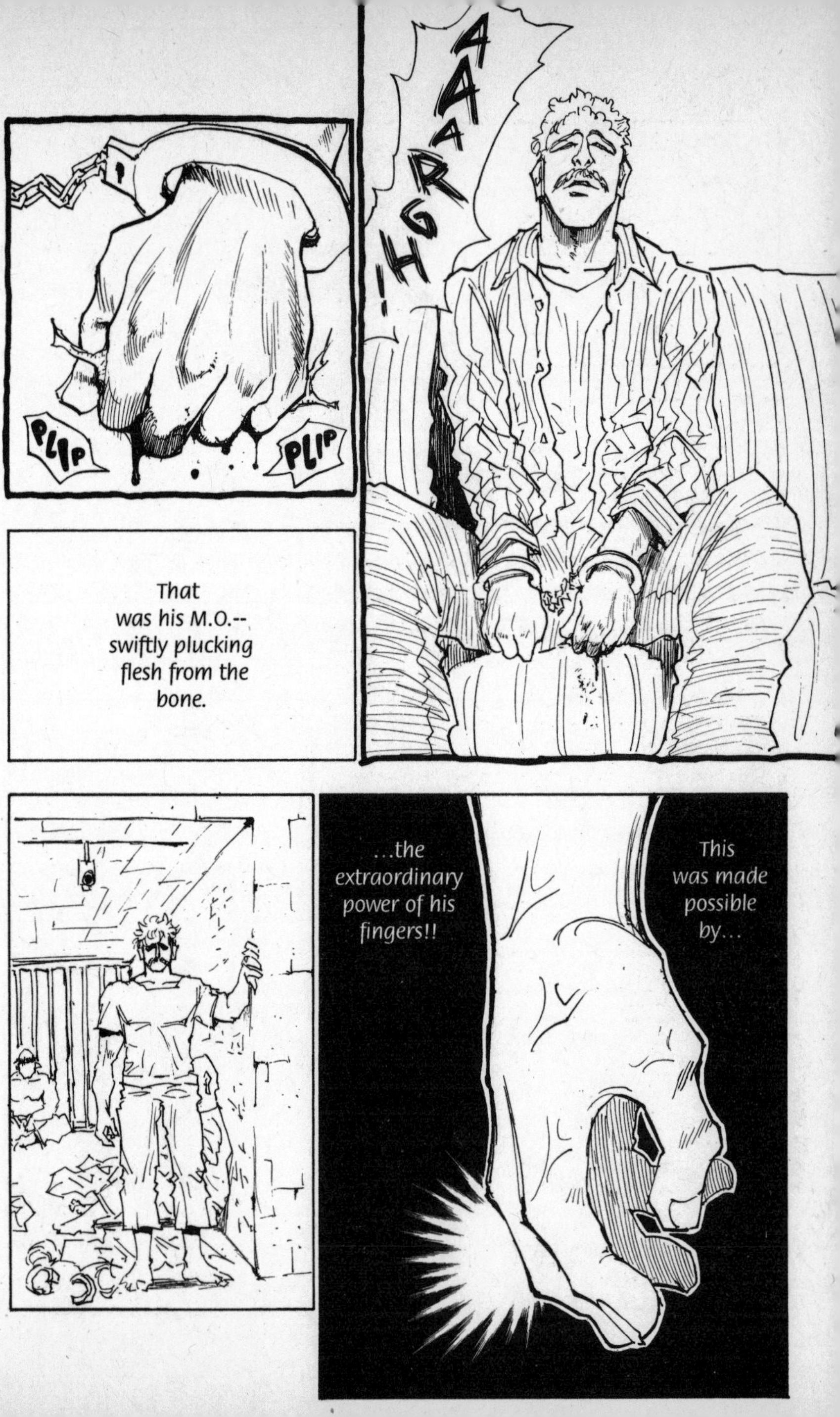
AAARGH!
PLIP
PLIP
That was his M.O.-- swiftly plucking flesh from the bone.
This was made possible by...
...the extraordinary power of his fingers!!

READ THIS WAY

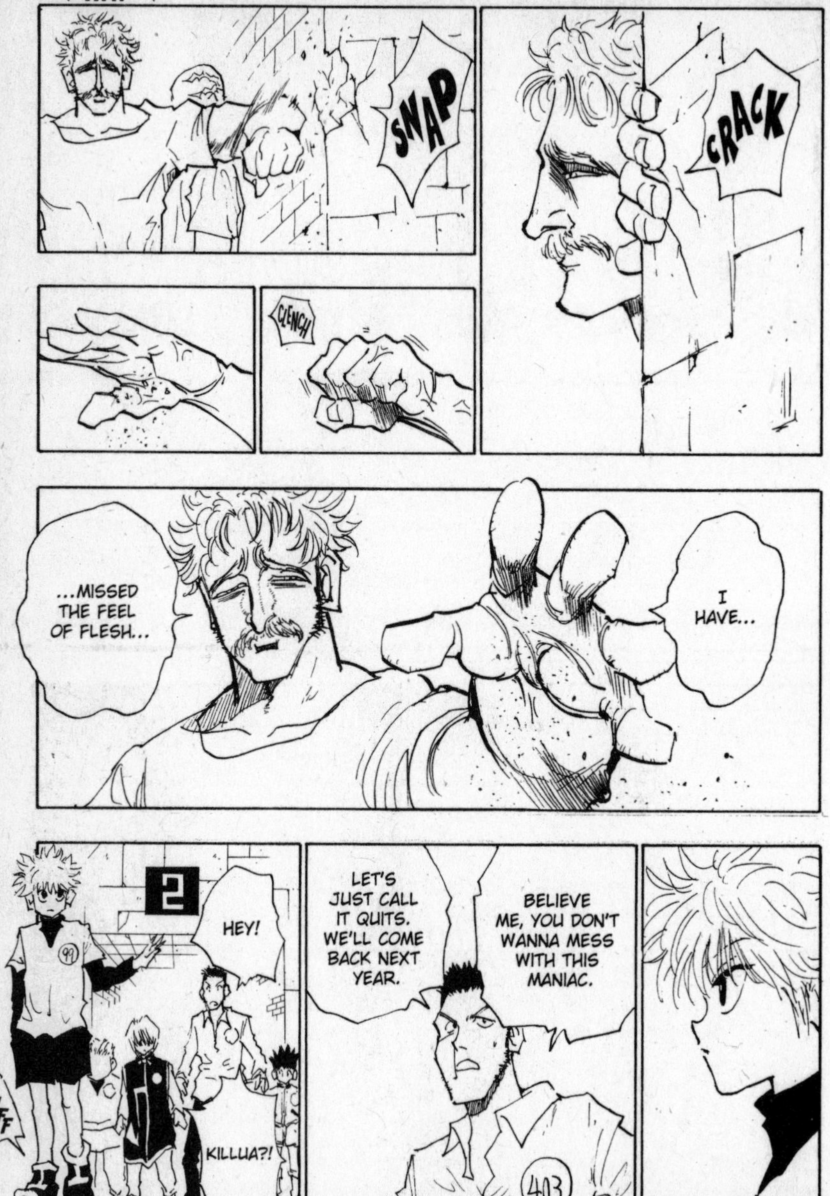
CRACK
SNAP
CLENCH
I HAVE...
...MISSED THE FEEL OF FLESH...
BELIEVE ME, YOU DON'T WANNA MESS WITH THIS MANIAC.
LET'S JUST CALL IT QUITS. WE'LL COME BACK NEXT YEAR.
403
HEY!
2
99
KILLUA?!
HUFF

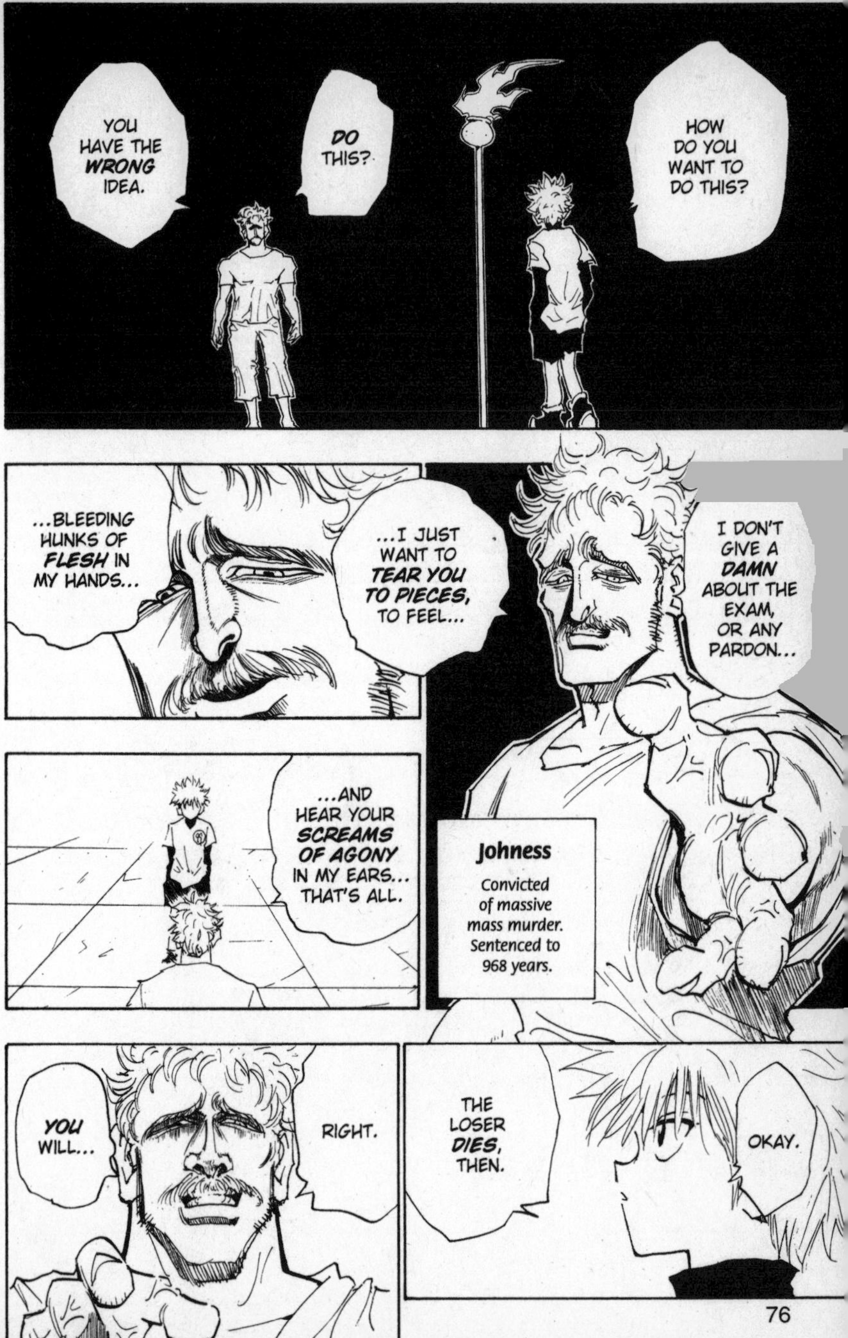
HOW DO YOU WANT TO DO THIS?
DO THIS?
YOU HAVE THE WRONG IDEA.
I DON'T GIVE A DAMN ABOUT THE EXAM, OR ANY PARDON...
Johness
Convicted of massive mass murder. Sentenced to 968 years.
...I JUST WANT TO TEAR YOU TO PIECES, TO FEEL...
...BLEEDING HUNKS OF FLESH IN MY HANDS...
...AND HEAR YOUR SCREAMS OF AGONY IN MY EARS... THAT'S ALL.
OKAY.
THE LOSER DIES, THEN.
RIGHT.
YOU WILL...

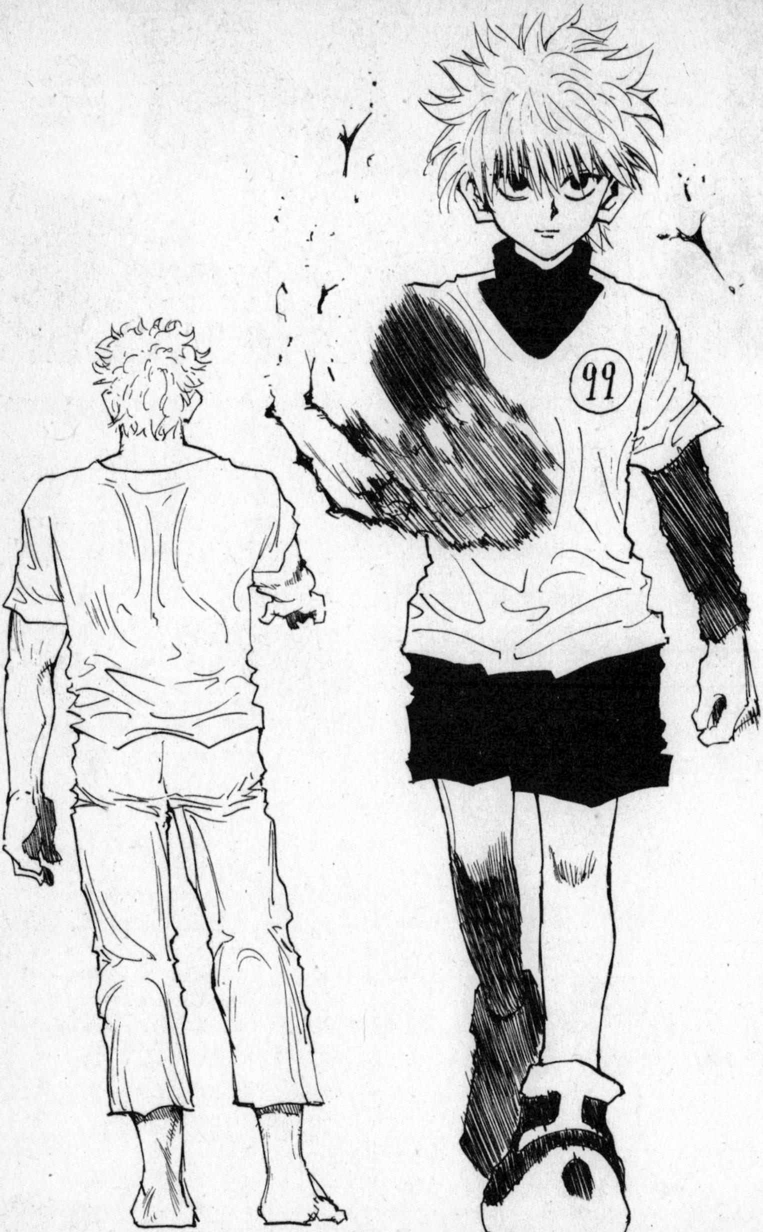
99

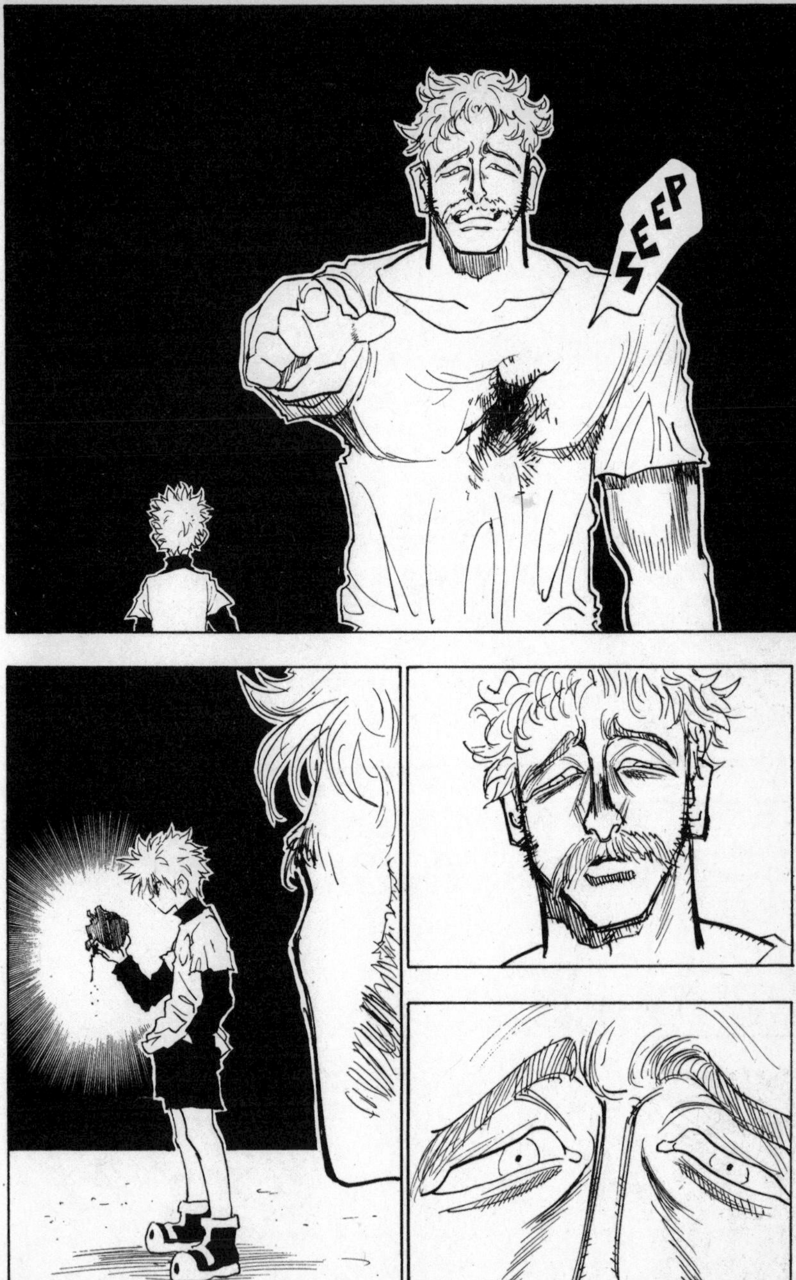
SEEP

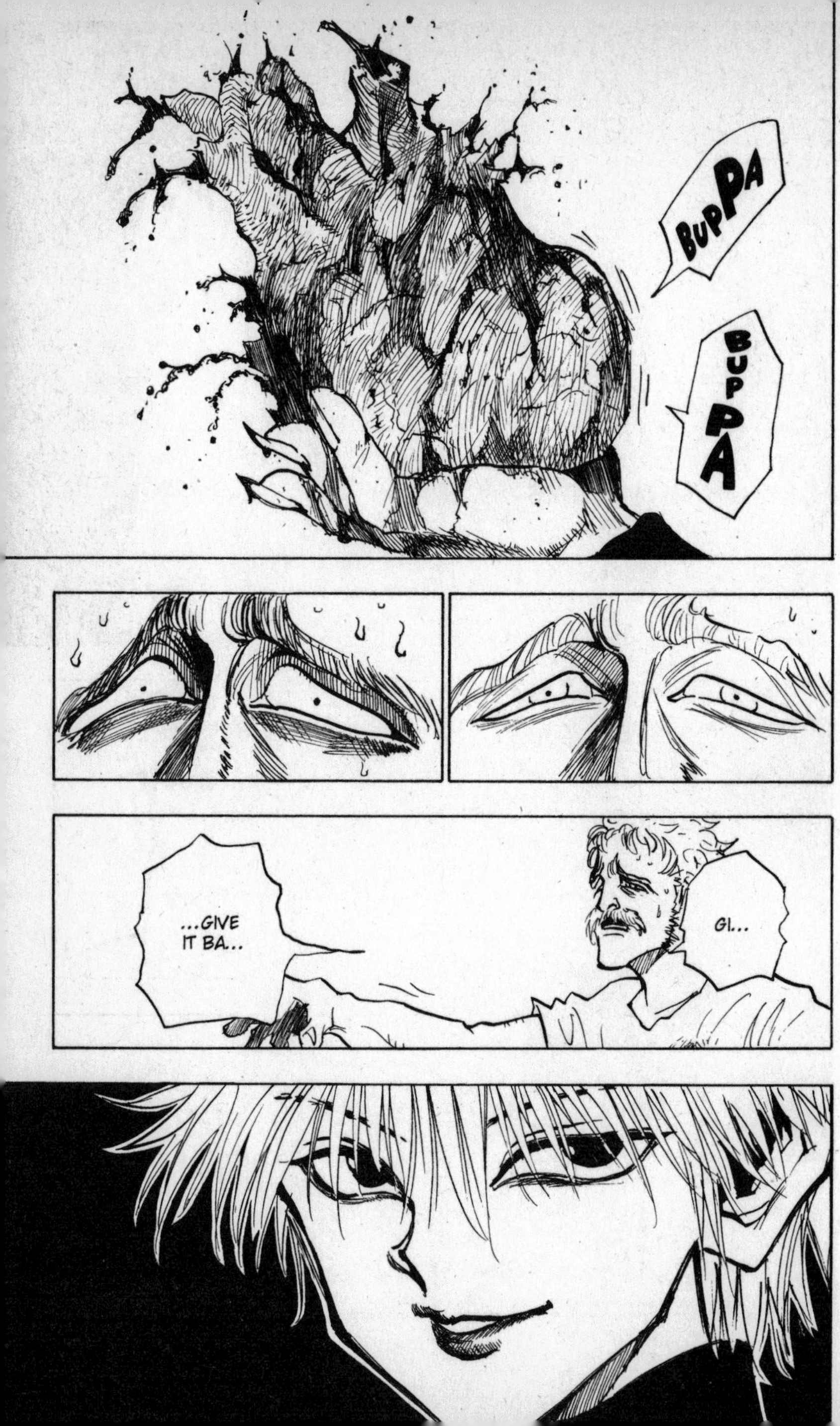
BUPPA
BUPPA
GI...
...GIVE IT BA...

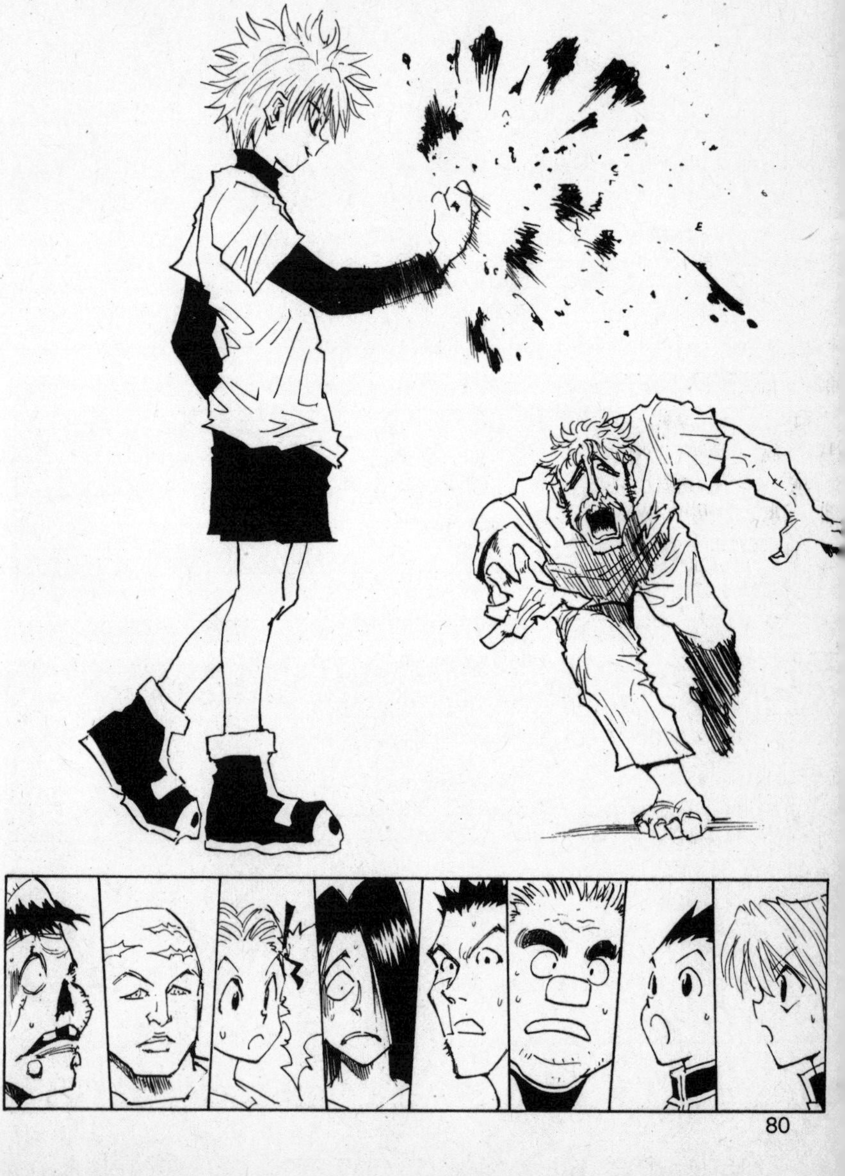

READ THIS WAY

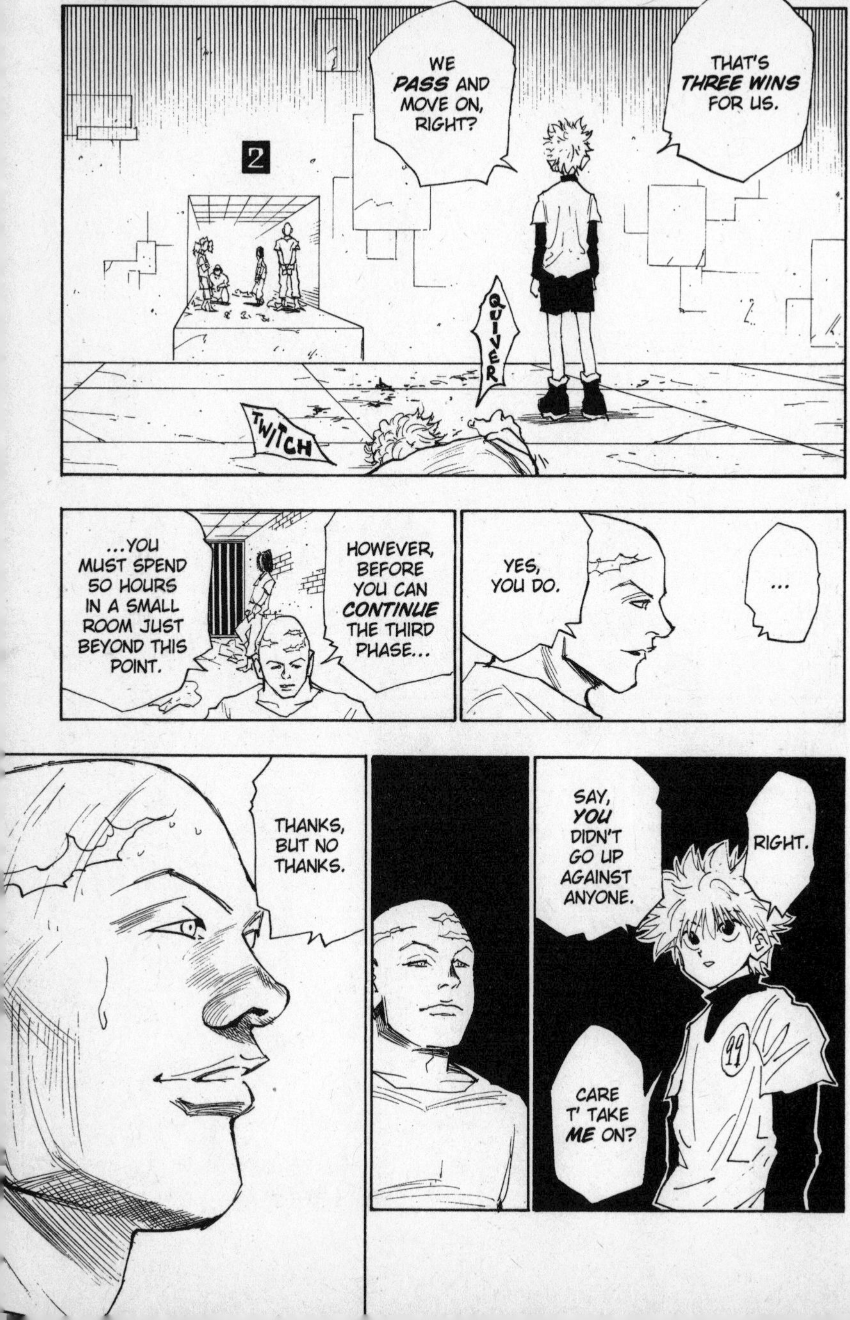
THAT'S *THREE WINS* FOR US.
WE *PASS* AND MOVE ON, RIGHT?
2
QUIVER
TWITCH
...
YES, YOU DO.
HOWEVER, BEFORE YOU CAN *CONTINUE* THE THIRD PHASE...
...YOU MUST SPEND 50 HOURS IN A SMALL ROOM JUST BEYOND THIS POINT.
RIGHT.
SAY, *YOU* DIDN'T GO UP AGAINST ANYONE.
CARE T' TAKE *ME* ON?
THANKS, BUT NO THANKS.

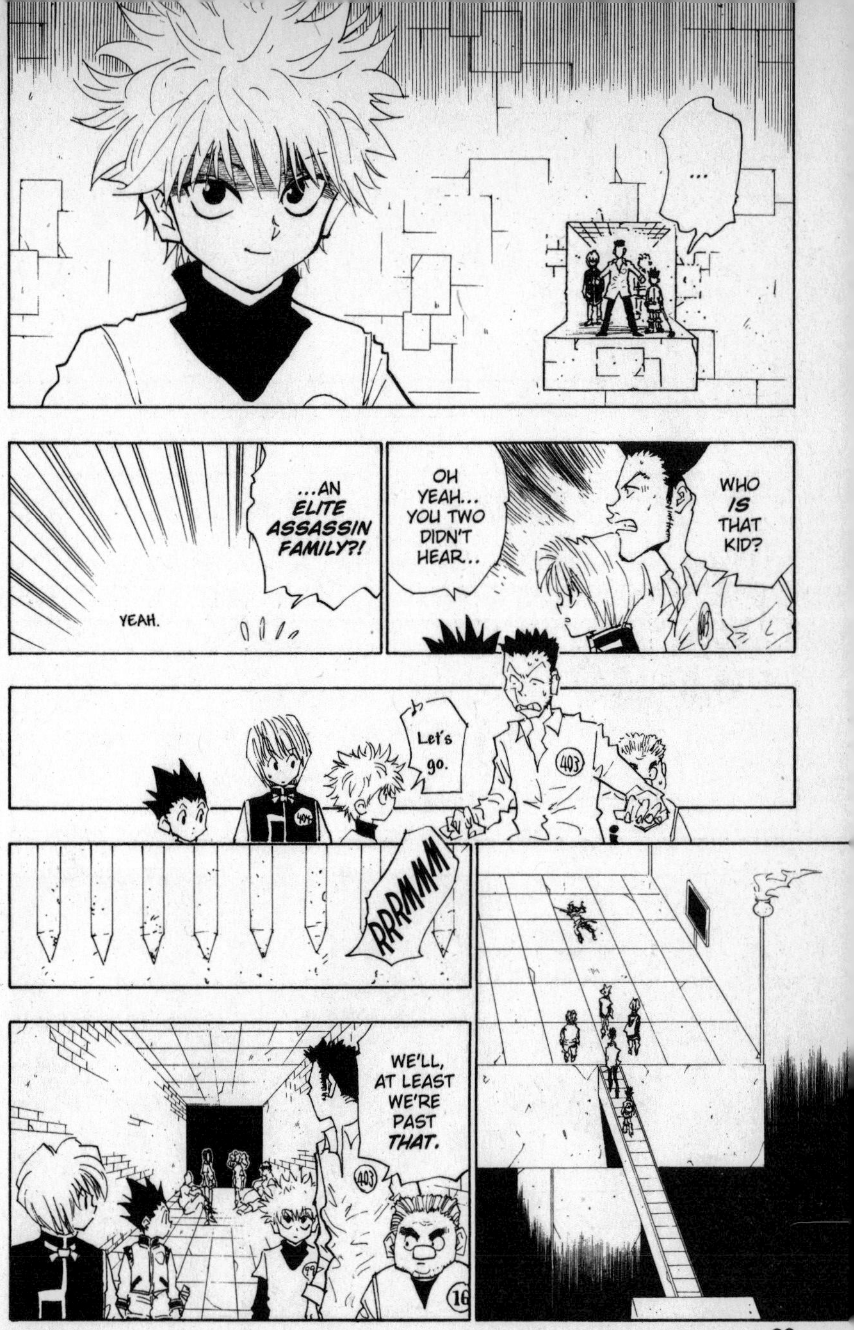
...
WHO IS THAT KID?
OH YEAH... YOU TWO DIDN'T HEAR...
...AN ELITE ASSASSIN FAMILY?!
YEAH.
Let's go.
RRRMMM
WE'LL, AT LEAST WE'RE PAST THAT.

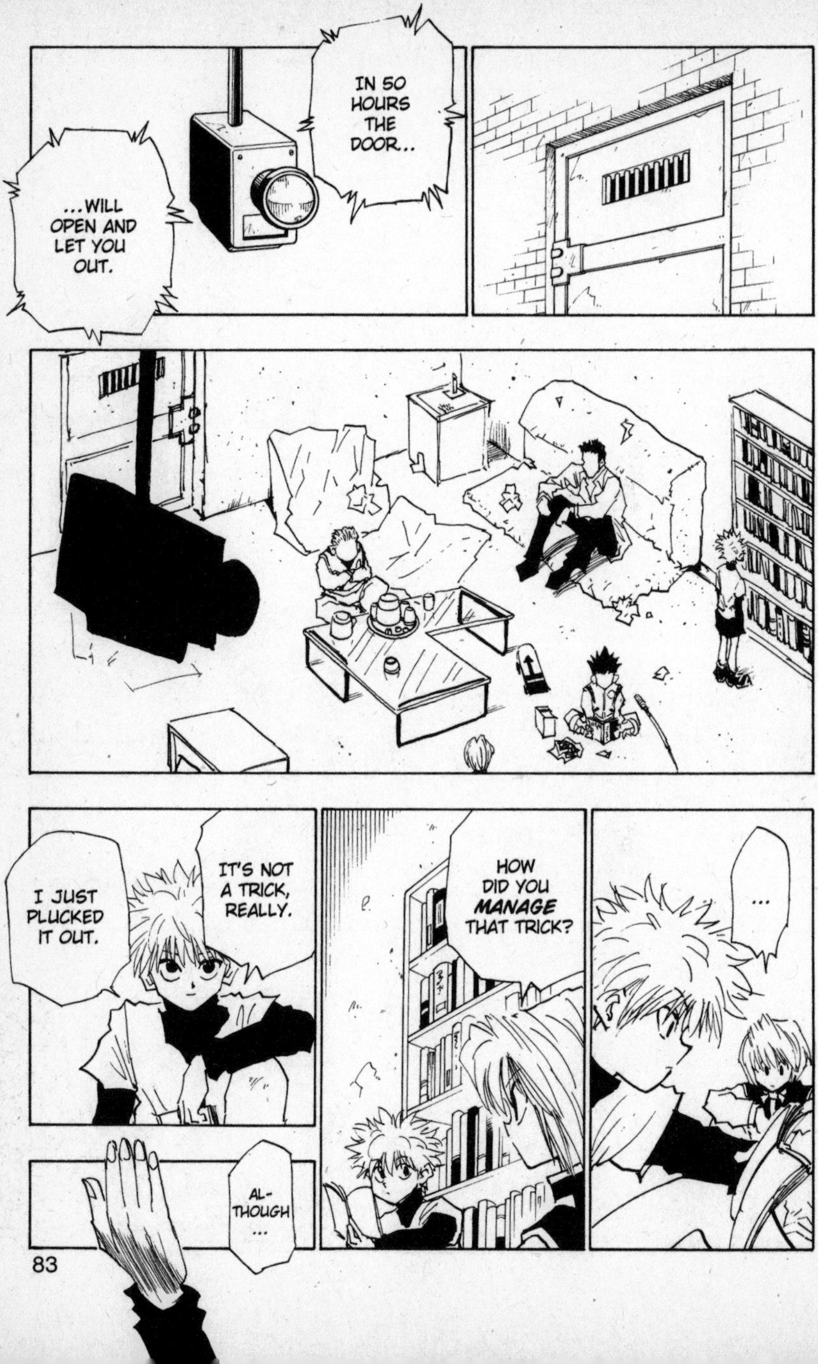
IN 50 HOURS THE DOOR...
...WILL OPEN AND LET YOU OUT.
...
HOW DID YOU ***MANAGE*** THAT TRICK?
IT'S NOT A TRICK, REALLY.
I JUST PLUCKED IT OUT.
AL-THOUGH ...

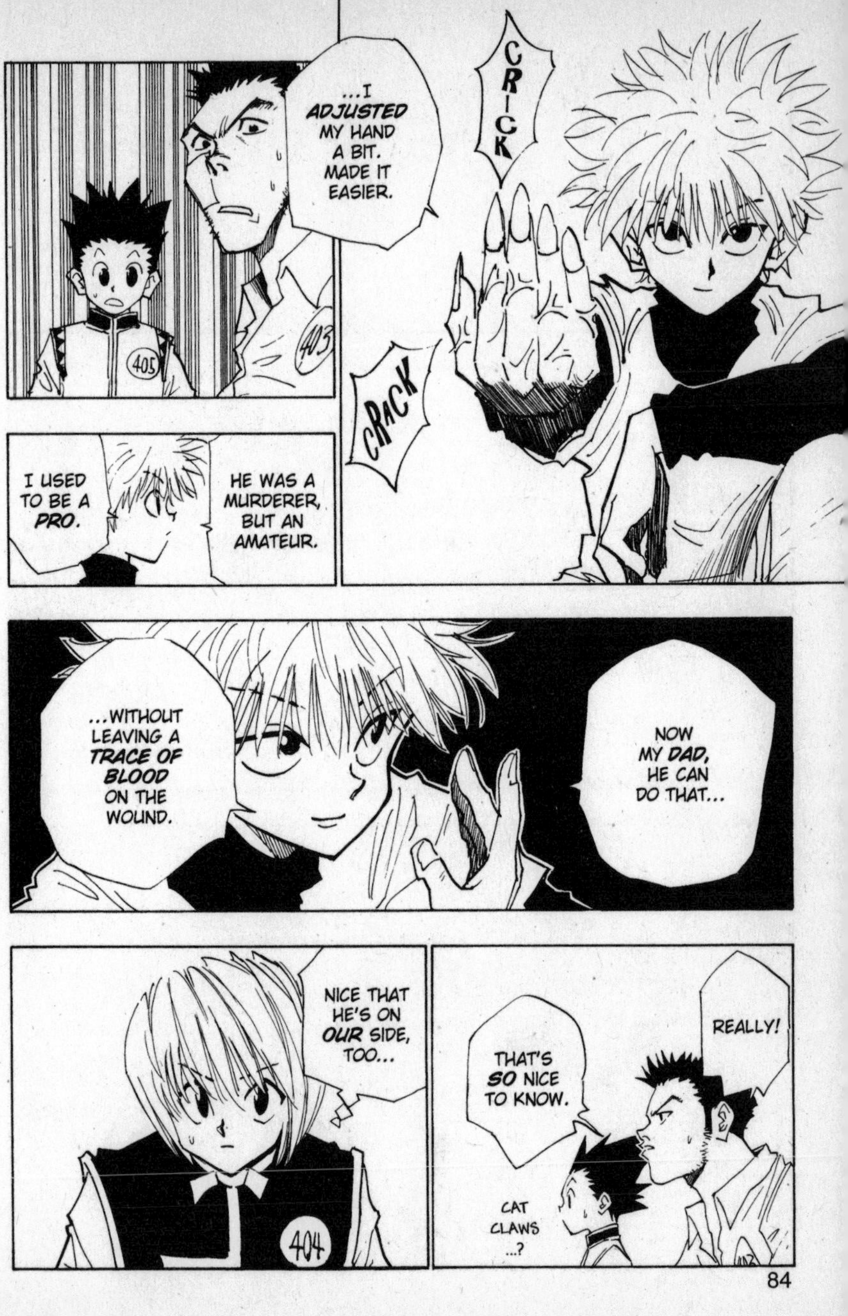
CRICK
...I ADJUSTED MY HAND A BIT. MADE IT EASIER.
CRACK
HE WAS A MURDERER, BUT AN AMATEUR.
I USED TO BE A PRO.
NOW MY DAD, HE CAN DO THAT...
...WITHOUT LEAVING A TRACE OF BLOOD ON THE WOUND.
REALLY!
THAT'S SO NICE TO KNOW.
CAT CLAWS ...?
NICE THAT HE'S ON OUR SIDE, TOO...

Fifty hours later...

RRMMM

DASH

LET'S HUSTLE.

`09:43:17`

X O

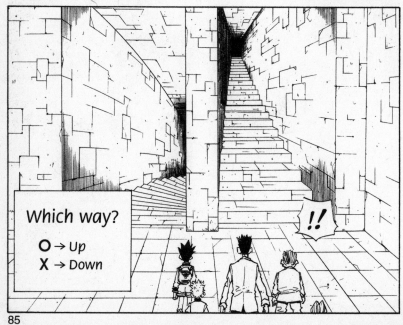

!!

Which way?

O → Up
X → Down

Khara

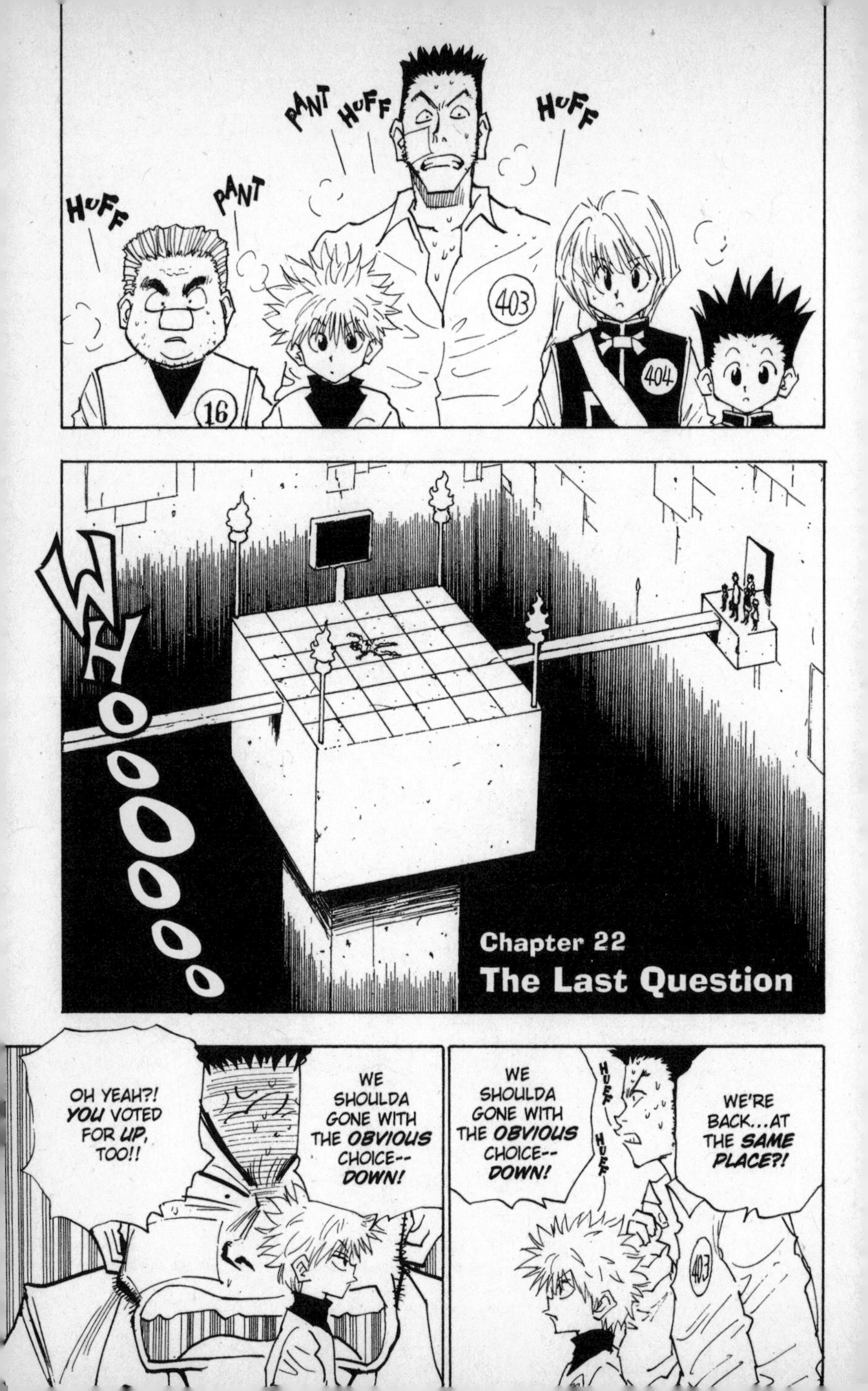
HUFF
HUFF
PANT
PANT
HUFF
WHOOOOOO
Chapter 22
The Last Question
WE'RE BACK...AT THE SAME PLACE?!
WE SHOULDA GONE WITH THE OBVIOUS CHOICE-- DOWN!
HUFF
HUFF
WE SHOULDA GONE WITH THE OBVIOUS CHOICE-- DOWN!
OH YEAH?! YOU VOTED FOR UP, TOO!!

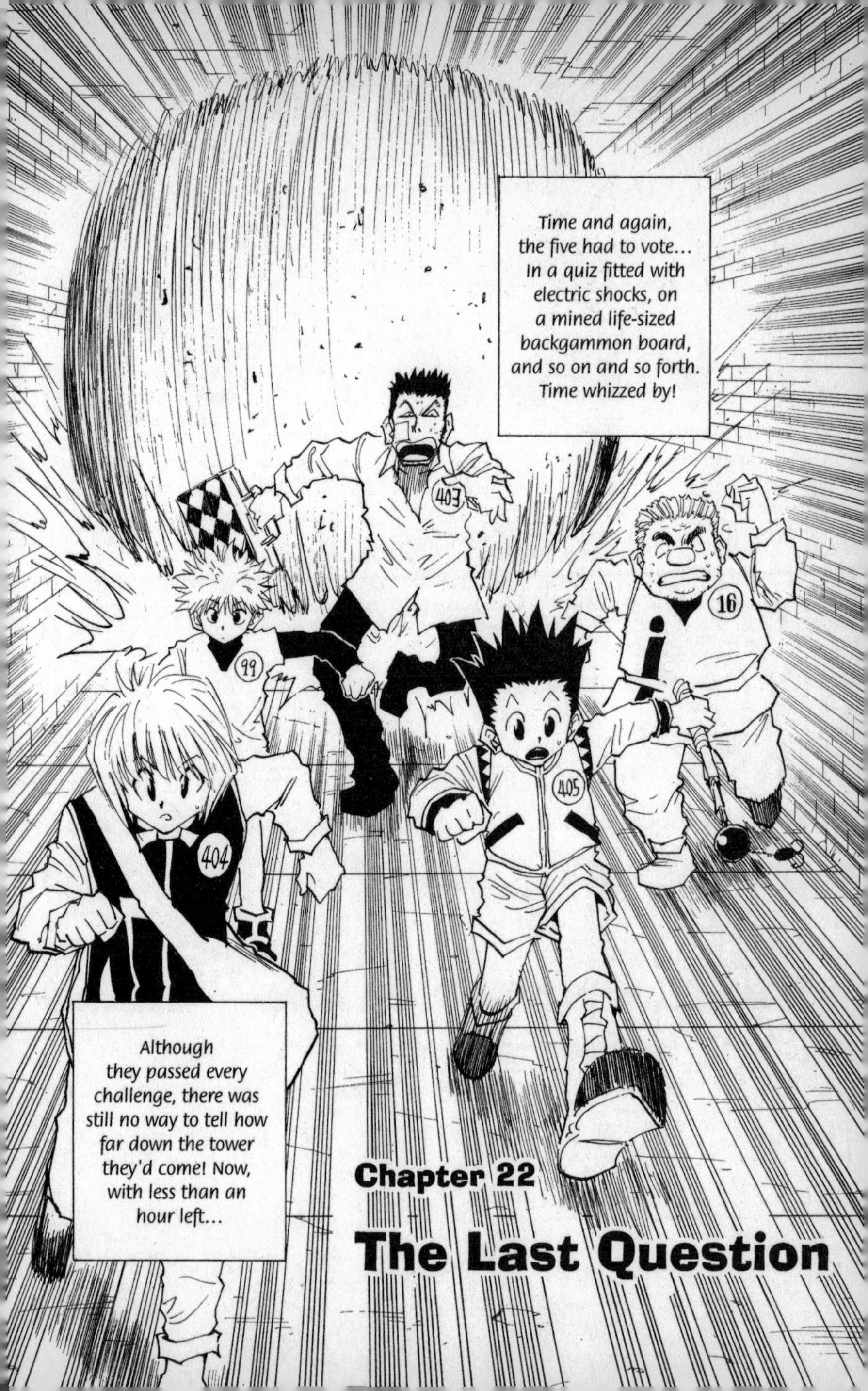
Time and again, the five had to vote... In a quiz fitted with electric shocks, on a mined life-sized backgammon board, and so on and so forth. Time whizzed by!
403
16
99
405
404
Although they passed every challenge, there was still no way to tell how far down the tower they'd come! Now, with less than an hour left...
Chapter 22
The Last Question

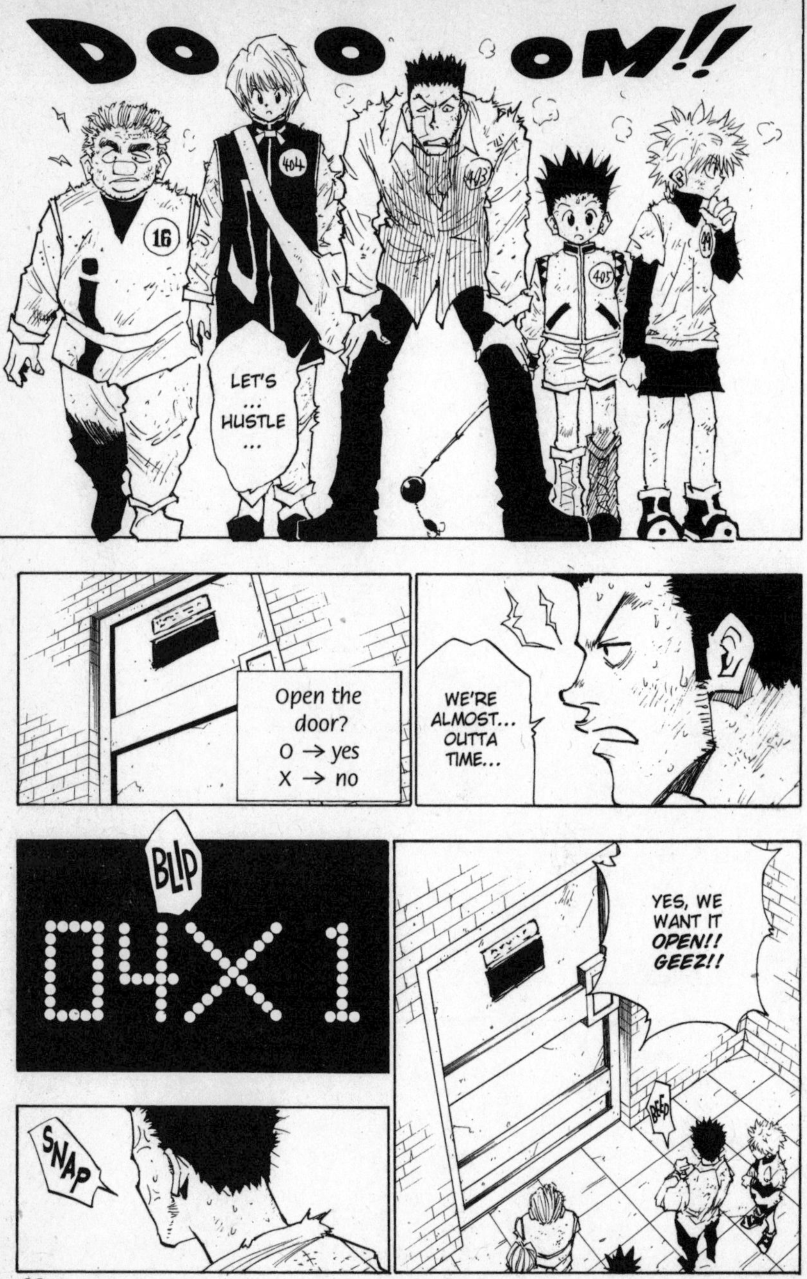
DO O OM!!
LET'S ... HUSTLE ...
WE'RE ALMOST... OUTTA TIME...
Open the door?
O → yes
X → no
YES, WE WANT IT *OPEN!! GEEZ!!*
BLIP
04X1
SNAP

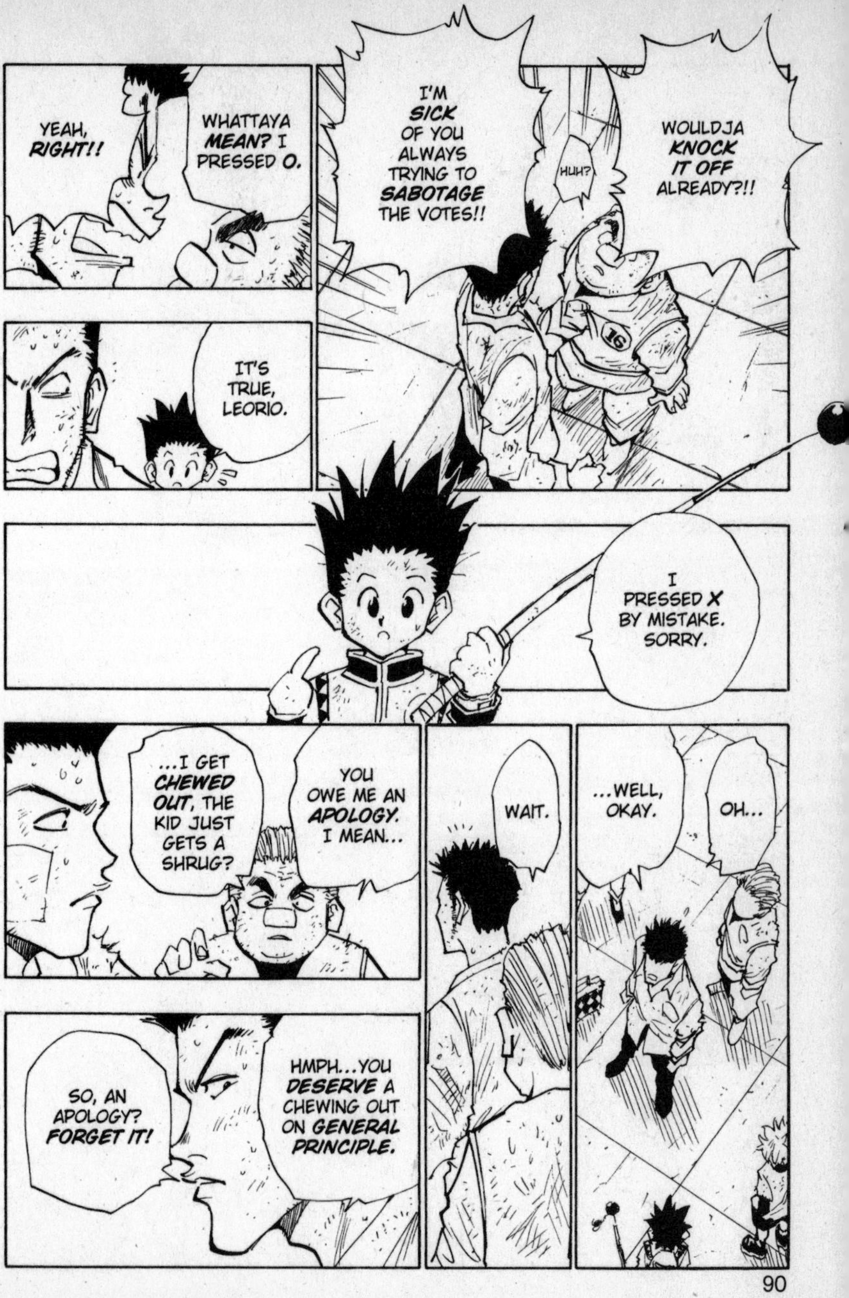
WOULDJA KNOCK IT OFF ALREADY?!!
I'M SICK OF YOU ALWAYS TRYING TO SABOTAGE THE VOTES!!
HUH?
WHATTAYA MEAN? I PRESSED O.
YEAH, RIGHT!!
IT'S TRUE, LEORIO.
I PRESSED X BY MISTAKE. SORRY.
OH...
...WELL, OKAY.
WAIT.
YOU OWE ME AN APOLOGY. I MEAN...
...I GET CHEWED OUT, THE KID JUST GETS A SHRUG?
HMPH...YOU DESERVE A CHEWING OUT ON GENERAL PRINCIPLE.
SO, AN APOLOGY? FORGET IT!

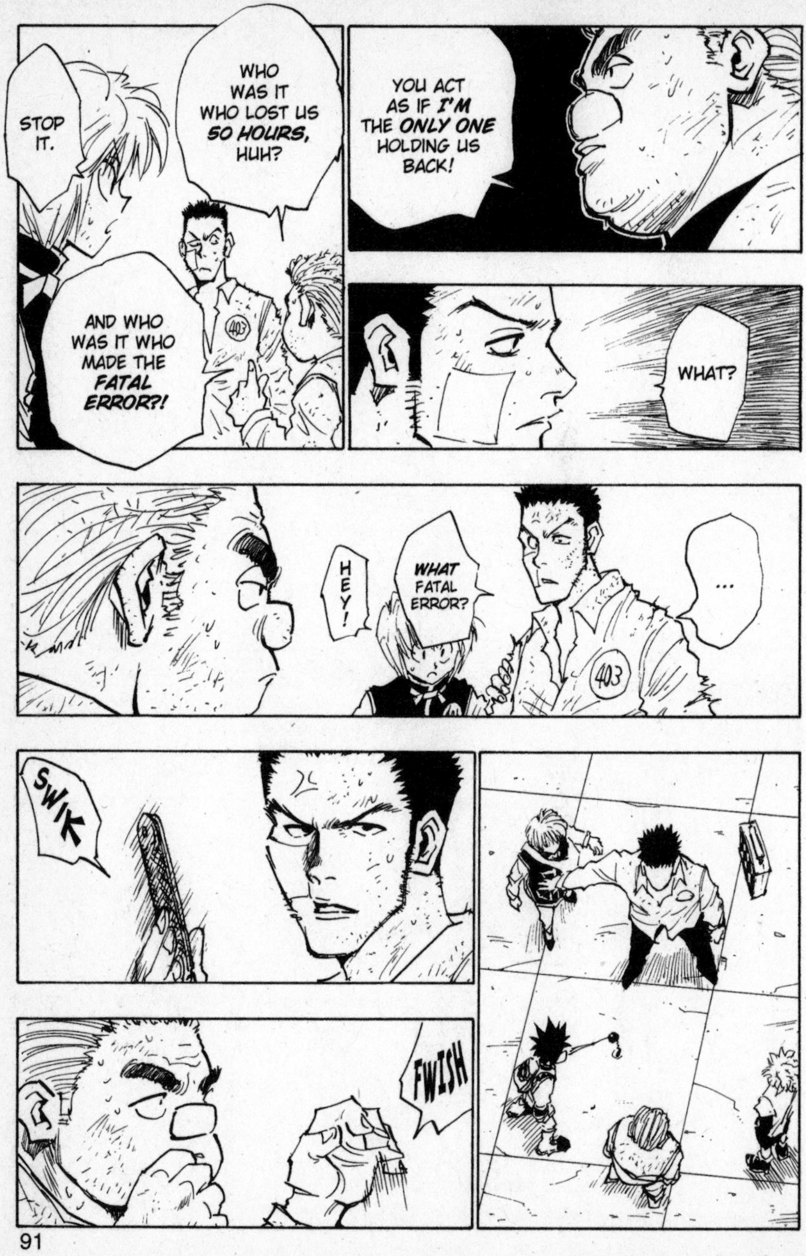
YOU ACT AS IF *I'M* THE *ONLY ONE* HOLDING US BACK!
WHAT?
WHO WAS IT WHO LOST US *50 HOURS,* HUH?
STOP IT.
AND WHO WAS IT WHO MADE THE *FATAL ERROR?!*
...
WHAT FATAL ERROR?
HEY!
SWIK
FWISH

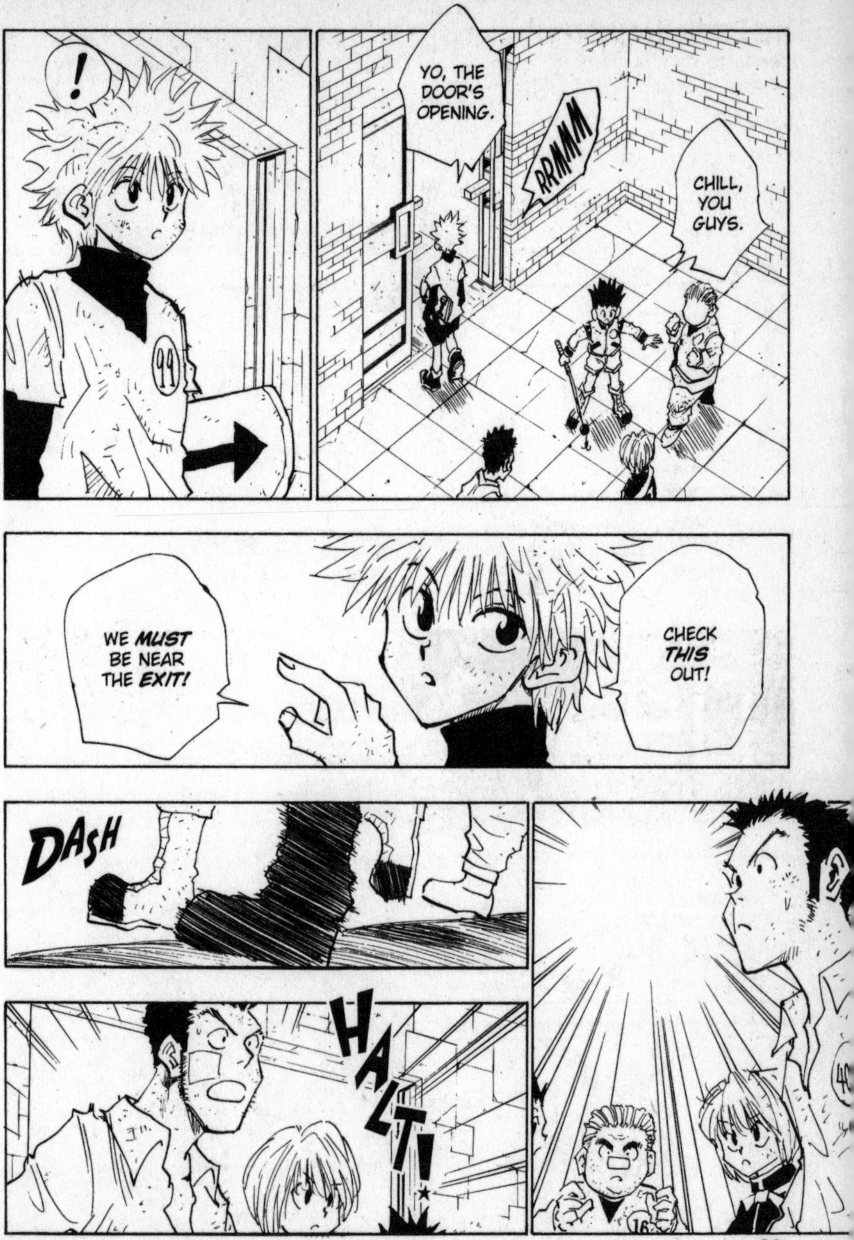
YO, THE DOOR'S OPENING.
RRMMM
CHILL, YOU GUYS.
!
CHECK THIS OUT!
WE MUST BE NEAR THE EXIT!
DASH
HALT!

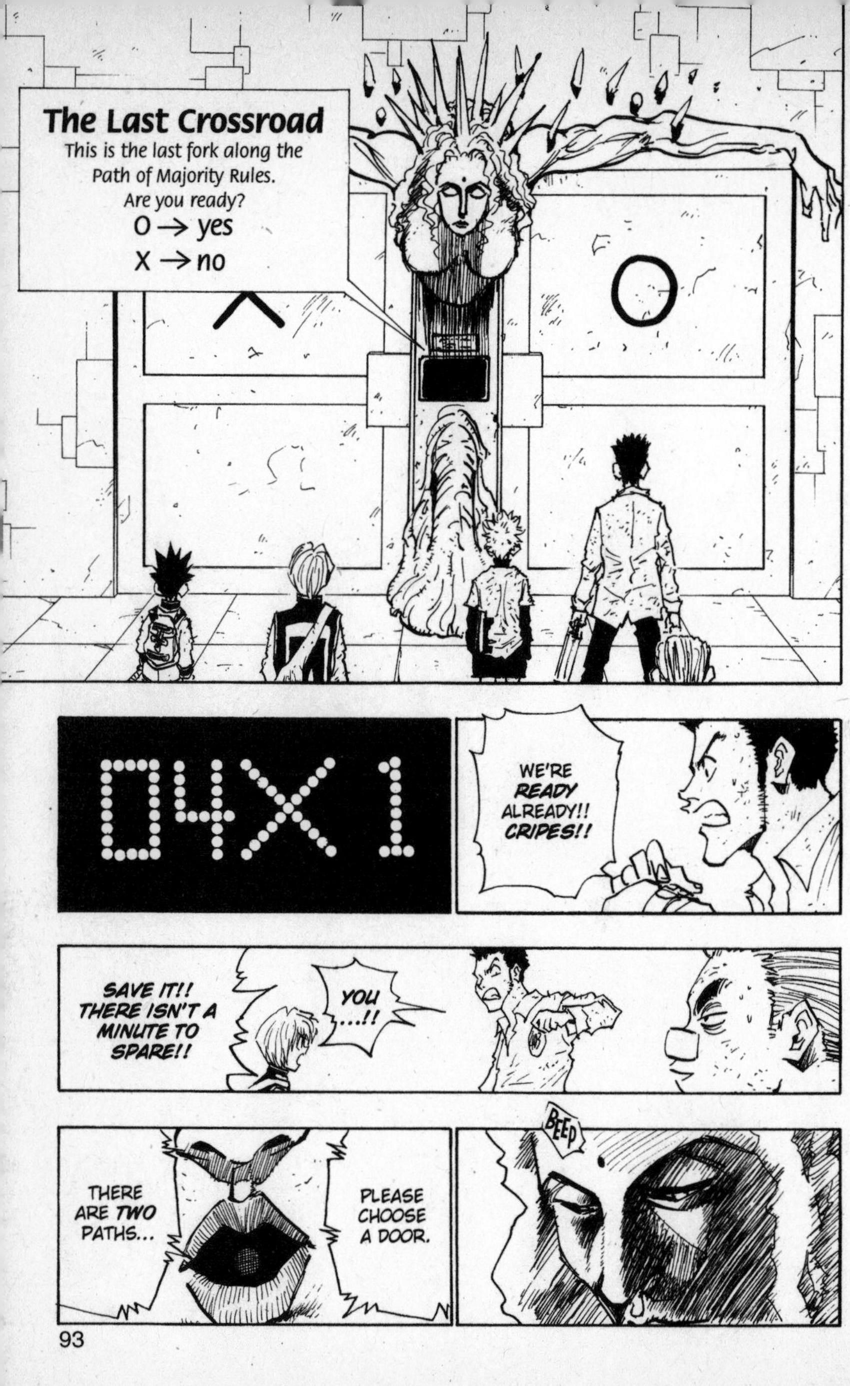
The Last Crossroad
This is the last fork along the Path of Majority Rules. Are you ready?
O → yes
X → no
O
WE'RE READY ALREADY!! CRIPES!!
O4X1
YOU ...!!
SAVE IT!! THERE ISN'T A MINUTE TO SPARE!!
BEEP
PLEASE CHOOSE A DOOR.
THERE ARE TWO PATHS...

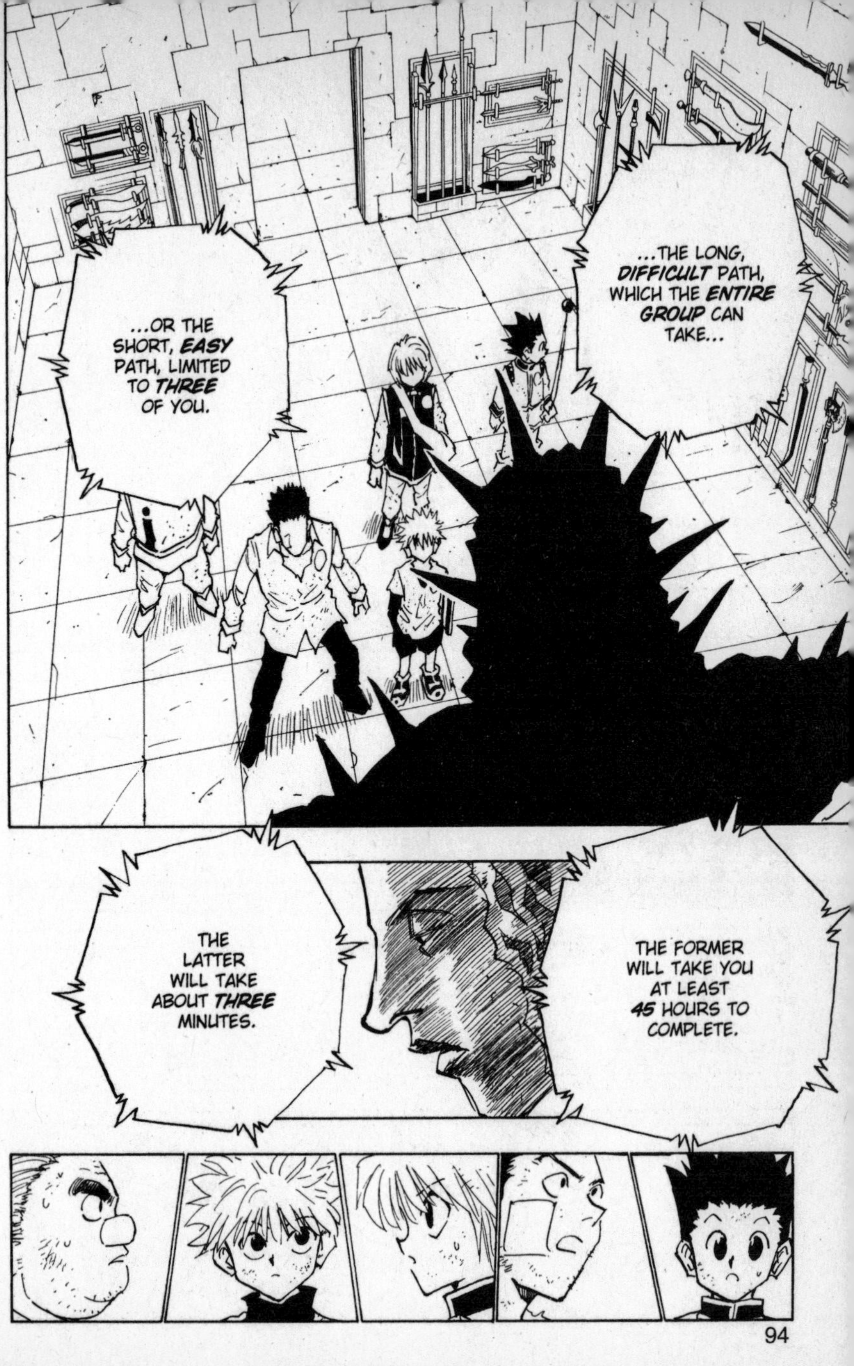
...THE LONG, DIFFICULT PATH, WHICH THE ENTIRE GROUP CAN TAKE...
...OR THE SHORT, EASY PATH, LIMITED TO THREE OF YOU.
THE FORMER WILL TAKE YOU AT LEAST 45 HOURS TO COMPLETE.
THE LATTER WILL TAKE ABOUT THREE MINUTES.

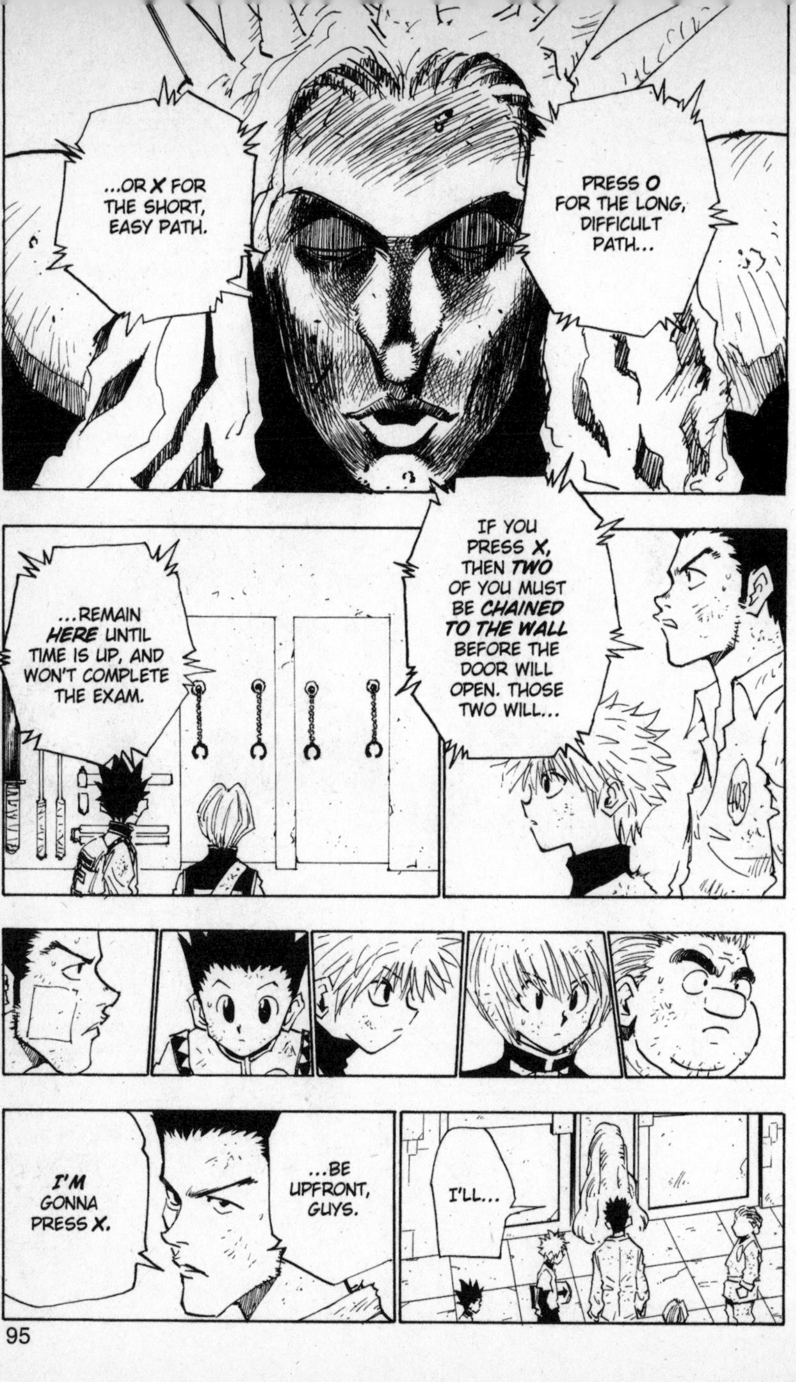
PRESS O FOR THE LONG, DIFFICULT PATH...
...OR X FOR THE SHORT, EASY PATH.
IF YOU PRESS X, THEN TWO OF YOU MUST BE CHAINED TO THE WALL BEFORE THE DOOR WILL OPEN. THOSE TWO WILL...
...REMAIN HERE UNTIL TIME IS UP, AND WON'T COMPLETE THE EXAM.
403
I'LL...
...BE UPFRONT, GUYS.
I'M GONNA PRESS X.

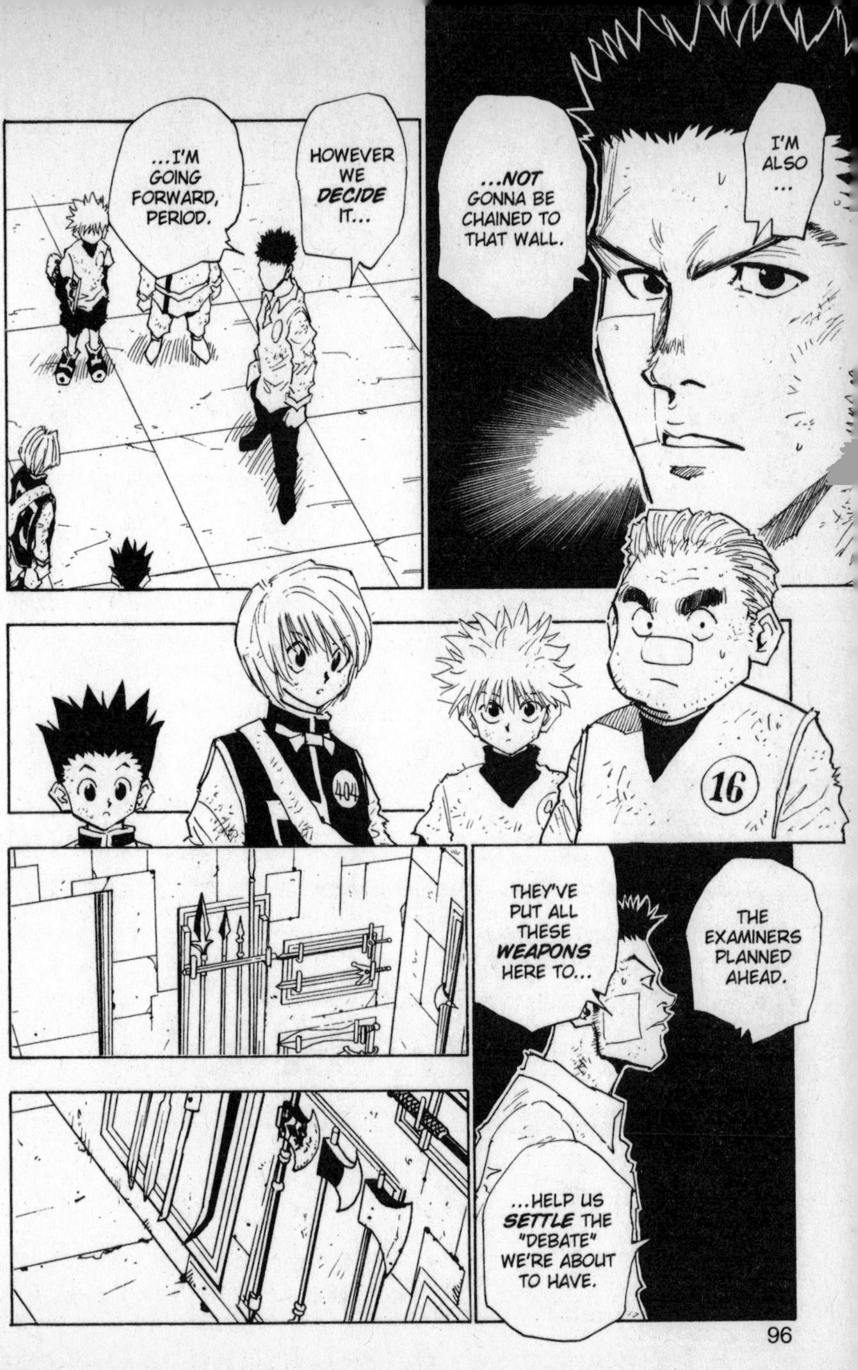
I'M ALSO ...
...NOT GONNA BE CHAINED TO THAT WALL.
HOWEVER WE DECIDE IT...
...I'M GOING FORWARD, PERIOD.
THE EXAMINERS PLANNED AHEAD.
THEY'VE PUT ALL THESE WEAPONS HERE TO...
...HELP US SETTLE THE "DEBATE" WE'RE ABOUT TO HAVE.

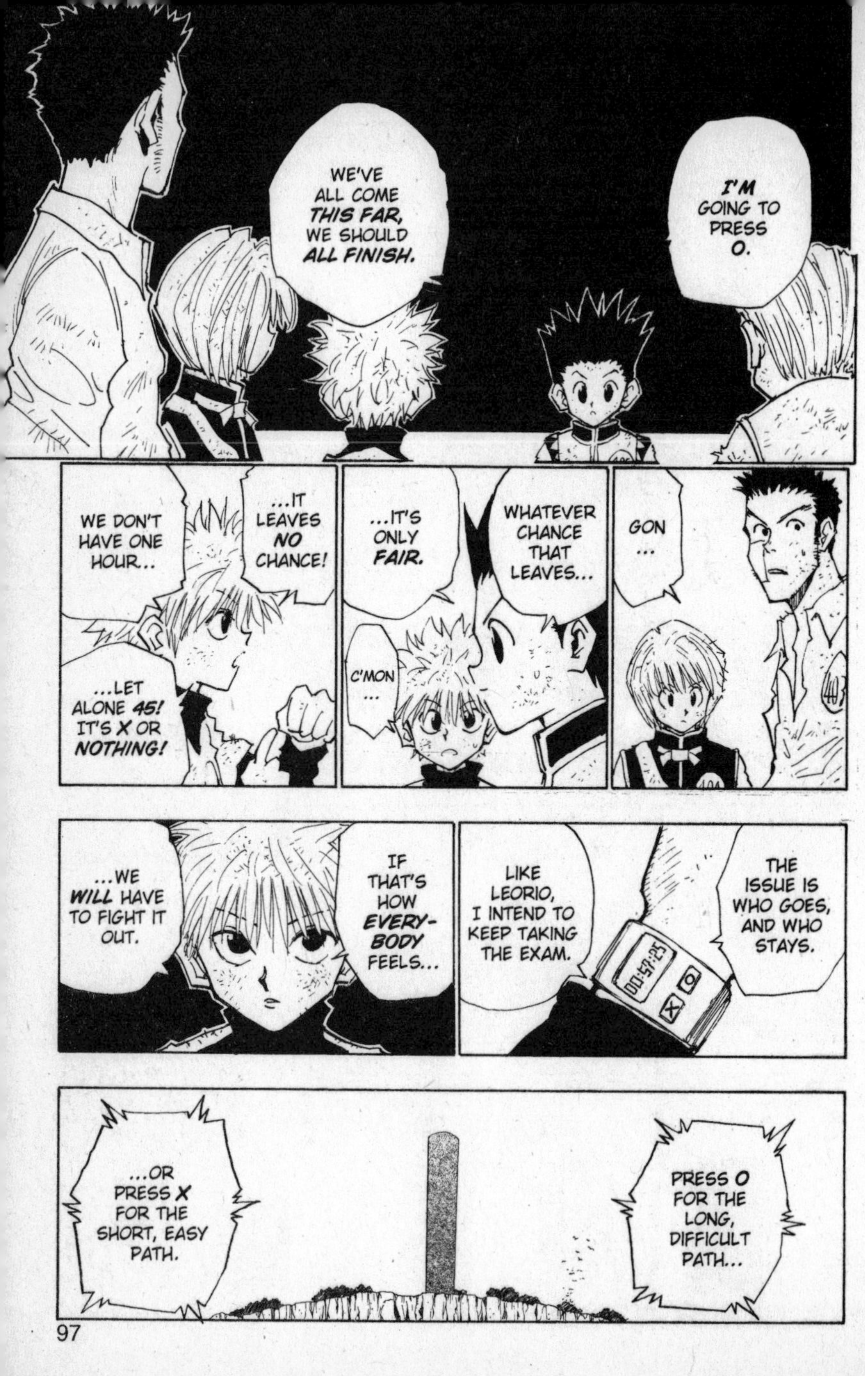
I'M GOING TO PRESS O.
WE'VE ALL COME THIS FAR, WE SHOULD ALL FINISH.
GON ...
WHATEVER CHANCE THAT LEAVES...
...IT'S ONLY FAIR.
C'MON ...
...IT LEAVES NO CHANCE!
WE DON'T HAVE ONE HOUR...
...LET ALONE 45! IT'S X OR NOTHING!
THE ISSUE IS WHO GOES, AND WHO STAYS.
LIKE LEORIO, I INTEND TO KEEP TAKING THE EXAM.
IF THAT'S HOW EVERY-BODY FEELS...
...WE WILL HAVE TO FIGHT IT OUT.
PRESS O FOR THE LONG, DIFFICULT PATH...
...OR PRESS X FOR THE SHORT, EASY PATH.

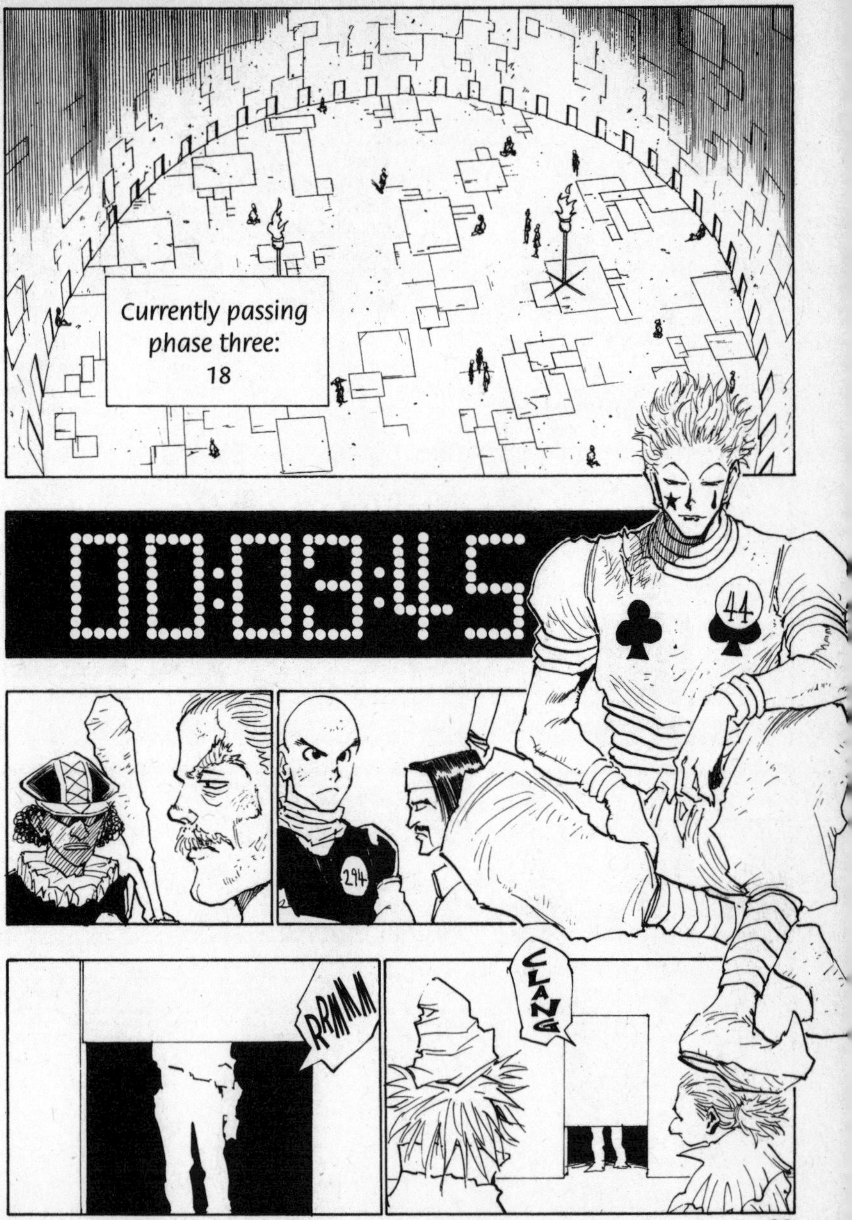

Currently passing phase three: 18
00:03:45
CLANG
RRMMM

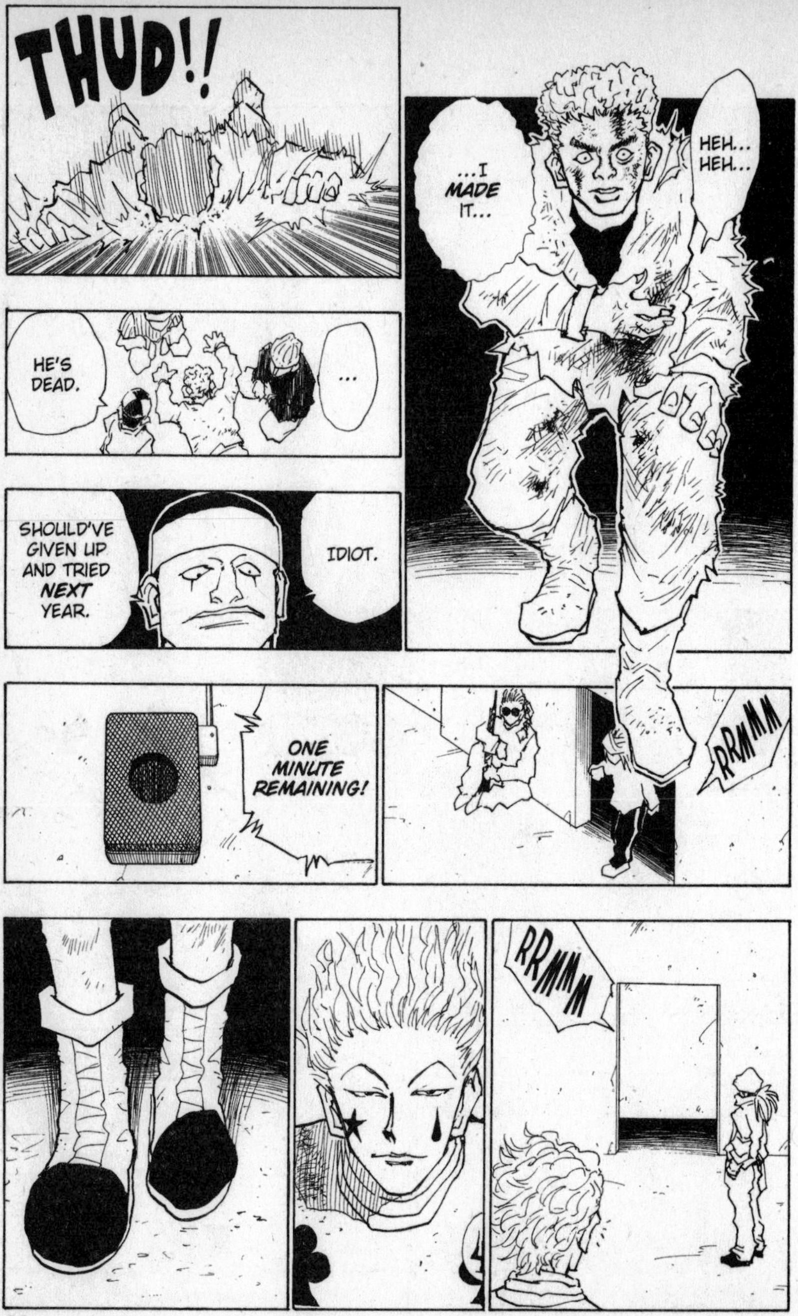
HEH... HEH...
...I MADE IT...
THUD!!
...
HE'S DEAD.
IDIOT.
SHOULD'VE GIVEN UP AND TRIED NEXT YEAR.
RRMMM
ONE MINUTE REMAINING!
RRMMM

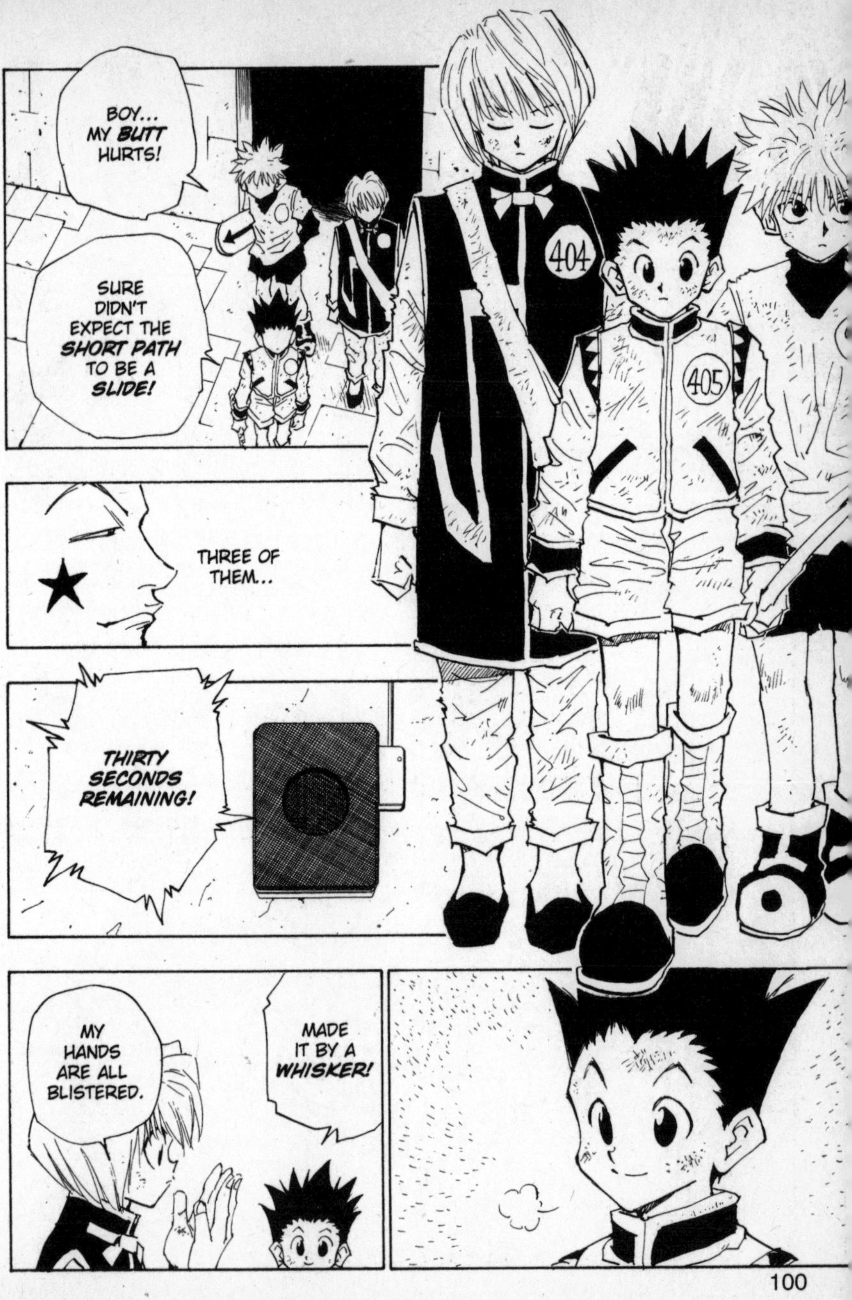
BOY... MY BUTT HURTS!
SURE DIDN'T EXPECT THE SHORT PATH TO BE A SLIDE!
THREE OF THEM...
THIRTY SECONDS REMAINING!
MADE IT BY A WHISKER!
MY HANDS ARE ALL BLISTERED.

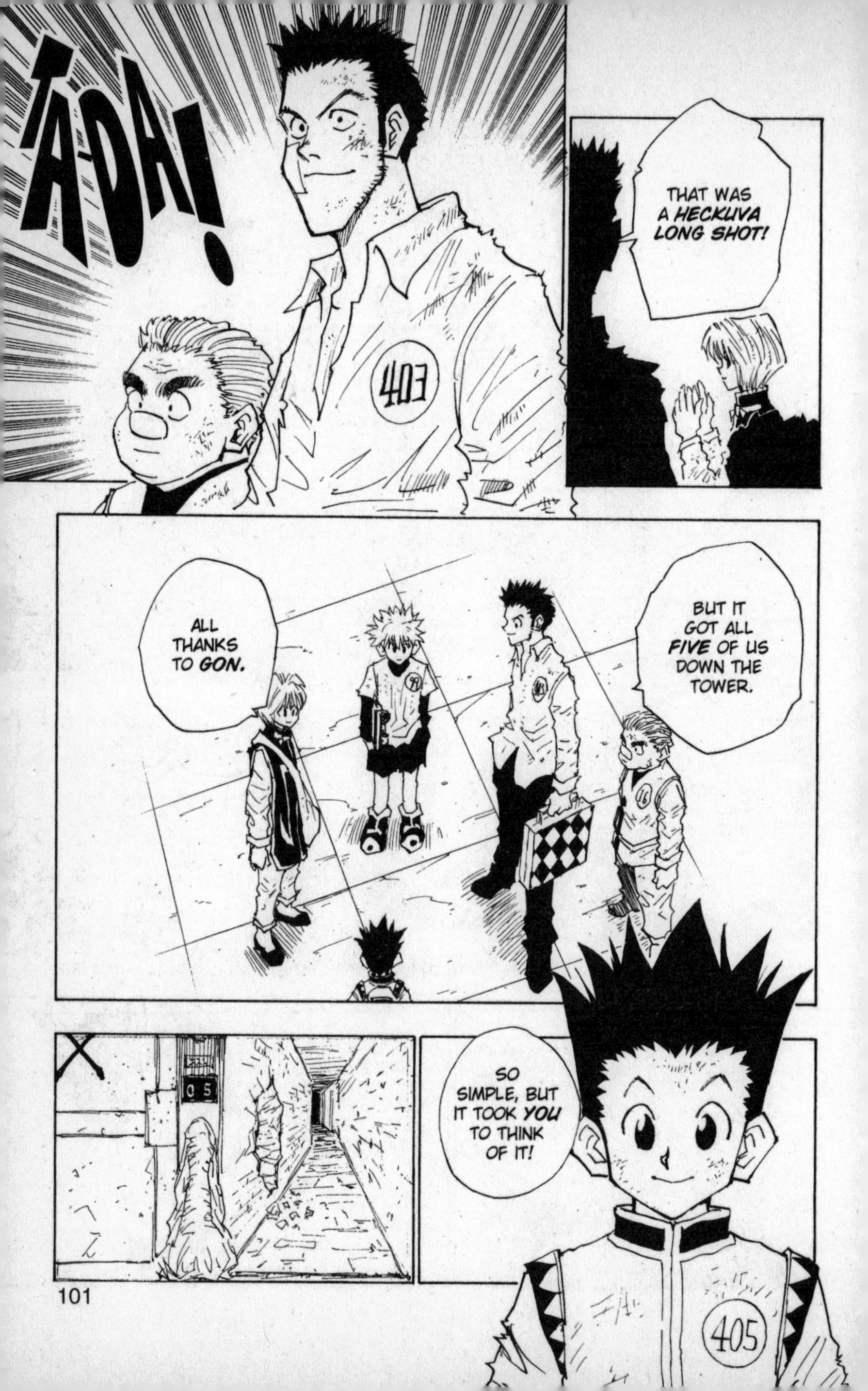
THAT WAS A HECKUVA LONG SHOT!
TA-DA!
BUT IT GOT ALL FIVE OF US DOWN THE TOWER.
ALL THANKS TO GON.
SO SIMPLE, BUT IT TOOK YOU TO THINK OF IT!
05

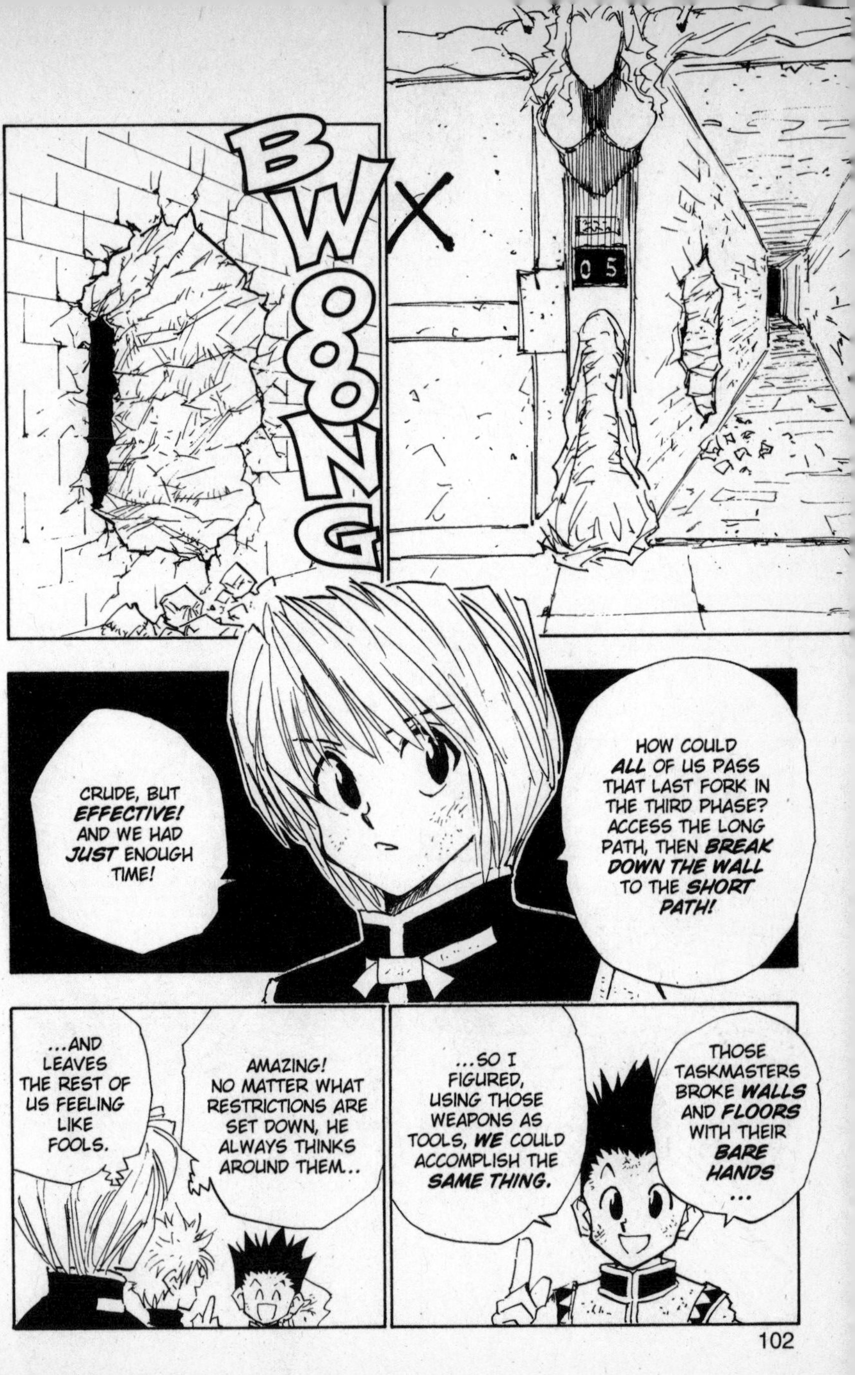
0 5
BWOOONG
HOW COULD ALL OF US PASS THAT LAST FORK IN THE THIRD PHASE? ACCESS THE LONG PATH, THEN BREAK DOWN THE WALL TO THE SHORT PATH!
CRUDE, BUT EFFECTIVE! AND WE HAD JUST ENOUGH TIME!
THOSE TASKMASTERS BROKE WALLS AND FLOORS WITH THEIR BARE HANDS ...
...SO I FIGURED, USING THOSE WEAPONS AS TOOLS, WE COULD ACCOMPLISH THE SAME THING.
AMAZING! NO MATTER WHAT RESTRICTIONS ARE SET DOWN, HE ALWAYS THINKS AROUND THEM...
...AND LEAVES THE REST OF US FEELING LIKE FOOLS.

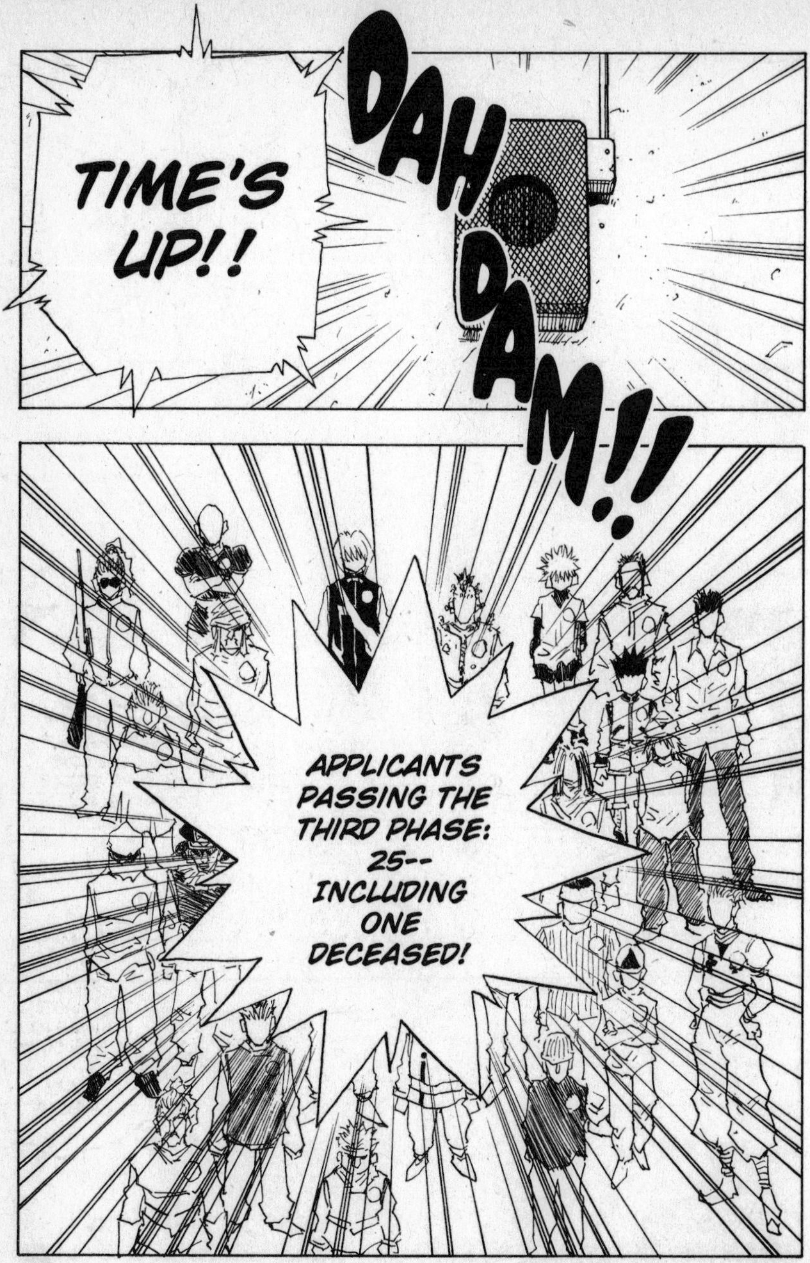
TIME'S UP!!
DAH DAM!!
APPLICANTS PASSING THE THIRD PHASE: 25-- INCLUDING ONE DECEASED!

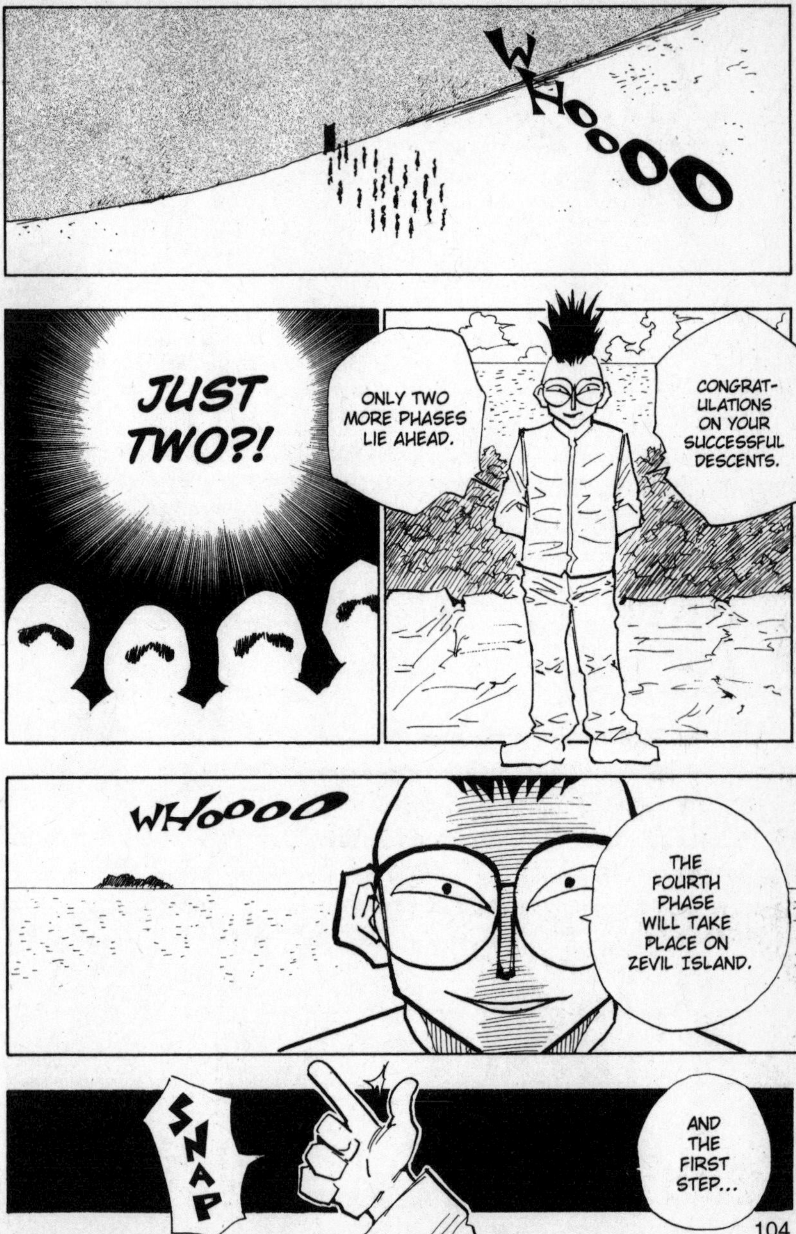
WHOOOO
CONGRAT-ULATIONS ON YOUR SUCCESSFUL DESCENTS.
ONLY TWO MORE PHASES LIE AHEAD.
JUST TWO?!
THE FOURTH PHASE WILL TAKE PLACE ON ZEVIL ISLAND.
WHOOOO
AND THE FIRST STEP...
SNAP

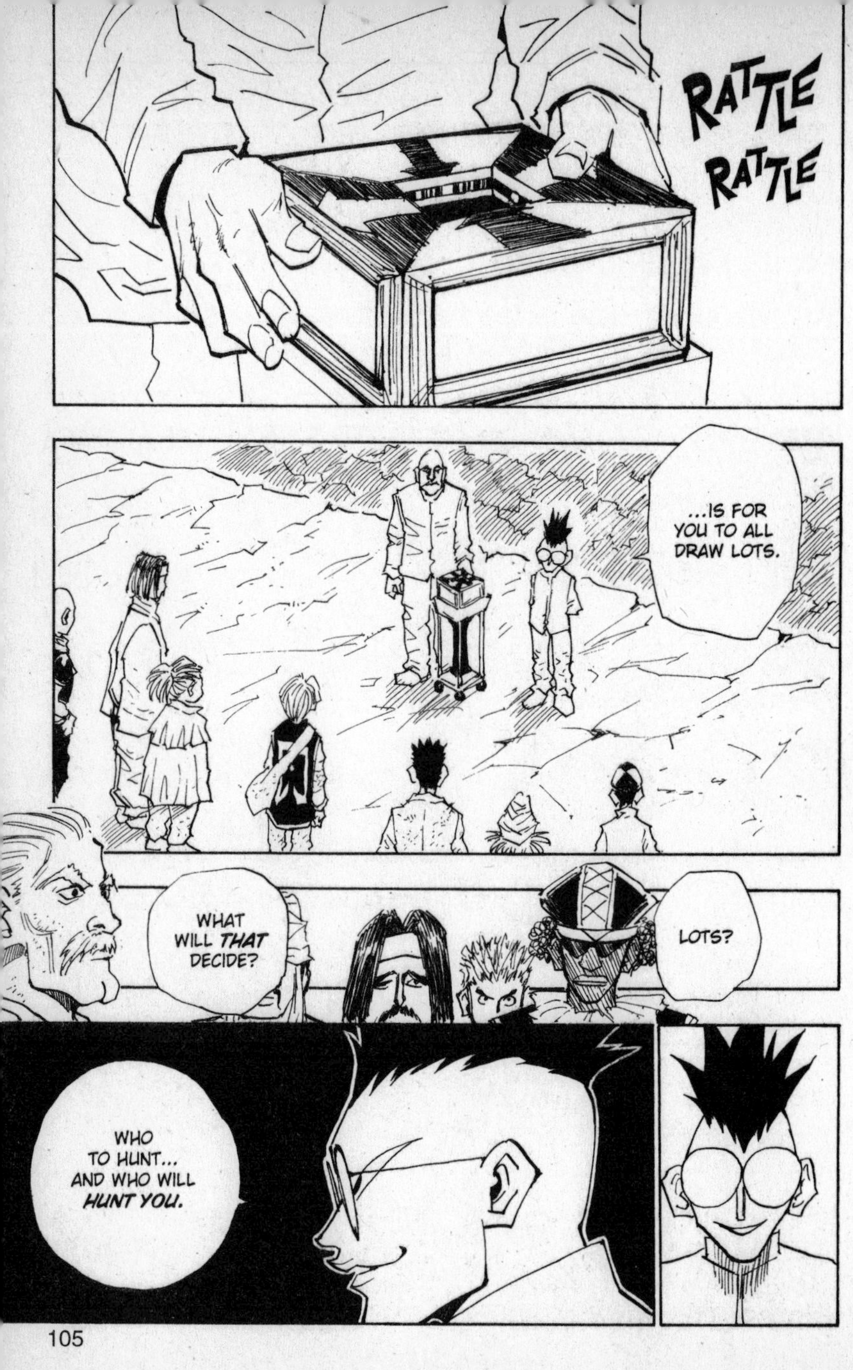
RATTLE RATTLE
...IS FOR YOU TO ALL DRAW LOTS.
LOTS?
WHAT WILL THAT DECIDE?
WHO TO HUNT... AND WHO WILL HUNT YOU.

Geretta

Chapter 23
Two Enemies

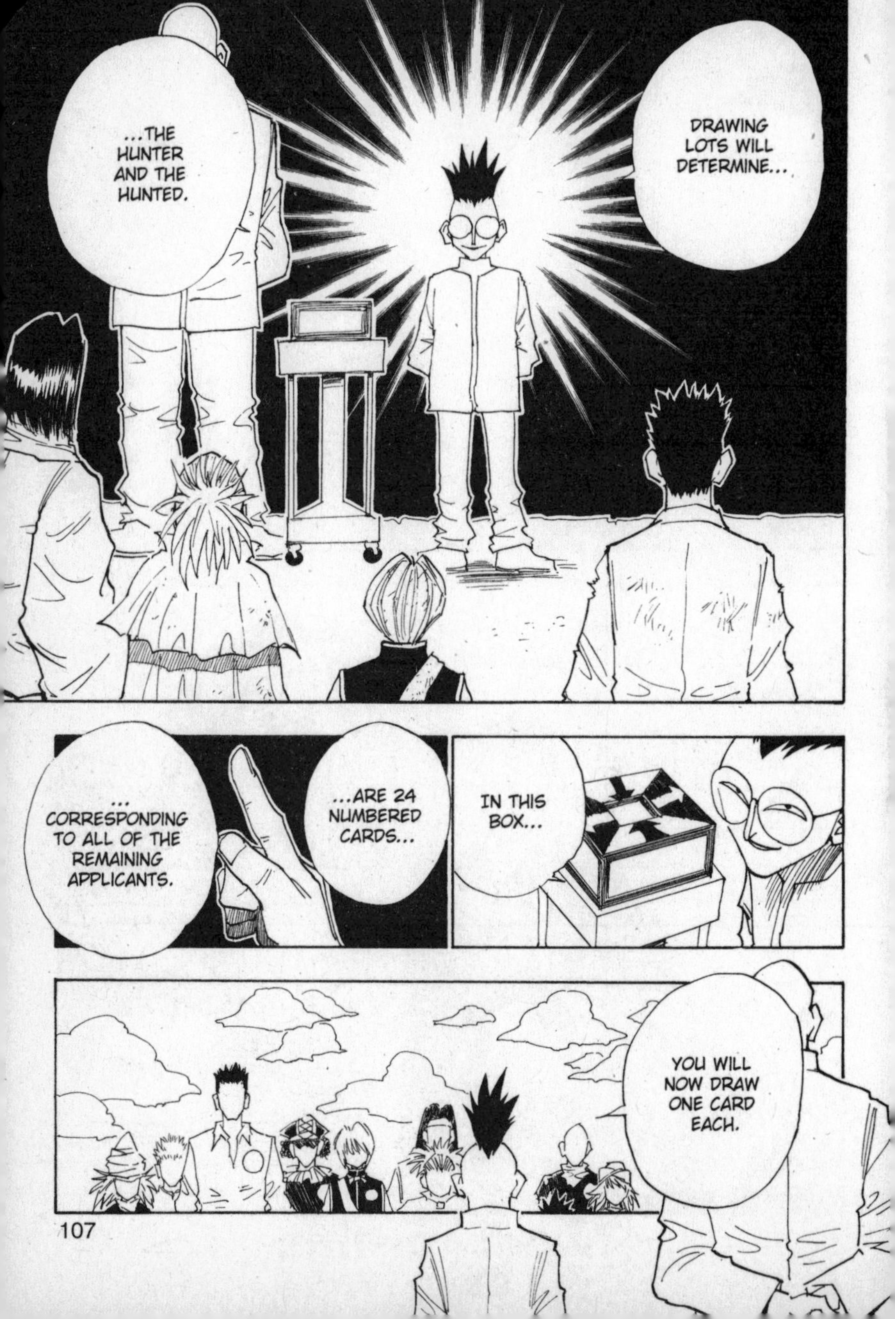
DRAWING LOTS WILL DETERMINE...
...THE HUNTER AND THE HUNTED.
IN THIS BOX...
...ARE 24 NUMBERED CARDS...
...CORRESPONDING TO ALL OF THE REMAINING APPLICANTS.
YOU WILL NOW DRAW ONE CARD EACH.

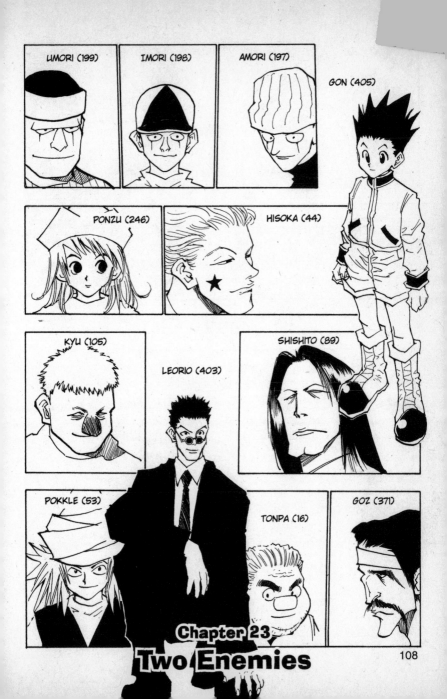

UMORI (199)

IMORI (198)

AMORI (197)

GON (405)

PONZU (246)

HISOKA (44)

KYU (105)

LEORIO (403)

SHISHITO (89)

POKKLE (53)

TONPA (16)

GOZ (371)

Chapter 23
Two Enemies

108

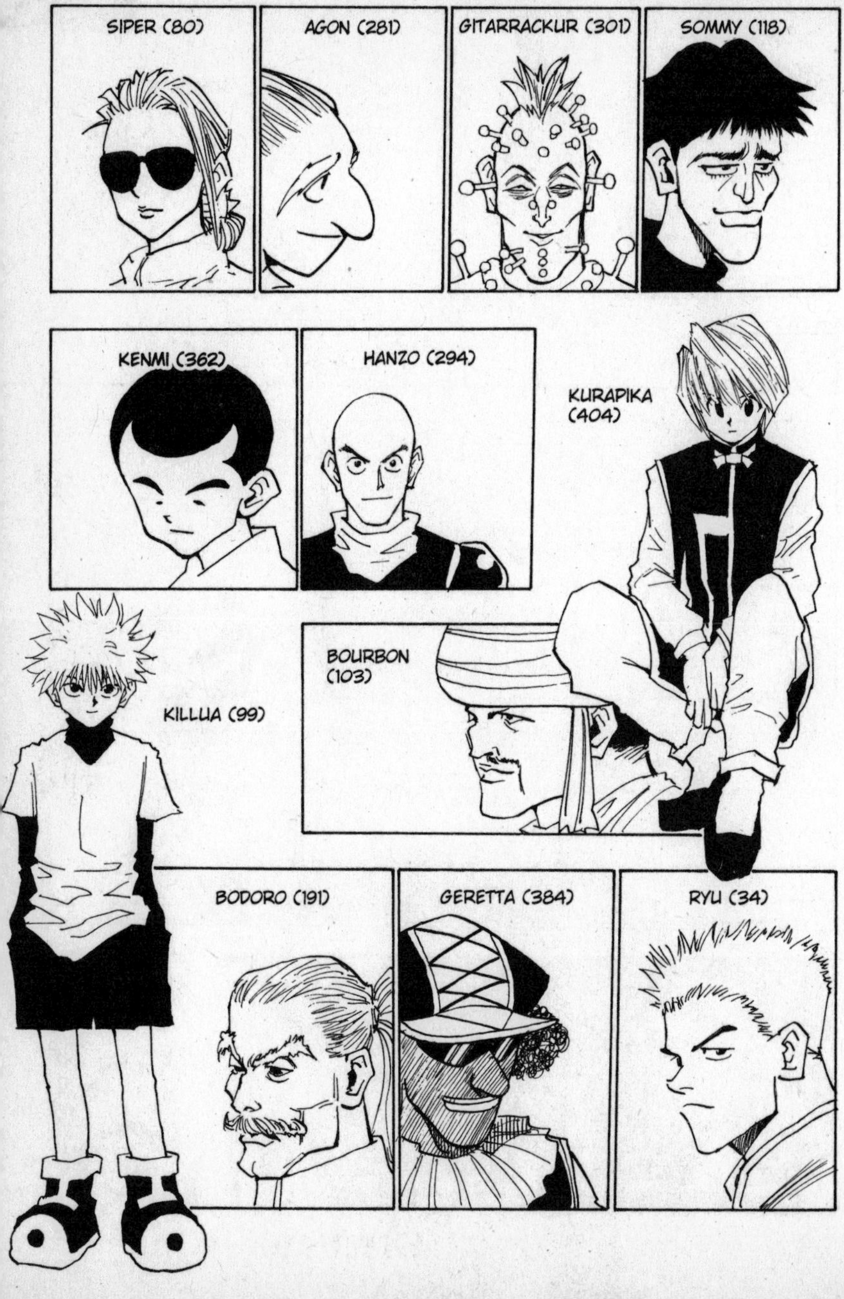
SOMMY (118)
GITARRACKUR (301)
AGON (281)
SIPER (80)
KURAPIKA (404)
HANZO (294)
KENMI (362)
BOURBON (103)
KILLUA (99)
RYU (34)
GERETTA (384)
BODORO (191)

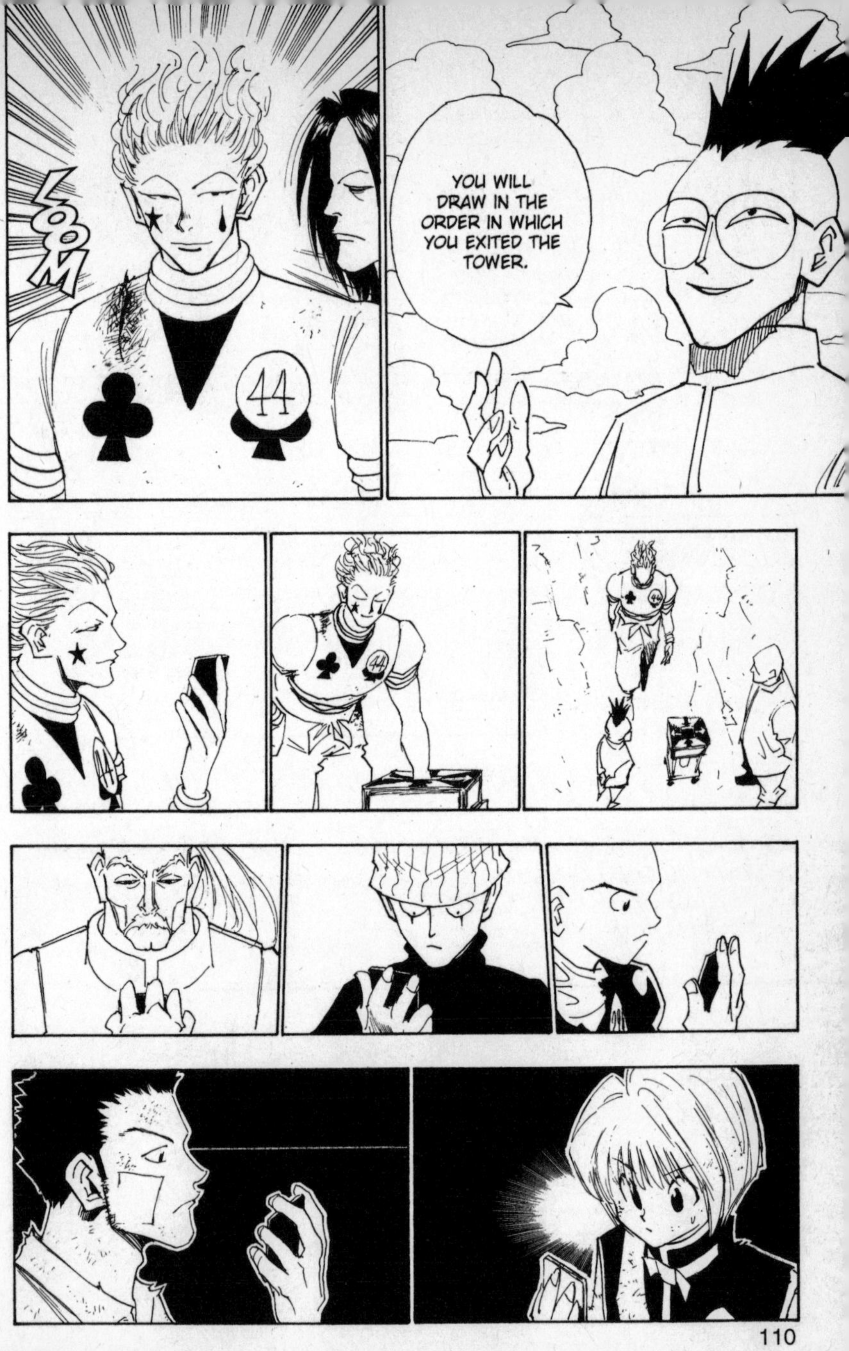
YOU WILL DRAW IN THE ORDER IN WHICH YOU EXITED THE TOWER.
LOOM

READ THIS WAY

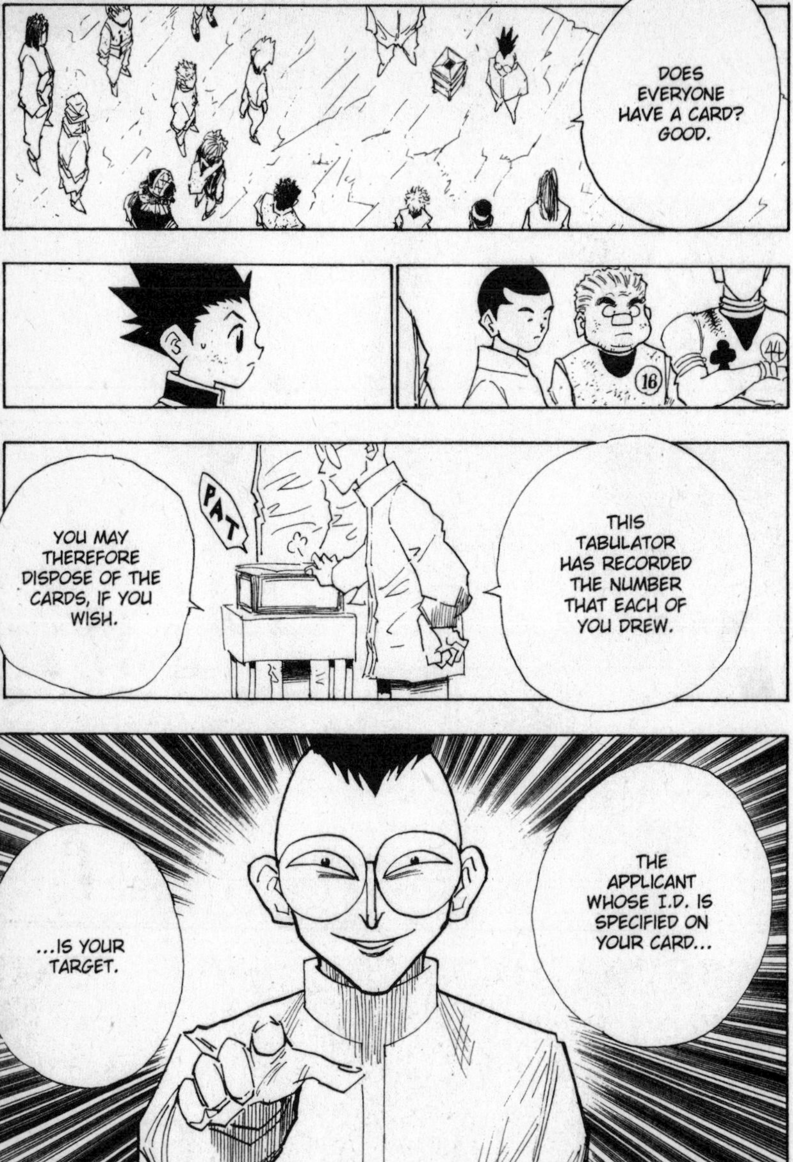
DOES EVERYONE HAVE A CARD? GOOD.
16
44
THIS TABULATOR HAS RECORDED THE NUMBER THAT EACH OF YOU DREW.
PAT
YOU MAY THEREFORE DISPOSE OF THE CARDS, IF YOU WISH.
THE APPLICANT WHOSE I.D. IS SPECIFIED ON YOUR CARD...
...IS YOUR TARGET.

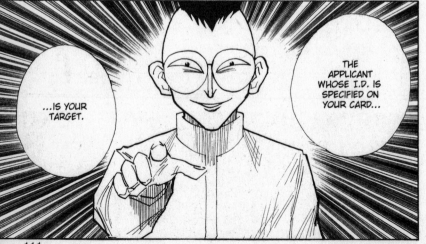

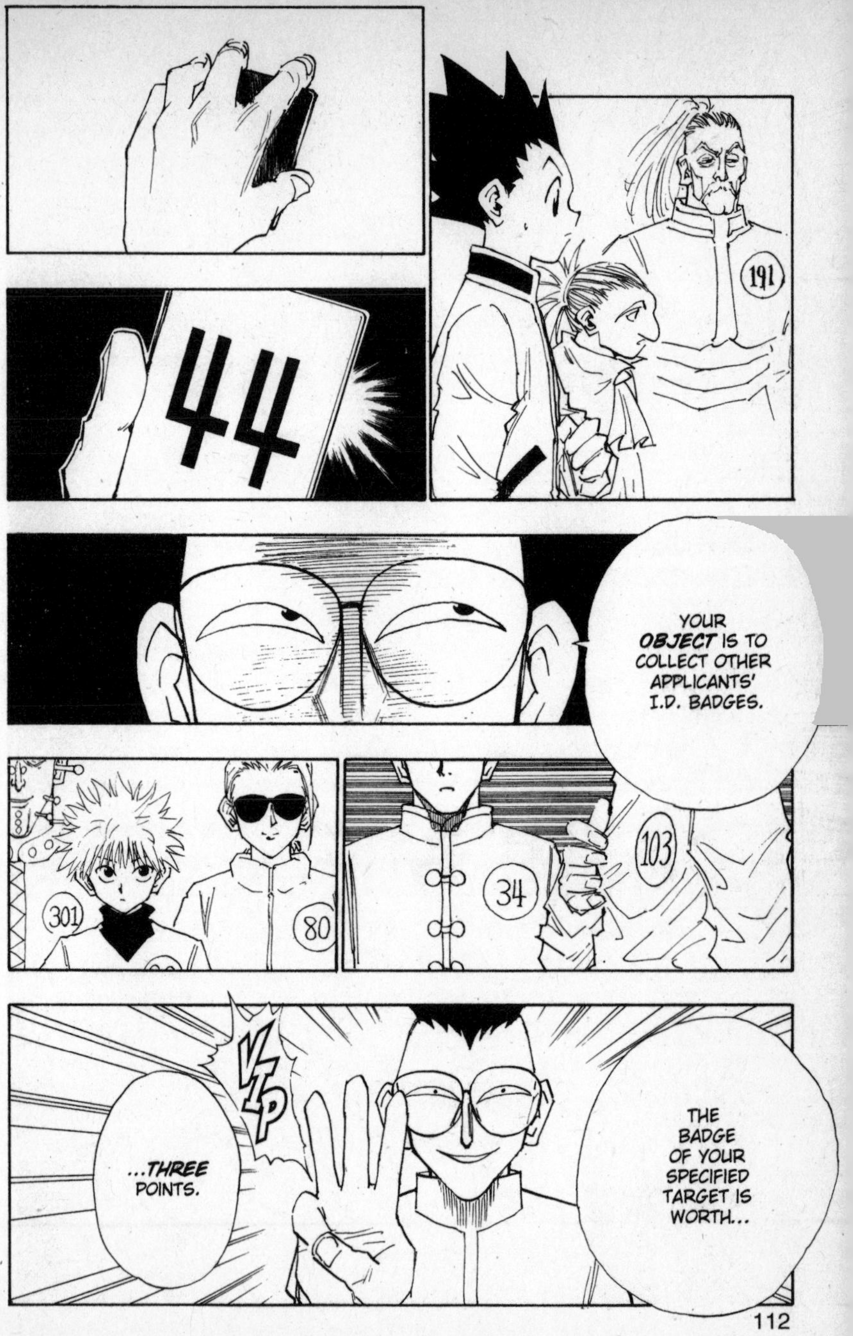
191
44
YOUR *OBJECT* IS TO COLLECT OTHER APPLICANTS' I.D. BADGES.
103
34
80
301
THE BADGE OF YOUR SPECIFIED TARGET IS WORTH...
VIP
...*THREE* POINTS.

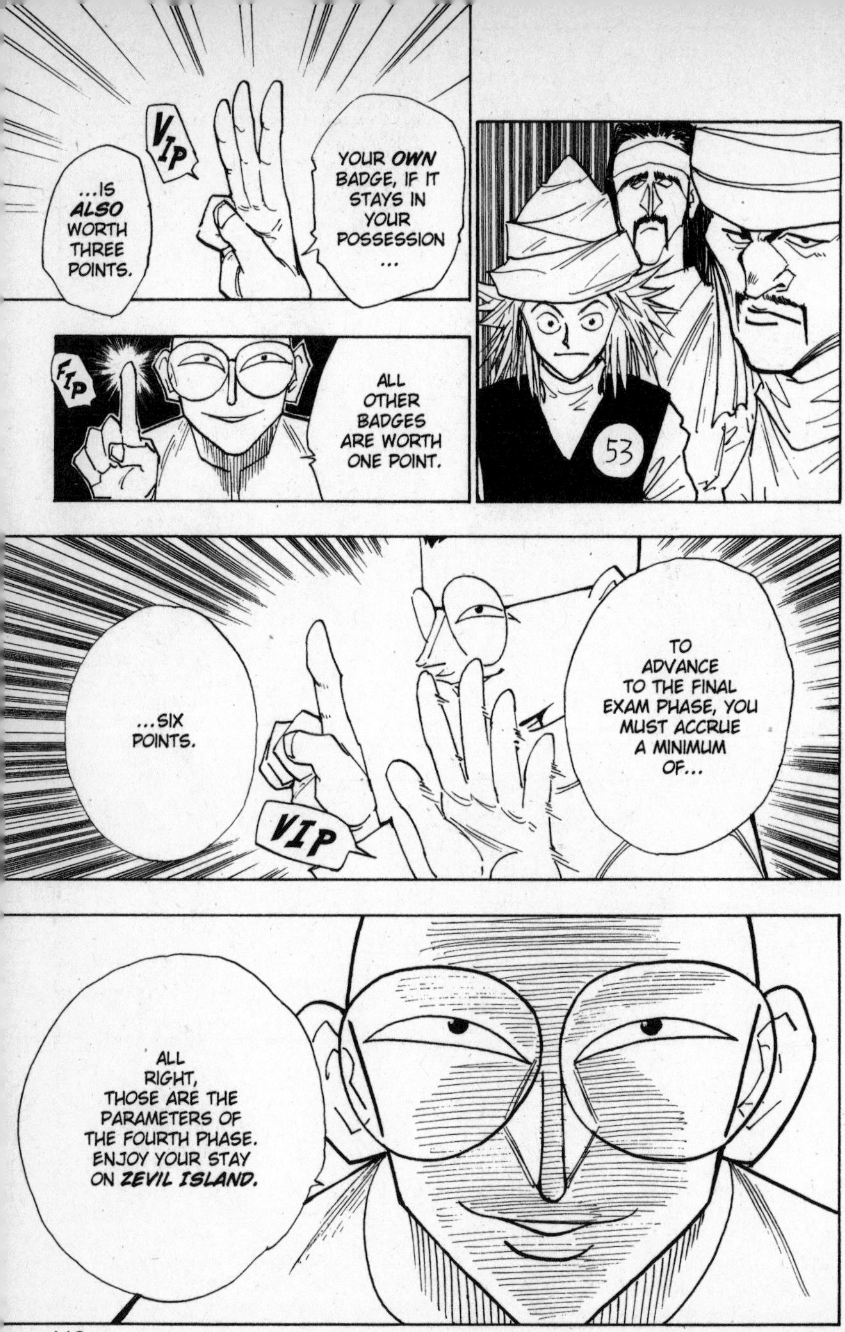
YOUR *OWN* BADGE, IF IT STAYS IN YOUR POSSESSION ...
VIP
...IS *ALSO* WORTH THREE POINTS.
FIP
ALL OTHER BADGES ARE WORTH ONE POINT.
53
TO ADVANCE TO THE FINAL EXAM PHASE, YOU MUST ACCRUE A MINIMUM OF...
VIP
...SIX POINTS.
ALL RIGHT, THOSE ARE THE PARAMETERS OF THE FOURTH PHASE. ENJOY YOUR STAY ON *ZEVIL ISLAND*.

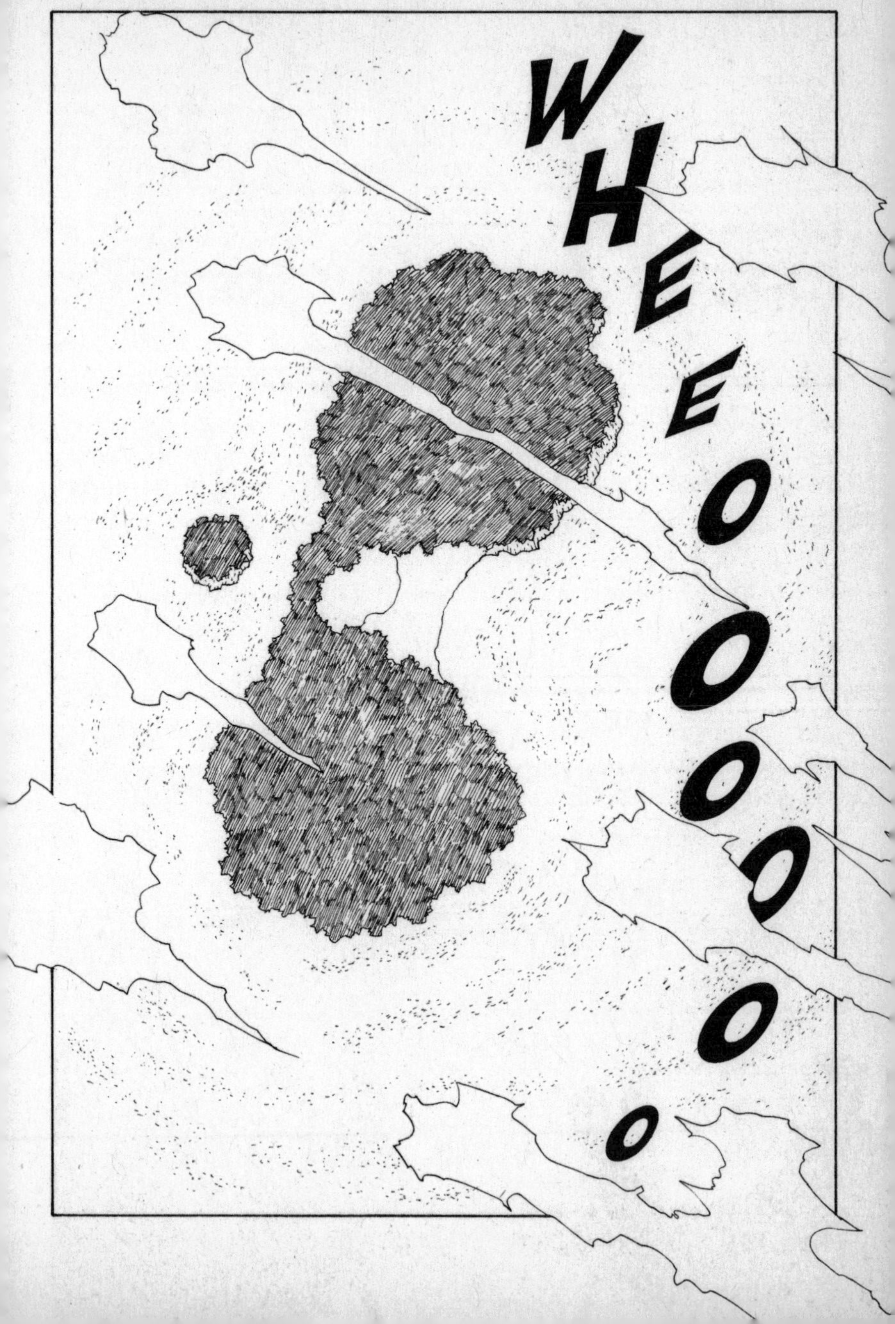
WHEEOOOOOo

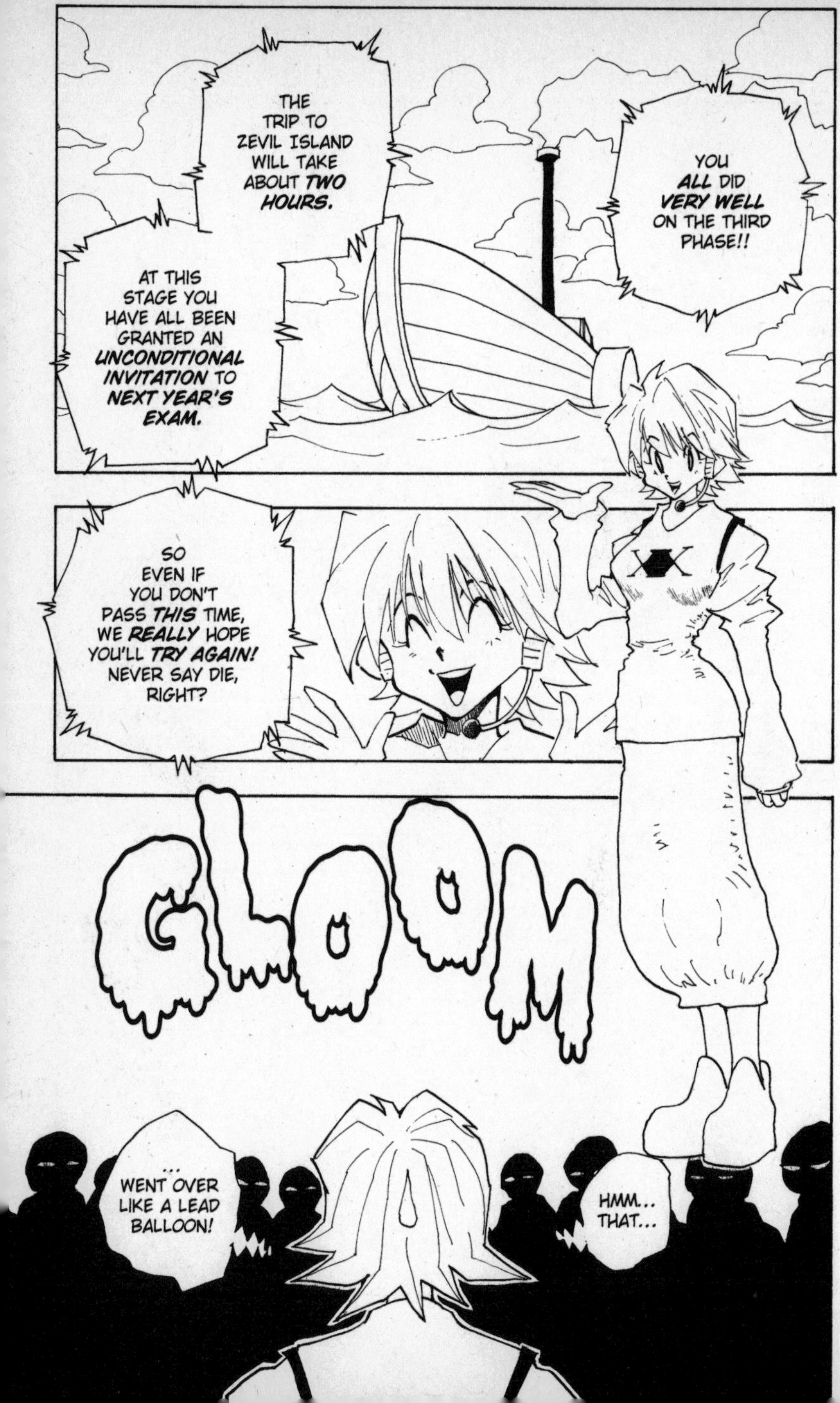
YOU ALL DID VERY WELL ON THE THIRD PHASE!!
THE TRIP TO ZEVIL ISLAND WILL TAKE ABOUT TWO HOURS.
AT THIS STAGE YOU HAVE ALL BEEN GRANTED AN UNCONDITIONAL INVITATION TO NEXT YEAR'S EXAM.
SO EVEN IF YOU DON'T PASS THIS TIME, WE REALLY HOPE YOU'LL TRY AGAIN! NEVER SAY DIE, RIGHT?
GLOOM
HMM... THAT...
...WENT OVER LIKE A LEAD BALLOON!

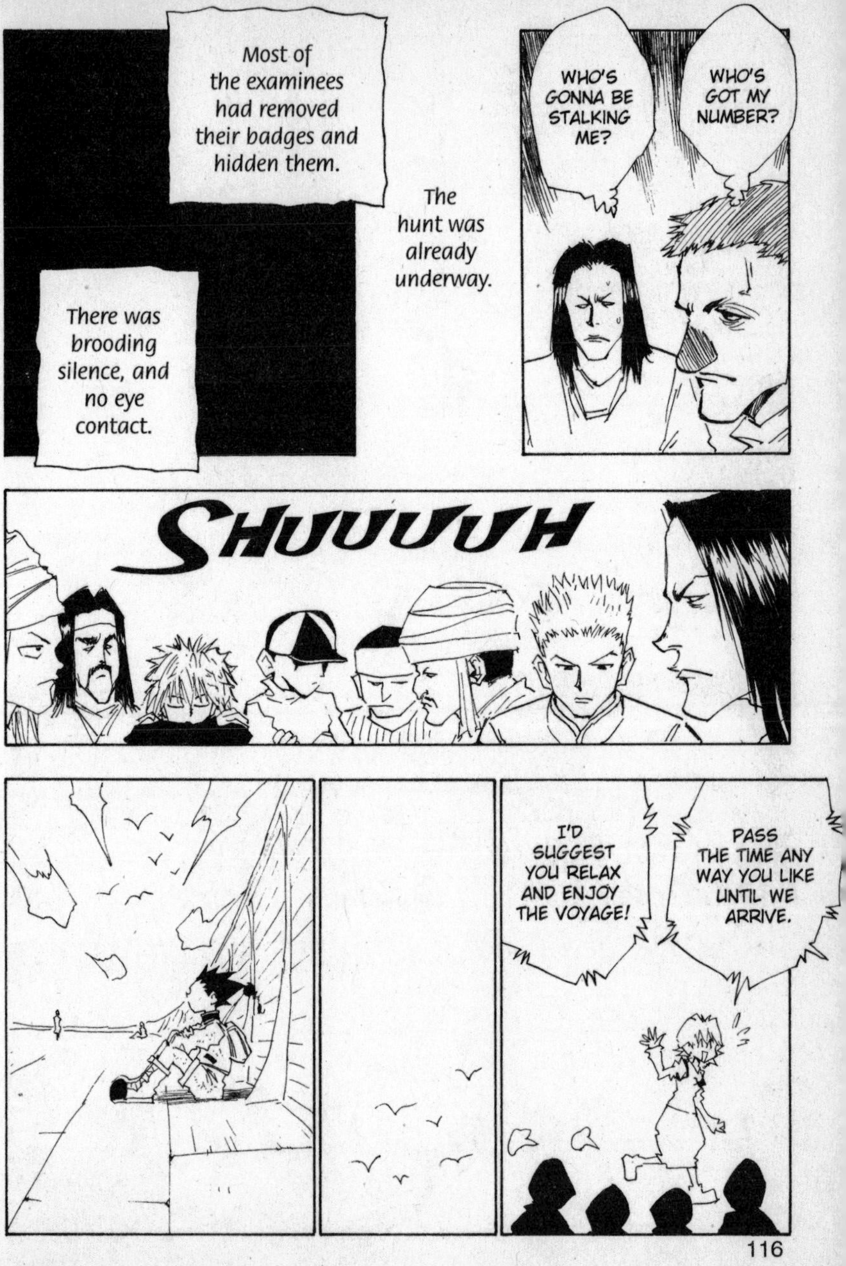
WHO'S GOT MY NUMBER?
WHO'S GONNA BE STALKING ME?
Most of the examinees had removed their badges and hidden them.
There was brooding silence, and no eye contact.
The hunt was already underway.
SHUUUUH
PASS THE TIME ANY WAY YOU LIKE UNTIL WE ARRIVE.
I'D SUGGEST YOU RELAX AND ENJOY THE VOYAGE!

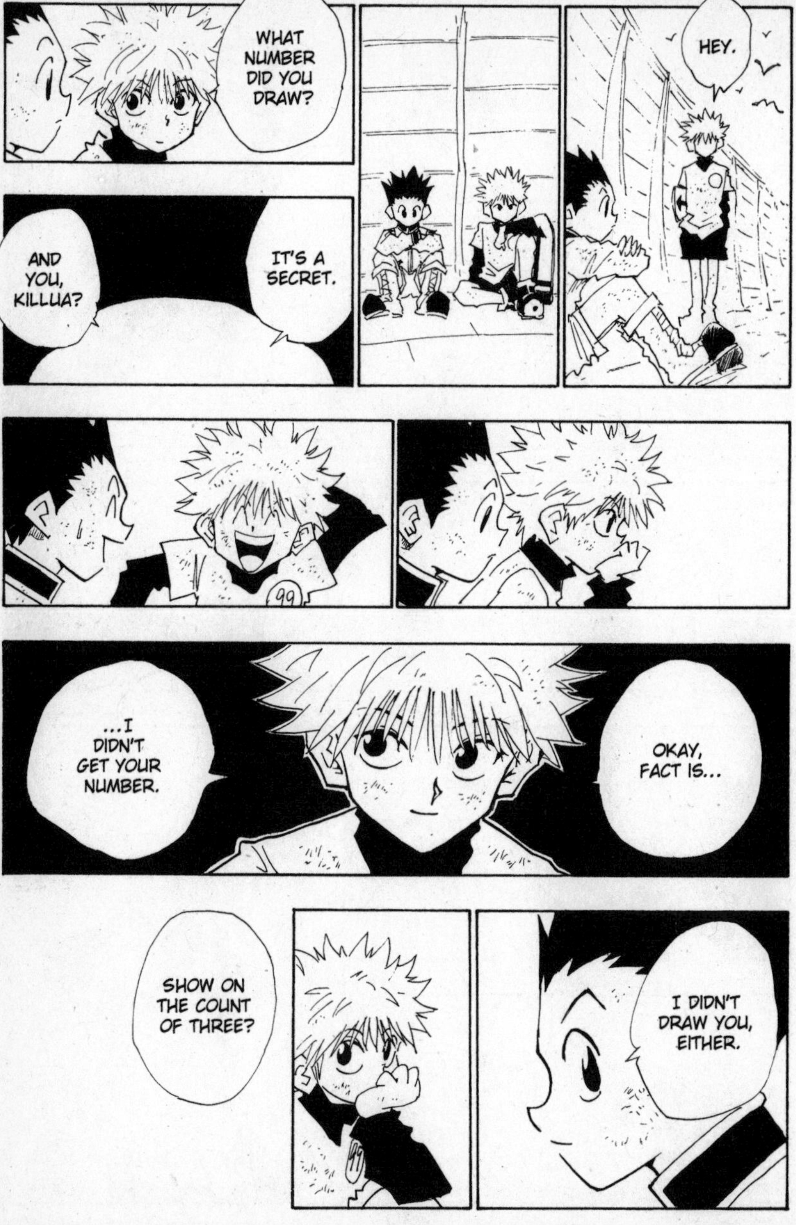
HEY.
WHAT NUMBER DID YOU DRAW?
IT'S A SECRET.
AND YOU, KILLUA?
OKAY, FACT IS...
...I DIDN'T GET YOUR NUMBER.
I DIDN'T DRAW YOU, EITHER.
SHOW ON THE COUNT OF THREE?

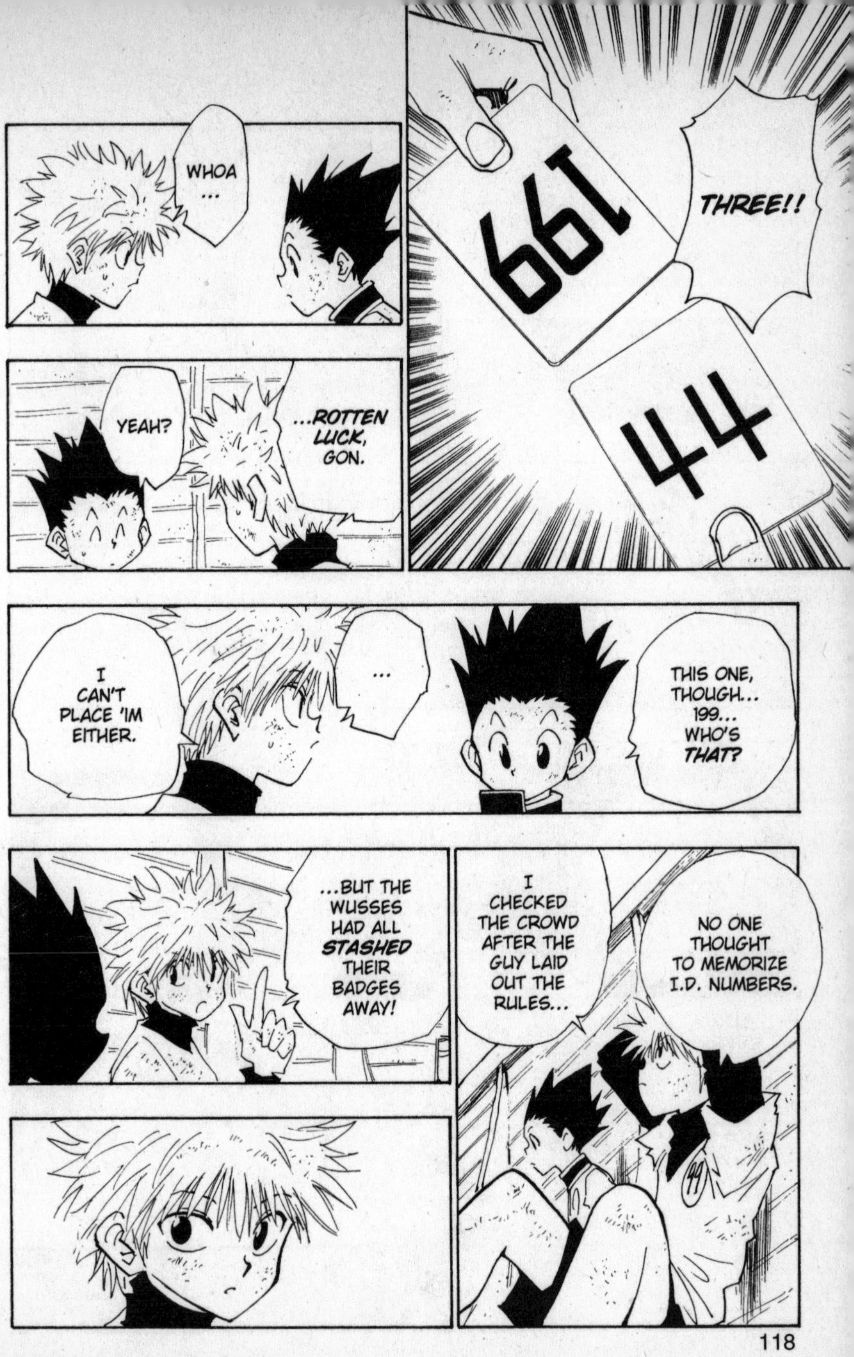
THREE!!
199
44
WHOA ...
...ROTTEN LUCK, GON.
YEAH?
THIS ONE, THOUGH... 199... WHO'S THAT?
...
I CAN'T PLACE 'IM EITHER.
NO ONE THOUGHT TO MEMORIZE I.D. NUMBERS.
I CHECKED THE CROWD AFTER THE GUY LAID OUT THE RULES...
...BUT THE WUSSES HAD ALL STASHED THEIR BADGES AWAY!
99

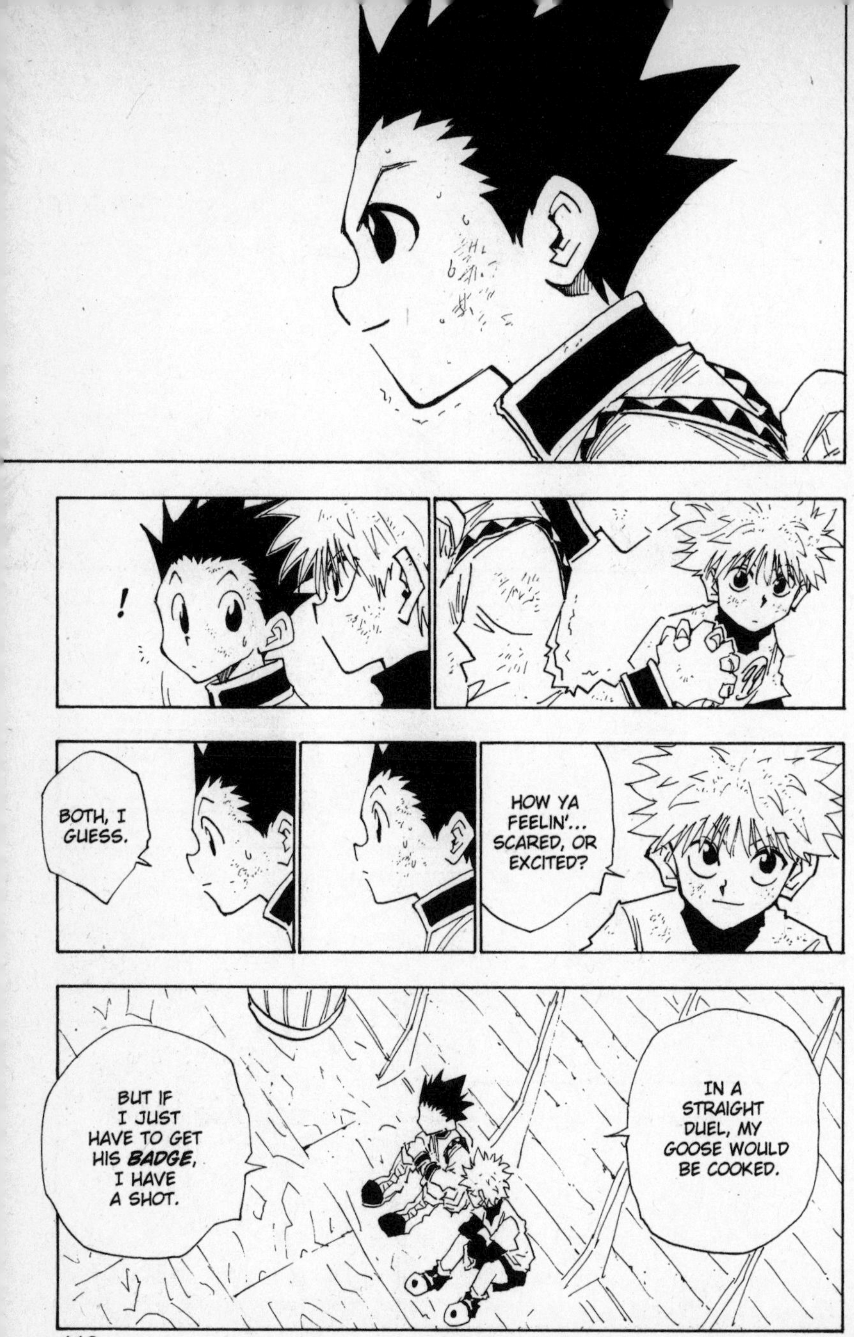
!
HOW YA FEELIN'... SCARED, OR EXCITED?
BOTH, I GUESS.
IN A STRAIGHT DUEL, MY GOOSE WOULD BE COOKED.
BUT IF I JUST HAVE TO GET HIS *BADGE*, I HAVE A SHOT.

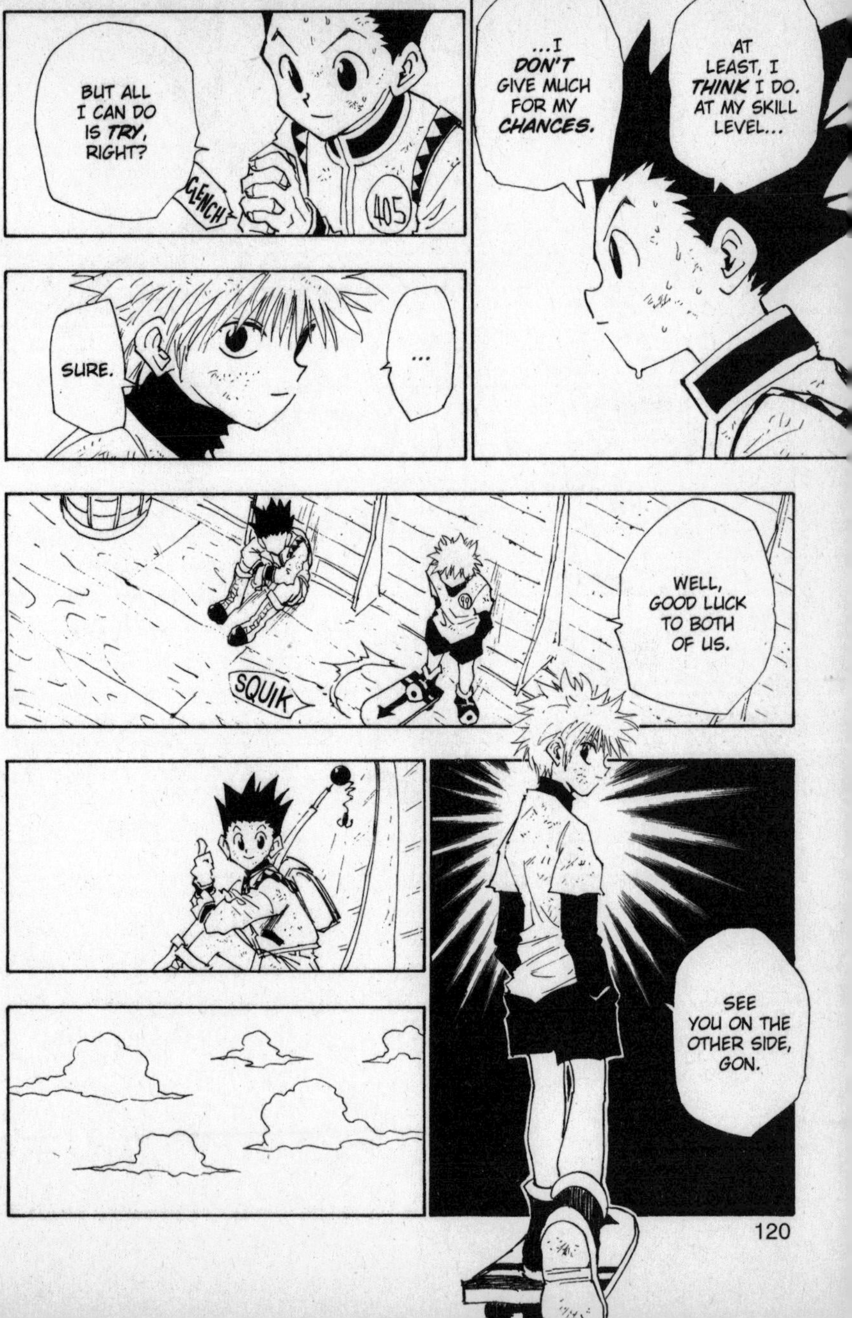
AT LEAST, I *THINK* I DO. AT MY SKILL LEVEL...
...I *DON'T* GIVE MUCH FOR MY *CHANCES.*
BUT ALL I CAN DO IS *TRY*, RIGHT?
CLENCH
...
SURE.
WELL, GOOD LUCK TO BOTH OF US.
SQUIK
SEE YOU ON THE OTHER SIDE, GON.

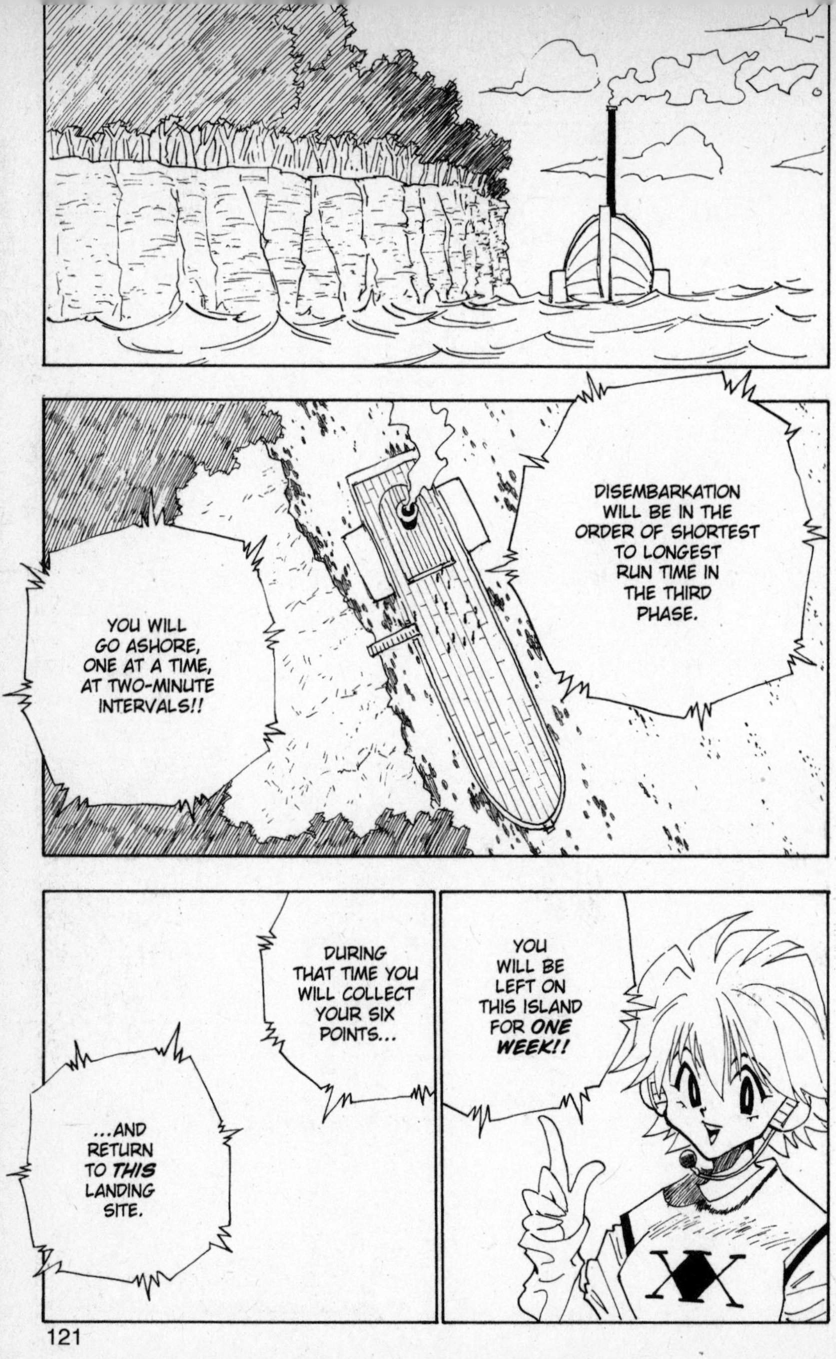
DISEMBARKATION WILL BE IN THE ORDER OF SHORTEST TO LONGEST RUN TIME IN THE THIRD PHASE.
YOU WILL GO ASHORE, ONE AT A TIME, AT TWO-MINUTE INTERVALS!!
YOU WILL BE LEFT ON THIS ISLAND FOR ***ONE WEEK!!***
DURING THAT TIME YOU WILL COLLECT YOUR SIX POINTS...
...AND RETURN TO ***THIS*** LANDING SITE.

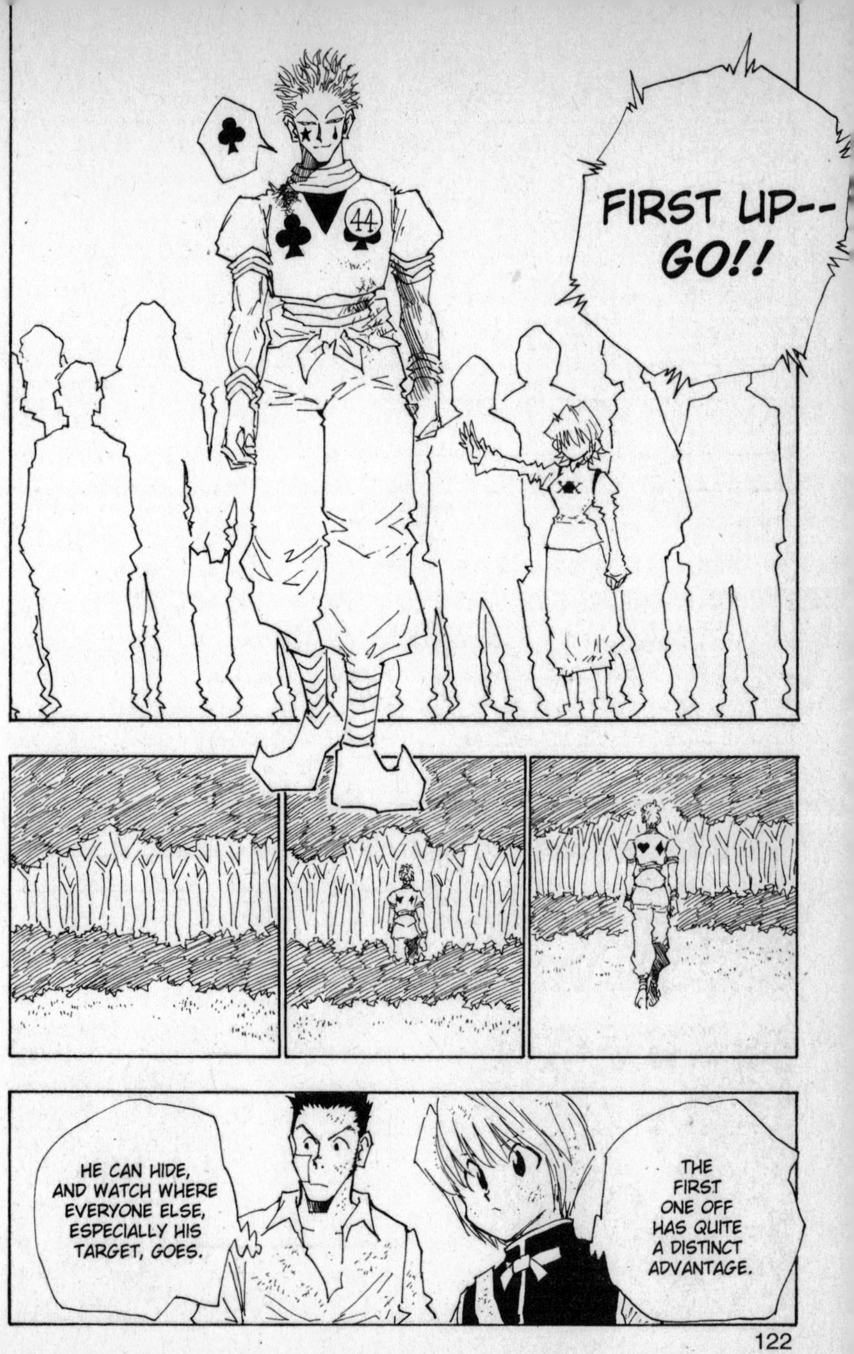
FIRST UP--GO!!
THE FIRST ONE OFF HAS QUITE A DISTINCT ADVANTAGE.
HE CAN HIDE, AND WATCH WHERE EVERYONE ELSE, ESPECIALLY HIS TARGET, GOES.

READ THIS WAY

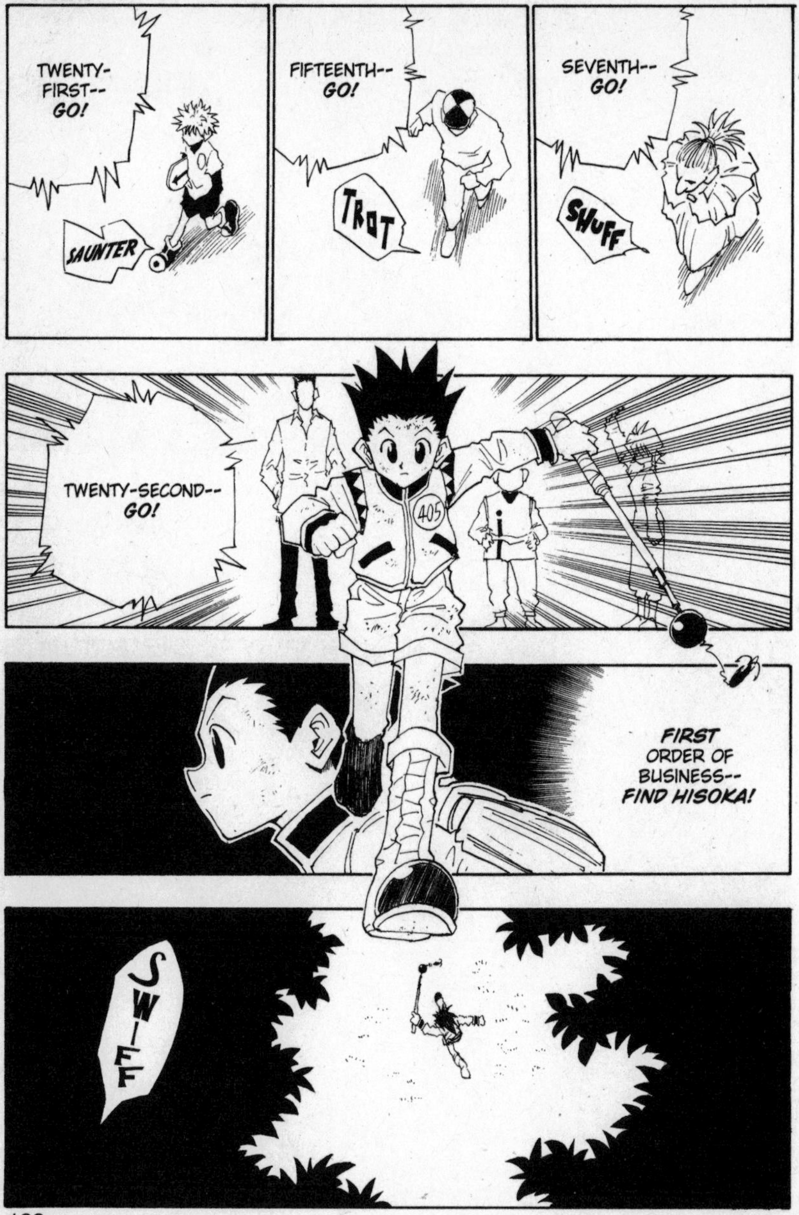
SEVENTH-- GO!
SHUFF
FIFTEENTH-- GO!
TROT
TWENTY-FIRST-- GO!
SAUNTER
405
TWENTY-SECOND-- GO!
FIRST ORDER OF BUSINESS-- FIND HISOKA!
SWIFF

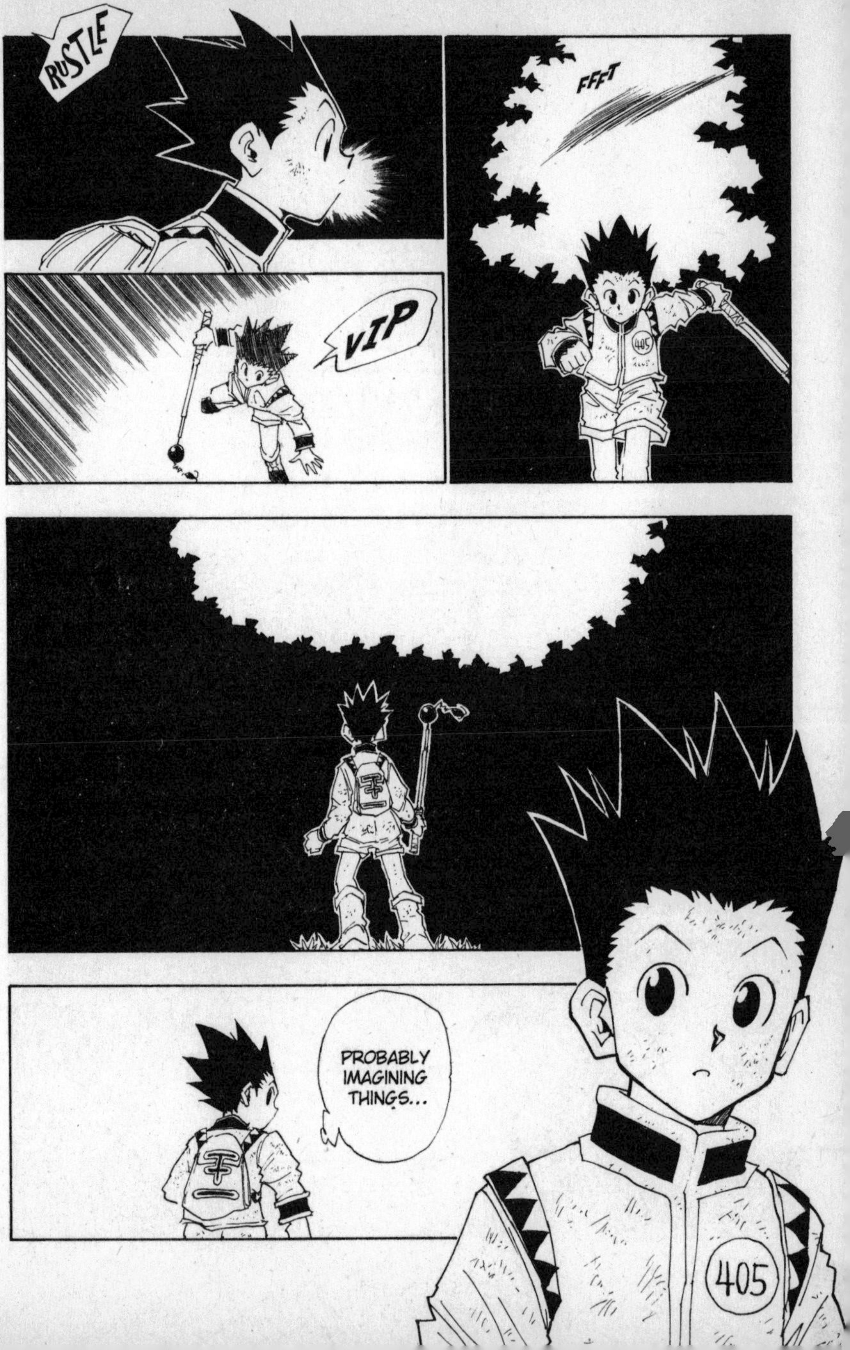
FFFT
RUSTLE
VIP
PROBABLY IMAGINING THINGS...

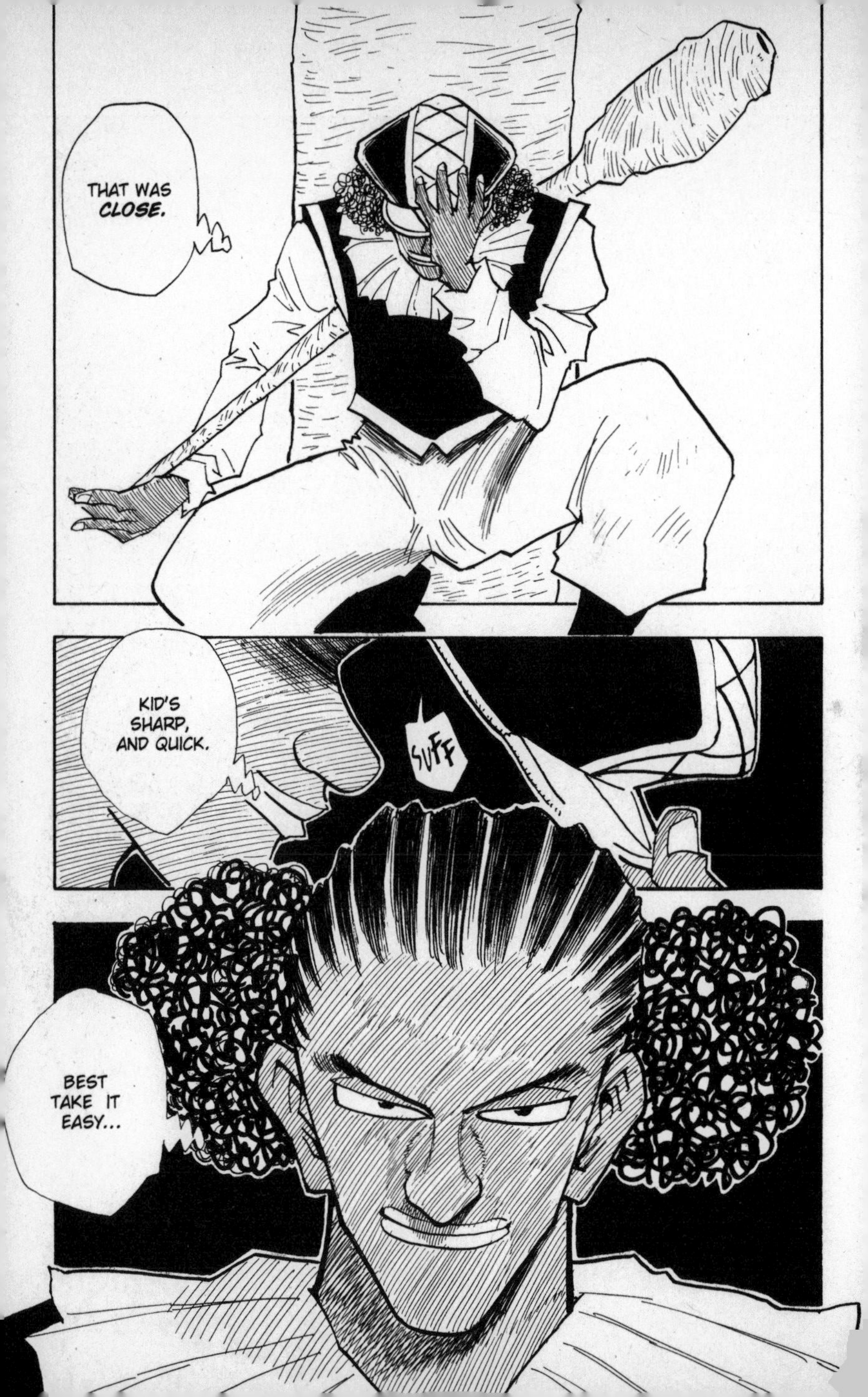
THAT WAS CLOSE.
KID'S SHARP, AND QUICK.
SUFF
BEST TAKE IT EASY...

Sommy

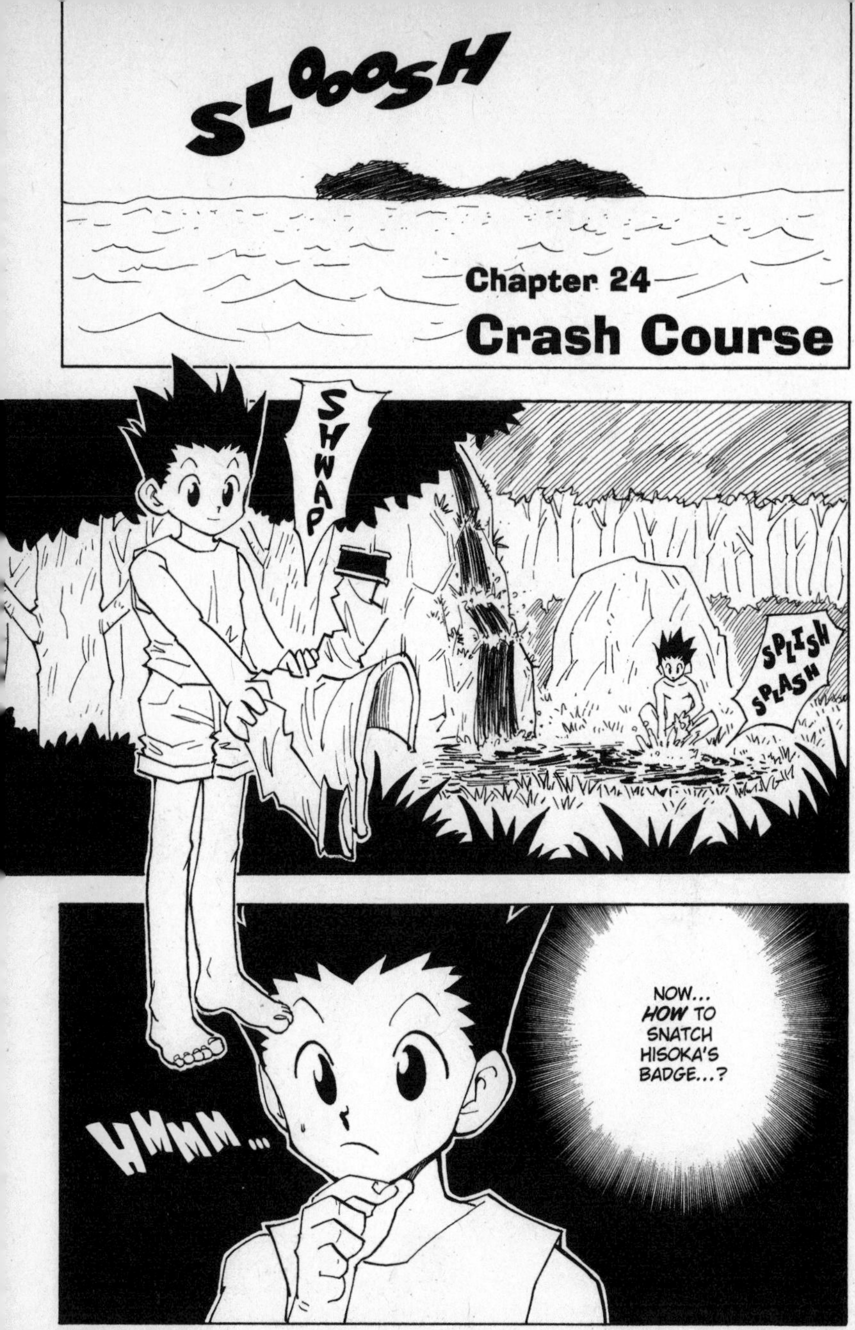
SLOOOSH
Chapter 24
Crash Course
SPLISH SPLASH
SHWAP
NOW... *HOW* TO SNATCH HISOKA'S BADGE...?
HMMM...

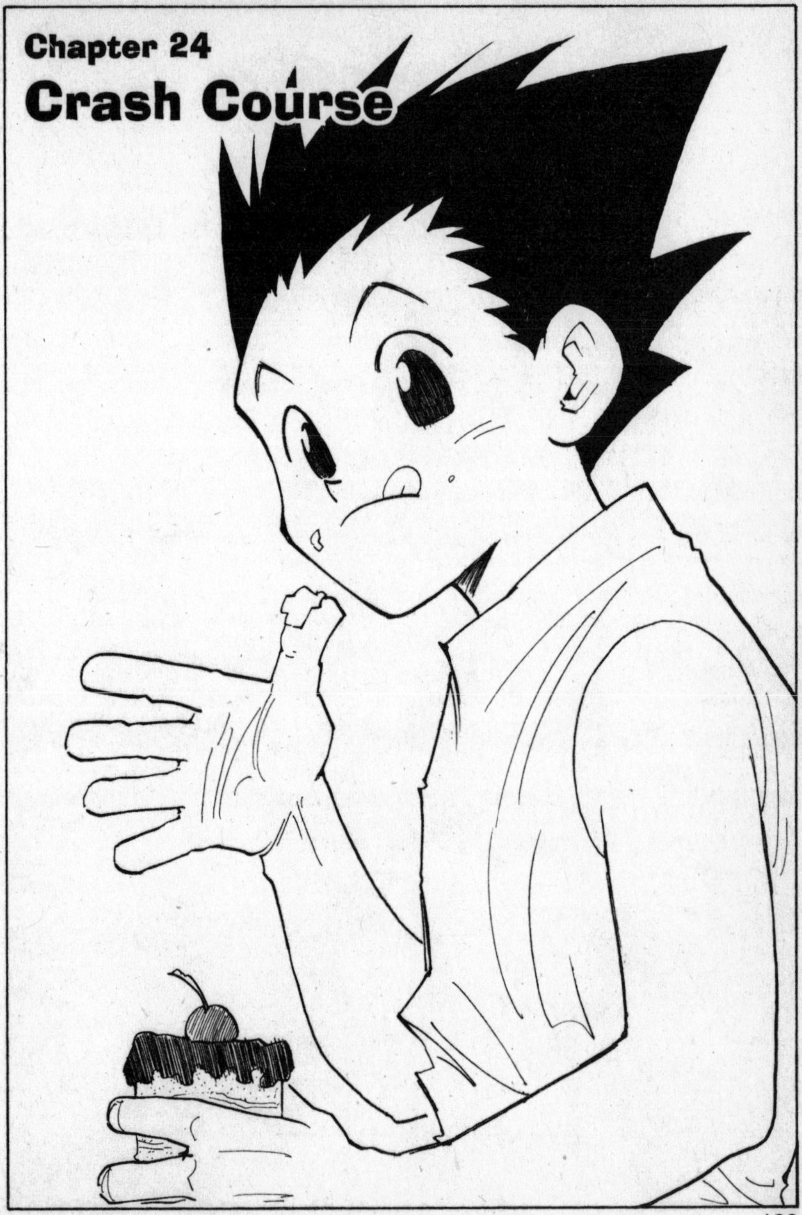
Chapter 24
Crash Course

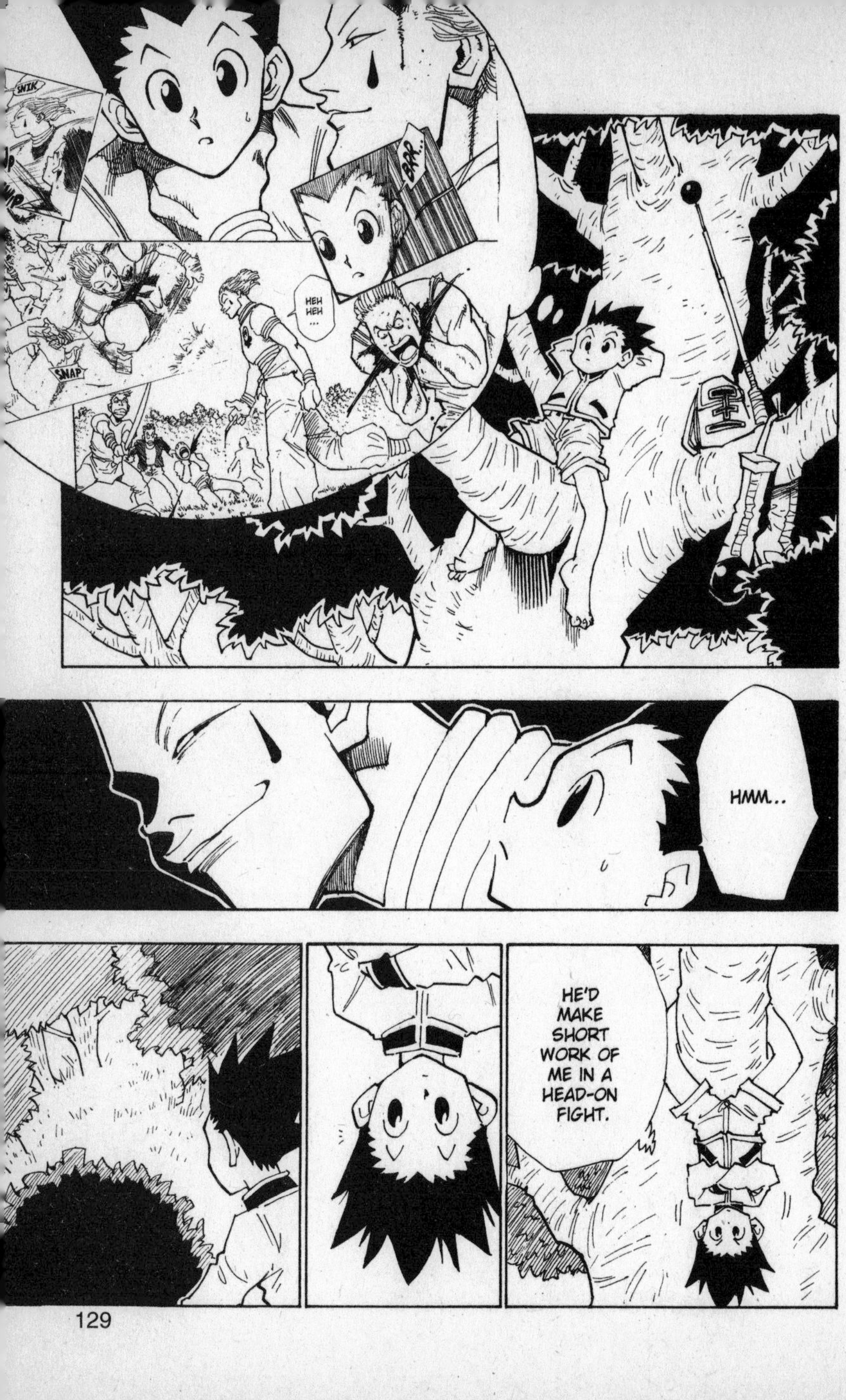
BRR...
HEH HEH ...
SNIK
SNAP
HMM...
HE'D MAKE SHORT WORK OF ME IN A HEAD-ON FIGHT.

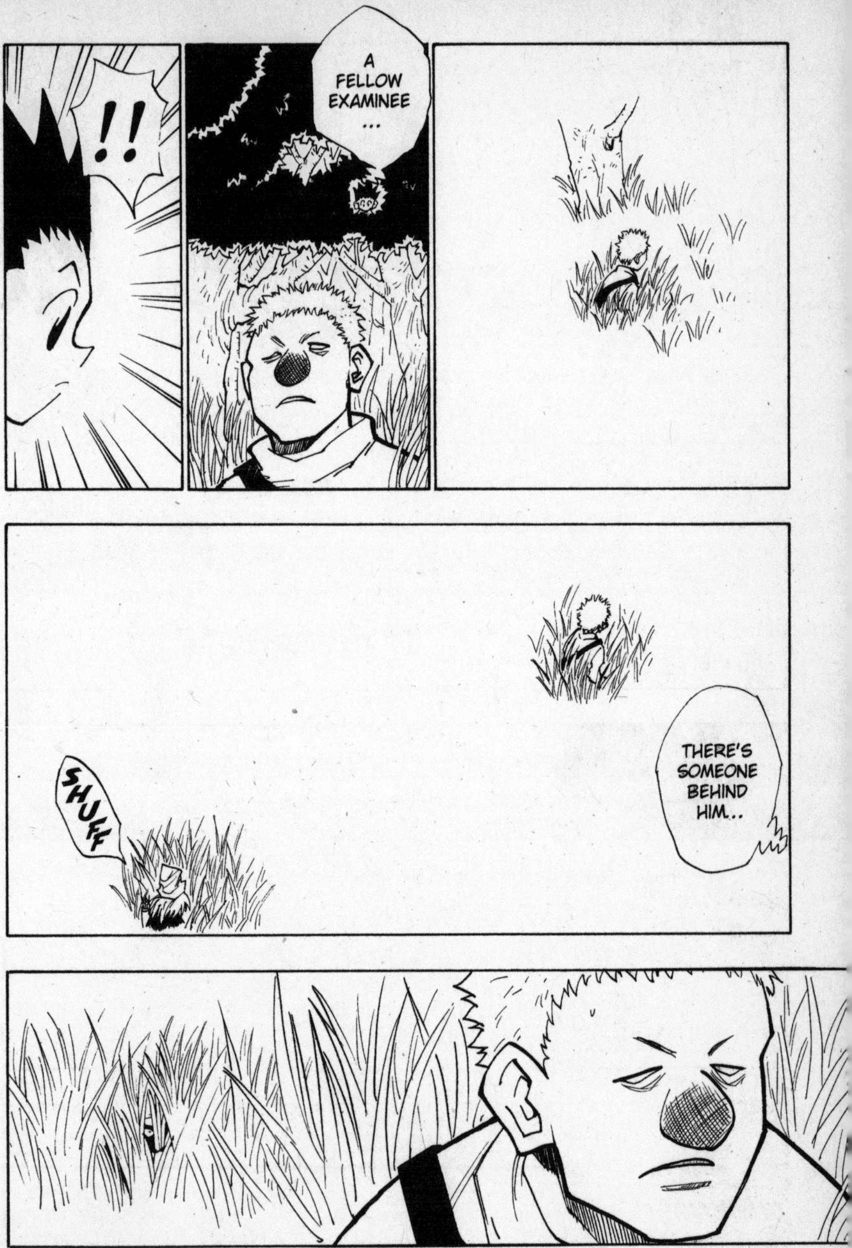

A FELLOW EXAMINEE ...
!!
THERE'S SOMEONE BEHIND HIM...
SHUFF

READ THIS WAY

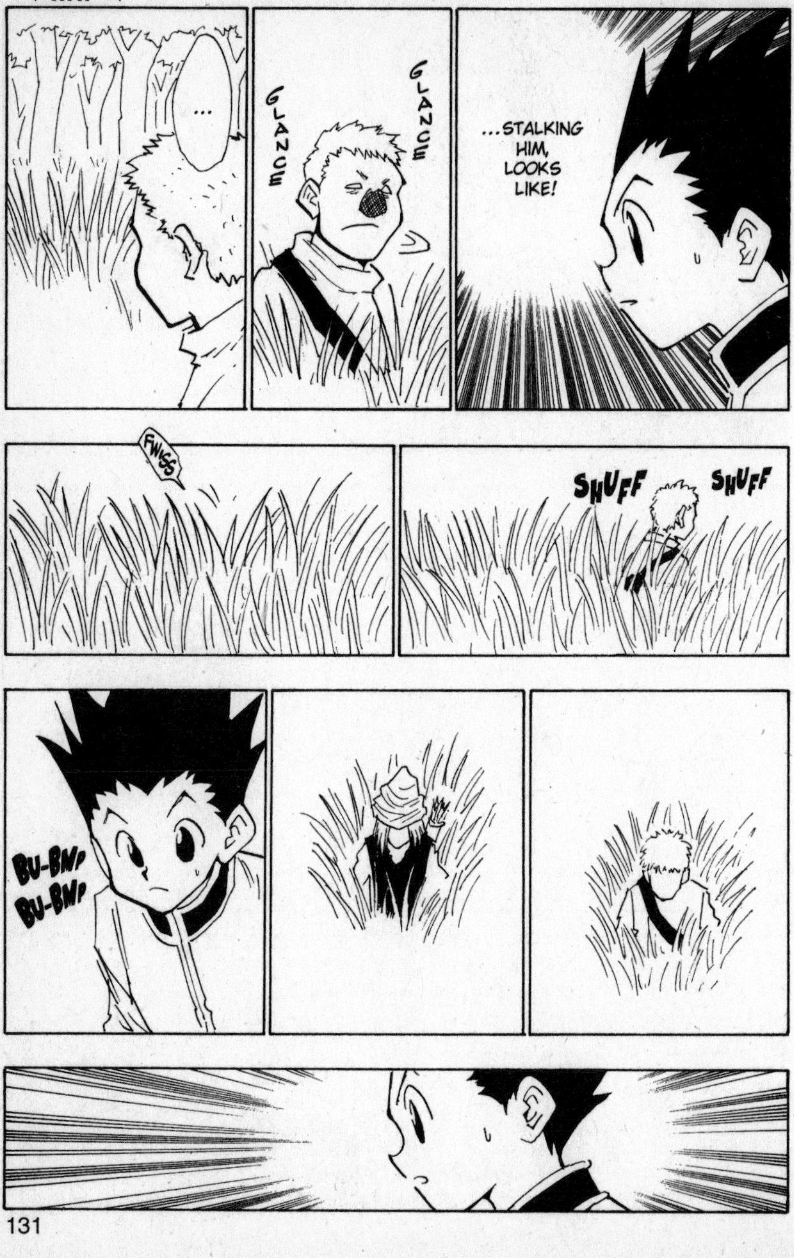
...STALKING HIM, LOOKS LIKE!
GLANCE
GLANCE
...
SHUFF
SHUFF
FWISS
BU-BMP
BU-BMP

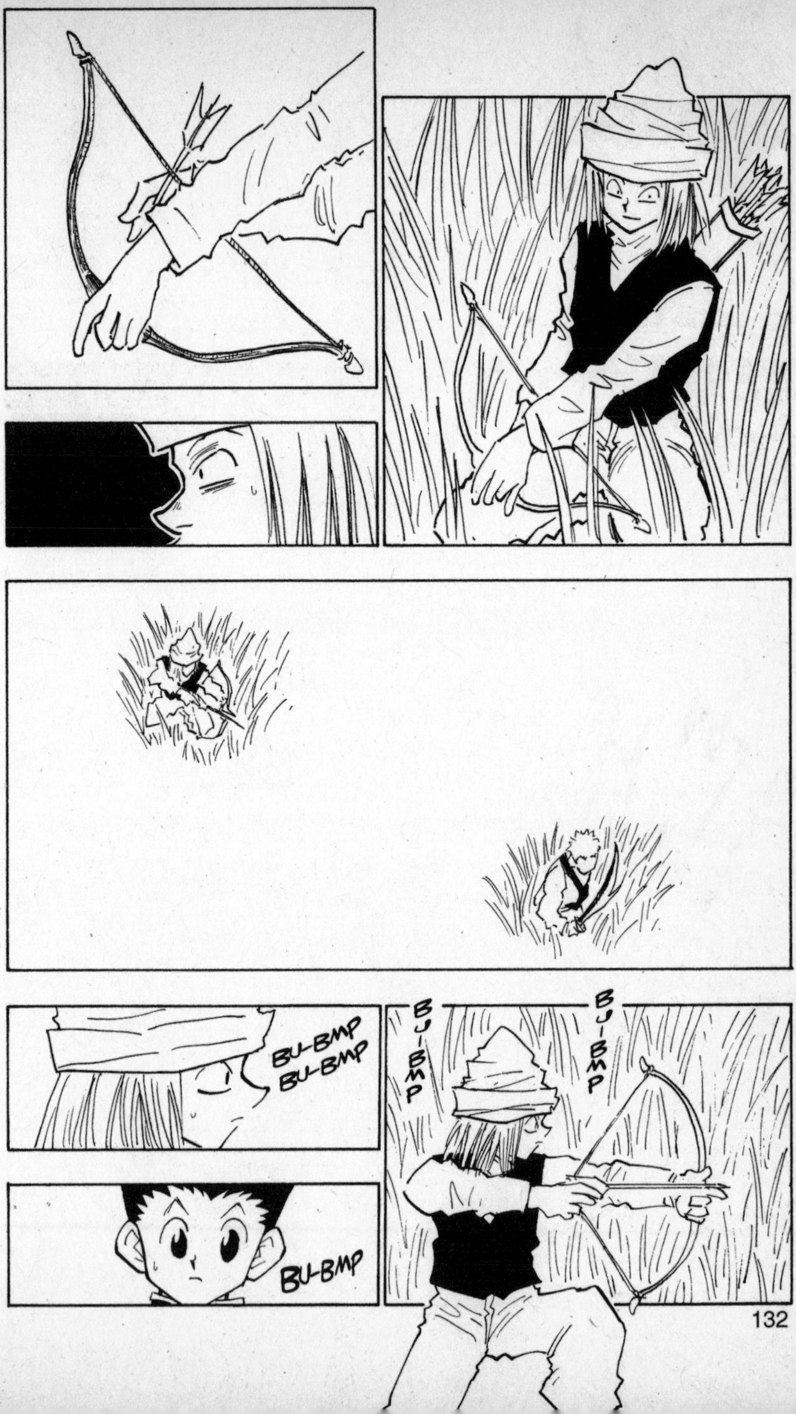
BU-BMP
BU-BMP
BU-BMP
BU-BMP
BU-BMP

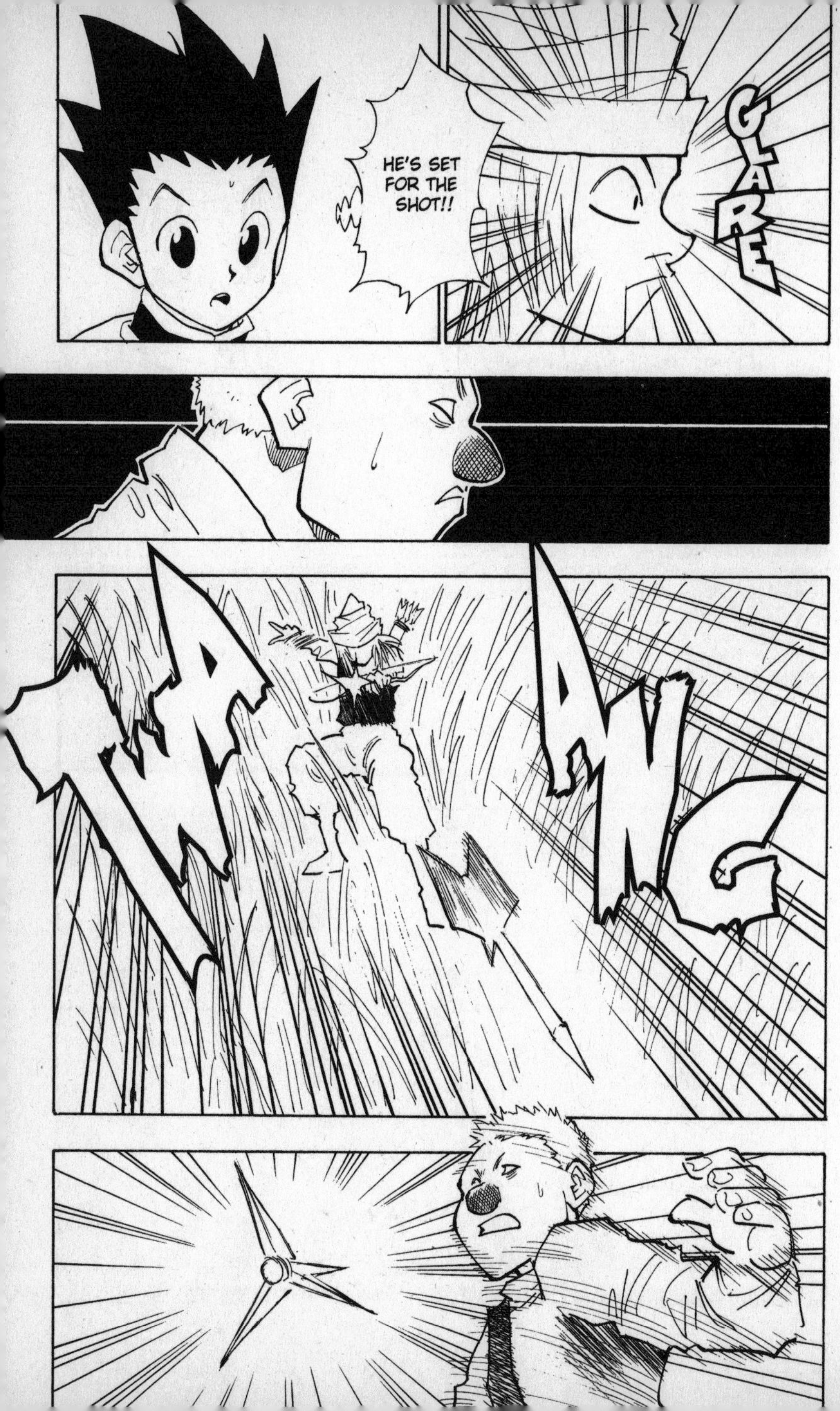
GLARE
HE'S SET FOR THE SHOT!!
TWANG

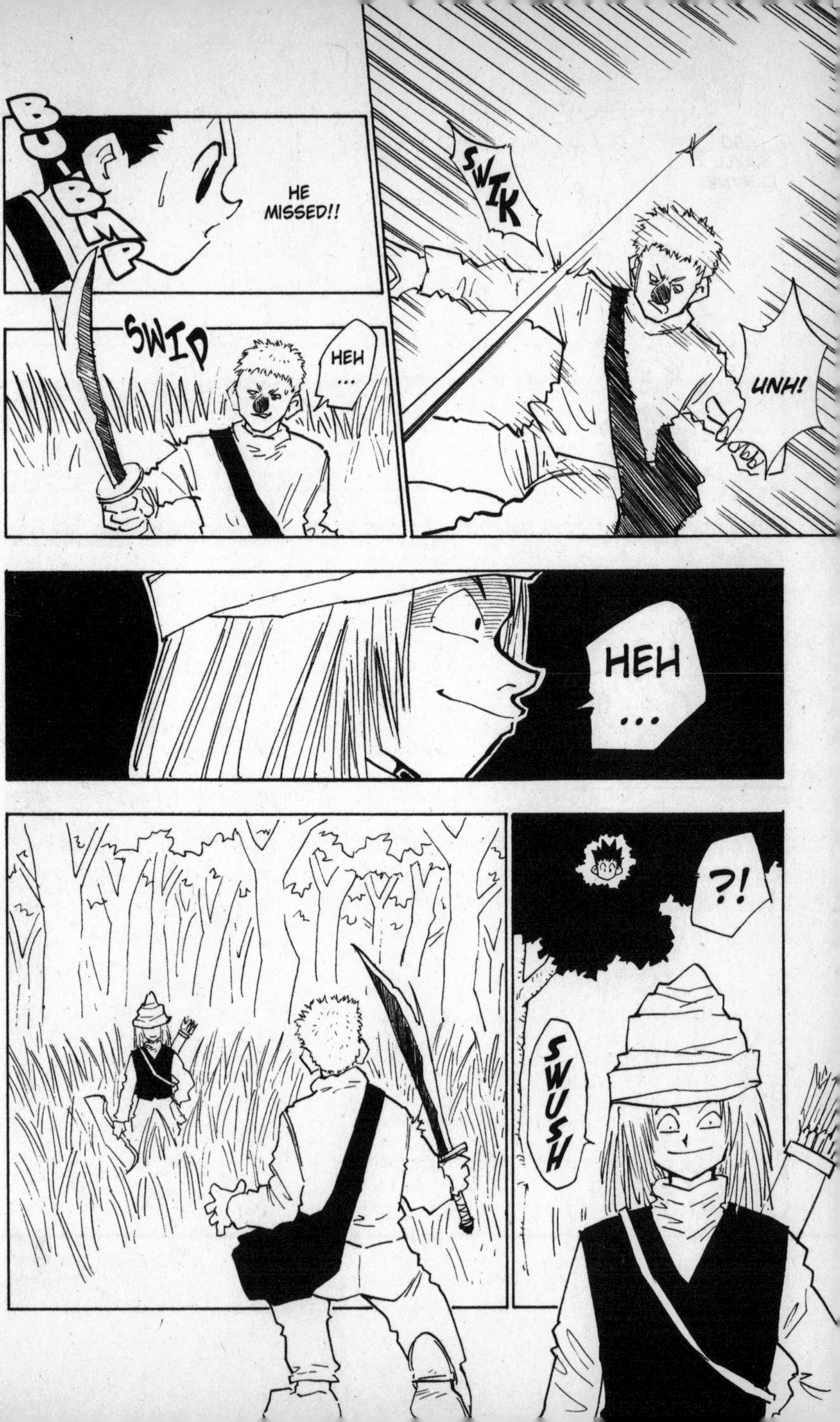
SWIK
UNH!
BU-BMP
HE MISSED!!
SWID
HEH ...
HEH ...
?!
SWUSH

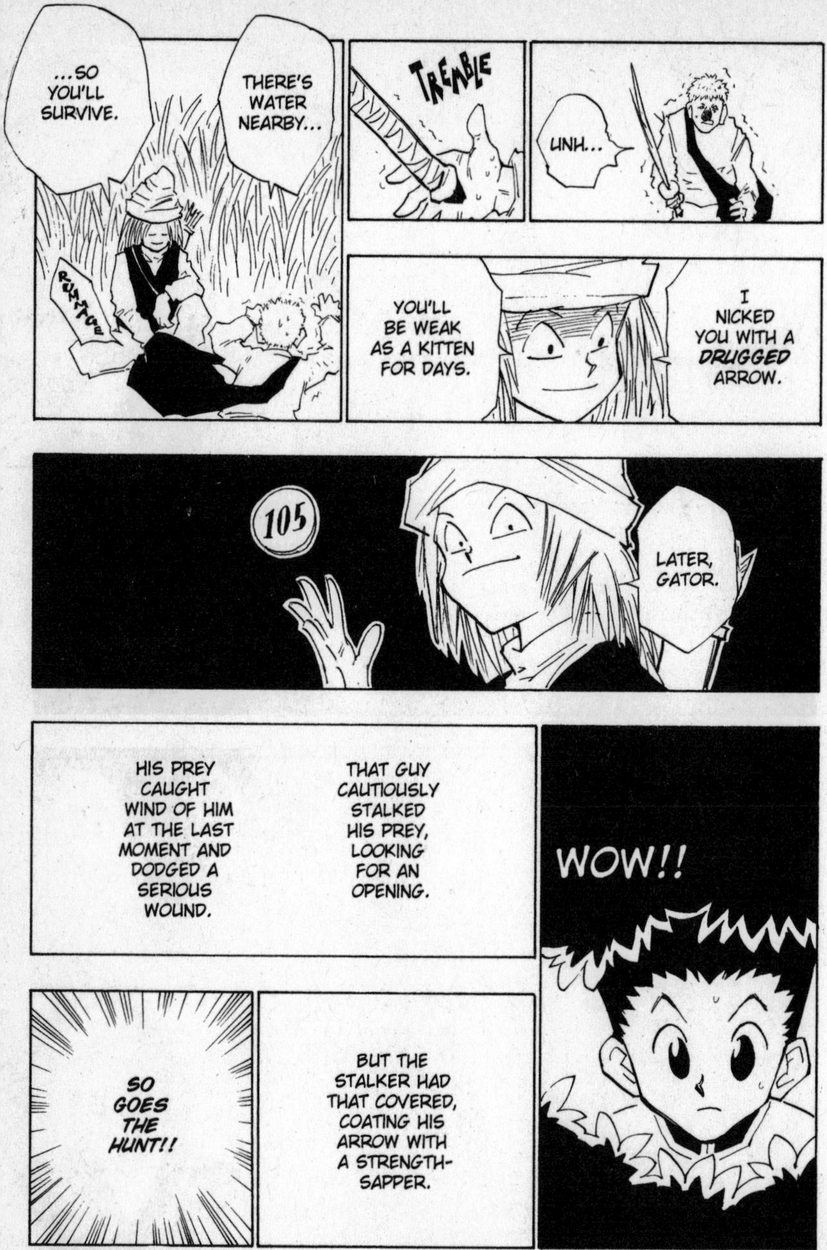
UNH...
TREMBLE
I NICKED YOU WITH A *DRUGGED* ARROW.
YOU'LL BE WEAK AS A KITTEN FOR DAYS.
THERE'S WATER NEARBY...
...SO YOU'LL SURVIVE.
RUMMAGE
105
LATER, GATOR.
WOW!!
THAT GUY CAUTIOUSLY STALKED HIS PREY, LOOKING FOR AN OPENING.
HIS PREY CAUGHT WIND OF HIM AT THE LAST MOMENT AND DODGED A SERIOUS WOUND.
BUT THE STALKER HAD THAT COVERED, COATING HIS ARROW WITH A STRENGTH-SAPPER.
SO GOES THE HUNT!!

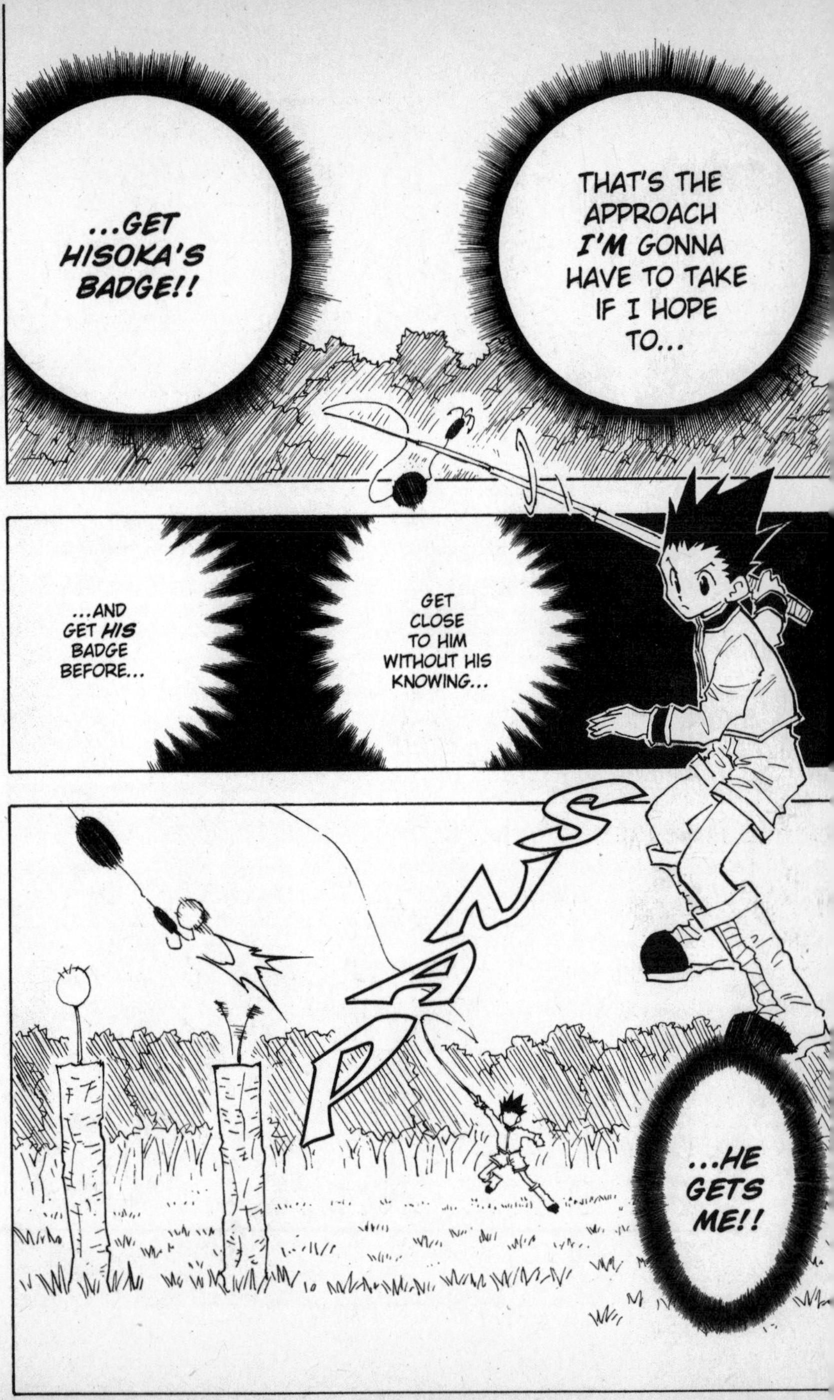
THAT'S THE APPROACH *I'M* GONNA HAVE TO TAKE IF I HOPE TO...
...GET HISOKA'S BADGE!!
GET CLOSE TO HIM WITHOUT HIS KNOWING...
...AND GET *HIS* BADGE BEFORE...
PANS
...HE GETS ME!!

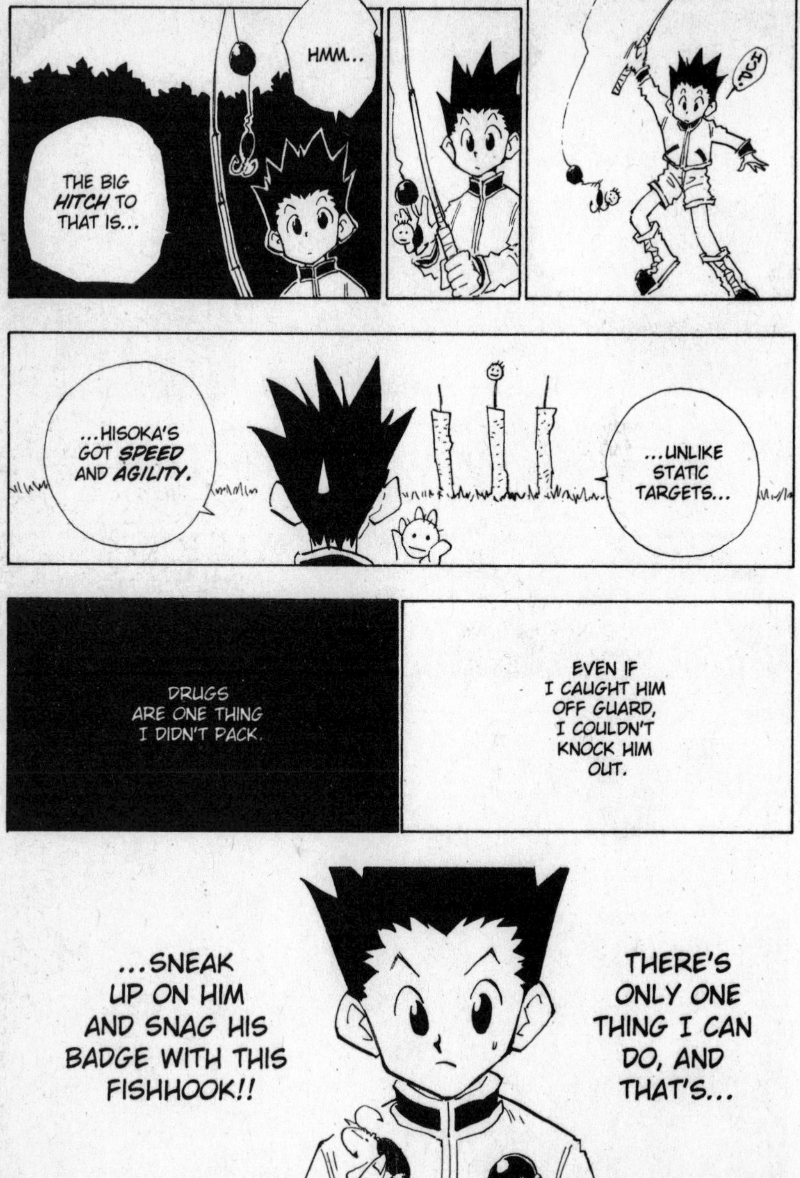
HUP.
HMM...
THE BIG *HITCH* TO THAT IS...
...UNLIKE STATIC TARGETS...
...HISOKA'S GOT *SPEED* AND *AGILITY*.
EVEN IF I CAUGHT HIM OFF GUARD, I COULDN'T KNOCK HIM OUT.
DRUGS ARE ONE THING I DIDN'T PACK.
THERE'S ONLY ONE THING I CAN DO, AND THAT'S...
...SNEAK UP ON HIM AND SNAG HIS BADGE WITH THIS FISHHOOK!!

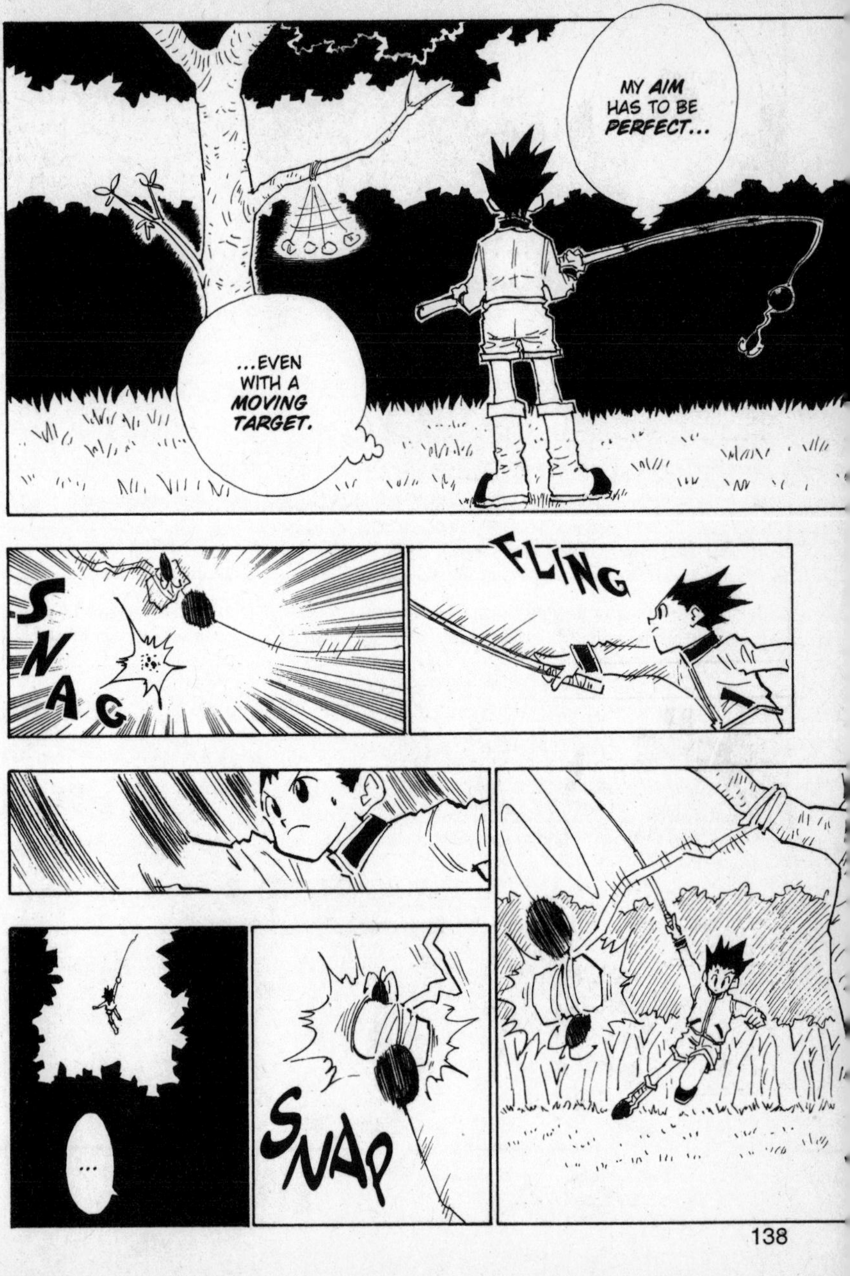
MY AIM HAS TO BE PERFECT...
...EVEN WITH A MOVING TARGET.
FLING
SNAG
SNAP
...

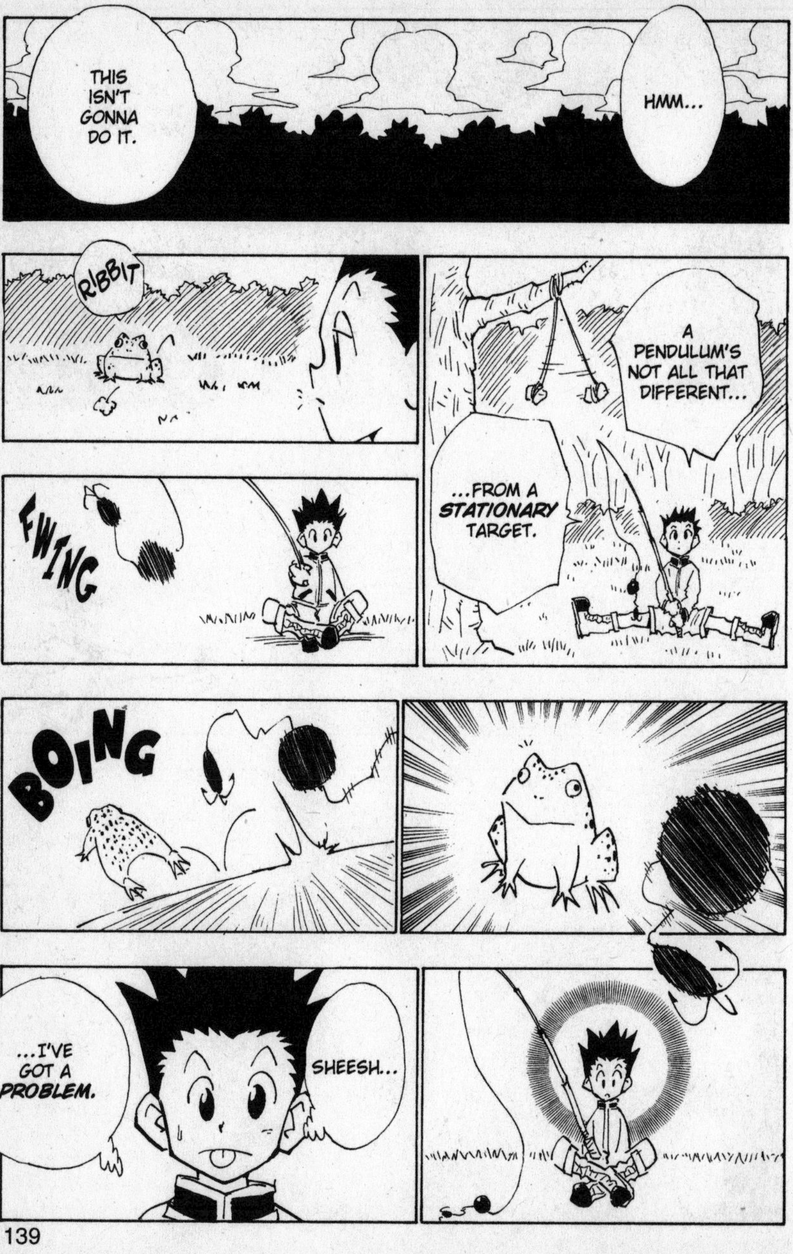

HMM...
THIS ISN'T GONNA DO IT.
A PENDULUM'S NOT ALL THAT DIFFERENT...
...FROM A STATIONARY TARGET.
RIBBIT
FWING
BOING
SHEESH...
...I'VE GOT A PROBLEM.

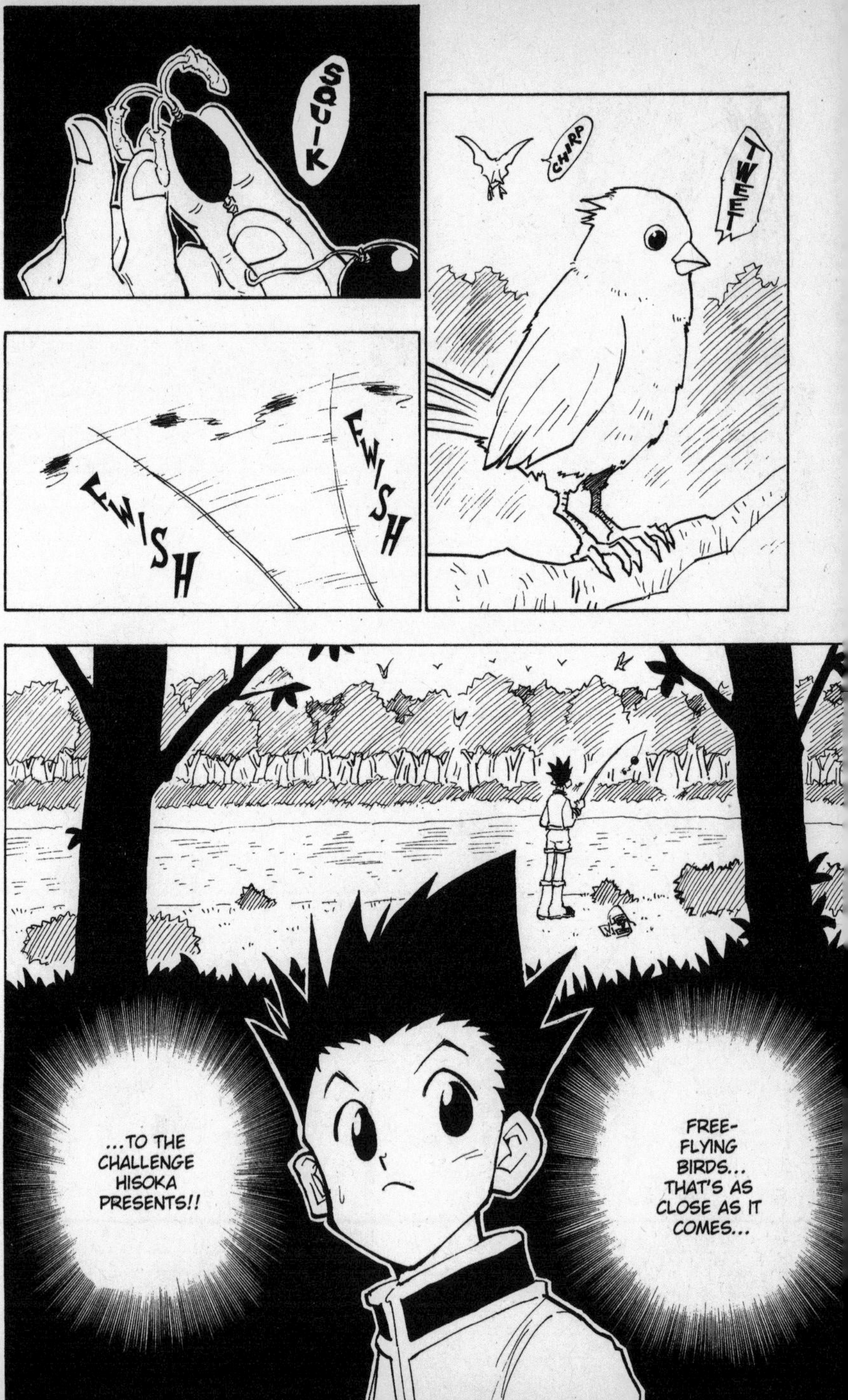
TWEET
CHIRP
SQUIK
FWISH
FWISH
FREE-FLYING BIRDS... THAT'S AS CLOSE AS IT COMES...
...TO THE CHALLENGE HISOKA PRESENTS!!

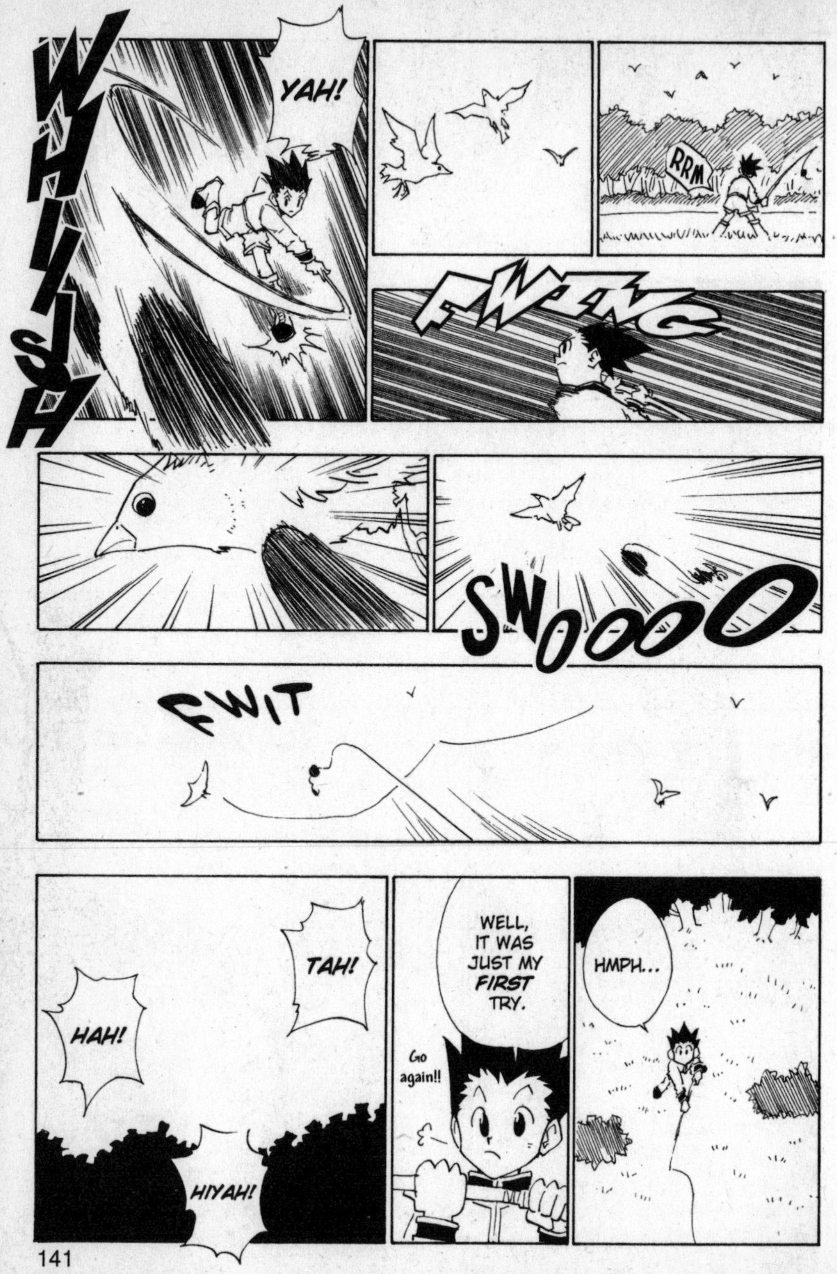
RRM
FWING
YAH!
WHIIISH
SWOOOO
FWIT
HMPH...
WELL, IT WAS JUST MY FIRST TRY.
Go again!!
TAH!
HAH!
HIYAH!

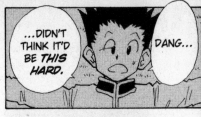

HUFF...
PUFF...
DANG...
...DIDN'T THINK IT'D BE THIS HARD.
I'LL START FRESH IN THE MORNING!
TAH!
HIYAH!
NO USE!
I'M NOT EVEN GETTING CLOSE!!
SNAGGING A BIRD IN FLIGHT IS IMPOSSIBLE!
BY THE TIME...
...I CAST AT 'EM, THEY'RE GONE.

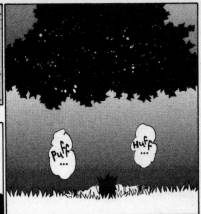

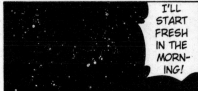

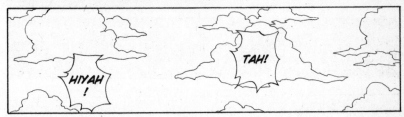

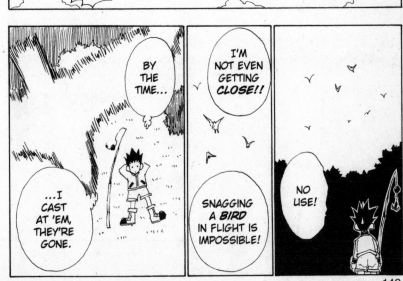

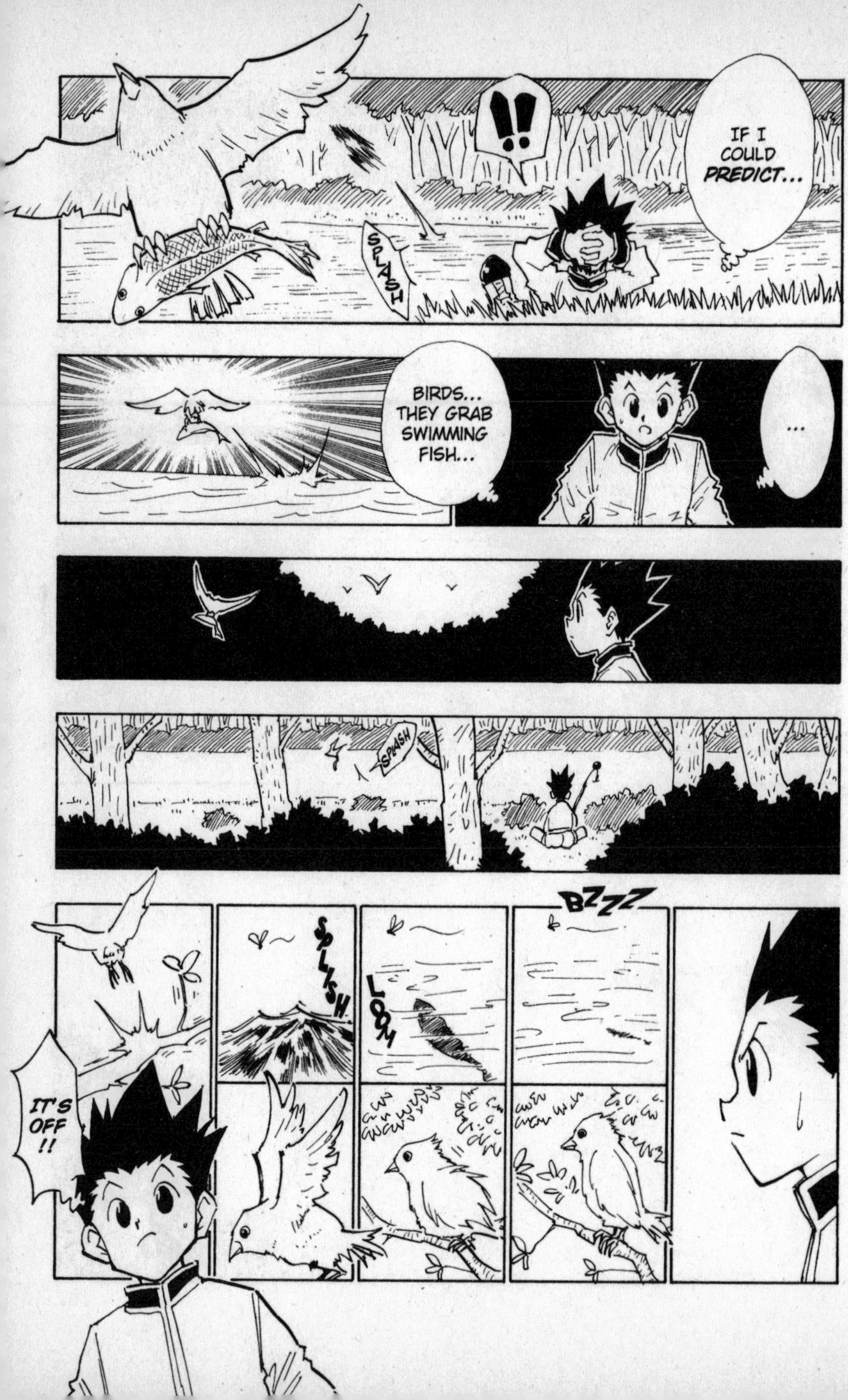
IF I COULD PREDICT...
!!
SPLASH
...
BIRDS... THEY GRAB SWIMMING FISH...
SPLASH
BZZZ
LOOM
SPLISH
IT'S OFF !!

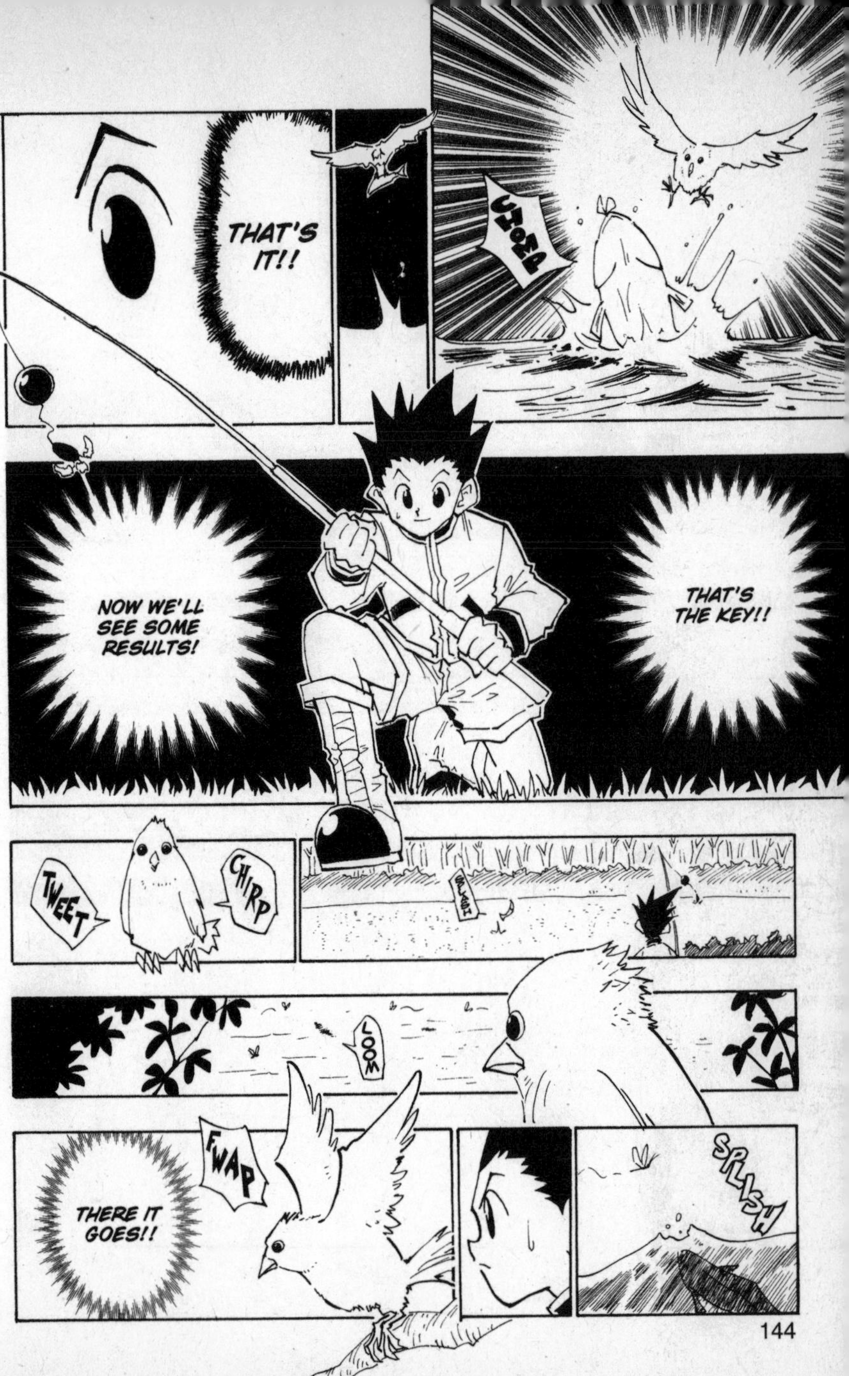
CHOMP
THAT'S IT!!
THAT'S THE KEY!!
NOW WE'LL SEE SOME RESULTS!
SPLISH
CHIRP
TWEET
LOOM
SPLISH
FWAP
THERE IT GOES!!

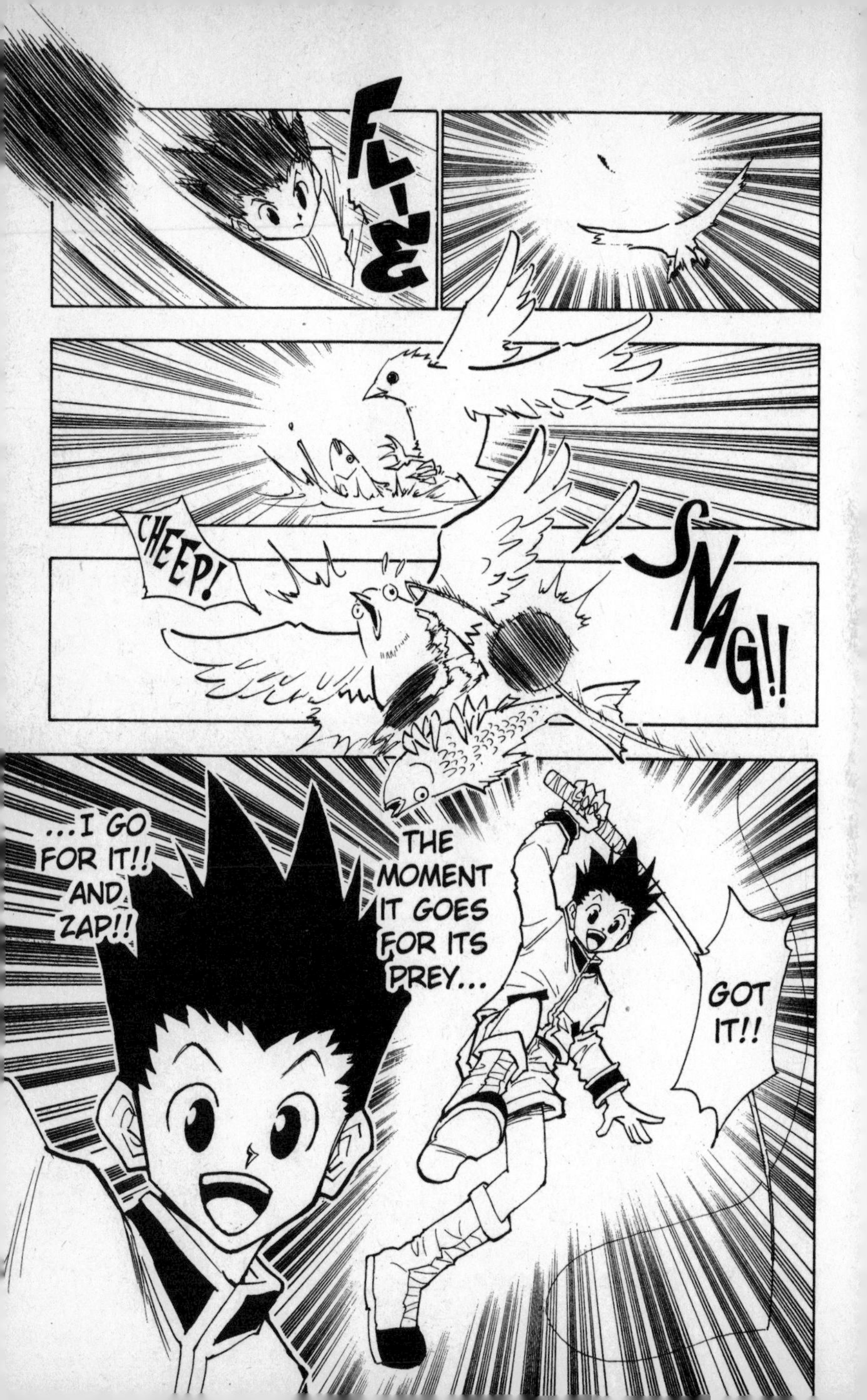
FLING
SNAG!!
CHEEP!
GOT IT!!
THE MOMENT IT GOES FOR ITS PREY...
...I GO FOR IT!! AND ZAP!!

Gittarackur
(alias)

Chapter 25

The Second Day

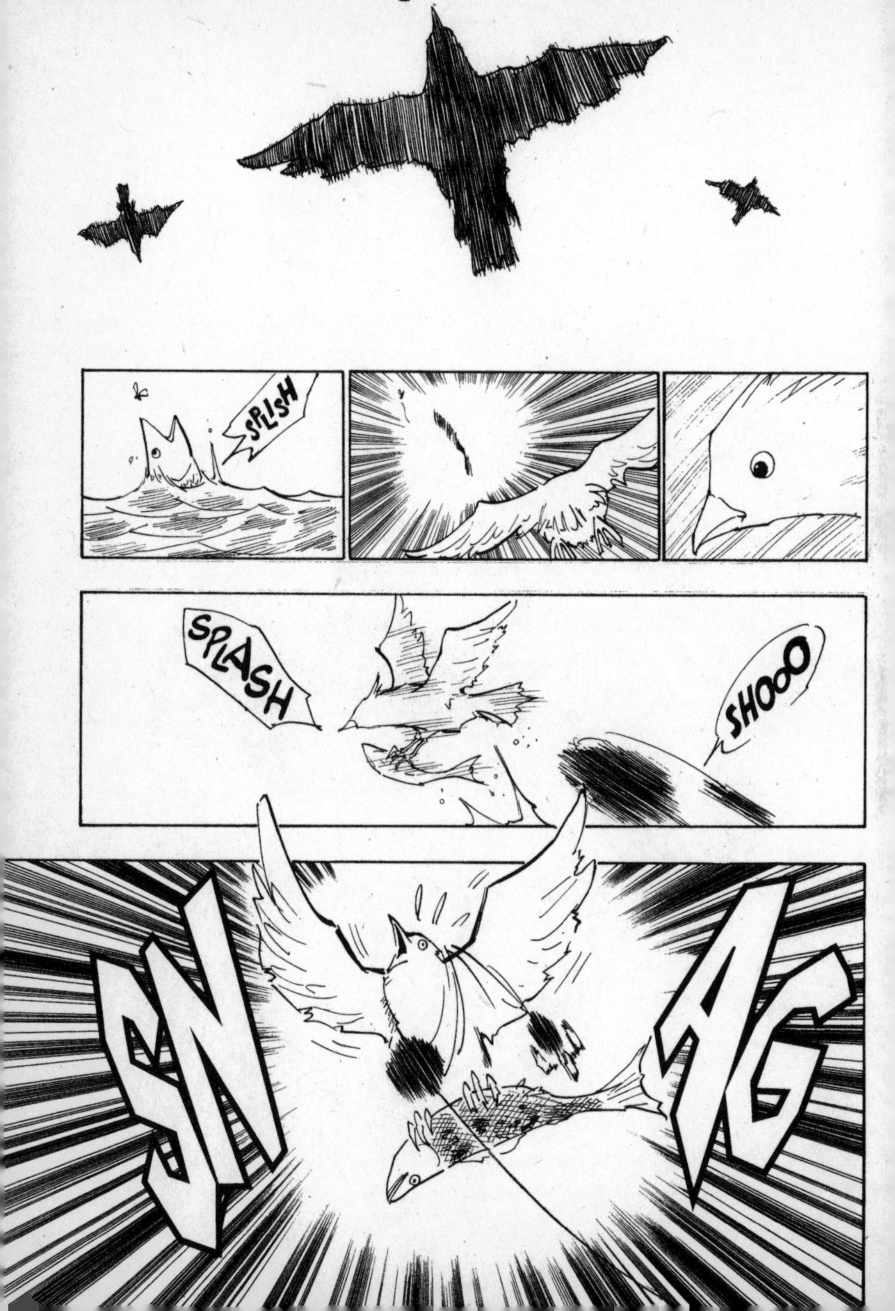
SPLISH
SHOOO
SPLASH
SNAG

Chapter 25
The Second Day

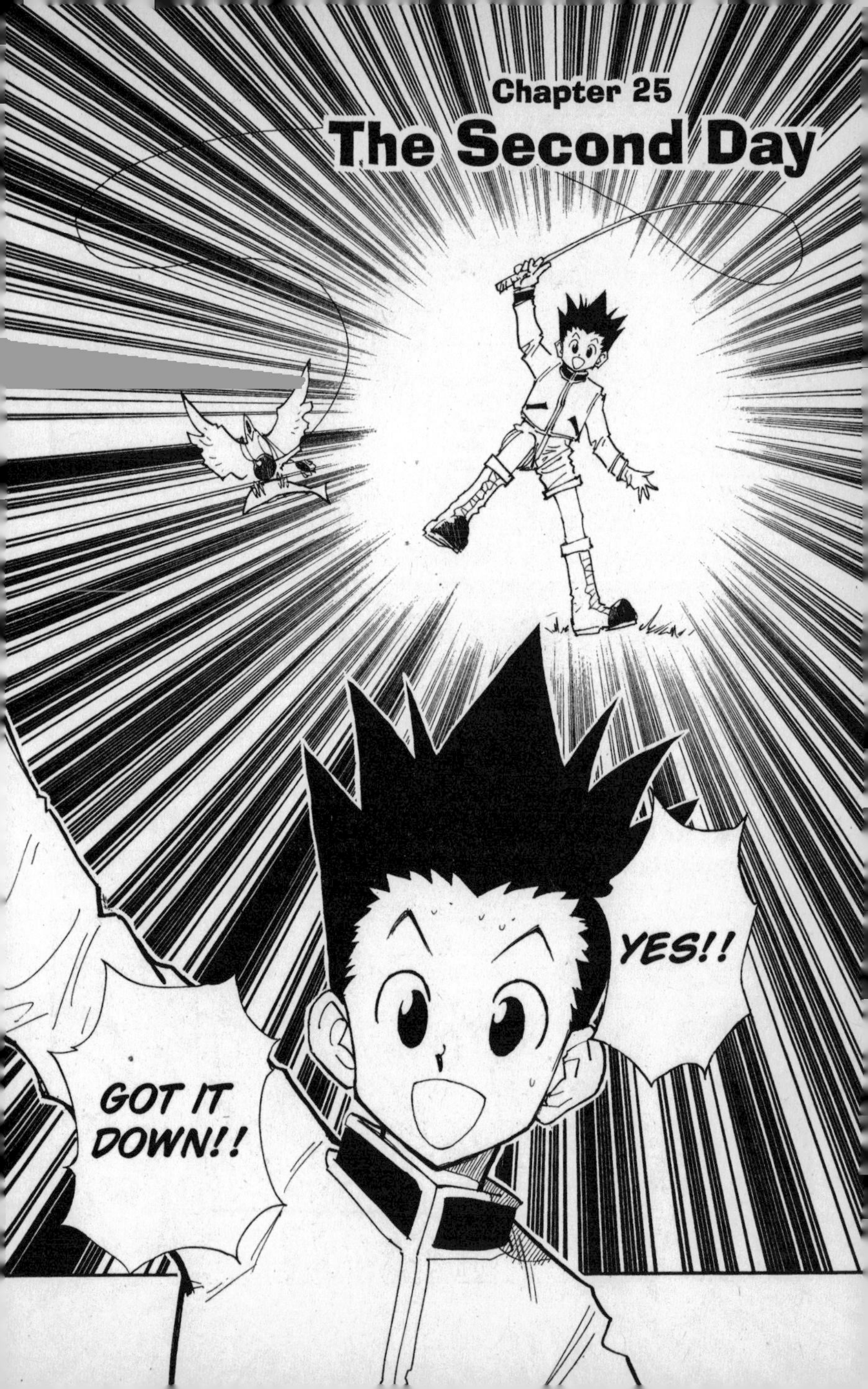
YES!!
GOT IT DOWN!!

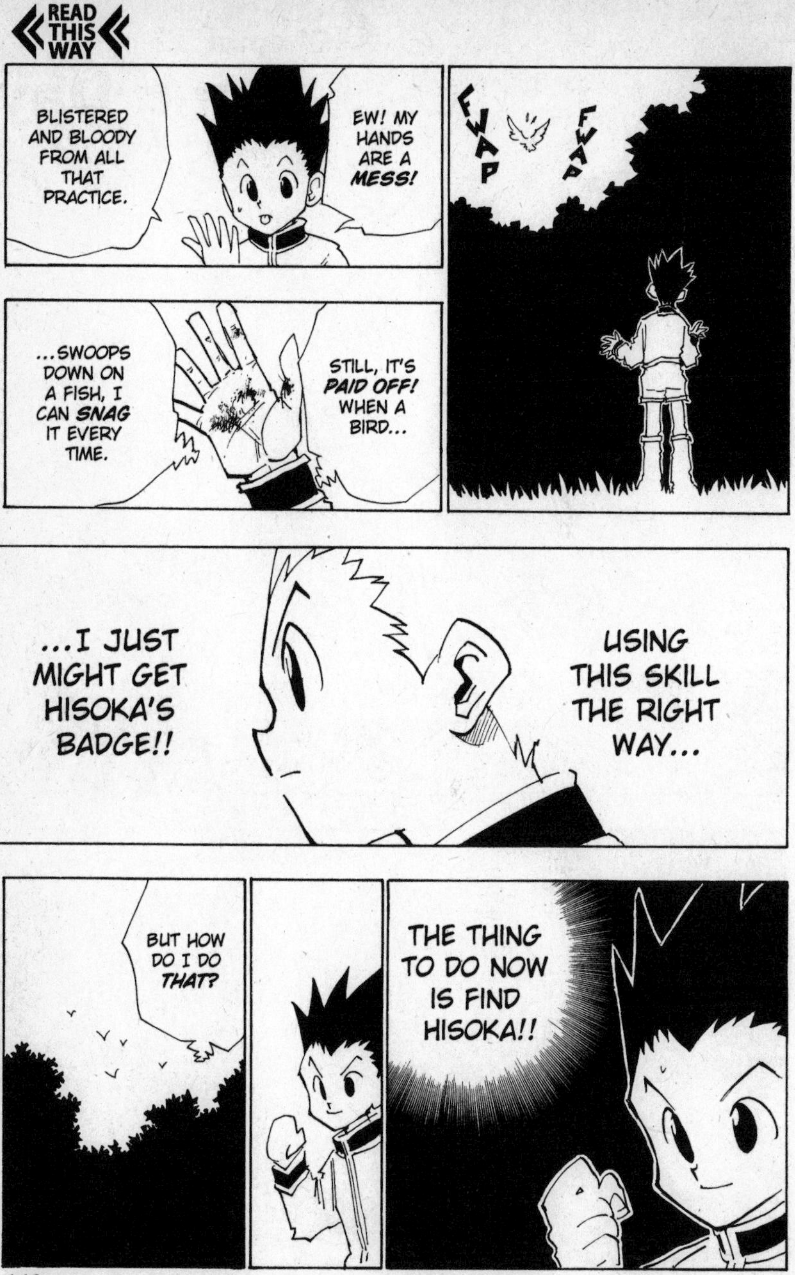
READ THIS WAY
FWAP
FWAP
EW! MY HANDS ARE A MESS!
BLISTERED AND BLOODY FROM ALL THAT PRACTICE.
STILL, IT'S PAID OFF! WHEN A BIRD...
...SWOOPS DOWN ON A FISH, I CAN SNAG IT EVERY TIME.
USING THIS SKILL THE RIGHT WAY...
...I JUST MIGHT GET HISOKA'S BADGE!!
THE THING TO DO NOW IS FIND HISOKA!!
BUT HOW DO I DO THAT?

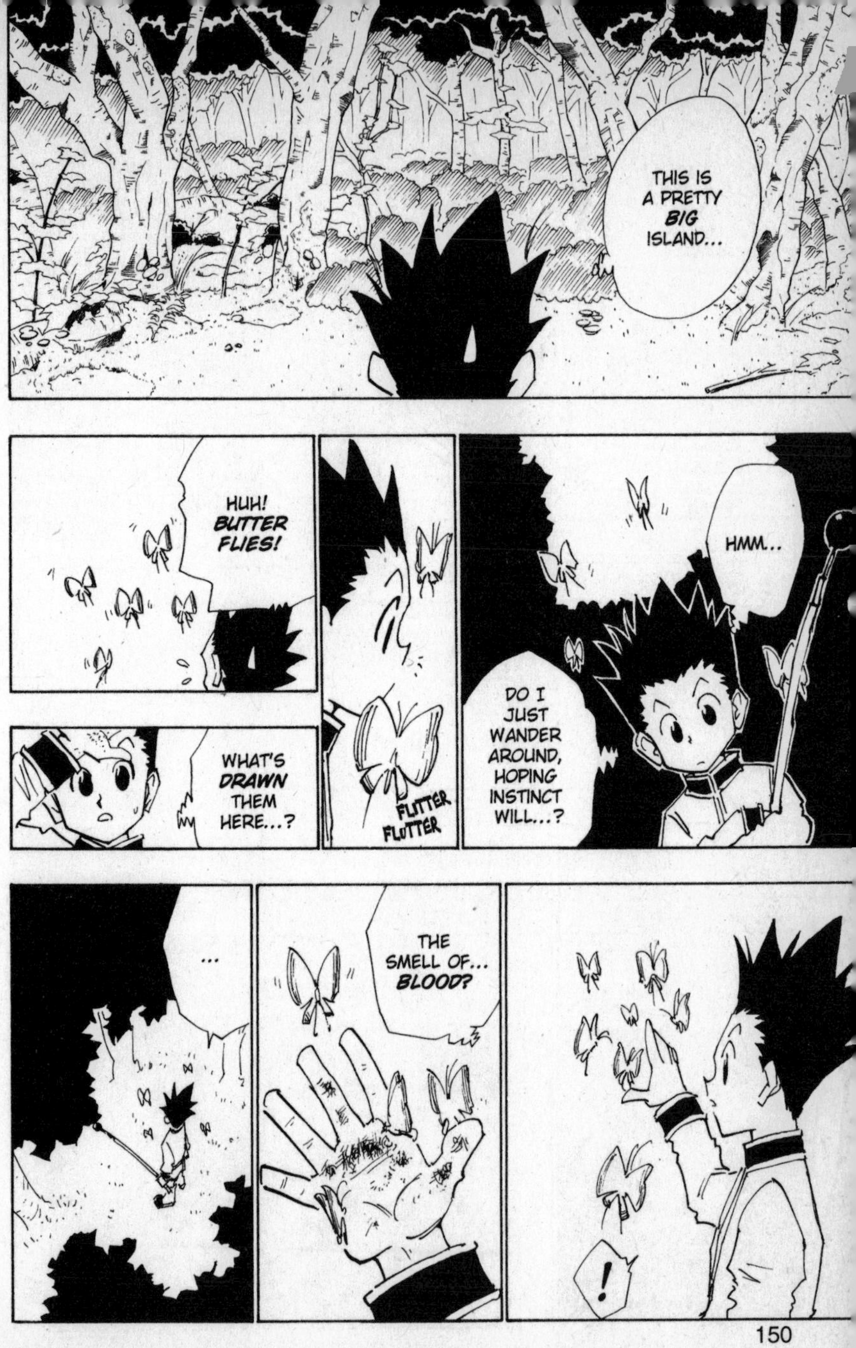
THIS IS A PRETTY BIG ISLAND...
HMM...
DO I JUST WANDER AROUND, HOPING INSTINCT WILL...?
FLUTTER FLUTTER
HUH! BUTTER FLIES!
WHAT'S DRAWN THEM HERE...?
!
THE SMELL OF... BLOOD?
...

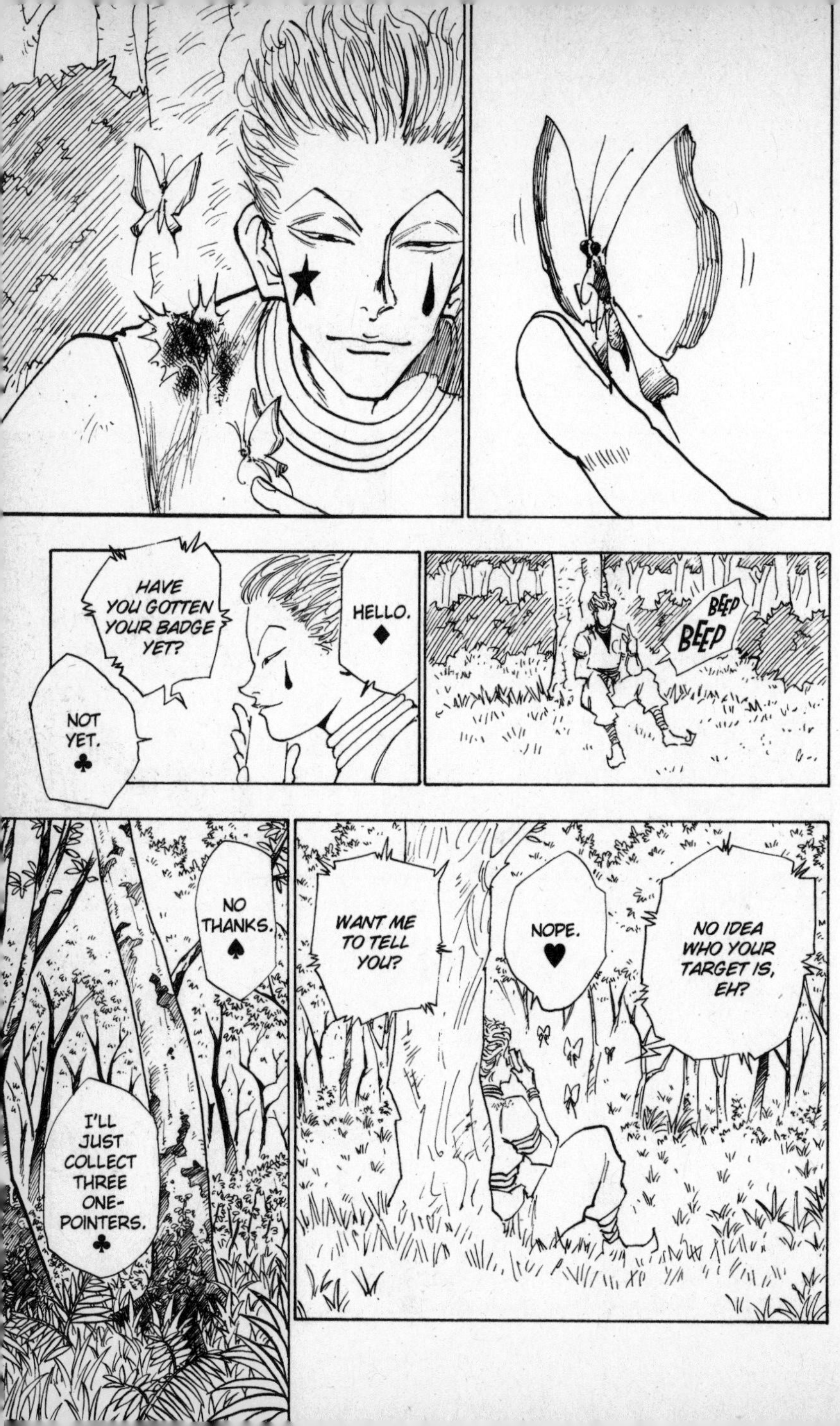
BEEP BEEP
HELLO. ♦
HAVE YOU GOTTEN YOUR BADGE YET?
NOT YET. ♣
NO IDEA WHO YOUR TARGET IS, EH?
NOPE. ♥
WANT ME TO TELL YOU?
NO THANKS. ♠
I'LL JUST COLLECT THREE ONE-POINTERS. ♣

AS I RECOLLECT, HISOKA GOT DOWN THE TOWER FIRST...

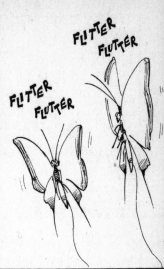

FLITTER FLITTER

FLITTER FLITTER

...BUT *NOT* WITHOUT GETTING *CUT UP* A BIT. I SHOULD FIND HIM BEFORE HIS INJURIES HEAL...

!!

SHUFF

OH, IT'S...

...THE GUY WHO GOT DRUGGED.

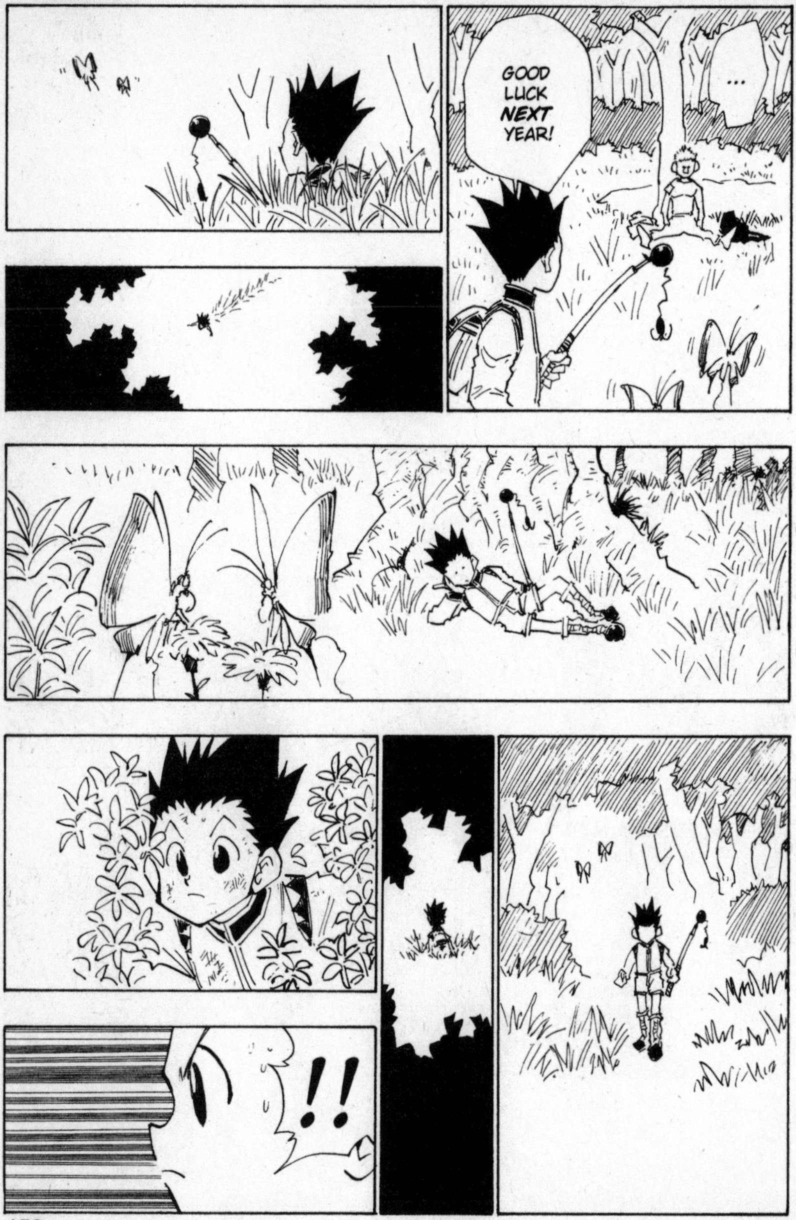
...
GOOD LUCK NEXT YEAR!
!!

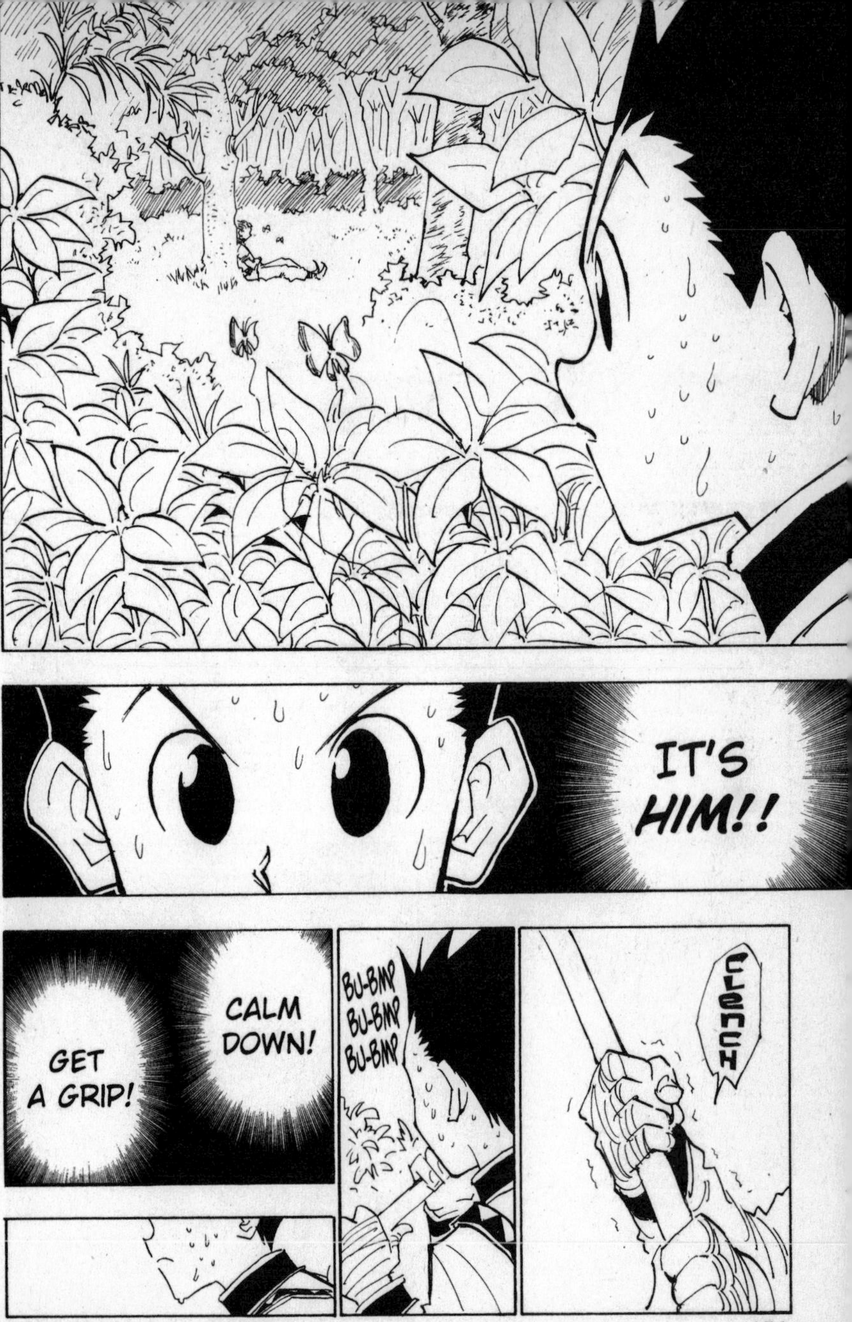
IT'S HIM!!
CLENCH
BU-BMP BU-BMP BU-BMP
CALM DOWN!
GET A GRIP!

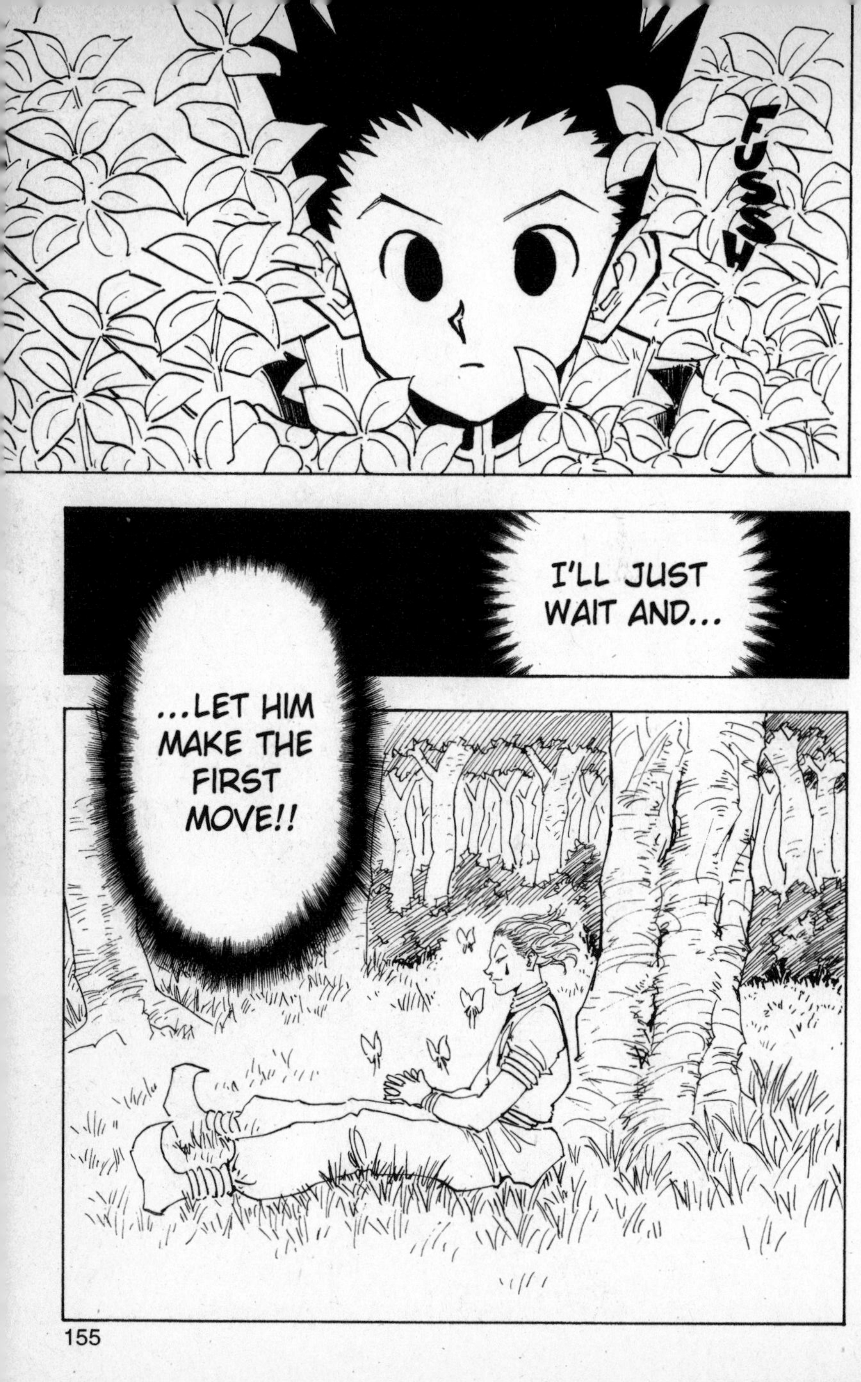
FUSSH
I'LL JUST WAIT AND...
...LET HIM MAKE THE FIRST MOVE!!

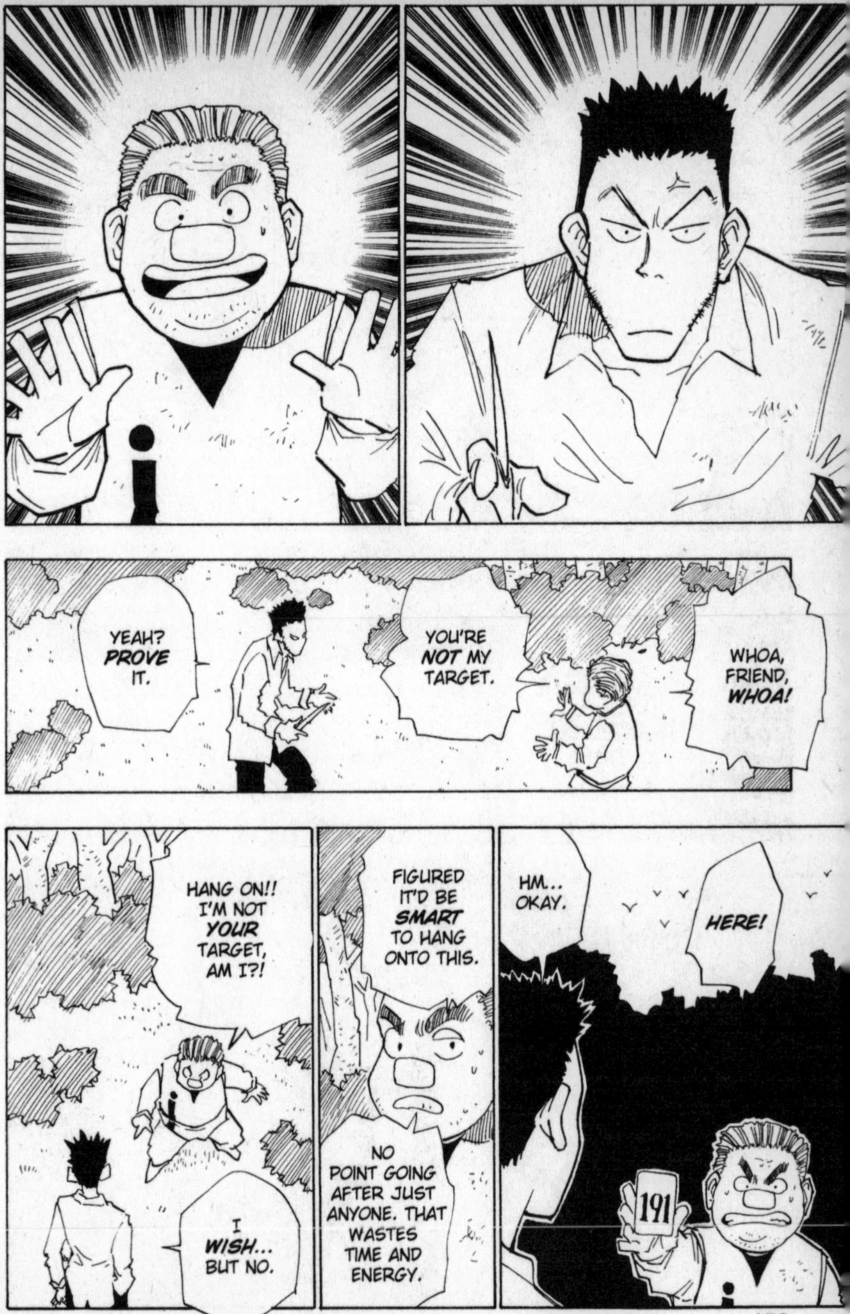
WHOA, FRIEND, WHOA!
YOU'RE NOT MY TARGET.
YEAH? PROVE IT.
HERE!
HM... OKAY.
191
FIGURED IT'D BE SMART TO HANG ONTO THIS.
NO POINT GOING AFTER JUST ANYONE. THAT WASTES TIME AND ENERGY.
HANG ON!! I'M NOT YOUR TARGET, AM I?!
I WISH... BUT NO.

READ THIS WAY

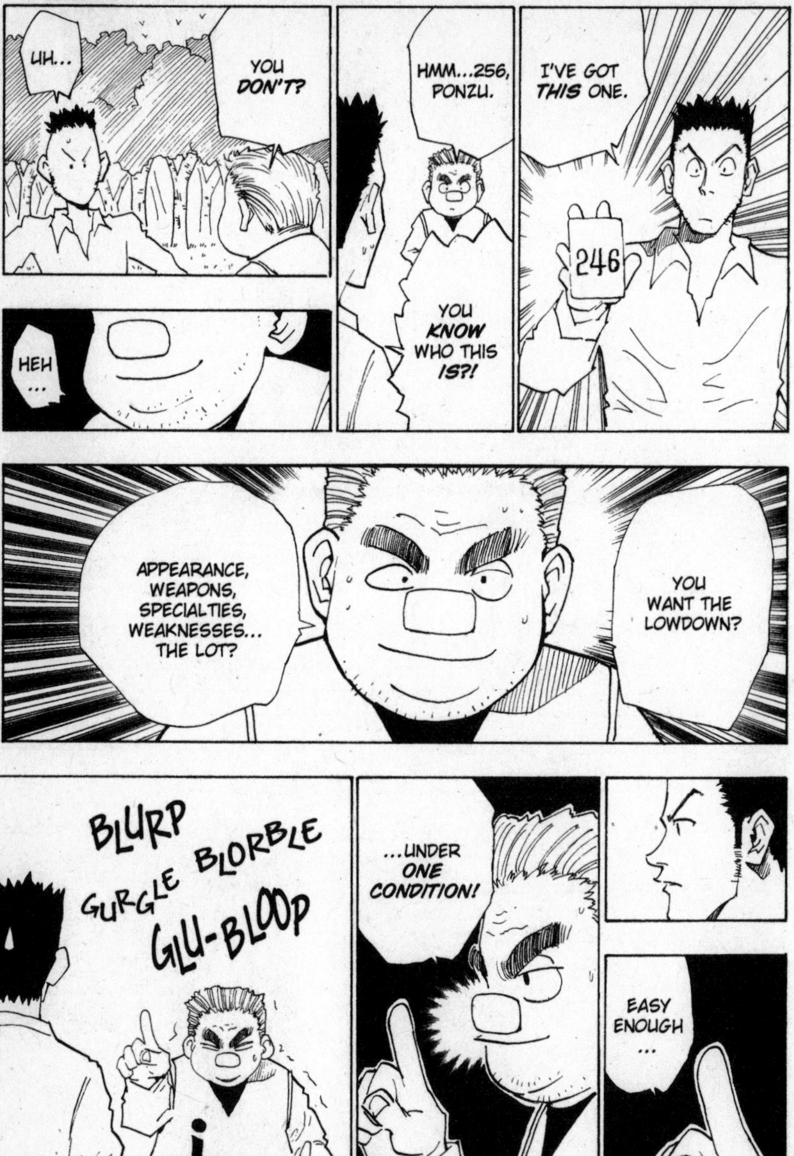
I'VE GOT THIS ONE.
HMM...256, PONZU.
YOU KNOW WHO THIS IS?!
YOU DON'T?
UH...
HEH ...
YOU WANT THE LOWDOWN?
APPEARANCE, WEAPONS, SPECIALTIES, WEAKNESSES... THE LOT?
EASY ENOUGH ...
...UNDER ONE CONDITION!
BLURP
GURGLE BLORBLE
GLU-BLOOP

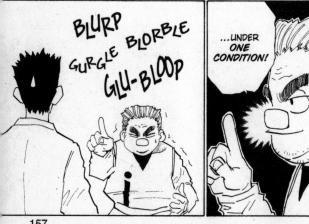

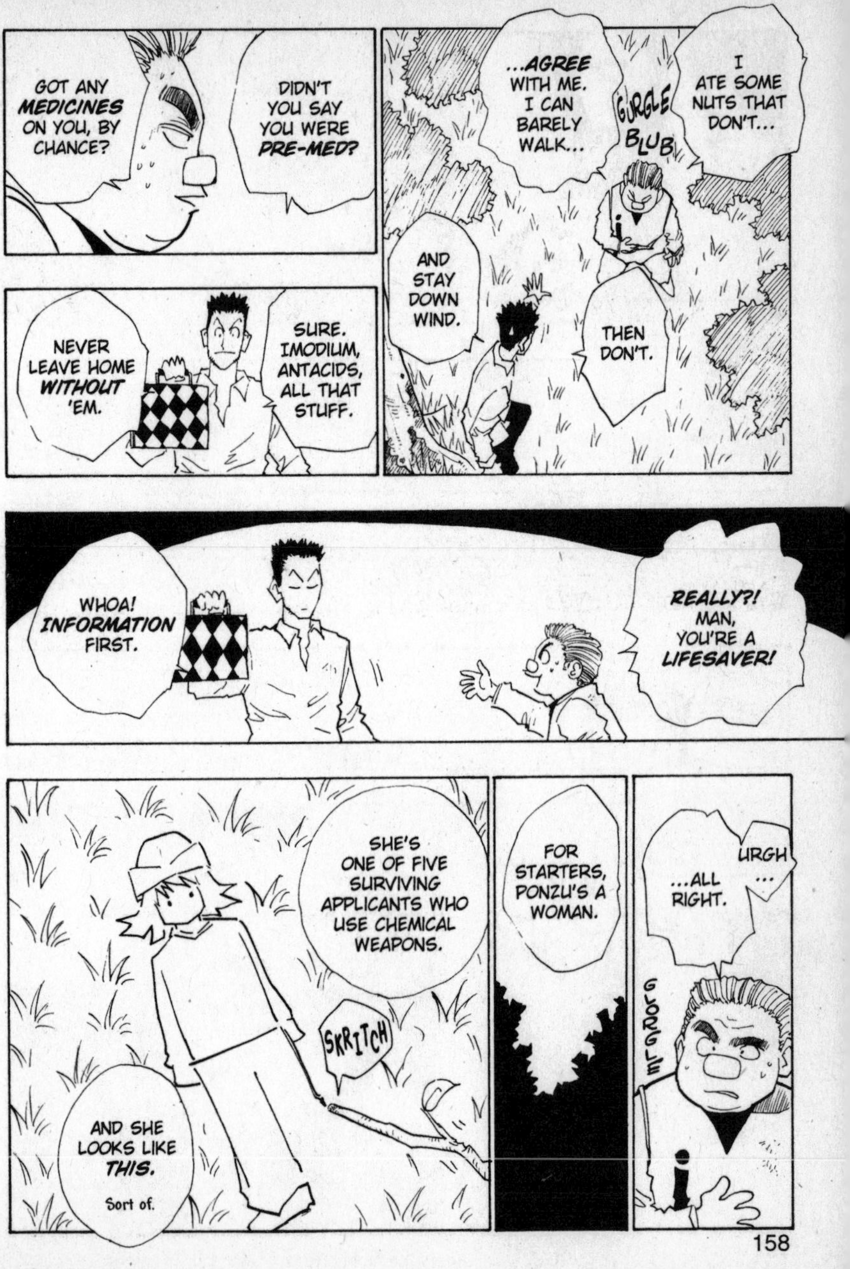
I ATE SOME NUTS THAT DON'T...
GURGLE BLUB
...AGREE WITH ME. I CAN BARELY WALK...
THEN DON'T.
AND STAY DOWN WIND.
DIDN'T YOU SAY YOU WERE PRE-MED?
GOT ANY MEDICINES ON YOU, BY CHANCE?
SURE. IMODIUM, ANTACIDS, ALL THAT STUFF.
NEVER LEAVE HOME WITHOUT 'EM.
REALLY?! MAN, YOU'RE A LIFESAVER!
WHOA! INFORMATION FIRST.
URGH ...
...ALL RIGHT.
GLORGLE
FOR STARTERS, PONZU'S A WOMAN.
SHE'S ONE OF FIVE SURVIVING APPLICANTS WHO USE CHEMICAL WEAPONS.
SKRITCH
AND SHE LOOKS LIKE THIS.
Sort of.

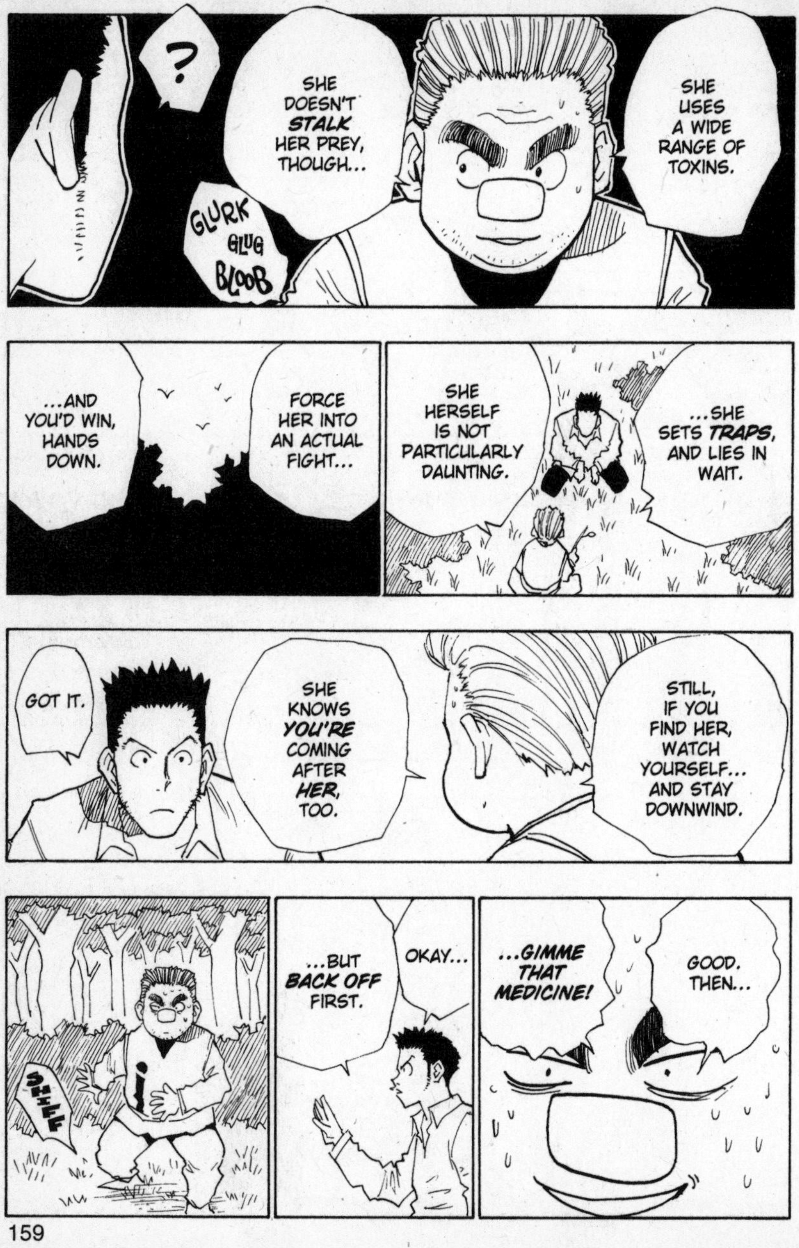
SHE USES A WIDE RANGE OF TOXINS.
SHE DOESN'T STALK HER PREY, THOUGH...
?
GLURK GLUG BLOOB
...SHE SETS TRAPS, AND LIES IN WAIT.
SHE HERSELF IS NOT PARTICULARLY DAUNTING.
FORCE HER INTO AN ACTUAL FIGHT...
...AND YOU'D WIN, HANDS DOWN.
STILL, IF YOU FIND HER, WATCH YOURSELF... AND STAY DOWNWIND.
SHE KNOWS YOU'RE COMING AFTER HER, TOO.
GOT IT.
GOOD. THEN...
...GIMME THAT MEDICINE!
OKAY...
...BUT BACK OFF FIRST.
SHIFF

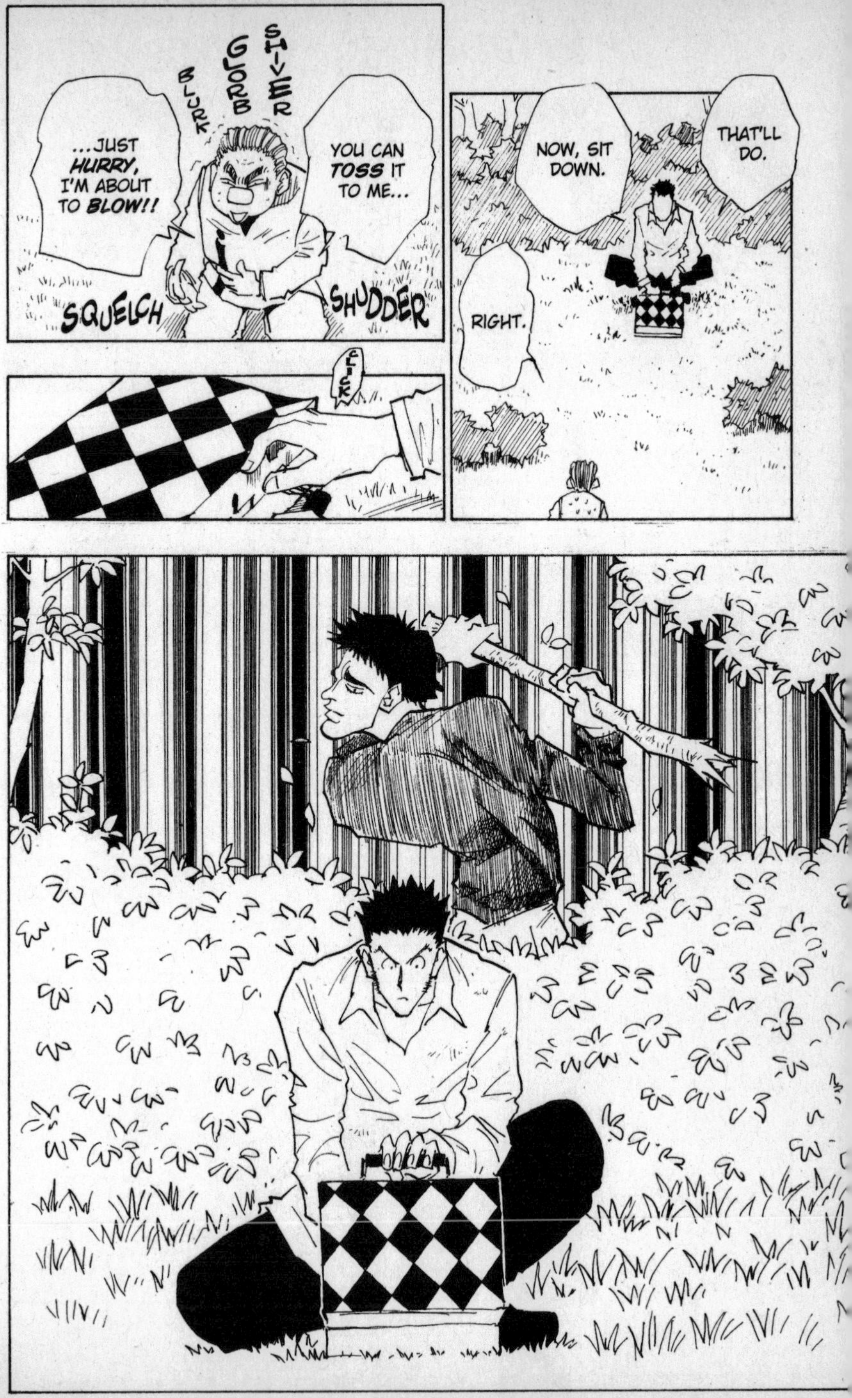
THAT'LL DO.
NOW, SIT DOWN.
RIGHT.
SHIVER
GLORB
YOU CAN TOSS IT TO ME...
BLURK
...JUST HURRY, I'M ABOUT TO BLOW!!
SHUDDER
SQUELCH
CLICK

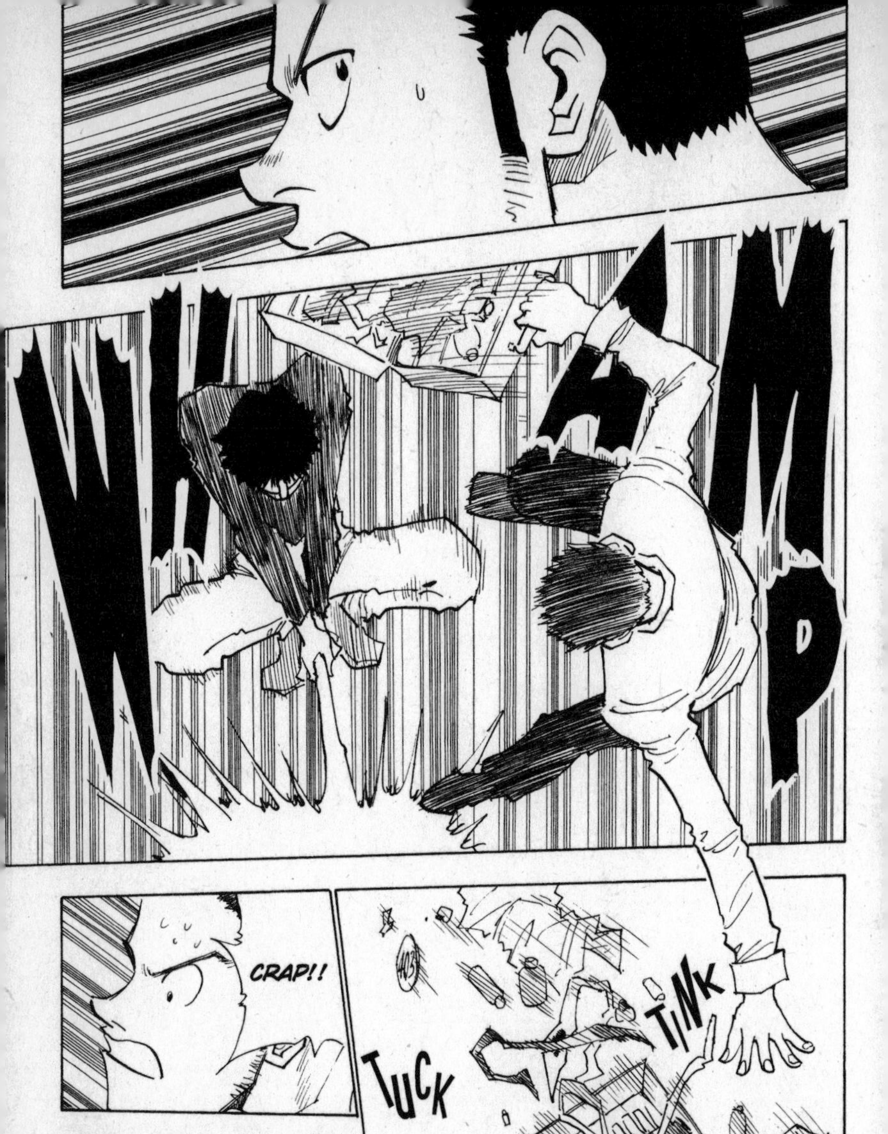
TINK
TUCK
CLATTER
CRAP!!
FWISH

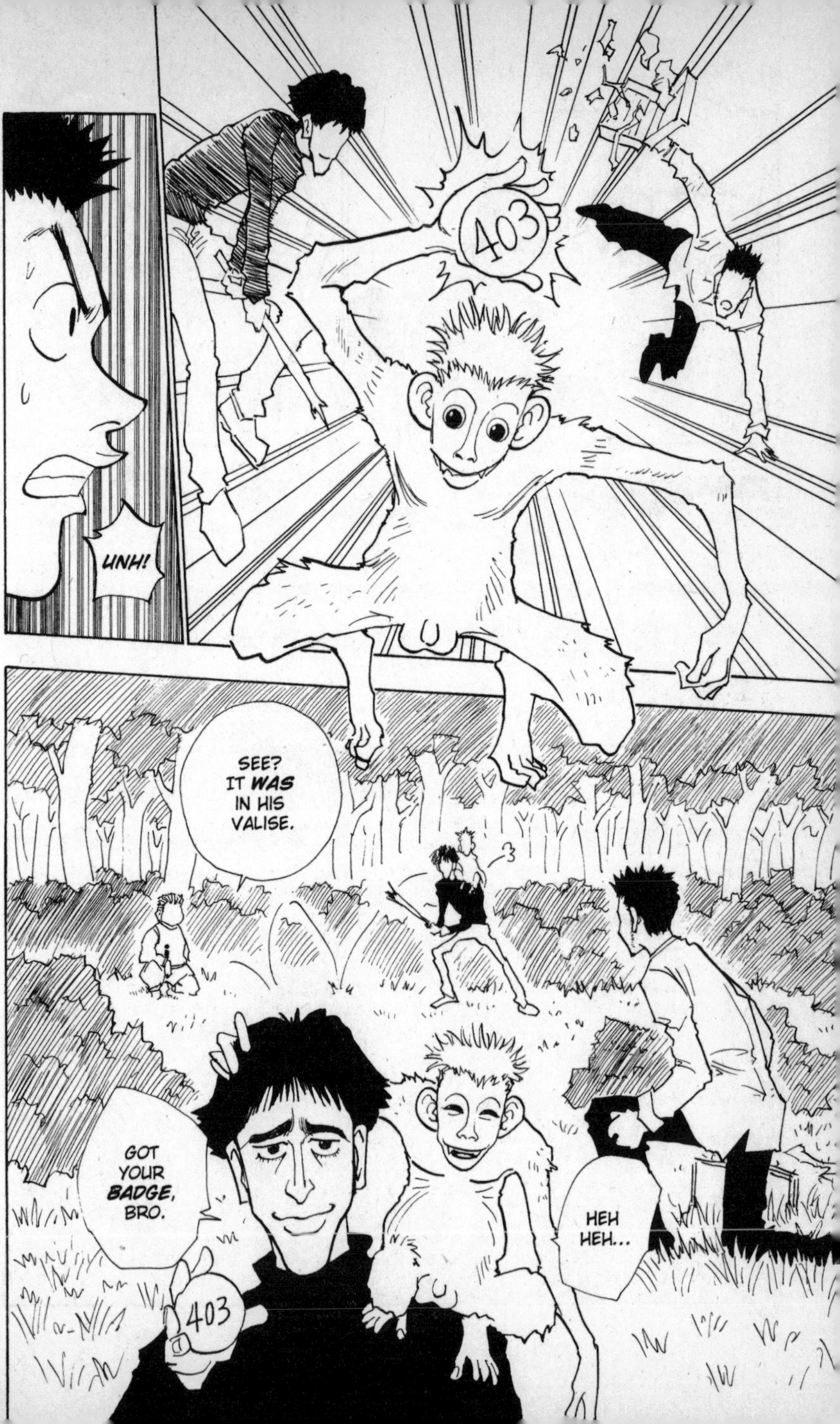
403
UNH!
SEE? IT WAS IN HIS VALISE.
GOT YOUR BADGE, BRO.
HEH HEH...
403

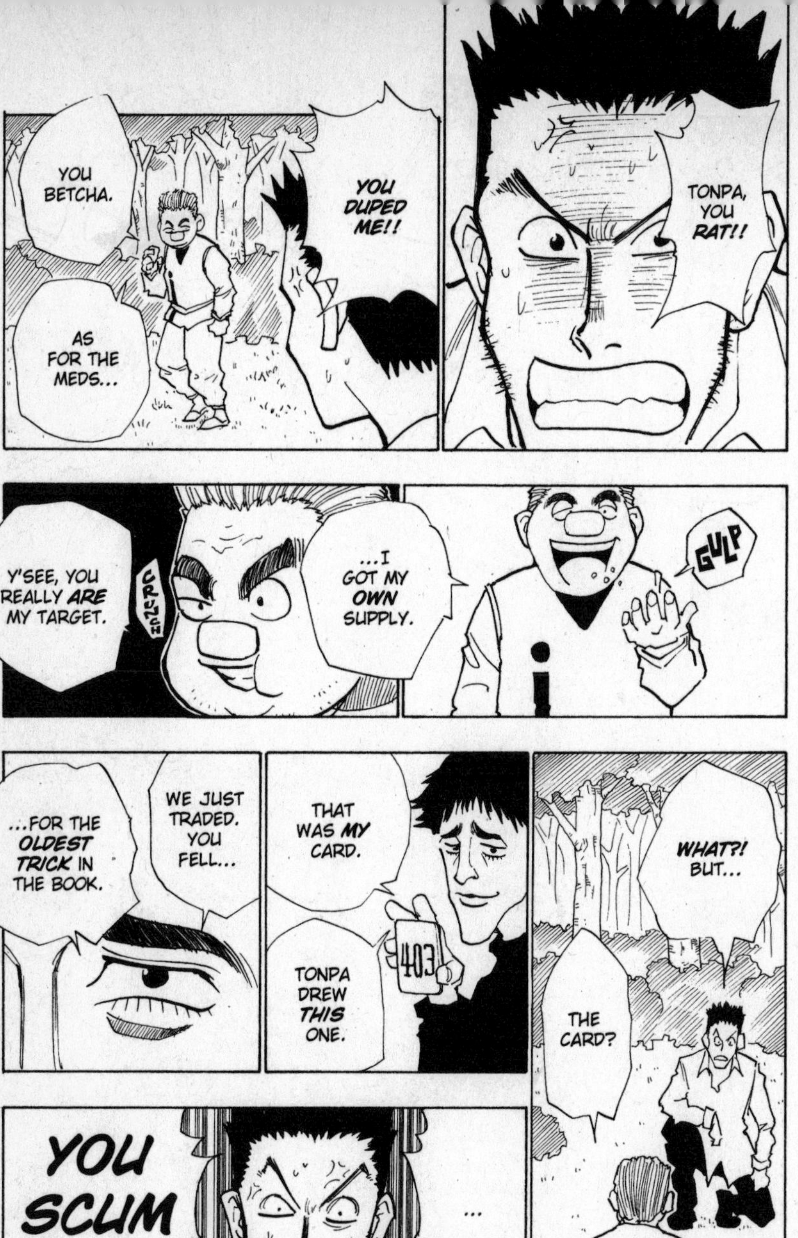
TONPA, YOU RAT!!
YOU DUPED ME!!
YOU BETCHA.
AS FOR THE MEDS...
GULP
...I GOT MY OWN SUPPLY.
CRUNCH
Y'SEE, YOU REALLY ARE MY TARGET.
WHAT?! BUT...
THE CARD?
THAT WAS MY CARD.
403
TONPA DREW THIS ONE.
WE JUST TRADED. YOU FELL...
...FOR THE OLDEST TRICK IN THE BOOK.
...
YOU SCUM!!!

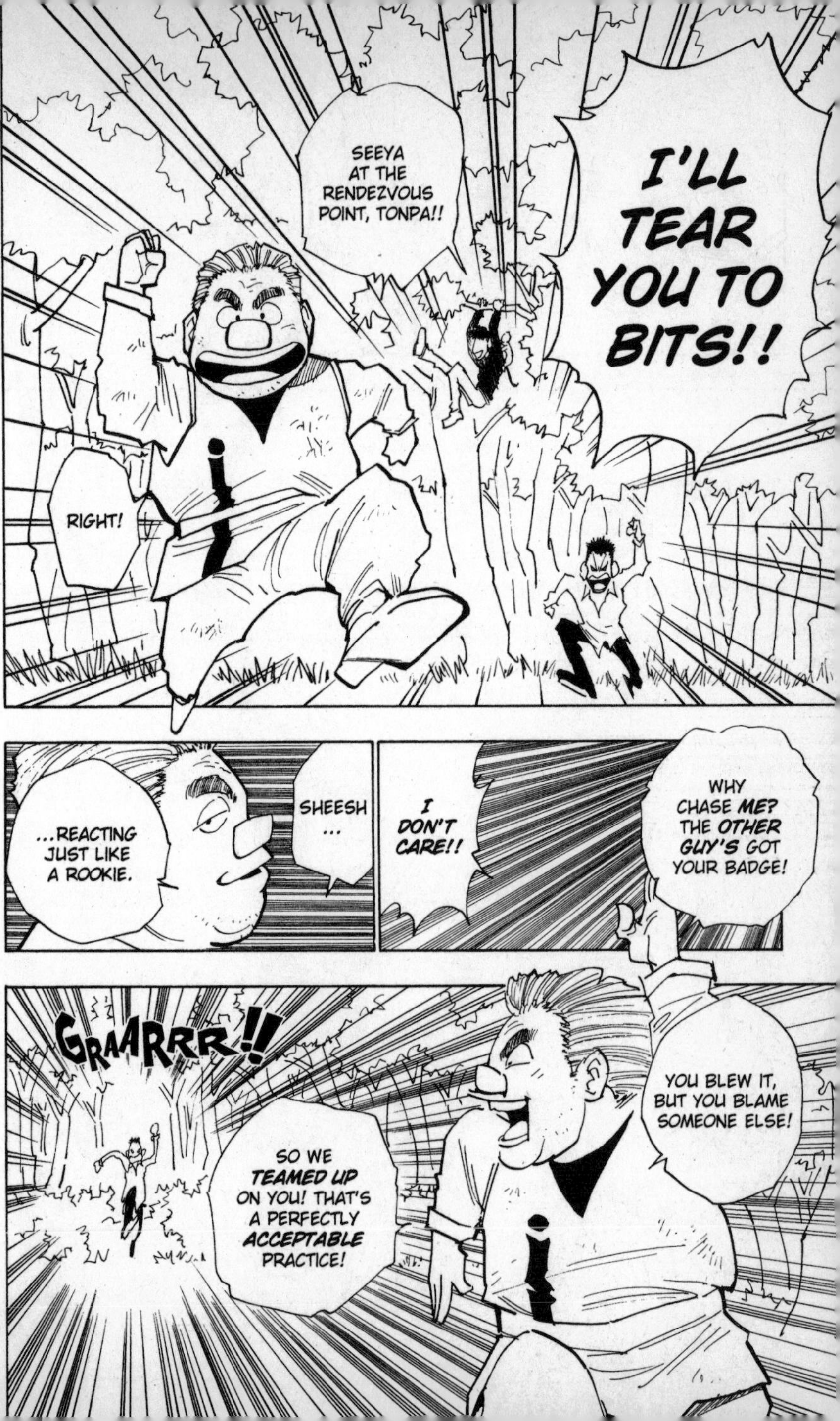
I'LL TEAR YOU TO BITS!!
SEEYA AT THE RENDEZVOUS POINT, TONPA!!
RIGHT!
WHY CHASE ME? THE OTHER GUY'S GOT YOUR BADGE!
I DON'T CARE!!
SHEESH ...
...REACTING JUST LIKE A ROOKIE.
YOU BLEW IT, BUT YOU BLAME SOMEONE ELSE!
SO WE TEAMED UP ON YOU! THAT'S A PERFECTLY ACCEPTABLE PRACTICE!
GRAARRR!!

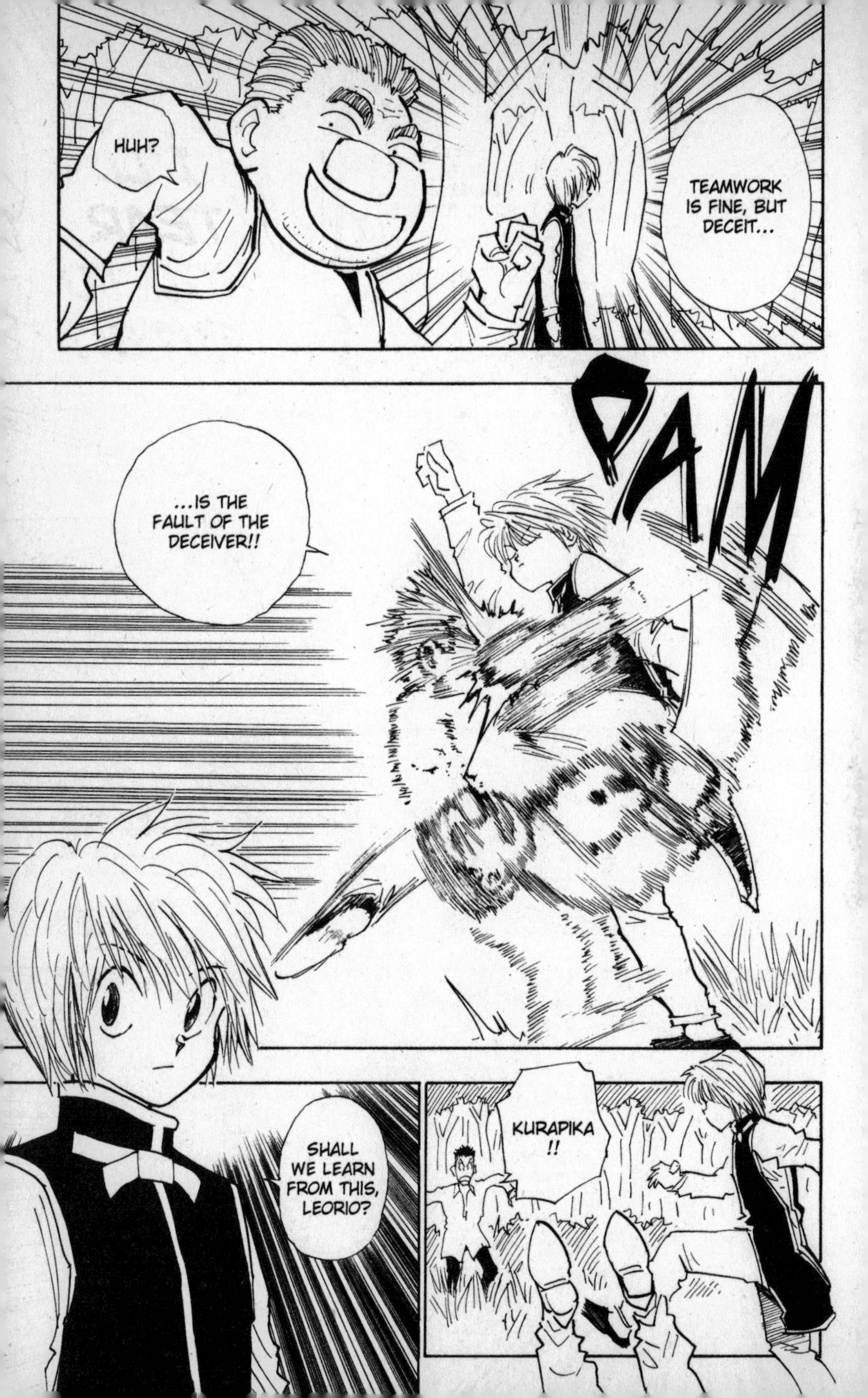
TEAMWORK IS FINE, BUT DECEIT...
HUH?
BAM
...IS THE FAULT OF THE DECEIVER!!
KURAPIKA !!
SHALL WE LEARN FROM THIS, LEORIO?

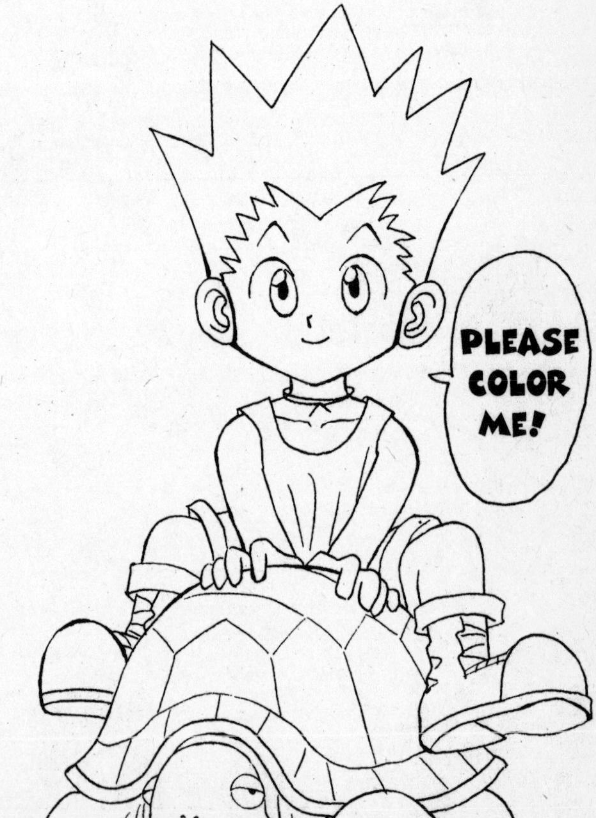
PLEASE COLOR ME!

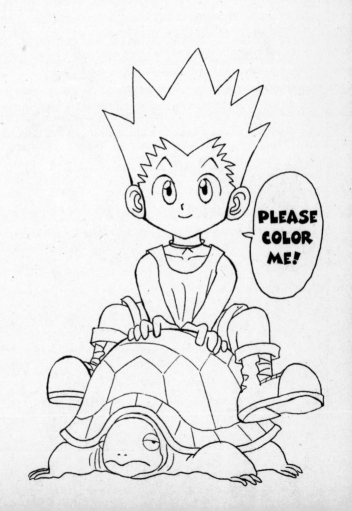

Chapter 26

The Night Before the Showdown

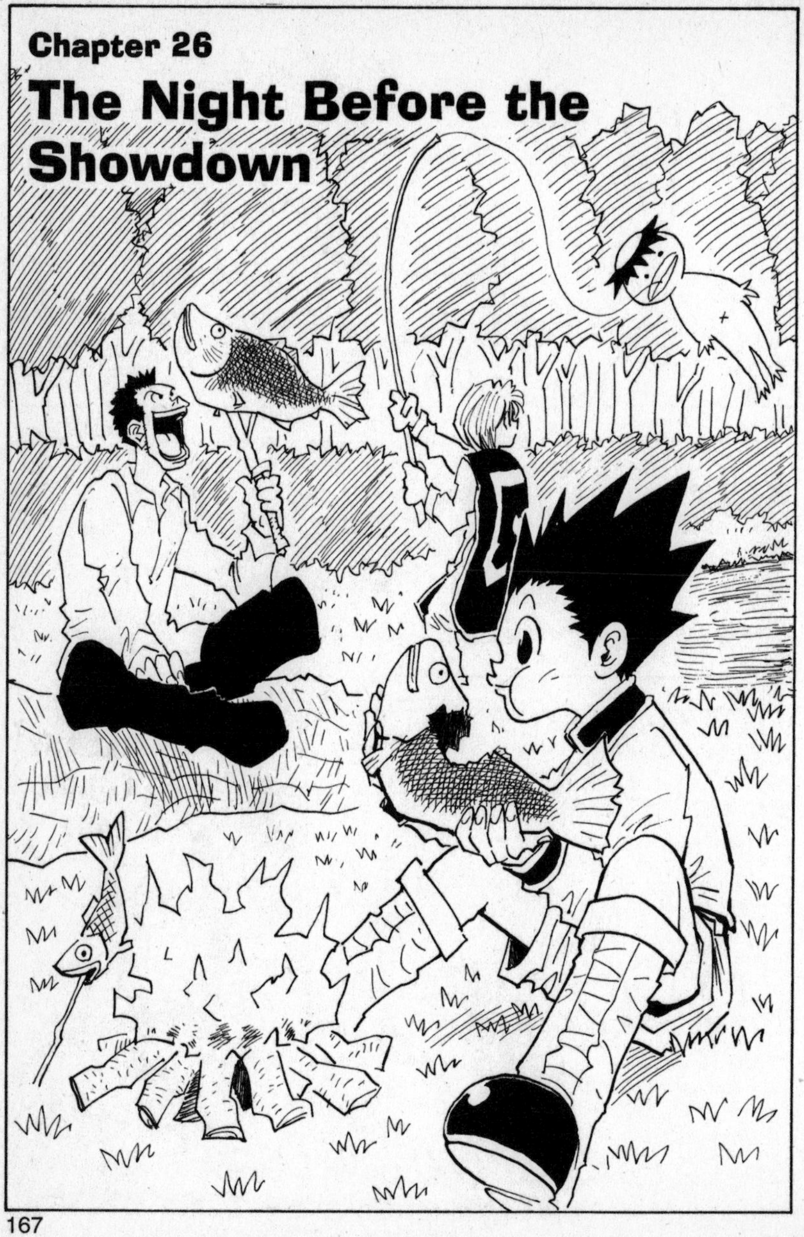

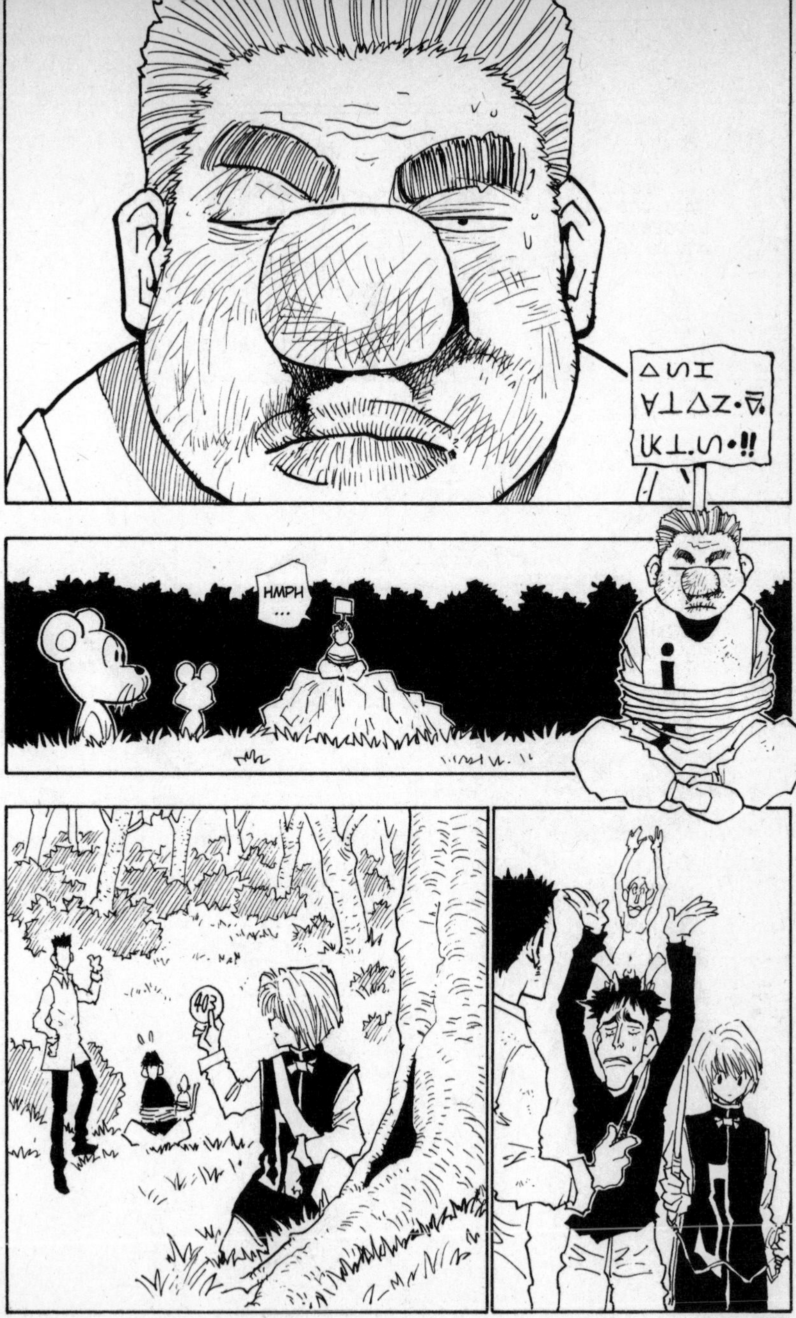
HMPH …

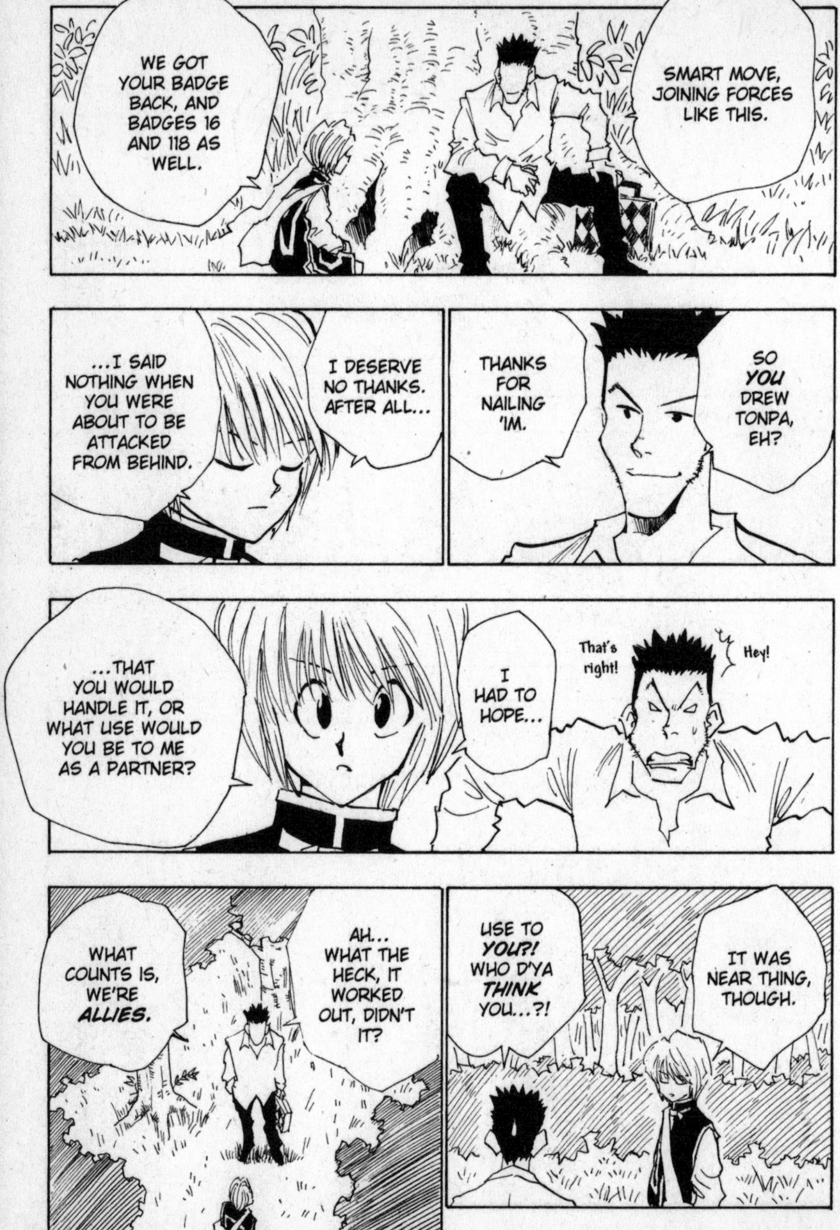
SMART MOVE, JOINING FORCES LIKE THIS.
WE GOT YOUR BADGE BACK, AND BADGES 16 AND 118 AS WELL.
SO *YOU* DREW TONPA, EH?
THANKS FOR NAILING 'IM.
I DESERVE NO THANKS. AFTER ALL...
...I SAID NOTHING WHEN YOU WERE ABOUT TO BE ATTACKED FROM BEHIND.
Hey!
That's right!
I HAD TO HOPE...
...THAT YOU WOULD HANDLE IT, OR WHAT USE WOULD YOU BE TO ME AS A PARTNER?
IT WAS NEAR THING, THOUGH.
USE TO *YOU?!* WHO D'YA *THINK* YOU...?!
AH... WHAT THE HECK, IT WORKED OUT, DIDN'T IT?
WHAT COUNTS IS, WE'RE ***ALLIES.***

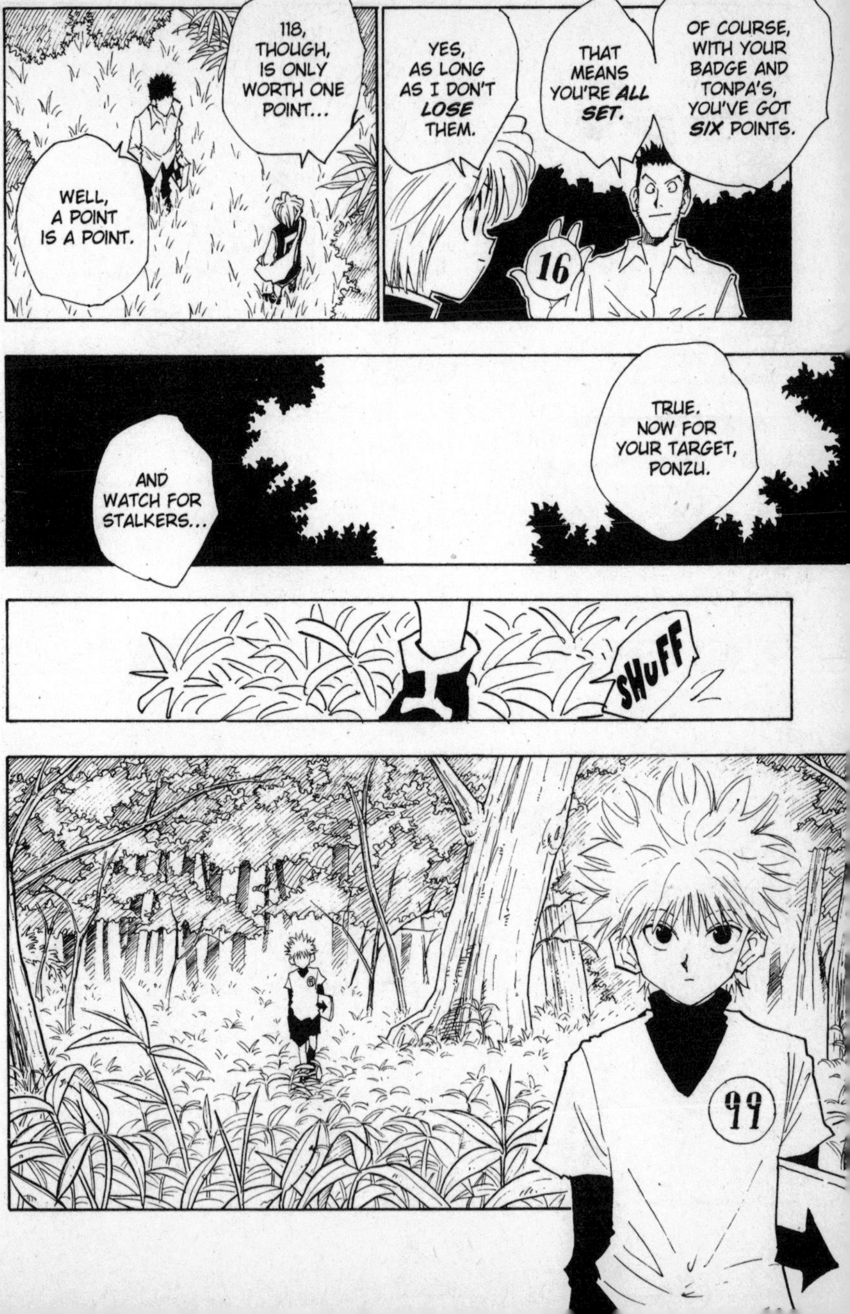

OF COURSE, WITH YOUR BADGE AND TONPA'S, YOU'VE GOT **SIX** POINTS.
THAT MEANS YOU'RE **ALL SET.**
16
YES, AS LONG AS I DON'T **LOSE** THEM.
118, THOUGH, IS ONLY WORTH ONE POINT...
WELL, A POINT IS A POINT.
TRUE. NOW FOR YOUR TARGET, PONZU.
AND WATCH FOR STALKERS...
SHUFF
99

READ THIS WAY

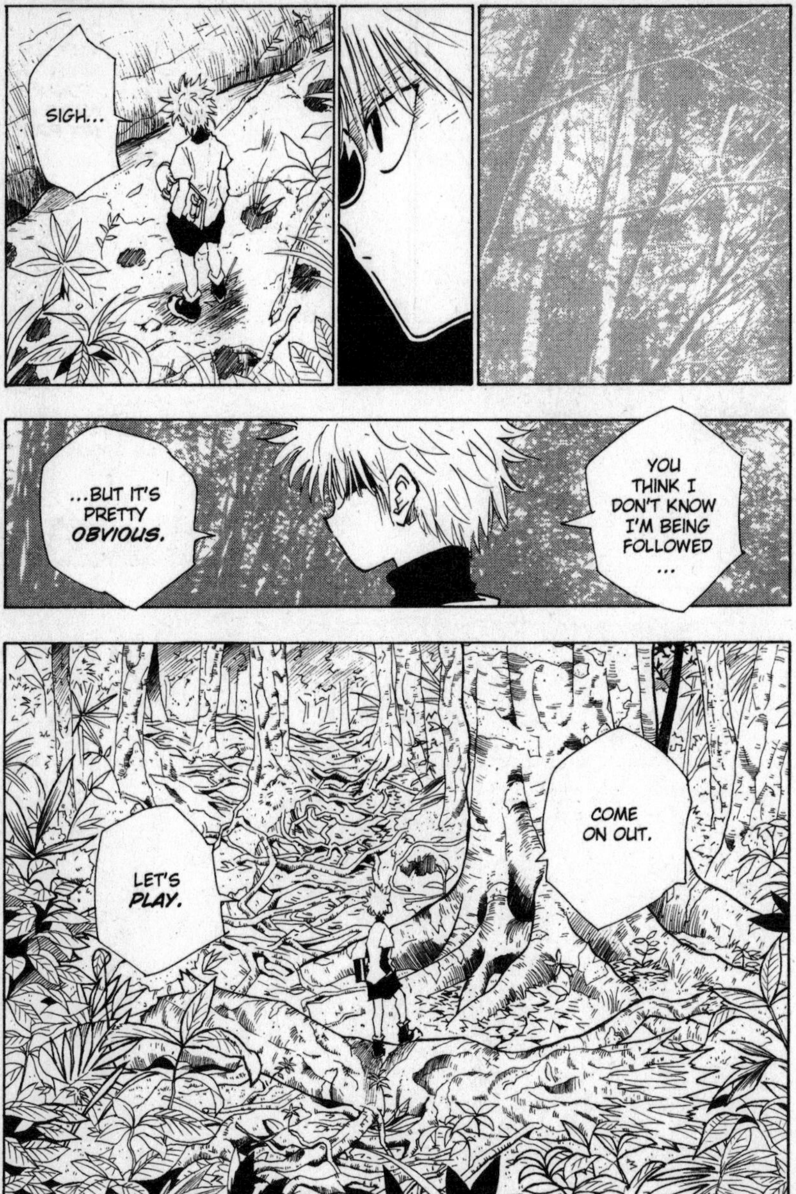
SIGH...
YOU THINK I DON'T KNOW I'M BEING FOLLOWED ...
...BUT IT'S PRETTY *OBVIOUS.*
COME ON OUT.
LET'S *PLAY.*

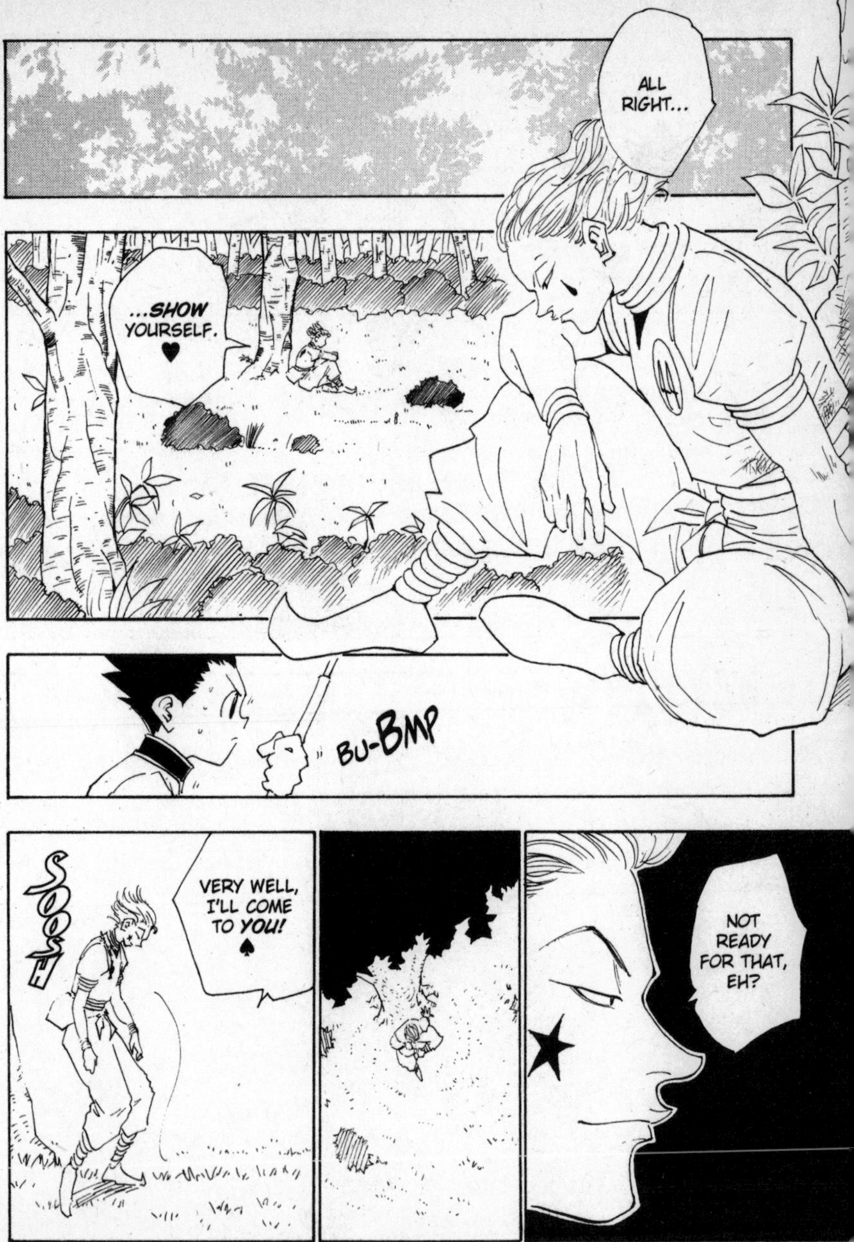
ALL RIGHT...
...SHOW YOURSELF. ♥
BU-BMP
NOT READY FOR THAT, EH?
VERY WELL, I'LL COME TO YOU! ♠
SOOSH

READ THIS WAY

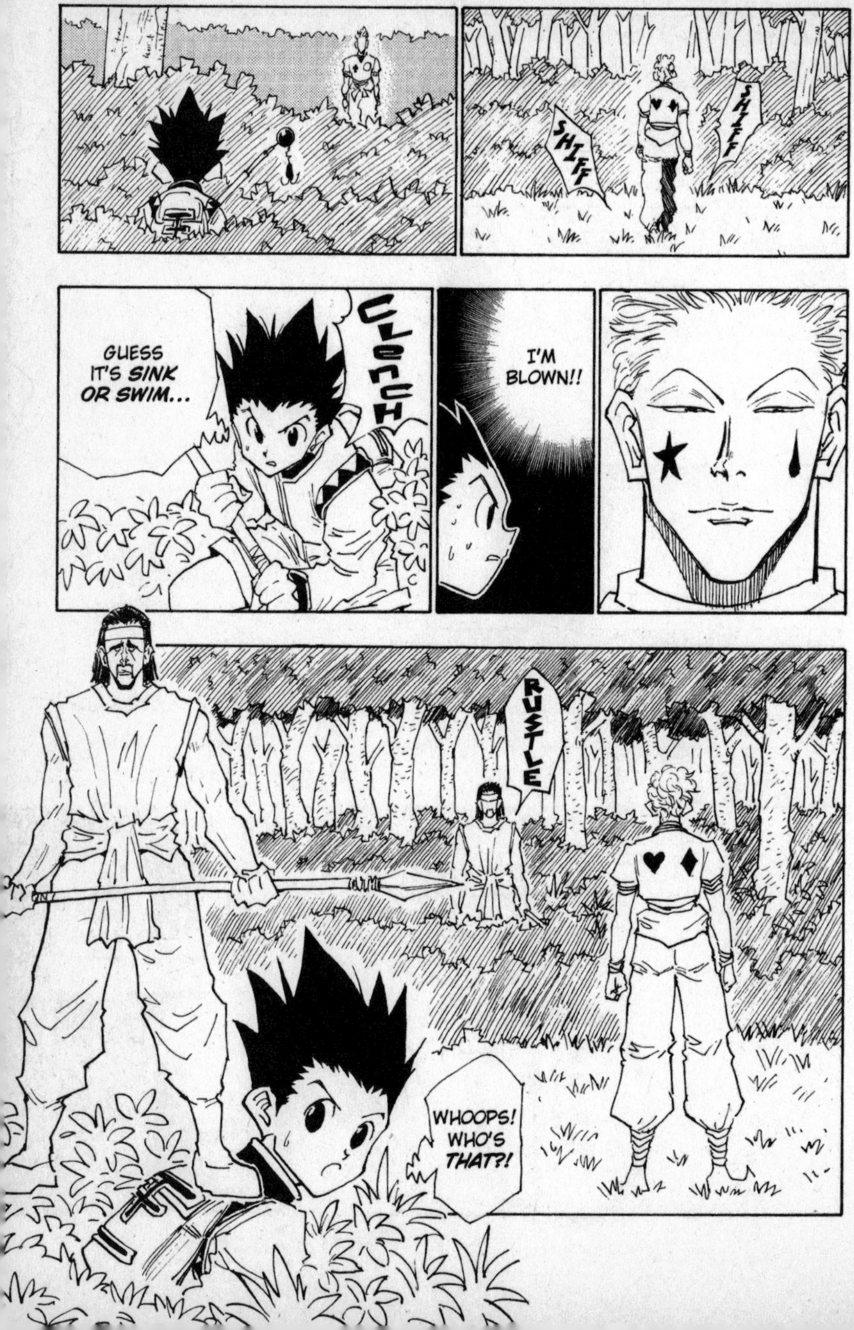
SHIFF
SHIFF
I'M BLOWN!!
CLENCH
GUESS IT'S *SINK* OR *SWIM*...
RUSTLE
WHOOPS! WHO'S *THAT?!*

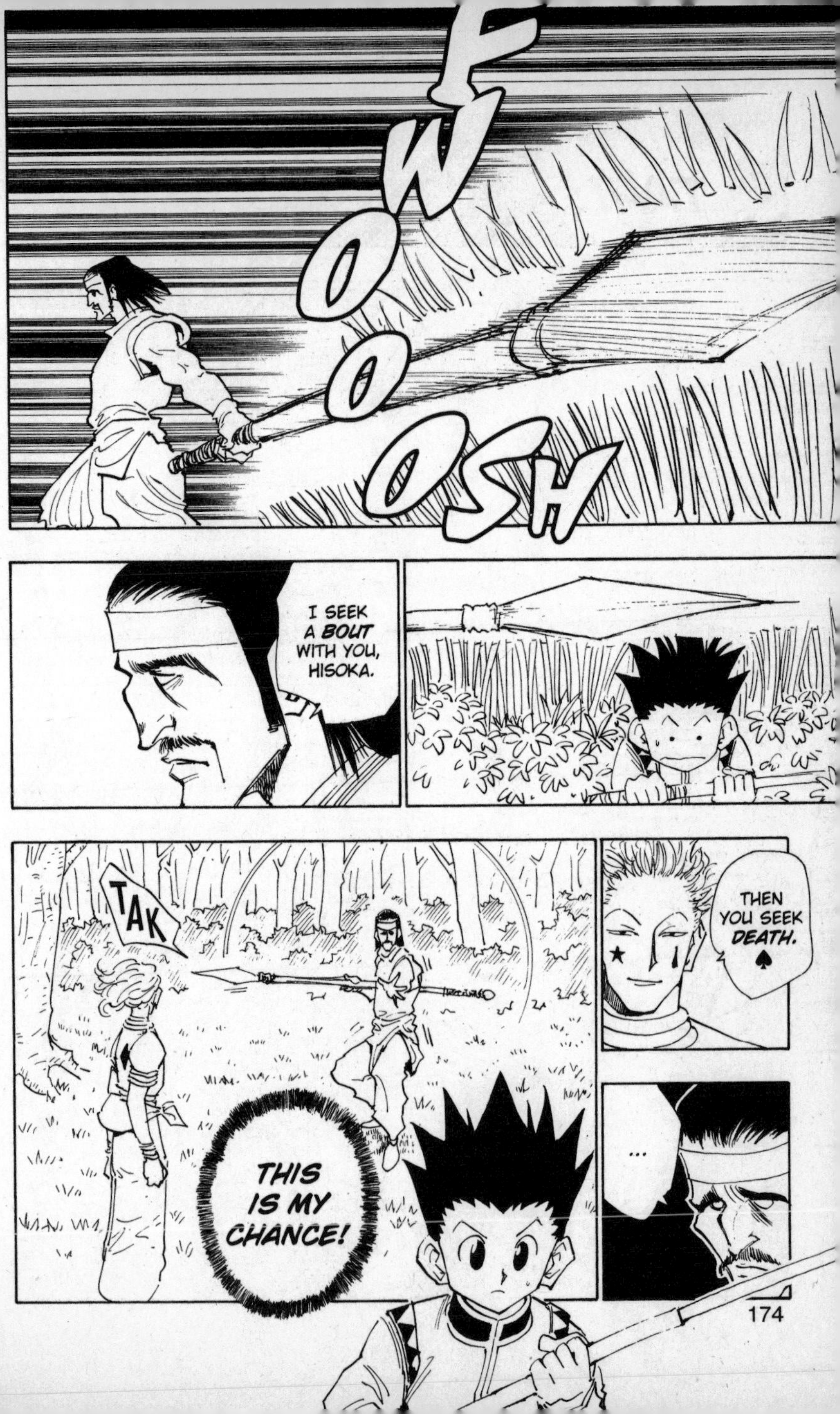
FWOOOOSH
I SEEK A *BOUT* WITH YOU, HISOKA.
THEN YOU SEEK *DEATH*. ♠
...
TAK
THIS IS MY CHANCE!

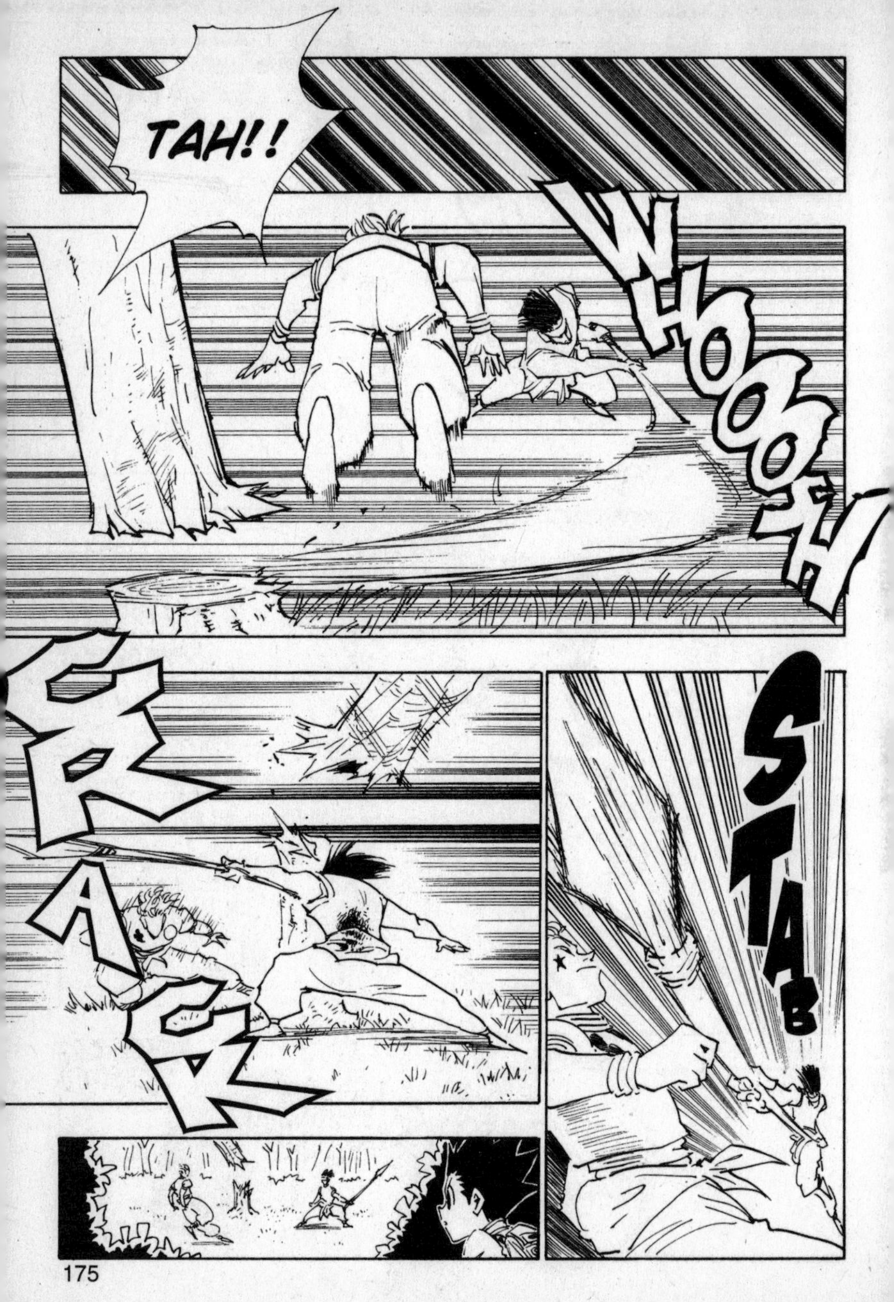
TAH!!
WHOOOOSH
STAB
CRACK

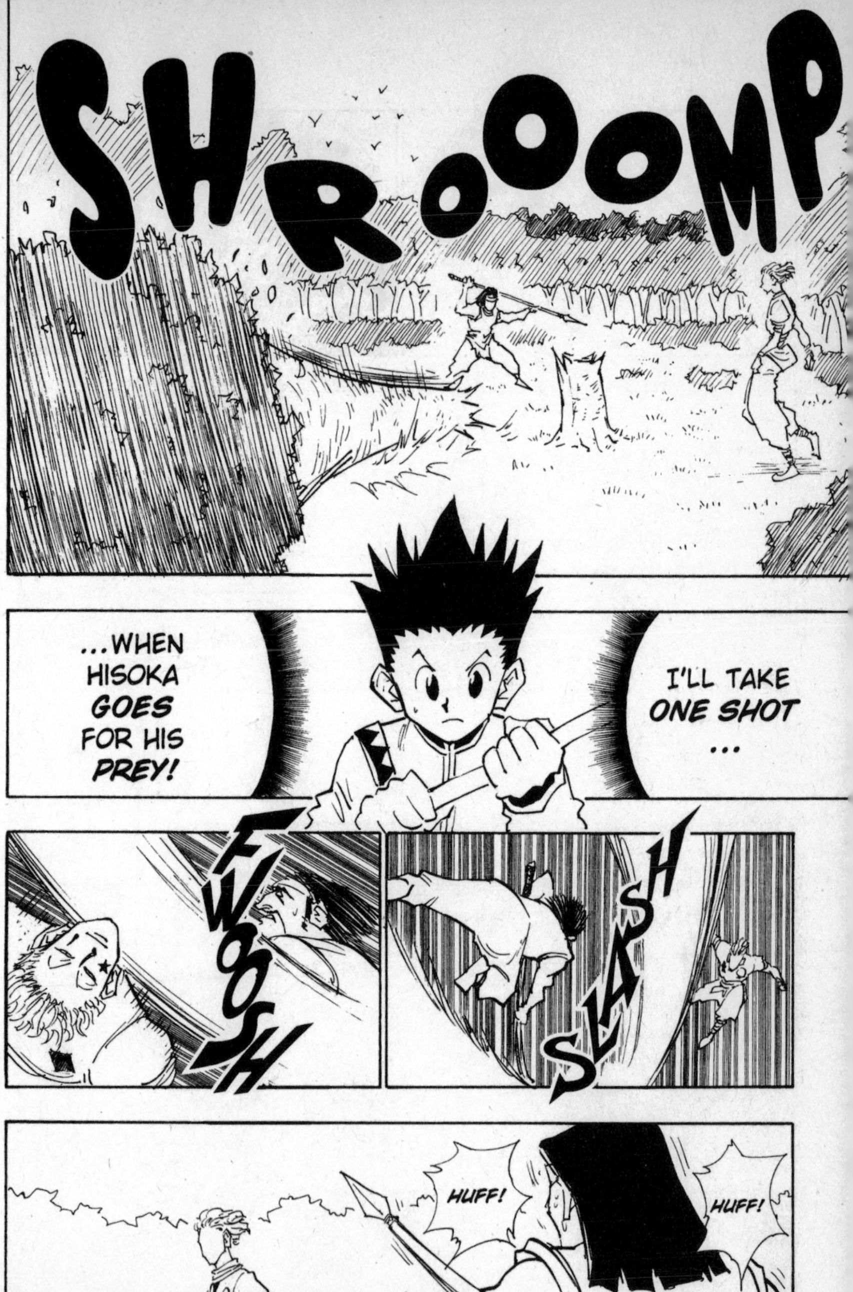
SHROOOMP
I'LL TAKE ONE SHOT ...
...WHEN HISOKA GOES FOR HIS PREY!
SLASH
FWOOSH
HUFF!
HUFF!

READ THIS WAY

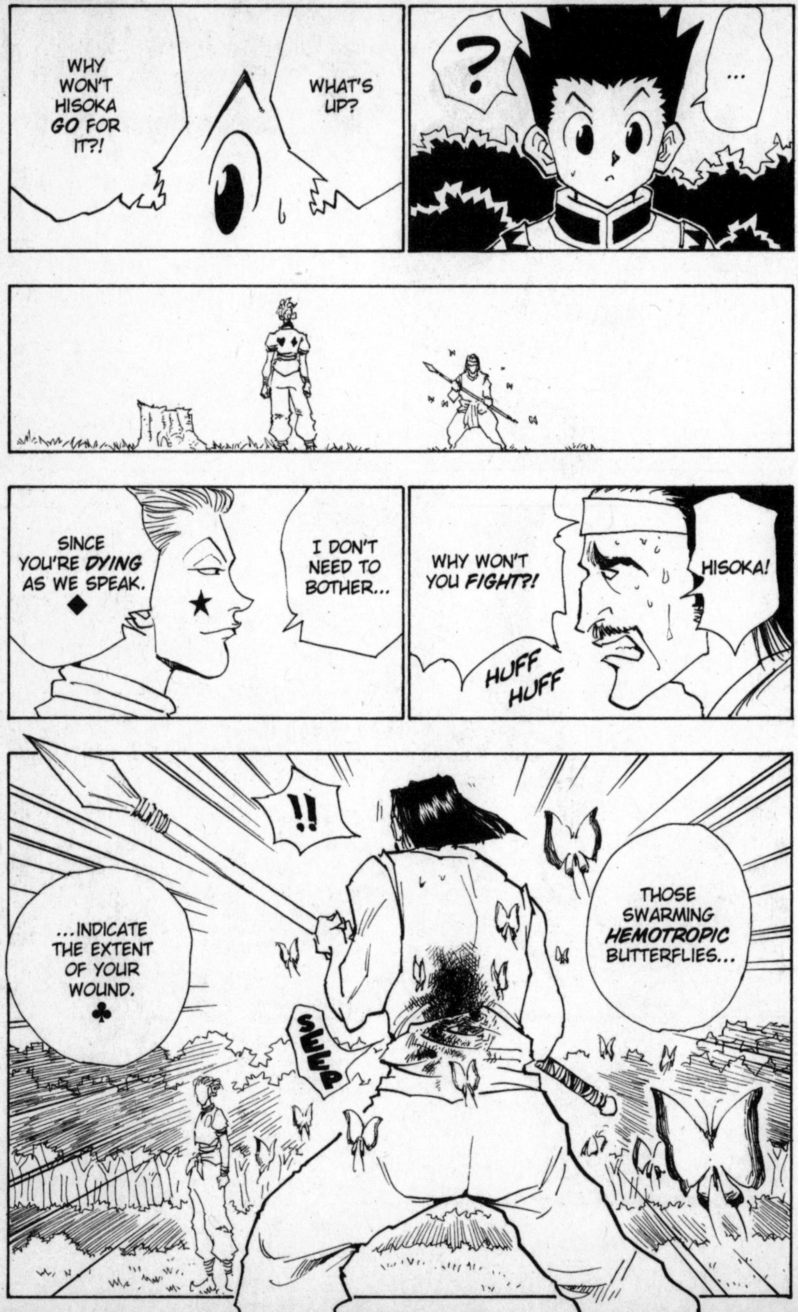
?
...
WHAT'S UP?
WHY WON'T HISOKA GO FOR IT?!
HISOKA!
WHY WON'T YOU FIGHT?!
HUFF HUFF
I DON'T NEED TO BOTHER...
SINCE YOU'RE DYING AS WE SPEAK. ♦
!!
THOSE SWARMING HEMOTROPIC BUTTERFLIES...
SEEP
...INDICATE THE EXTENT OF YOUR WOUND. ♣

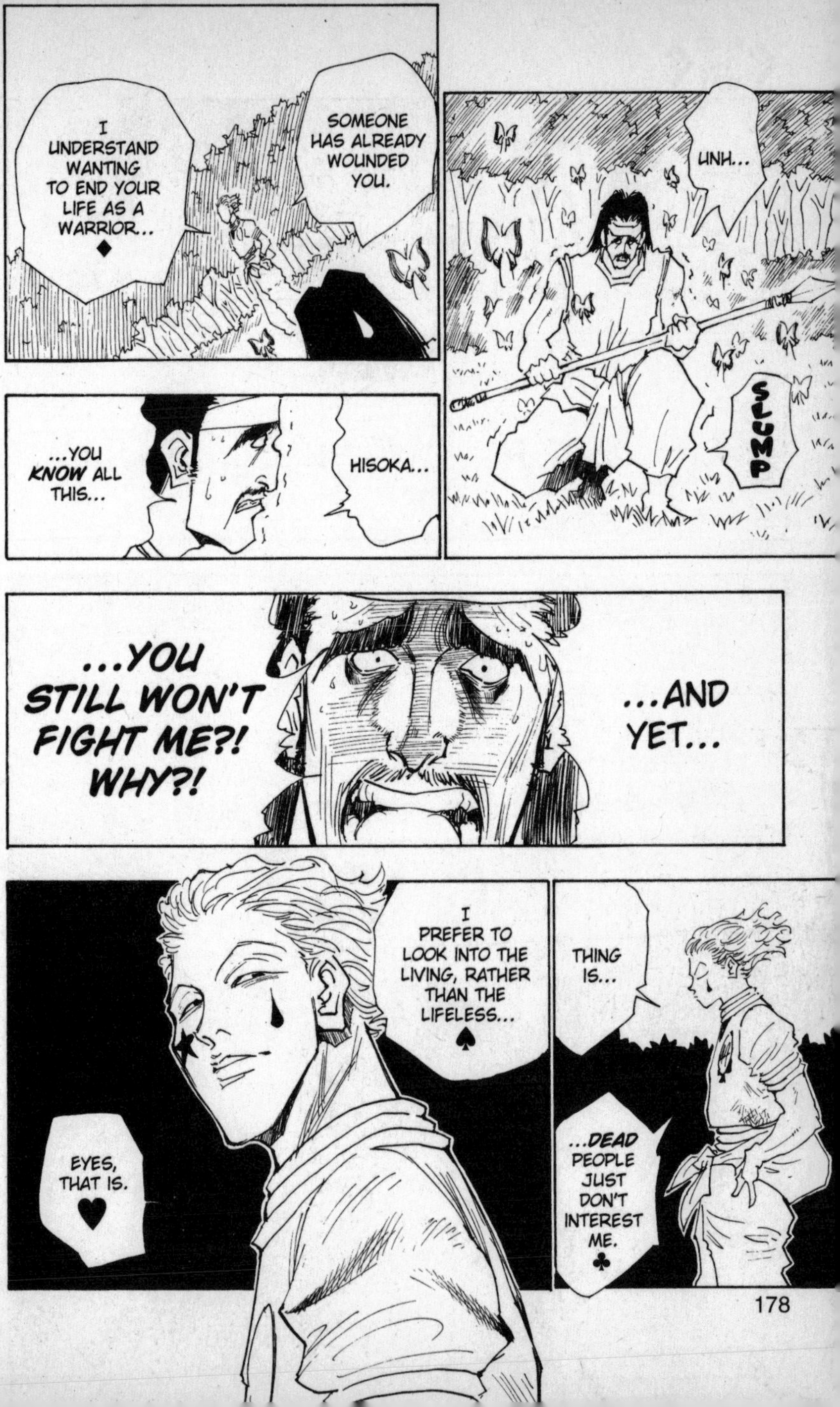
UNH...
SLUMP
SOMEONE HAS ALREADY WOUNDED YOU.
I UNDERSTAND WANTING TO END YOUR LIFE AS A WARRIOR... ◆
HISOKA...
...YOU KNOW ALL THIS...
...AND YET...
...YOU STILL WON'T FIGHT ME?! WHY?!
THING IS...
...DEAD PEOPLE JUST DON'T INTEREST ME. ♣
I PREFER TO LOOK INTO THE LIVING, RATHER THAN THE LIFELESS... ♠
EYES, THAT IS. ♥

READ THIS WAY

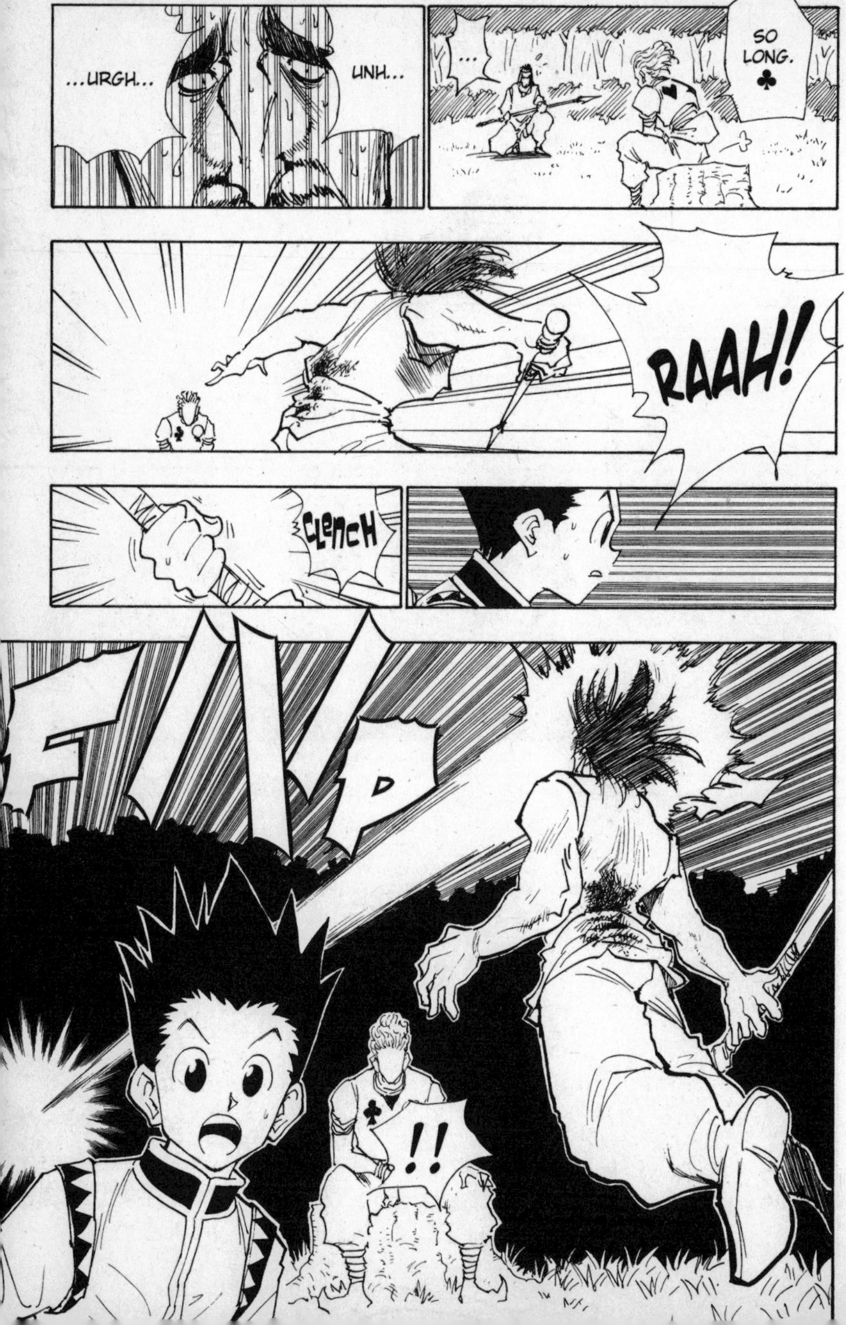
SO LONG. ♣
...
UNH...
...URGH...
RAAH!
CLENCH
!!

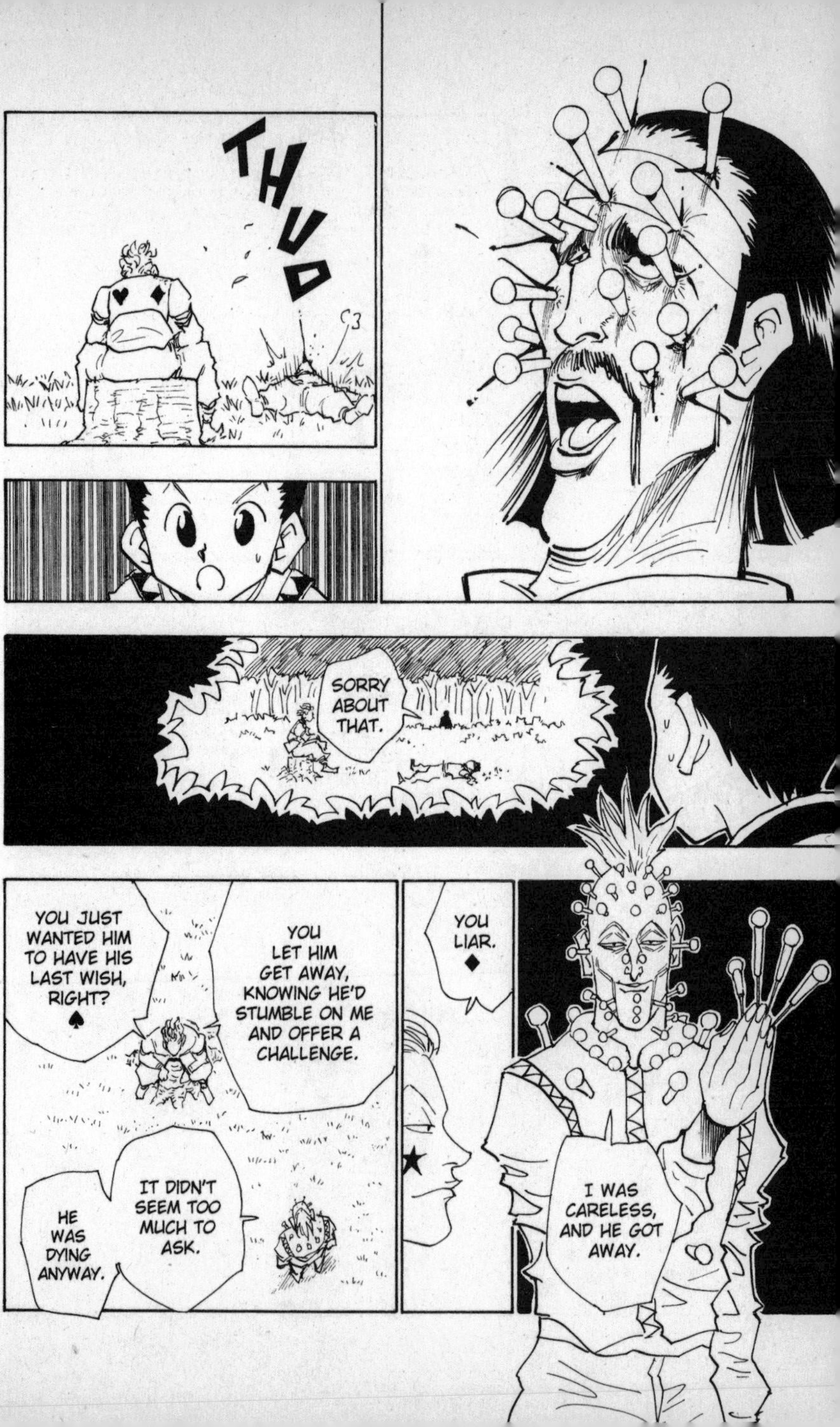
THUD
SORRY ABOUT THAT.
I WAS CARELESS, AND HE GOT AWAY.
YOU LIAR. ♦
YOU LET HIM GET AWAY, KNOWING HE'D STUMBLE ON ME AND OFFER A CHALLENGE.
YOU JUST WANTED HIM TO HAVE HIS LAST WISH, RIGHT? ♠
IT DIDN'T SEEM TOO MUCH TO ASK.
HE WAS DYING ANYWAY.

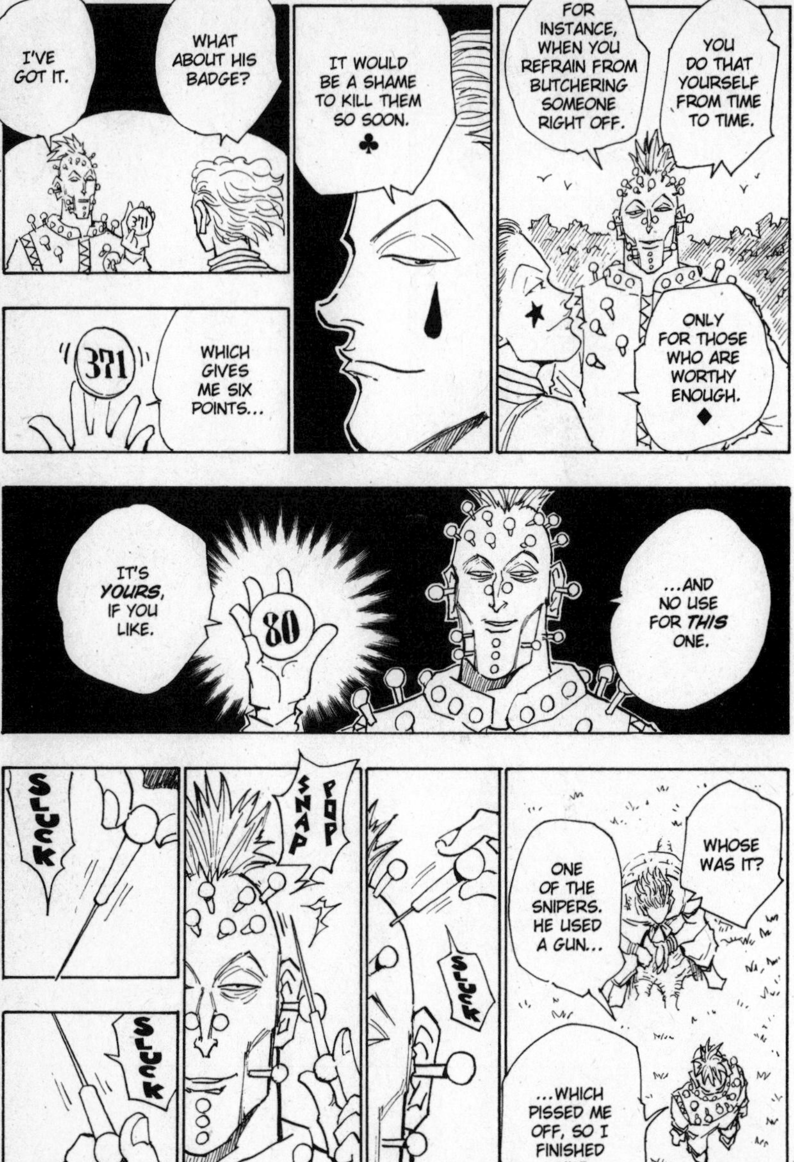
YOU DO THAT YOURSELF FROM TIME TO TIME.
FOR INSTANCE, WHEN YOU REFRAIN FROM BUTCHERING SOMEONE RIGHT OFF.
ONLY FOR THOSE WHO ARE WORTHY ENOUGH. ◆
IT WOULD BE A SHAME TO KILL THEM SO SOON. ♣
WHAT ABOUT HIS BADGE?
I'VE GOT IT.
371
371
WHICH GIVES ME SIX POINTS...
...AND NO USE FOR *THIS* ONE.
80
IT'S *YOURS*, IF YOU LIKE.
WHOSE WAS IT?
ONE OF THE SNIPERS. HE USED A GUN...
...WHICH PISSED ME OFF, SO I FINISHED HIM.
SLUCK
POP
SNAP
SLUCK
SLUCK

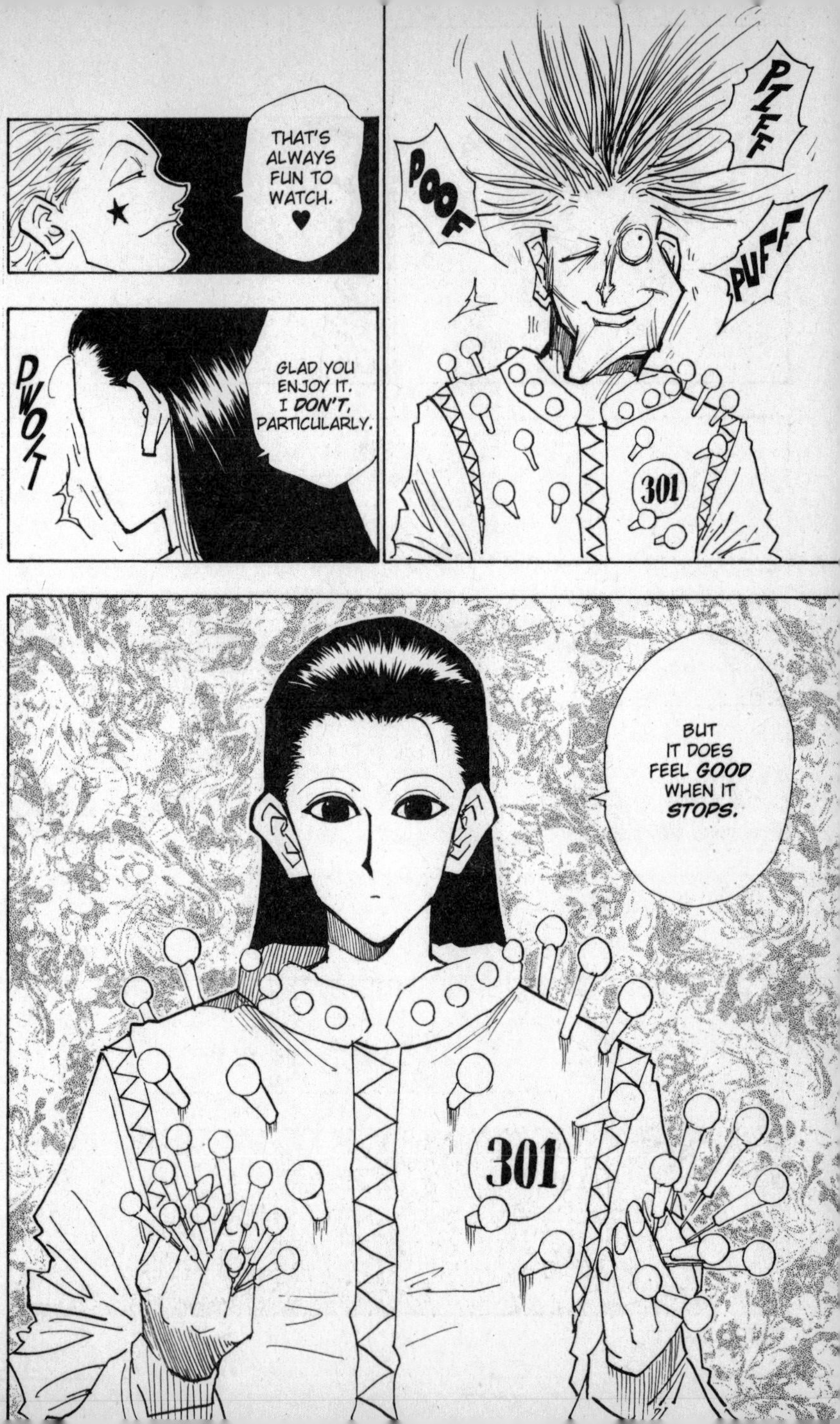
PIFF
POOF
PUFF
THAT'S ALWAYS FUN TO WATCH. ♥
GLAD YOU ENJOY IT. I *DON'T*, PARTICULARLY.
DWOIT
301
BUT IT DOES FEEL *GOOD* WHEN IT *STOPS*.
301

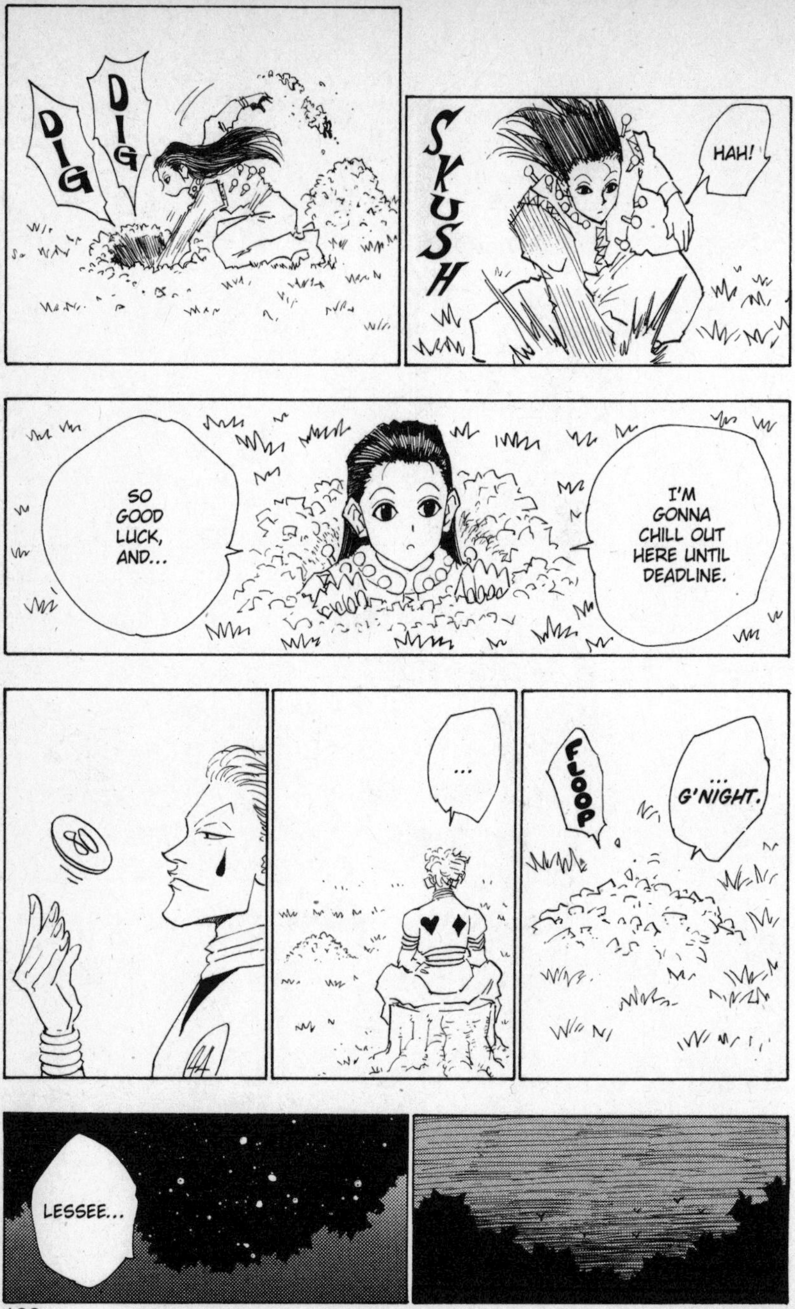
SKUSH
HAH!
DIG
DIG
I'M GONNA CHILL OUT HERE UNTIL DEADLINE.
SO GOOD LUCK, AND...
FLOOP
... G'NIGHT.
...
LESSEE...

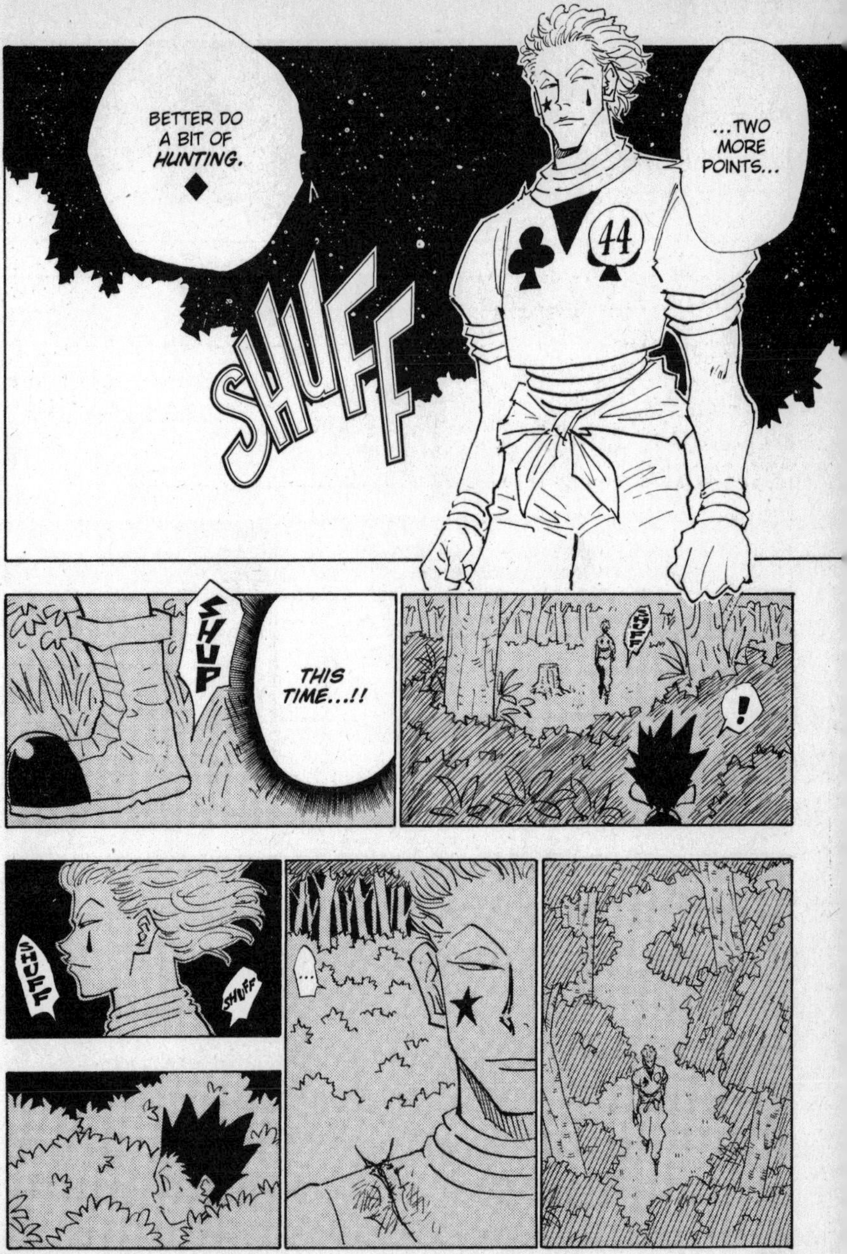
...TWO MORE POINTS...
BETTER DO A BIT OF HUNTING. ◆
SHUFF
SHUFF
!
SHUP
THIS TIME...!!
...
SHUFF
SHUFF

READ THIS WAY

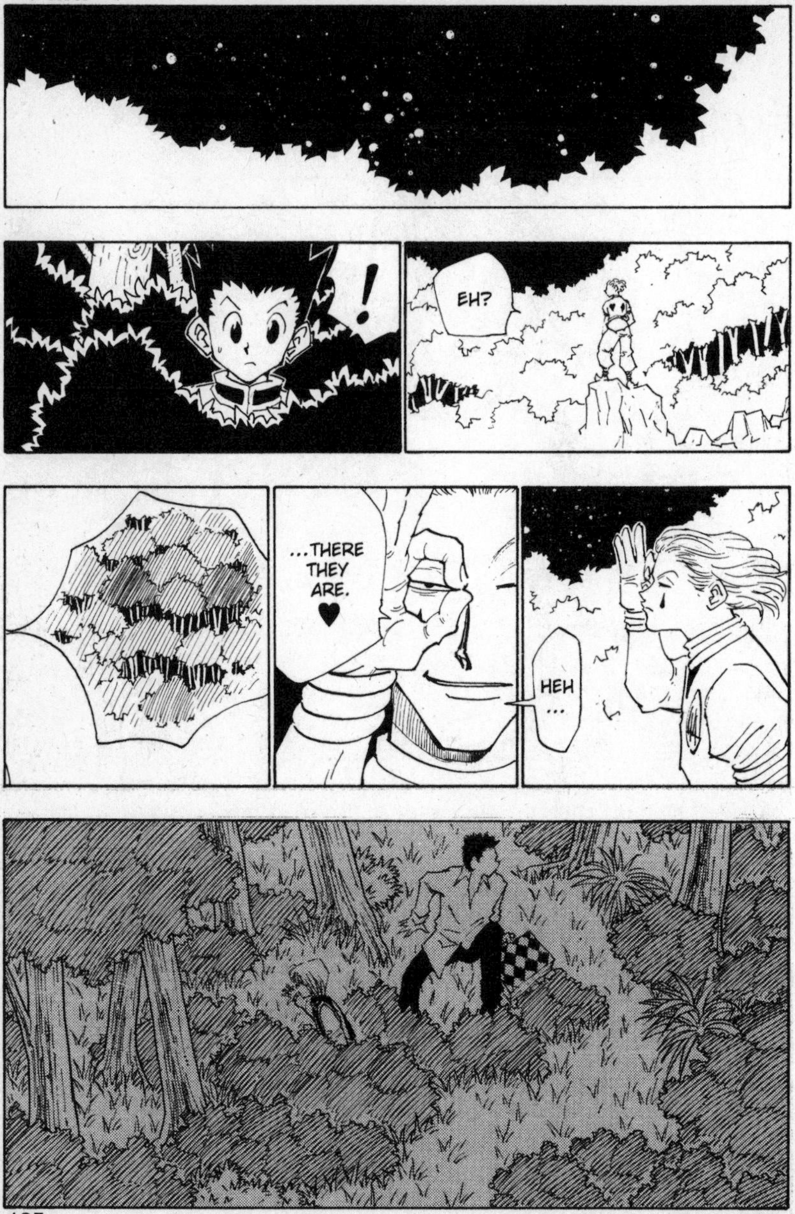
!
EH?
HEH ...
...THERE THEY ARE. ♥

Coming Next Volume...

The final test of the Hunter Exam is looming large, but first the applicants have to survive the fourth phase and get off the deserted island. Gon manages to escape Hisoka's murderous whimsy—and even manages to earn a few points. But a trap full of killer bees and poisoous snakes serves as an unexpected pit stop for Gon and his friends Kurapika and Leorio. Will it be a deadly delay?

Available in September 2005!

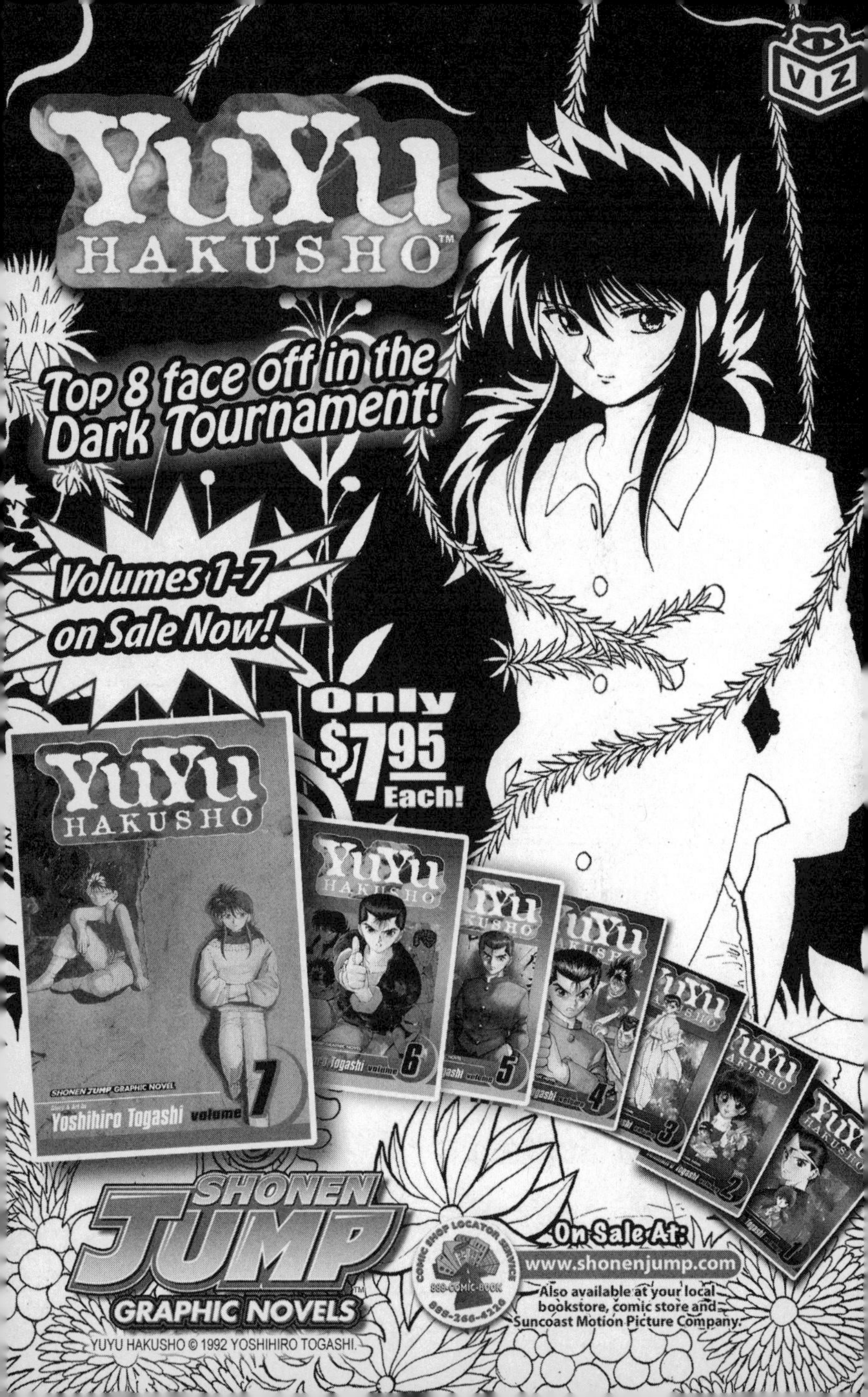
VIZ
YuYu HAKUSHO™
Top 8 face off in the Dark Tournament!
Volumes 1-7 on Sale Now!
Only $7.95 Each!
SHONEN JUMP GRAPHIC NOVELS
On Sale At:
www.shonenjump.com
Also available at your local bookstore, comic store and Suncoast Motion Picture Company.
COMIC SHOP LOCATOR SERVICE
888-COMIC-BOOK
888-266-4226
YUYU HAKUSHO © 1992 YOSHIHIRO TOGASHI.

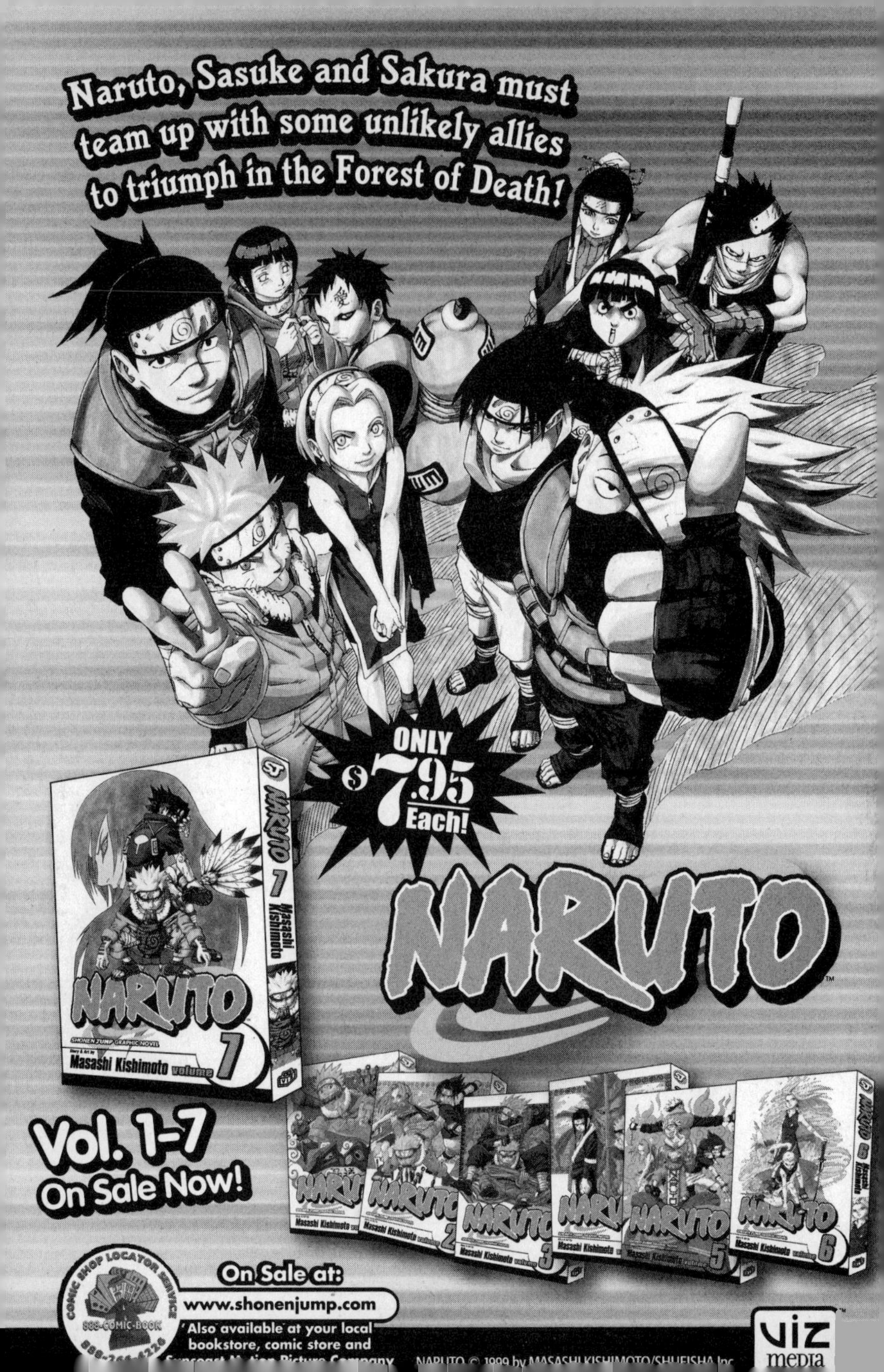
Naruto, Sasuke and Sakura must team up with some unlikely allies to triumph in the Forest of Death!
ONLY $7.95 Each!
NARUTO™
NARUTO 7
Masashi Kishimoto
SHONEN JUMP GRAPHIC NOVEL
Masashi Kishimoto volume 7
Vol. 1-7
On Sale Now!
COMIC SHOP LOCATOR SERVICE
888-COMIC-BOOK
On Sale at:
www.shonenjump.com
Also available at your local bookstore, comic store and
viz media

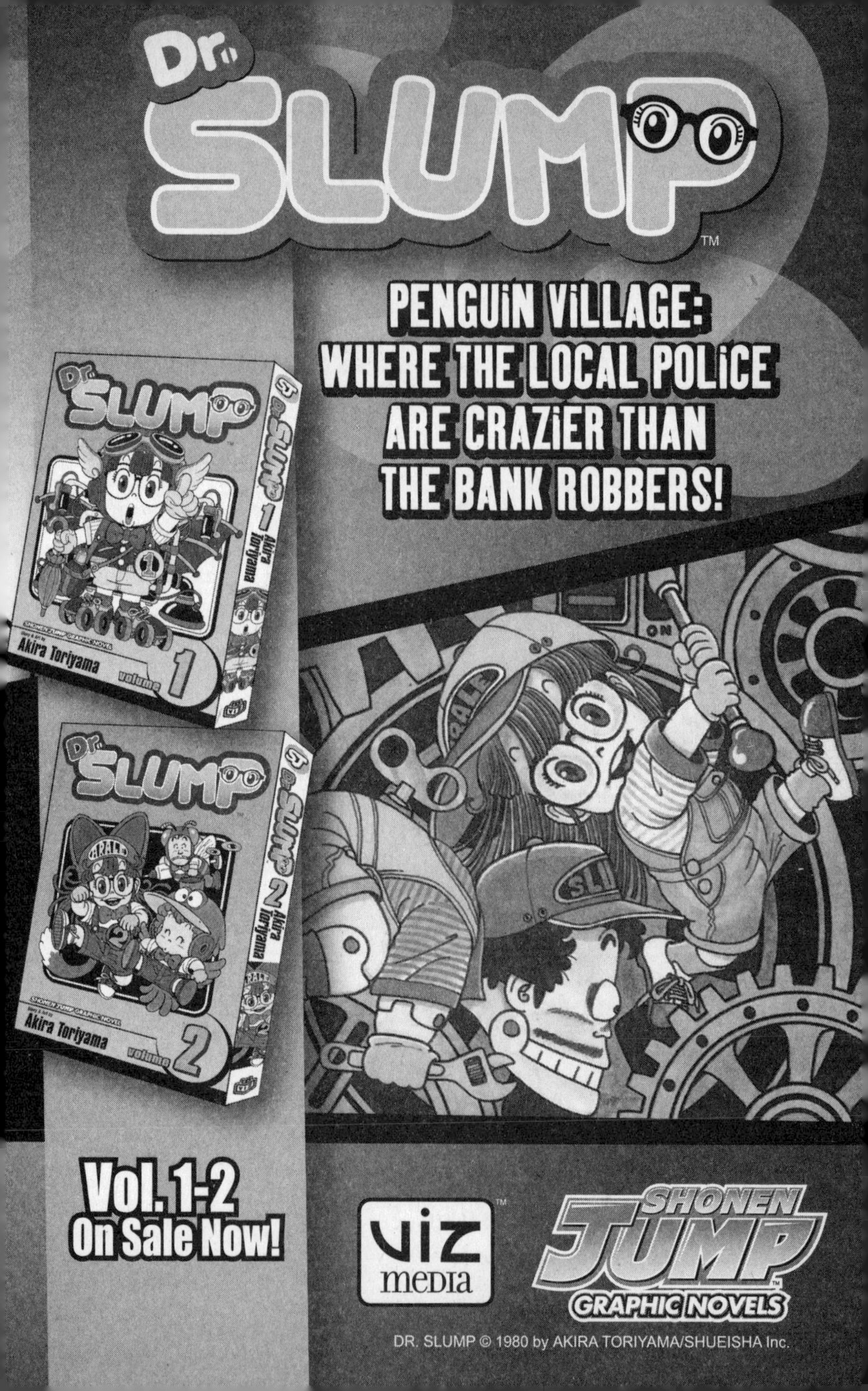

Dr. SLUMP™
PENGUIN VILLAGE: WHERE THE LOCAL POLICE ARE CRAZIER THAN THE BANK ROBBERS!
Dr. SLUMP
Akira Toriyama
volume 1
Dr. SLUMP
Akira Toriyama
volume 2
Vol. 1-2 On Sale Now!
viz media
SHONEN JUMP GRAPHIC NOVELS
DR. SLUMP © 1980 by AKIRA TORIYAMA/SHUEISHA Inc.

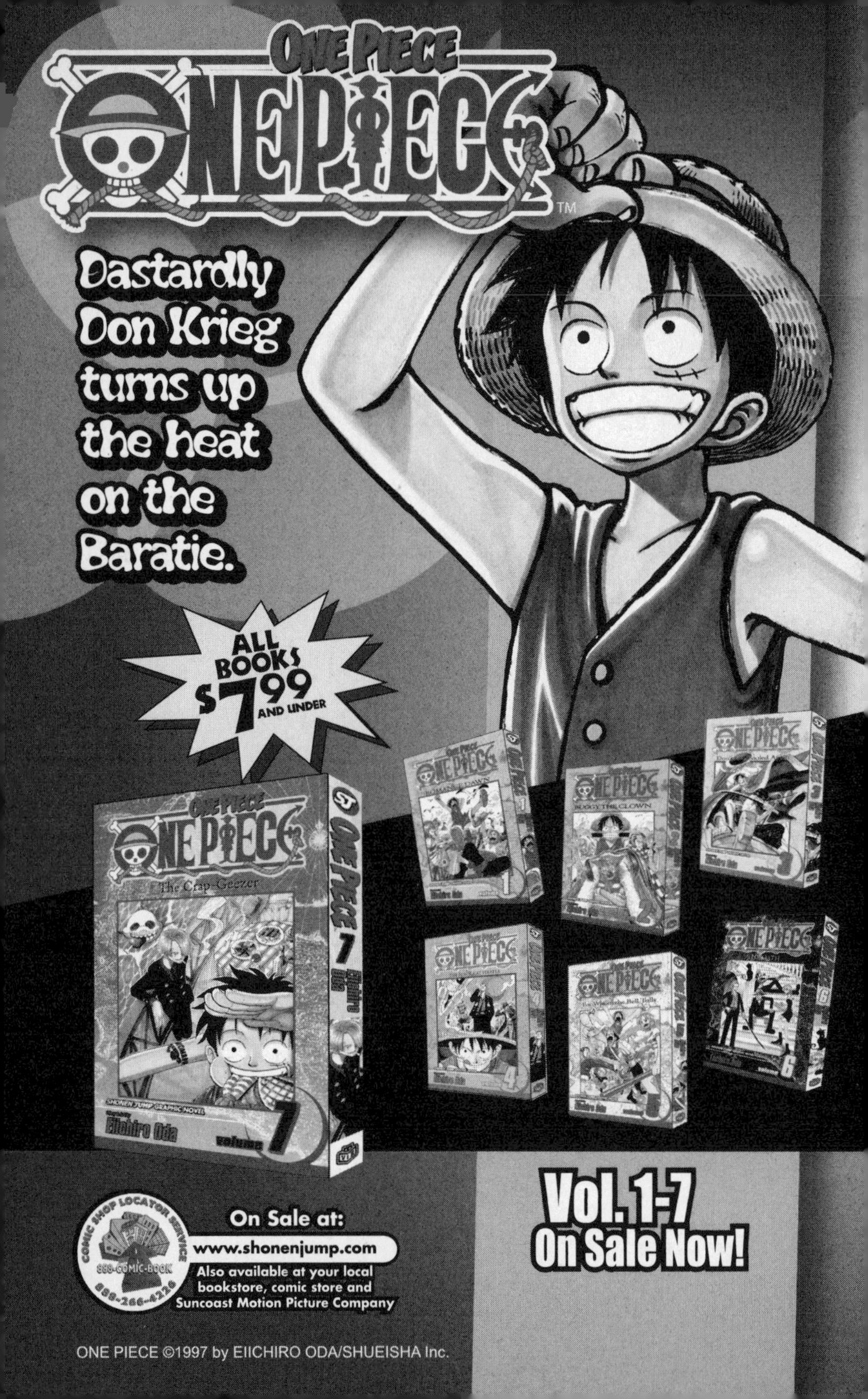
ONE PIECE
ONE PIECE
TM
Dastardly Don Krieg turns up the heat on the Baratie.
ALL BOOKS $7.99 AND UNDER
ONE PIECE
The Crap-Geezer
ONE PIECE 7
SHONEN JUMP GRAPHIC NOVEL
Eiichiro Oda
volume 7
Vol. 1-7 On Sale Now!
COMIC SHOP LOCATOR SERVICE
888-COMIC-BOOK
888-266-4226
On Sale at:
www.shonenjump.com
Also available at your local bookstore, comic store and Suncoast Motion Picture Company
ONE PIECE ©1997 by EIICHIRO ODA/SHUEISHA Inc.

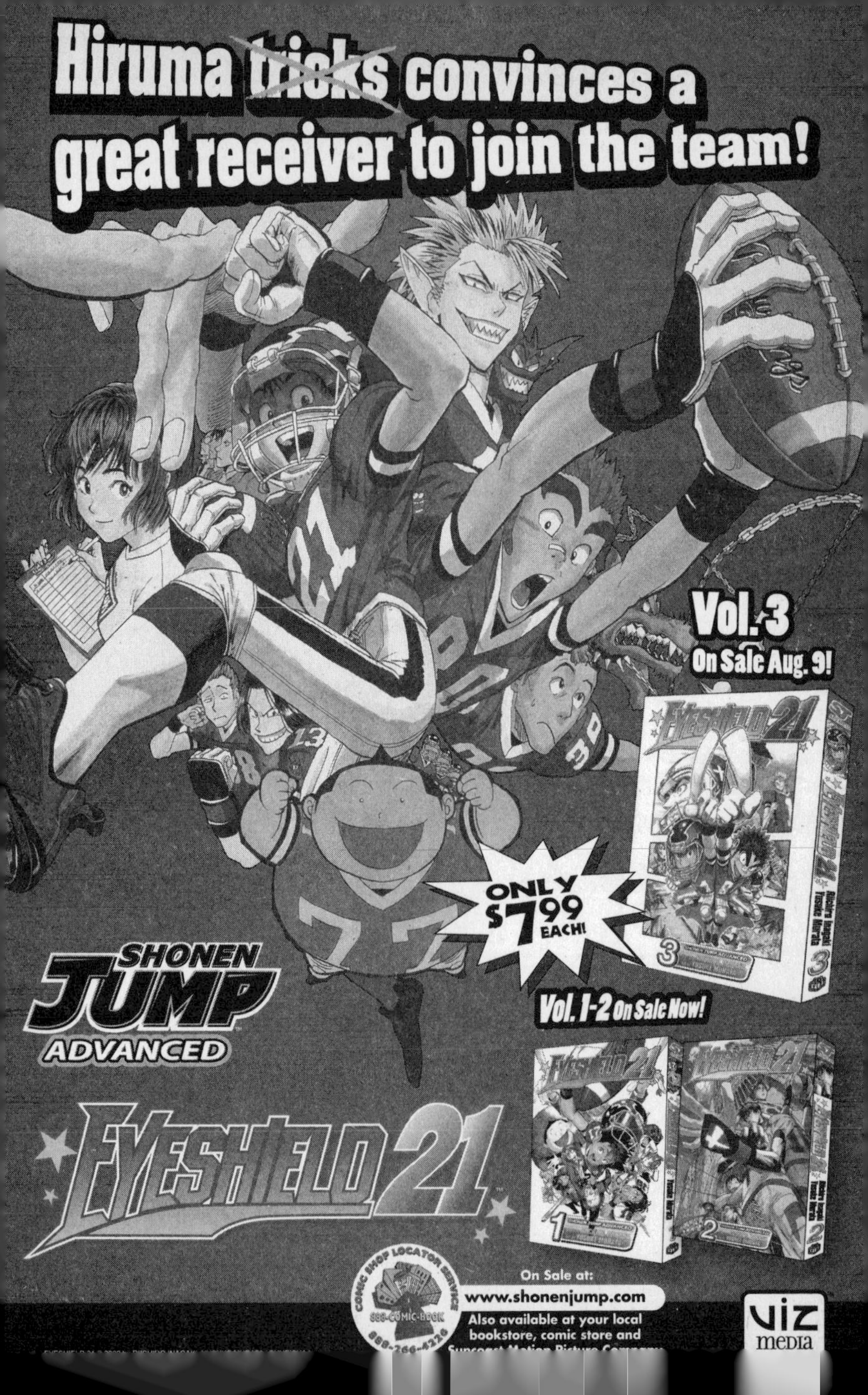
Hiruma tricks convinces a great receiver to join the team!
Vol. 3
On Sale Aug. 9!
ONLY $7.99 EACH!
SHONEN JUMP ADVANCED
EYESHIELD 21
Vol. 1-2 On Sale Now!
COMIC SHOP LOCATOR SERVICE
888-COMIC-BOOK
888-266-4226
On Sale at:
www.shonenjump.com
Also available at your local
bookstore, comic store and
viz media

SHONEN JUMP
THE WORLD'S MOST POPULAR MANGA

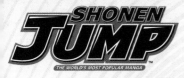

COMPLETE OUR SURVEY AND LET US KNOW WHAT YOU THINK!

☐ Please do NOT send me information about VIZ and SHONEN JUMP products, news and events, special offers, or other information.

☐ Please do NOT send me information from VIZ's trusted business partners.

Name: ______________________________

Address: ______________________________

City: ______________ **State:** ________ **Zip:** ______________

E-mail: ______________________________

☐ **Male** ☐ **Female** **Date of Birth** **(mm/dd/yyyy):** ___/___/_____ **(Under 13? Parental consent required)**

1 Do you purchase SHONEN JUMP Magazine?

☐ Yes ☐ No **(if no, skip the next two questions)**

If **YES**, do you subscribe?

☐ Yes ☐ No

If **NO**, how often do you purchase SHONEN JUMP Magazine?

☐ 1-3 issues a year

☐ 4-6 issues a year

☐ more than 7 issues a year

2 Which SHONEN JUMP Graphic Novel did you purchase? **(please check one)**

☐ Beet the Vandel Buster ☐ Bleach ☐ Dragon Ball

☐ Dragon Ball Z ☐ Dr. Slump ☐ Eyeshield 21

☐ Hikaru no Go ☐ Hunter x Hunter ☐ I"s

☐ Knights of the Zodiac ☐ Legendz ☐ Naruto

☐ One Piece ☐ Rurouni Kenshin ☐ Shaman King

☐ The Prince of Tennis ☐ Ultimate Muscle ☐ Whistle!

☐ Yu-Gi-Oh! ☐ Yu-Gi-Oh!: Duelist ☐ YuYu Hakusho

☐ Other ______________________________

Will you purchase subsequent volumes?

☐ Yes ☐ No

3 How did you learn about this title? **(check all that apply)**

☐ Favorite title ☐ Advertisement ☐ Article

☐ Gift ☐ Read excerpt in SHONEN JUMP Magazine

☐ Recommendation ☐ Special offer ☐ Through TV animation

☐ Website ☐ Other ______________________________

4 Of the titles that are serialized in SHONEN JUMP Magazine, have you purchased the Graphic Novels?

☐ Yes ☐ No

If **YES**, which ones have you purchased? (check all that apply)

☐ Dragon Ball Z ☐ Hikaru no Go ☐ Naruto ☐ One Piece
☐ Shaman King ☐ Yu-Gi-Oh! ☐ YuYu Hakusho

If **YES**, what were your reasons for purchasing? (please pick up to 3)

☐ A favorite title ☐ A favorite creator/artist ☐ I want to read it in one go
☐ I want to read it over and over again ☐ There are extras that aren't in the magazine
☐ The quality of printing is better than the magazine ☐ Recommendation
☐ Special offer ☐ Other

If **NO**, why did/would you not purchase it?

☐ I'm happy just reading it in the magazine ☐ It's not worth buying the graphic novel
☐ All the manga pages are in black and white unlike the magazine
☐ There are other graphic novels that I prefer ☐ There are too many to collect for each title
☐ It's too small ☐ Other ______________________

5 Of the titles NOT serialized in the Magazine, which ones have you purchased?
(check all that apply)

☐ Beet the Vandel Buster ☐ Bleach ☐ Dragon Ball ☐ Dr. Slump
☐ Eyeshield 21 ☐ Hunter x Hunter ☐ I"s ☐ Knights of the Zodiac
☐ Legendz ☐ The Prince of Tennis ☐ Rurouni Kenshin ☐ Whistle!
☐ Yu-Gi-Oh!: Duelist ☐ None ☐ Other ______________________

If you did purchase any of the above, what were your reasons for purchase?

☐ A favorite title ☐ A favorite creator/artist
☐ Read a preview in SHONEN JUMP Magazine and wanted to read the rest of the story
☐ Recommendation ☐ Other

Will you purchase subsequent volumes?

☐ Yes ☐ No

6 What race/ethnicity do you consider yourself? (please check one)

☐ Asian/Pacific Islander ☐ Black/African American ☐ Hispanic/Latino
☐ Native American/Alaskan Native ☐ White/Caucasian ☐ Other

THANK YOU! Please send the completed form to: VIZ Survey
42 Catharine St.
Poughkeepsie, NY 12601

All information provided will be used for internal purposes only. We promise not to sell or otherwise divulge your information.